Roland Hayes

Roland Hayes

The Legacy of an American Tenor

Christopher A. Brooks
and Robert Sims

INDIANA UNIVERSITY PRESS

Bloomington & Indianapolis

This book is a publication of

INDIANA UNIVERSITY PRESS
Office of Scholarly Publishing
Herman B Wells Library 350
1320 East 10th Street
Bloomington, Indiana 47405 USA

iupress.indiana.edu

Telephone   800-842-6796
Fax   812-855-7931

⊗ The paper used in this publication
meets the minimum requirements of
the American National Standard for
Information Sciences – Permanence of
Paper for Printed Library Materials,
ANSI Z39.48–1992.

*Manufactured in the
United States of America*

*Library of Congress
Cataloging-in-Publication Data*

Brooks, Christopher Antonio, [date].
  Roland Hayes : the legacy of
an American tenor / Christopher
A. Brooks and Robert Sims.
    pages cm
    Includes bibliographical
references and index.
    ISBN 978-0-253-01536-5 (cloth : alkaline
paper) – ISBN 978-0-253-01539-6 (ebook)
1. Hayes, Roland, 1887-1977. 2. Tenors
(Singers) – United States – Biography. I.
Sims, Robert (Baritone), author. II. Title.
    ML420.H25B76 2015
    782.42168092 – dc23
    [B]

                                    2014021653

1 2 3 4 5   20 19 18 17 16 15

This work is dedicated to all of those who were influenced by the musical legacy of Roland Hayes, including Benjamin Matthews, William Warfield, and W. Hazaiah Williams.

Contents

Foreword

AS A YOUTH IN INDIANAPOLIS, MY HEROES WERE A QUARTET OF African Americans, only three of whom were musical: the great concert tenor Roland Hayes; the stunning contralto Marian Anderson; the robust basso Paul Robeson; and the unbeatable Brown Bomber, Joe Louis.

I placed Roland Hayes as the point man in this corps of luminaries. Although slight of physical stature when compared to Robeson and Louis – and, possibly, to Anderson – he was in every other aspect of his life and career a giant. His voice was delicate, but his artistic use of it placed him at the pinnacle of accomplishment, ensuring his place in the international annals of musical attainment.

When I was eight years old, my family moved to Detroit and held membership in the Ebenezer AME Church. In 1942, the church presented the legendary tenor in recital.

After being spellbound by Hayes's singing, along with his charismatic and dignified presence, I tasted a future that would one day enlist me in the service of Orpheus. Following the recital, my parents introduced their wide-eyed little boy to this full-maned "Aframerican" paragon. This encounter was the first of precious few to follow over the course of time. My prepubescent singing efforts in the congregation after hearing him earned me the sobriquet "The Young Roland Hayes."

Twenty years later, in 1962, I was among the near-capacity audience at Carnegie Hall that attended Roland Hayes's seventy-fifth birthday celebration, which marked his extraordinary career. Time again stood still as his performance rekindled memories of two decades past when I had sat in my church pew, mesmerized by the power of his incomparable artistry.

In 1964, I performed Rodolfo in Puccini's *La bohème* in Boston with the Metropolitan Opera Spring Tour. Following the first act, an usher handed me a business card with a handwritten message, "Bravo!," on the back. Imprinted on the front was the name "Roland W. Hayes." When I caught my breath, I uttered a prayer of thanks that my high C in the first act aria "Che gelida manina" had spun forth without incident.

A decade later, I was approached by WQXR-FM in New York about hosting a new series of broadcasts devoted to the careers of African Americans in classical music. I was to create the format and select performing artists and composers for live interviews. I was also to choose musical excerpts I felt best represented their work. My first guests were to be Roland Hayes, Marian Anderson, and Paul Robeson. (Joe Louis unfortunately did not fit the format.)

To my great disappointment, ill health made an interview with Mr. Robeson impossible. Miss Anderson agreed and was interviewed at the WQXR-FM studios in Manhattan. Mr. Hayes, who was eighty-seven at that time, agreed to meet with me at his home in Brookline, Massachusetts. In anticipation of this opportunity, I packed my tape recorder and set forth on a journey I knew would provide a recorded moment unequaled in the history of sound capture.

I arrived at the elegant Hayes home and was greeted by Mrs. Hayes, who showed me to their beautiful living room. While I waited, I summoned visions of Mr. Hayes rehearsing at his grand piano with some of the accompanists with whom he had collaborated – Lawrence Brown, Percival Parham, William Lawrence, and Reginald Boardman, among others. My reveries halted when the tenor himself stepped into the room.

Mr. Hayes was immaculately dressed. He admitted to having experienced a difficult winter, but when he smiled – a smile I shall never forget – his drawn visage radiated an astonishing glow of youth.

As I explained my mission to the elder musical statesman, I swallowed hard at his request that our time together not be electronically recorded, for I so wanted to share this incredible experience with my listening audience. I could well imagine him leery of interviews at this point in his long life and that the final product of such give and take may not always have accurately represented his views. He may also have wished just to speak more freely and candidly with me without having to monitor his comments. Whatever his reasons were, I respected his wishes. To do otherwise was not an option.

In any case, the hour that followed some forty years ago remains emblazoned on my psyche. We spoke of his life and career, much with which I was already familiar. However, reading it from a book could never match hearing it from the source. When our time together drew to its close, I parted company – as it turned out, for the last time – with one of the most spiritual human beings I have ever known. I left his presence feeling blessed beyond description and beyond measure.

This frail man, who possessed such a powerful soul, had lifted me, once again, beyond the mundane into the metaphysical realm where God's angels soar and sing. And on this occasion, he accomplished this miracle without singing a note! Although I did not record my hour with Roland Hayes for posterity, the words and presence of this spiritual giant remain inscribed in my heart forever. I extend my heartfelt gratitude to Drs. Christopher Brooks and Robert Sims for bringing Roland Hayes to the world in this exhaustive appraisal of, and tribute to, his momentous life and ineradicable legacy.

George Shirley
Joseph Edgar Maddy Distinguished University
Emeritus Professor of Voice
University of Michigan
Ann Arbor

Foreword

ALTHOUGH I DID NOT HAVE THE HONOR OF SEEING ROLAND Hayes onstage, I, like most African American artists of my generation, was influenced by his presence and stature. In some of his concert reviews that I read when I was a young man, he was always described as a consummate and musical artist. This feat was all the more remarkable because Roland Hayes was just one generation removed from legal enslavement in this country. During the course of his long career and life, he understood the challenges facing African American musicians, especially the plight of African American male performers.

In February 2007 I was in Chicago performing with Robert Sims, and at a reception afterward I casually mentioned to him and Christopher Brooks that it was a shame that no one had written a comprehensive biography of the late great tenor. Totally unbeknownst to me, not only did these two scholars embark on the work, but the result, *Roland Hayes: The Legacy of an American Tenor,* will no doubt be the definitive work on his life and career and will capture its readers. Brooks and Sims's research has taken them throughout this country and Europe to uncover this complex artist who many of us knew by reputation but will really come to understand better as a result of this work.

Their interviews with relatives and other great African American artists who were directly and indirectly influenced by this hero of the stage have been very revealing. I heartily congratulate Christopher Brooks and Robert Sims on the publication of *The Legacy of an American Tenor.* Their achievement of reviving this important musical icon for a

new generation will go far and earn for Roland Hayes the attention he
so richly deserves.

Simon Estes
Wartburg College,
Waverly, Iowa

Introduction

"I'LL MAKE ME A MAN"

ONCE KNOWN AS THE "BLACK CARUSO," ROLAND HAYES WAS
hailed as one of the greatest concert performers of the twentieth century. During his sixty-year career, the gifted American singer packed
concert halls across the globe.[1] At the height of his popularity, along with
Fritz Kreisler, Ignaz Paderewski, Nellie Melba, Feodor Chaliapin, and
Pablo Casals, he was one of the few artists who could sell out venues like
Carnegie Hall and the Hollywood Bowl, among other major auditori-
ums throughout the United States and Europe. In 1923, he was the first
African American musician to perform with a major symphony orches-
tra, leading him to sing under the batons of celebrated conductors like
Eugene Ormandy, Leopold Stokowski, Otto Klemperer, Bruno Walter,
Pierre Monteux, Walter Damrosch, and Gabriel Pierné, among others.
Like other acclaimed musicians, he sang for crowned heads of Europe,
prime ministers, presidents, and other heads of state.

The Roland Hayes story brings from the shadows a portrait of a man
as complex as the music he performed. His trailblazing career carved
the paths for Paul Robeson, Marian Anderson, Todd Duncan, Dorothy
Maynor, and a host of other African American concert artists. He was
one of the first concert artists to routinely program African American
spirituals, thereby beginning a tradition that continues among African
American classical singers today. He transcended cultural, geographical, and musical boundaries with his mastery of genres and a repertory
from some of history's greatest composers. His vocal nuance and ability
to sing *messa di voce* (the art of gradually crescendoing and decrescendo-

ing on a single note) could spontaneously send shivers throughout his audiences.

Such was the case on the evening of February 7, 1926, when the tenor confidently strode onstage to the applause of four thousand concertgoers to sing with the New York Symphony Orchestra. The singer stood more than a foot shorter than lanky conductor Otto Klemperer, who followed him onstage. Their height difference was punctuated further when the bushy-headed, bespectacled Klemperer took the podium. Hayes stood perfectly still with his head slightly elevated, eyes closed, and hands clasped, suggesting deep prayer. The conductor raised his arms and motioned for the ensemble to begin. Hayes seemed to come alive as the strings introduced the melody to Mozart's concert aria for tenor and orchestra "Si mostra la sorte" (Fate proves itself) K. 209. He opened his eyes slightly and gestured as if he were painting the words he sang. The relatively brief, up-tempo aria did not display the singer's full vocal range, but it turned into a preview of what was to come. When he next sang the challenging "Un'aura amorosa" (A loving breeze) from Mozart's *Così fan tutte,* the audience experienced the full measure of his talent and vocal artistry.

His was not a stentorian sound but was like the lilting, plaintive quality of a viola, capable of reaching high and low registers. His sound was rich in the middle range, and his pianissimos were nothing short of stunning. The audience held its collective breath as the tenor drew out the passage in the Mozart aria, "Un dolce ristoro . . ." (A sweet refreshment), that rises and falls. He also employed a vocal technique in which he would purposefully sing at half-voice to condition the audience to a softer volume. Then, when he produced a fuller sound, it gave the impression that his voice was larger than it first seemed.

After the intermission, he took the audience on a musical journey of a very different nature. Using the same gifts that he had employed to sing Mozart, the tenor essayed several African American spirituals set for keyboard and orchestra. The practice of including spirituals with European art music in the same concert proved to be one of his enduring legacies. The headline of the *New York Times'* review of this concert was predictable: "Hayes Sings with New York Symphony – Negro Tenor Heard in Mozart Aria and 'Spirituals' – Klemperer Conducts Before 4,000!"

Nearing forty years old, the celebrated tenor was at the height of his vocal power, commanding a fee of $2,500 per recital – in some cases more. His American engagements alone numbered more than eighty concerts during the 1925–26 concert season. As the darling of both the African American and the white press, Hayes scrupulously avoided any negative attention that could tarnish his reputation.

Between the 1920s and the 1970s, Hayes's life was peppered with relationships that would place him among some of the most influential thinkers and artists of the twentieth century. He counted George Washington Carver, Eleanor Roosevelt, W. E. B. Du Bois, Mary McLeod Bethune, General Dwight D. Eisenhower, Alain Locke, Carter G. Woodson, Sterling Brown, and Langston Hughes among his friends and acquaintances. He also crossed paths professionally with Booker T. Washington, A. Philip Randolph, Thurgood Marshall, and – with great stealth – the exiled "Lion of Judah," Emperor Haile Selassie I.

At the same time, Roland Hayes was forced to confront the struggles of his era, such as whether to play the "race man" and challenge Jim Crow segregation laws (like his contemporary Marcus Garvey) or to cater to his mostly European and white American audiences. He understood quite early the importance of placing his name before the public as a career-building strategy and advertised in well-respected media outlets of his day, including the opinion-making NAACP-sponsored *Crisis* magazine. But when he had multiple opportunities to be featured in radio broadcasts, perform at the White House (during the presidency of Franklin D. Roosevelt), or record during his vocal zenith – all of which would have catapulted his career to yet a higher level – he declined them because he believed that doing so would compromise his art.

Roland Hayes was conflicted in many ways. He would have gladly embraced a movie career like that of his slightly younger contemporary Paul Robeson, but he was dismissive, if not disdainful, of Robeson because he believed the Rutgers-educated, Columbia Law School graduate had not properly refined his "natural" talent.

Not given to underestimate his abilities or willingness to share his art with others, Roland Hayes always intended that his story be told. The artist dictated his life story to the writer MacKinley Helm, who published the biography now long out of print, titled *Angel Mo' and Her*

Son, Roland Hayes, in 1942. To document his rich life further, he left more than 100,000 personal papers, photographs, pieces of correspondence, manuscripts, recordings, and other ephemera, which are now available for researchers at the Detroit Public Library. However, our search for Roland Hayes went well beyond Detroit, as Robert Sims and I examined additional documents in archival collections in Boston; New York; Washington, D.C.; Calhoun and Rome, Georgia; Carmel and San Francisco, California; and Memphis and Chattanooga, Tennessee; not to mention several collections in Europe. In order to uncover this important story, we interviewed direct descendants and relatives along with many others who were in some way connected to this historical figure. We discovered that while Hayes went through great pains to carefully construct and preserve his legacy, there were aspects of his life he was determined to keep private. When this information began to be leaked to the press, he fought to stop it.[2]

Roland Hayes operated in an era when African American men did not speak or display their feelings publicly, which added a layer of complexity to researching this book. It is also important to note that Robert Sims and I have come to this work from different perspectives – Sims as a renowned performing artist who has specialized in the African American folk song repertoire, much of which Roland Hayes performed, and I as an anthropologically trained Africanist interested in exploring Hayes's continental African and diasporan importance in an era of racial exclusion. We were both interested in exploring the complex issues surrounding this once-famous personality in an era of segregation and censorship and how Hayes negotiated his way through the sometimes-volatile concert music world. This combination of backgrounds offers a reflective and exhaustive account of this long-forgotten musician and historical figure whom the world once recognized as great.

Christopher A. Brooks

Roland Hayes

Prologue

AFTER COMPLETING A MAJOR ENGAGEMENT IN ATLANTA IN
November 1926, Roland Hayes traveled seventy-five miles north to still-
rural Gordon County, Georgia, where there was once a town called Curryville.[1] Although Hayes was in the area on other business, he met with
Joseph Mann, an impoverished, elderly white man who had enslaved
Hayes's forebears. Roland solicited the meeting with the feeble Joe Mann
because gaps in the tenor's maternal lineage could be filled only by his
family's former enslaver. As is true for many Americans of African descent, it was difficult to document the life of his forebears who had been
seized in Africa and sold into enslavement in the American South. And
so, determined to understand the origins of his family, Roland returned
to the countryside of his youth, where his own story begins.

Joe Mann was born in the 1830s and had once lived a life of opportunity and privilege. Like his father, Edward Mann, he farmed two sizable
plantations in the antebellum South. By 1926, however, the once-wealthy
landowner and his sickly, bedridden wife had been reduced to living in
a drafty shed, outfitted with makeshift furniture. His living quarters
were scarcely better than those of the blacks who had once worked that
very land.

The difference in the two men's appearances could not have been
more striking. Hayes's freshly shaven, flawless, dark skin contrasted with
the old man's pale, weather-beaten, and unshaven face. Roland was impeccably dressed in a tailor-made wool suit, a stiff, white high-collared
shirt with cuff links, a dark tie, and polished black shoes, while Joe Mann

wore a threadbare dark suit and a vest without a tie. His tattered hat covered his thinning, matted white hair.

With the aid of his cane, the old man made his way to a chair near Hayes, who alternately knelt or stood beside him. Despite the dramatic difference in current social status and appearances, Mann still felt entitled to address the thirty-nine-year-old as a servant: "Roland, are you that boy of Pony's who got caught settin' down on a plow and ringin' a cowbell?"[2]

Finally, Mann gave the tenor what he sought. The Roland Hayes story, according to Mann, was traceable to the final decade of the eighteenth century, when Hayes's great-grandfather Abá 'Ougi had been captured near the interior of West Africa, in modern-day Ivory Coast.[3] Like millions of others, Abá 'Ougi was shipped by way of the Middle Passage from West Africa to Savannah, Georgia. After being processed, bid on, and sold, was he given the Christian name Charles Weaver by the family that had purchased his body and labor, presumably for the rest of his life. According to Mann, Abá 'Ougi was proud and independent and had a well-known musical talent. Mann told Hayes, "You come of a great family for singin'."[4] Mann remembered Abá 'Ougi singing "He Never Said a Mumberlin' Word." Perhaps Mann was aware that Hayes had sung the dramatic "Mumberlin' Word" in many European capitals, reducing his audience members to tears.[5] Abá 'Ougi converted to Christianity and eventually became an overseer, charged with enforcing discipline and productivity.

"Weaver" was often heard singing, and his owners saw it as his normal behavior. But the enslaved men and women understood those songs as encoded messages.[6] The descendants of the African American Mann family explained during their reunions that Abá 'Ougi used musical signals to assemble occasional clandestine meetings. Although their origins aren't actually verifiable, Roland attributed many songs, including "Mumberlin' Word" and "Steal Away," to his African great-grandfather. They subsequently became standards within African American spiritual repertory.

Hayes was well versed in the story told by the black side of the Mann family, which had evolved over generations. It held that Abá 'Ougi ultimately lost his life because of his strong Christian faith. One of his religious assemblies for laborers had just begun when the gathered were set upon by bounty hunters. Only after seeing that the others got off safely did the self-appointed leader attempt to flee. Abá 'Ougi met his fate at the hands of those determined to see him remain enslaved.

Like many Africans who were bartered and sold, Abá 'Ougi had been obliged to provide breeding services for plantation owners in neighboring areas. The Weavers had paired him with a young woman from Edward Mann's plantation.[7] Resulting from this transaction was Roland's maternal grandfather, Peter Weaver, who was reputed to be a vibrant man with a legendary temper. When Peter was twenty, he was allowed to marry Mandy, a young woman from Edward Mann's enslaved population. The Weavers agreed to sell Peter to the Manns, who then adopted that surname for himself.[8]

This union produced five children, including Roland's mother, Fannie (also known as "Pony" while enslaved), who was most likely born in 1847.[9] Because she was told it was hot when she was born, she concluded that she had been born in August.

Joe Mann had not been particularly kind to those souls whom he had inherited from his father. According to Roland's mother, Mann had physically abused her as a teenager, supposedly for stealing sugar, and he threw Roland's pregnant grandmother into a tub of cold water at the close of the Civil War.[10]

After Joe Mann had promised Roland's quick-tempered grandfather a whipping for some minor infraction, he ran off and lived in the woods for more than a year during the war. During one of his periodic visits to his wife and their children, Peter was discovered. Joe Mann and his hounds chased and treed Roland's grandfather, who was ultimately caught, beaten mercilessly, and died from the heinous treatment routinely administered to captured fugitives. Peter Mann never lived to see the end of the war and never knew any freedom beyond that which he had taken when he fled the inhumane treatment on the Mann plantation.[11]

Fully aware of the significance of his meeting with Joe Mann, Roland had brought along a photographer. He had already begun to prepare his story for a future public. At the conclusion of the two-hour visit, Roland and Joe Mann posed together for pictures. If he had feelings of anger against the old man, the photos do not reveal them. After all, the black man now represented wealth, affluence, and opportunity, while the white man presented the very antithesis.

Roland shook hands with Mann, gave him a few dollars, and told him that he expected to see him in the not-too-distant future. If Joe Mann wondered why Roland had not taken his moment of revenge for the misery endured by his forebears, his final humiliation came when he learned he would end his days living on ground that now belonged to Hayes, who had just finished purchasing it. As a former planter, Joe Mann knew all too well the power inherent in landowning and that his future was now in Roland's hands. They bid farewell and continued on very separate roads. Roland's road was to greater recognition, higher performing fees, and bigger audiences, while Joe Mann, who had enslaved and abused men, women, and children, would die a squatter on land that he formerly owned but now belonged to Roland Hayes.

All who knew Roland, from boyhood through his life as a distinguished concert artist, remarked upon his drive and determination. That same tenacity served him well in uncovering the story of his ancestors and the beginnings of his own.

ONE

A New Jerusalem

1887–1911

CURRYVILLE IN GORDON COUNTY, GEORGIA, IN AN AREA known as the Flatwoods, was mostly a backwater village when Roland Wiltsie Hayes was born there on June 3, 1887. The summit of Horn Mountain beheld an unobstructed panorama of hills, grasslands, creeks, woods, falling rocks, waterfalls, animal-worn dirt trails, and a smattering of houses and plots of farmland.[1]

Roland's worldview was shaped by the racially segregated environment of his parents, William Hayes and Fannie. Black landowners eventually became the new reality in post–Civil War Georgia, but only in the context of die-hard racial animus. African Americans were still required to show deference to their white counterparts lest they become subject to racial attack from organizations like the Ku Klux Klan, among others. The people who populated this part of the country and shared Roland's ethnic heritage and lower social status found themselves as part of a permanent underclass; they had managed to survive because they knew "their place" when interacting with the white majority.

William Hayes had built a two-room log cabin at the foot of Horn Mountain using trees from nearby woods.[2] By the time Roland was born, the cabin was equipped with a large wood-burning fireplace and chimney. There were a few other adornments in the house, and of course the cabinets and other furniture were expertly made by William.[3] Off from the house was a kitchen that William had also built, where Fannie cooked for her growing family.

As the disciplinarian, William had a somewhat detached relationship with his children. The nurturing and housework were left to his wife. When a boy reached a certain age (around eight), he was expected to shoulder his responsibility for the household. Roland helped to stick the hogs for curing in the family's smokehouse, to fetch wood and water for cooking, and, when he was a little older, to join in the hunt for wild game with his father and older brothers.[4]

Roland's somewhat idyllic – as he later described it – picture of his childhood depicts a boy roaming in the woods and hunting with his father. Hunting, however, was not Roland's favorite activity. Because he was the youngest at the time, he was obliged to carry the dead catch.[5] As he grew older, he became deft at snaring rabbits and other small game, following the example of William and his older brothers.[6]

Roland had four older brothers and an older sister; later, "Baby" Jesse was born. Roland's vivid recollections of his older brothers William Jr. (or "Willie") and Nathaniel "Tench" centered on their sometimes troubled relationship with their father because of the latter's strict ways. Before Roland was born, Willie had reached adolescence and run away from home. Although he was permanently disabled from a knee injury, Willie returned to Curryville with an education from Chattanooga. His schooling there had surpassed that of the local teachers in the Curryville school for the African American children, and Willie likely became his younger brother's first formal grade school teacher.

Nathaniel "Tench" Hayes would have been eleven when Roland was born, and young Roland would have been no more than six or seven when Tench left home. Tench would return to the Hayes household over the next several years with various illnesses and eventually died sometime in the late 1890s.[7] He was probably no more than twenty-one years old.

As his only sister, Mattie Hayes would have been in her fourteenth year when Roland was born. She, too, met with an untimely and unexplained death, but unlike her brothers she at least had the opportunity to wed, although it was a short and unhappy marital experience. Hayes recollected that the only time he remembered seeing his mother cry was when his sister died. Letting down her guard for the display of emotion was not a luxury she could often afford.[8] Of Fannie Hayes's seven children, three died within a short time frame, and only four survived to see the twentieth century.

Churchgoing was an integral part of life in Curryville, and Fannie insisted on a strict Baptist religious foundation for all of her children.

She taught them to fear and respect the Lord and to believe in his power to change people's hearts and minds. Roland received his earliest music lessons from his father, which included witnessing William's uncanny sensitivity to sounds. He remembered his father's "shimmering" and mellow tenor voice, which he used to summon his hogs.[9] He also learned to sing his career-defining *messa di voce* from his father and not from formal voice lessons.

Roland once remembered asking his father about his ability to imitate natural sounds so expertly. William explained to his son that all humans had some manifestation of nature within themselves and that everyone possessed the ability to understand and imitate the sounds if they were willing to look deep inwardly and tap into it.[10] Roland's assertion years later that when he performed it was not him but the spirit expressing itself through him was a direct outgrowth of his father's teachings on vocal production.

While William Hayes had many talents, farming was not among them. He was known to have employed a trick using a cowbell to rhythmically simulate the family's cow plowing the fields while he sat and smoked under a tree. Joe Mann, the former enslaver of Fannie in Gordon County, mistakenly associated Roland with the cowbell incident when it had actually been his father. The story is still recounted among the Hayes family members more than one hundred years later.[11]

In the small, rural, southern dwellings of northwest Georgia, there were relatively few social outlets. Thus, the religious life of the community took on enhanced significance. Mount Zion Baptist Church was made up of mostly preliterate African Americans and was an important foundation in Roland's religious and musical formation. As the young boy grew more confident in his ability to speak before audiences, he was tasked with learning new songs to teach to the congregation. These songs also formed the basis of the "Aframerican" (as Hayes called them) folk songs that he would arrange and perform on the concert stage many years later.[12]

Fannie wanted Roland to become a preacher, as he began to display signs of an oratorical gift from a young age. Although Roland did not formally enter the pulpit, he routinely spoke about his singing and his art as a "message," which he felt compelled to deliver. He regarded his "work" in religious terms. In his later years, he routinely spoke about his religious beliefs but seemed not to have had a formal denominational affiliation. There is no question, however, that he considered himself a spiritual person and that his religious conditioning was based on his early days at Mount Zion Baptist Church.

Other social forces had a major impact on his worldview. Roland spoke of Peter Vaughn, who taught him how to read music from hymnals when Vaughn came to the Flatwoods to conduct his seasonal singing school.[13] Other influences included two of Fannie's younger brothers, Wiltsie and Simon, who were seasoned banjoists. These uncles of Roland were regular churchgoers but "scandalously" played (from their big sister's perspective) at social events at which peopled danced.

Roland's musical training under Peter Vaughn was quite extensive, but he also identified Jim Kirby (whom he called "Uncle Nat") as yet another teacher. It was from Uncle Nat that young Roland learned a number of African songs as a child. He apparently forgot many of them until meeting several continental Africans in England and France in the early 1920s. When these songs combined with the stories of his fabled African great-grandfather Abá 'Ougi, Roland developed a fascination, commitment, and affinity for the African continent that manifested itself in various ways throughout his career and the remainder of his life.

Roland's formal classroom education was different from what he experienced in the informal settings of his religious upbringing. This education was typical for a young black boy in the rural South in the late nineteenth century. That is, there was very little of it. The meager education that was available to him was seasonal at best. He described how it was the practice for the African American children to attend school in the winter months, only after the responsibilities of the fall harvest were completed. The teachers themselves had minimal skills, and the lessons did not go beyond the basics of reading, reciting, and perhaps some rudimentary mathematics. The highest level available to African American children in the Flatwoods during Roland's youth was the seventh grade. The lack of educational opportunities available would ultimately be a factor in Fannie's decision to move her younger children to Chattanooga, Tennessee, after the turn of the century.

Roland himself was unequivocal in his assessment of his early school years in the Flatwoods – he hated it.[14] Young Roland was especially terrified by the weekly recitations in which the students had to present memorized speeches.[15] Even when he desperately wanted to stand up to recite so as not to disappoint his teacher, whom he loved, fear and shyness overcame him.[16]

Fortunately in 1896, a young graduate from Atlanta Baptist College named Wilkin Green boarded with the Hayes family for a time and helped young Roland conquer his timidity.[17] Green also began telling the young boy of great African and African diasporan leaders, such as the legendary Haitian revolutionary Toussaint L'Ouverture, who inspired the young Roland and captured his interest into adulthood. As a result of Wilkin Green's confidence-building exercises, young Roland gave speeches in other African American schools and churches throughout the county, developing and displaying his oratorical talents.[18]

Although records do not make clear when or how it occurred, William Hayes suffered a severe spinal injury from a logging accident sometime in the latter half of the 1890s.[19] The accident was serious enough to keep him bedridden and in constant agony. His eventual death in 1898, while traumatic for his family, was not altogether unexpected. The funeral song of triumph, "Roun' about de Mountain," was sung at William Hayes's home-going procession. Roland's own performance of this song, with its prophetic refrain "the Lord loves a sinner, and he'll rise in his arm," became celebrated for many years and was included in his collection *My Songs, Aframerican Religious Folk Songs.*

Facing economic hardship with three young sons at home (Robert Brante, fifteen; Roland, eleven; and Jesse, less than ten), the pragmatic Fannie had to quickly assess the family's financial circumstances. It would take about two years of working the fields for her family to rise out of debt, at which point Fannie could take her sons to Chattanooga for a proper education. Roland and Robert Brante dropped out of school temporarily to run the Hayes family farm and the additional acres that Fannie leased.[20] Because of the family's extreme need, the brothers also hired themselves out to work on other area farms.

By 1900, the family had retired its farm debt, and Fannie carried on with her plans to get her sons educated in Chattanooga. Robert Brante and Roland (seventeen and thirteen), along with the family cow, traveled to the city by foot with another Curryville family. Fannie and "Baby" Jesse took the train. The Hayes matriarch left the management of her ten acres to her cousin Obie Mann. Although she leased the land for others to work, she continued to pay property taxes, and it remained in her family. The adolescent Roland was bound for a new city where a world he could barely imagine awaited him.

Like the Flatwoods area of northwest Georgia, the comparatively urbanized Chattanooga, Tennessee, had been once occupied by the Cherokee Nation prior to the infamous Trail of Tears. The city saw many dramatic battles during the Civil War, when Ulysses S. Grant had attempted to pound the region into submission. Chattanooga held a good mixture of black and white citizens, but as was the case throughout the South, social and racial lines were pronounced.

Fannie's arrival in Chattanooga by rail with her youngest son was a homecoming of sorts. Her mother, Mandy, had moved to the city after the Civil War to raise her family, and Fannie had begun her married life with William Hayes in Chattanooga before settling in the Flatwoods of Georgia. Fannie's younger sister Harriet, who lived in the Fort Wood area of the city, met Fannie when she arrived, and Roland and Robert eventually made it after their fifty-five-mile trek, having walked barefoot with their supplies and furniture, reluctantly pulled by the family cow. Harriet provided temporary housing for her older sister and her three sons until they could get themselves established.[21]

The boys' introduction to city life was dramatic. They saw things that they could not have fathomed, even in their wildest imaginations. Streetlights and paved roads were just a few of the wonders to behold in this "New Jerusalem."[22]

Roland recalled one of the earliest adjustments was in their religious worship. Having recently arrived from the country with their mended clothes, brass-tipped brogan shoes, rural accents, and "backwoods" mannerisms, the newly arrived Hayes family felt sorely out of place in their aunt's middle-class church, the First African Baptist Church. Once Fannie and her family could afford their own living accommodations, they established membership at the less "Hoity-toity! Madam-is-in-her airs" Monumental Baptist Church.[23]

Roland and his brothers also met several of their cousins for the first time. Roland recalled that this was when he first met Uncle Robert and Aunt Katie's daughter, Helen Alzada Mann. Born September 24, 1893, Alzada was among the oldest of fourteen children. Roland offered a fanciful tale of this meeting with his first cousin and future wife. As he told it, she was more impressed with his recently purchased, "squeaky high-pitched bright" yellow shoes.[24] Roland was thirteen and Helen Alzada was a mere seven when they met. This was hardly a fateful first encounter for the two, as his account suggested. In fact, the path to their marriage some thirty-two years later was far more complex with many roads and detours than Roland's simplified version intimates.[25]

Fannie had moved her sons to Chattanooga to take advantage of better educational opportunities. Her strategy, then, required that Robert and Roland alternate going to school. While one son spent the year being educated, the other would work to support the family. Robert, who was older and presumably more educated than Roland, began school in Chattanooga, while Roland found work. Because of his age, "Baby" Jesse was able to attend school full-time.

Before he turned fourteen in 1901, Roland had found a job at the Price-Evans Foundry Company, which produced iron door and window weights. He persuaded his employer to hire him, citing his family's dire need for him to work, and he was initially compensated at eighty cents a day.[26] The young Roland described his work at the foundry as the hardest work he had ever done. Along with an adult employee, he loaded iron from a nearby freight yard from the early morning to the midafternoon. Once they returned to the foundry with the metal, they began melting the iron in large vats and pouring it into molds to create the weights.

While transporting the molten hot iron from the vats to the molding casts, Roland wore his old brass-tipped brogans without shoestrings. In the very likely event that hot iron spilled, he could easily kick off the shoes. Even with this precaution, the boy sustained permanent scars on his feet and legs from the occasional hot iron flake.[27] Roland eventually graduated to the less physically taxing job of working with the casts used in molding the iron. Because he developed a more efficient method of blending the formula in this process, he was promoted to foreman with a higher salary and shorter working hours.[28]

Roland worked this job for more than a year before returning to school and kept it, at least part time, while he attended school in the afternoon. The muscle-bound, nearly sixteen-year-old wage earner and head of his household struck a clear contrast with the rest of the class of young children learning basic skills. But for the times, such a contrast was not that unusual. During the oratorical lessons, he lost a little of his southern drawl but not his somewhat affected pronunciation of words beginning with the letter *t*, which sounded more like a *td* combination.[29]

Fannie had not abandoned her plan for Roland to enter the pulpit. In 1903, Roland and his brothers were baptized in the Tennessee River after being inspired by the word as delivered through Reverend William G. Ward. Reverend Ward led more than twenty-five converts (among them Roland) to the waters of salvation wearing their white baptism gowns. In accepting Jesus Christ into his life, Roland had to give up certain practices, such as buck and toe dancing (a popular dance step of the time), and he had to dissociate himself from non-churchgoing boys.[30] He reached a compromise in the latter category by requiring his friends not to swear, take the Lord's name in vain, or engage in other blasphemous activities when he was around. Had it been left up to Fannie, the restrictions would have been even more severe, as she had routinely warned him to "come out from amongst them" after his baptism.[31]

Roland did not, however, concede to stop singing. In fact, he sang whether he was at work or in casual settings and saw no contradiction between singing and his newly acquired spiritual status. Roland recalled hearing a young African American man, Lemus Hardison, singing on the streets in the Fort Wood area of Chattanooga during this period; his tenor voice was strangely and profoundly reminiscent of Roland's late father's. Roland frequently sat in on the rehearsals of Hardison's singing group.[32]

Whether it was in response to Hardison's group is not clear, but Roland did join an a cappella vocal group, the Silver-Toned Quartet. It included Robert Igoe (who eventually married one of Roland's cousins), Ben Ingram, and Roland's brother Robert Brante.[33] The group sang at train stations and in affluent neighborhoods, where appreciative listeners responded by tossing them nickels and quarters. As choir members of the Monumental Baptist Church, the Silver-Toned Quartet had to adhere to the singing requirements of musical director Mrs. Jane Kennedy, who also played a pivotal role in young Roland's career aspirations and goals.[34]

A life-changing event occurred shortly after Roland's spiritual conversion. He offered different accounts of the incident at the Casey-Hedges Foundry but always came to the same conclusion – his survival was nothing short of miraculous.[35]

While standing too close to the conveyor machinery, Roland's clothes got caught in one of the belts. He was dragged onto the machine, which rotated at least three times on the pulley before it could be stopped. Mercifully, he was knocked unconscious by the belt's first rotation, but his rescuers initially thought he had been killed by the accident. After being revived, he was taken to a doctor's office and treated. Eventually the battered young Roland was taken home in a full body cast. When Fannie saw her son in this condition, she lost her composure and ran from the house, fearing that she would be told he was dead.[36] Because African Americans were rarely hospitalized in those days, the foundry provided Fannie with a full-time nurse to assist her in bringing Roland back to health. The owners of Casey-Hedges were also prepared to guarantee Roland a lifetime position with the company as additional compensation for his accident.

Elsewhere, Roland likened his conveyor belt incident to that of the apostle Paul, who similarly had to be prepared (through his temporary blindness on the road to Damascus) for his mission. Describing the incident in Pauline terms, Roland said: "There was nothing at all to save me . . . except the power of God. That I WAS saved convinced me that I was spared to fulfill a Divine Purpose. I saw the accomplishment of that Purpose through the musically artistic gifts with which the ALMIGHTY had endowed me."[37] During his ten-week convalescence, he reflected on what he had experienced and the severity of the incident that he had miraculously survived. When he returned to his old job, Roland could no longer stand the sight of the conveyor machine. When he passed the huge contraption, he again questioned how someone could have survived being pulled through the machine three times.

Even before the accident at the foundry, Roland had a reputation for singing at work. His employers at the foundry, as well as in his previous jobs, made exceptions to the rules and allowed him to do so. Once he was fit enough, Roland resumed his membership in the Silver-Toned Quartet, as well as in the Monumental Baptist Church choir, again under the direction of Mrs. Kennedy. The stage was now set for the next phase of Roland's formal musical development.

Roland's first formal voice teacher learned through Mrs. Kennedy that he could sing. She arranged for him to perform at a commencement program where W. Arthur Calhoun, Mrs. Kennedy's brother and a student at the well-regarded Oberlin College Conservatory of Music, was also present.[38] Calhoun, who would spur Roland on to the next phase in his career, had taken a year away from his studies to earn money for school by returning to Chattanooga to teach voice and piano.[39] Calhoun also gave small programs in area churches for extra money and staged such a program at Monumental Baptist Church.[40] After hearing Roland's small solo, Calhoun attempted to persuade him that his voice was worth developing. During a walk after that service, Calhoun took Roland's hand and said, "Boy, but you have a fine tenor voice! What are you going to do with it?" The still shy Roland responded, "I don't know, Sir. I just sing because I like to."[41]

Encouraging him to take his talent seriously, the Oberlin-trained keyboardist and voice teacher walked Roland to his house, convincing him that his instrument was worthy of cultivation and training. Persuading Fannie that her son should spend fifty cents per lesson, twice a week, was an entirely different matter. Roland quite vividly remembered Calhoun approaching his mother about studying voice with him:

> When he [Calhoun] talked to my mother about it he had an even more discouraging reception. I only laughed at the idea; but *she* resented it.
>
> To her it was worse than nonsense. She was rather proud of me – a good, steady, hard-working boy, earning better wages than many older men received. She knew no colored people who made a living out of music, except those who sang and played in dance halls and places of that sort. She didn't want any boy of hers to take up *that* kind of life. So she and my friend were decidedly at swords' points.
>
> He was so persistent that I consented to let him teach me, or try to, and for a while he gave me lessons. But I still wasn't very much interested.[42]

Roland made reference to some of the repertoire that he worked on with Calhoun, such as the once-popular wedding song "I Love You Truly," "Forgotten," and "The End of a Perfect Day."[43] Calhoun exposed the young Roland to other standard art music repertoire. Within months of studying with Calhoun, Roland's voice lessons stretched his imagination, and he became dedicated to pursuing a singing career.

Shortly thereafter, a local lodge staged the Hezekiah Butterworth cantata *David the Shepherd Boy,* and Roland (with Calhoun's influence and coaching) was assigned the lead role. The mostly white audience's reaction to the young singer was "tremendous." But Roland still wavered, heeding Fannie's warnings,[44] weighing her often-stated opposition to a singing career against his own desire, and wondering, "Does God want me to sing instead of making stoves?"[45]

Among Calhoun's other pupils were the daughters of Civil War colonel and editor of the highly regarded *Chattanooga Times* William Stone. After Roland had been studying for about a year, Calhoun arranged an introduction between the young singer and Stone, who played a defining role in Hayes's development. Roland recalled the fateful meeting of early autumn of 1904, when Calhoun first took him to Stone's house to sing. Roland recalled that he was eventually invited into a parlor where Stone, his wife, and their daughters were present.[46] Following the protocol of the period, Mrs. Stone and her daughters immediately excused themselves from the room upon the young black man's arrival. As Hayes began to sing, however, they returned, one by one.[47]

While the setting was unique for Roland (the tenor had mostly visited the homes of poor African Americans), the experience at Stone's home was memorable for another reason. After Roland had sung for the family, Stone introduced Hayes to the recordings of Dame Nellie Melba, Emma Ames, and Marcella Sembrich on his gramophone.[48] Roland likened the experience to being reborn and later referred to it as akin to a blind person being given sight; it was one of three epiphanies that he experienced during his formative years.

It was Stone's recording of the celebrated tenor Enrico Caruso, however, that would have the most profound impact on Roland.[49] The wealthy editor played the Italian singer's rendition of "Vesti la giubba" (Put on your costume) from Ruggero Leoncavallo's decade-old verismo

opera *I Pagliacci* (The Clowns). The beauty, clarity, and power of Caruso's
voice seared Roland's being. He sat in the parlor, nearly speechless. If,
after studying with Calhoun for only a few brief weeks, Roland was dedicated to a singing career, the experience at William Stone's house that
evening sparked him to set yet another new goal: that of being a great
artist in the tradition of Caruso himself. Pursuing his ambition of becoming a great singer became Roland's life's work, and from that point
on he pursued it with missionary zeal.[50]

Roland Hayes studied with Arthur Calhoun for at least another year,
but he (and no doubt Calhoun) realized his teacher's limitations. Roland
credited Calhoun, however, with exposing him to the necessary people
and circumstances that would eventually lead him to greatness.[51]

In spite of Roland's clear commitment to an artistic career, in 1906
Fannie remained the doubting Thomas. She often stated, "They tell me
Negroes can't understand good music, and white people don't want to
hear it from us. So it seems to me you are making a mistake."[52] Based on
her enslaved background and lack of exposure to such an unimaginable
world, her observation was sound. Roland, at the same time, was committed to moving forward with his goal, which meant furthering his
vocal studies. For some time, Calhoun had wanted Hayes to enroll at
Oberlin College in Ohio, and Roland was more than willing to comply.
To address the obvious issue of resources, Roland asked Fannie for some
of the family's collective savings. With fifty dollars, most of which he had
earned himself, and an incredible amount of determination, he set off for
Nashville on the first leg of his journey.

After arriving in the city – which, by the turn of the century, had
become an important trading center as state capital with a population
of 90,000[53] – Roland went to African American churches to seek the
assistance of those ministers. Encouraged by what he had learned from
Calhoun, Hayes gave concerts at local churches, charging ten cents for
admission, which he would share with the church. He had begun this
practice in Chattanooga. Of course, Roland had to pay from his share
the accompanist and other performance-related expenses. This arrangement actually depleted his resources.[54] In order to avoid returning to
Chattanooga in defeat, which young Roland considered unthinkable,
he adjusted his plans. Instead of attending Oberlin, he would choose a

school closer to home. A public school teacher in Nashville, Miss Margaret Stubbs, who was familiar with other music teachers in the city, suggested that Roland try nearby Fisk University.[55] Founded in 1866 by the American Missionary Association, a collection of Protestant denominations dedicated in the nineteenth century to abolition, Fisk University was one of several institutions committed to educating young African Americans who had either been enslaved or who were the children of Africans who had been held in bondage.[56] Roland, however, understood that his fifth grade education and lack of resources would be a hindrance to such a suggestion.[57]

Roland was understandably shy when he and Stubbs entered Fisk's well-manicured campus and was awed by the magnificence of Jubilee Hall, built through a donation by the renowned Jubilee Singers in the 1870s. Roland's intimidation grew when he and Stubbs approached the tall and severe Miss Jennie Robison, director of the music department. After much pleading, Stubbs persuaded Robinson to give Roland an informal hearing. Stubbs accompanied Hayes at the keyboard while he nervously sang Robert A. King's "Beyond the Gates of Paradise" and "Forgotten." Although the well-known and often-performed "Beyond the Gates" was a standard at the turn of the twentieth century, Robinson appeared unmoved by the singing. Her specific remarks were, "Where did you learn such sentimental rubbish?"[58] Predictably, Robinson vetoed even the possibility of a place for Roland for the approaching fall school term. Stubbs rose again to his defense and prevailed upon her to speak to Fisk president Dr. James G. Merrill on Roland's behalf.[59]

The following day, a now genuinely frightened Roland appeared before Merrill, whose long Roman nose impressed the apprehensive youth. Hayes thought the man looked like the American eagle itself.[60] After rapidly administering a battery of questions and asking Hayes what gave him the temerity to present himself without adequate preparation, Merrill sent the thoroughly cowed young man for a formal admission examination. That test measured Roland's mathematical ability, reading comprehension, geographical knowledge, and ability to recite poetry. Quite expectedly, the test revealed that Hayes was at the fifth grade level at best.[61] Yet Roland had evidently stirred the heart of the institution's otherwise stern president, because after thoroughly scrutinizing the test's results and informing him of his deficiencies, he granted Hayes a provisional month-long admission, during which his performance would determine his future at the school.

Roland was admitted to Fisk's lower school – like a high school – in a program designed to assist students who needed remedial work prior to collegiate admission. Less than two generations after enslaved Africans were legally freed in the United States, Roland Hayes's admission scenario was not that uncommon. In addition to granting Roland provisional admission, Merrill took the extraordinarily generous step of securing the newly admitted student a job as a butler and furnace boy to a local judge and his family. It included his accommodations, meals, and a stipend of one dollar per week.[62] Roland admitted that he worked mind and body at school as well as at his job off-campus to prove himself worthy.

His relationship with his employers, the Childress family, was long lasting, even though he worked for them only for his first year at Fisk.[63] While he served the Childress family, Roland learned all of the niceties of polite society, including how to set tables, among other activities which displayed his polish.

But the most pivotal personality in Hayes's years at Fisk, and perhaps throughout his life, was Jennie Asenath Robinson. Born in Topeka, Kansas, in 1857, Robinson's family had moved to the territory from Michigan with Christian missionary intent and abolitionist sympathies.[64] She received a bachelor's degree from Highland College in 1875 and later matriculated at Oberlin, where she studied until 1887, when she took a position as director of the fledgling music department at Fisk University. Robinson arrived in Nashville as a single thirty-two-year-old; she was imposing, severe, and strict and always wore her blonde, full-length hair neatly in a bun on top of her head. She was the definition of modesty. She wore no frills and very little jewelry. Robinson came to the institution with clear standards about what constituted an appropriate music education and recruited like-minded faculty members from Oberlin to support her in establishing the budding program.[65] The great eighteenth- and nineteenth-century European music composers were her ideal for instructing her students in voice culture, music theory, and other aspects of vocal production. Even late nineteenth-century composers like Richard Strauss and Hugo Wolf, whom Roland would come to love, were considered "too modern" for this classical music purist. She equipped all of her aspiring teachers with other necessary tools they would need to be successful and directed them to stay current with the latest vocal techniques and avoid repertory like popular "Negro spirituals," which she felt might demean their knowledge of great composers of previous centuries. Her thirty-two-year legacy was rich as she trained and placed students in strategic music-related teaching and administration positions throughout the South.[66]

To the chagrin of her Fisk colleagues, notably John W. Work II, the Nashville-born, Harvard-trained African American professor of classics and the leader of the Jubilee Singers at the time of Hayes's arrival,[67] Jennie Robinson was dismissive, if not disdainful, of the music being performed and promoted by the celebrated Jubilee singing group. From her standpoint and musical training, the Jubilee vocal tradition was uncultured and unprogressive, as it employed demeaning black dialect and advanced practices contrary to the standard she set for her students. Unfortunately for Roland, he arrived at the institution as these clearly delineated musical philosophies were most pronounced.[68]

At the end of Hayes's first year at Fisk, he was summoned to President Merrill's office for his "one-month" probationary assessment. Merrill reported to the young student that it had been a "long one-month probation." He offered Hayes a scholarship and employment with a family on campus for the following year.[69] Roland was properly elated but had learned to show polite restraint in public. He formed a closer bond with his next employer than that which he had enjoyed with the Childress family.

In the fall of 1907, the second-year Fisk student began working for Professor Warren G. Waterman, whom he described as a "tall Yankee chemist with sunburned skin and a consumptive stoop."[70] As with the Childresses, Roland maintained a relationship with the Waterman family, even after they left Nashville. Warren Waterman, like William Stone years prior, possessed a Victrola Talking Machine, on which he played recordings of European art music singers for Roland. This exposure to the great operatic repertory would be useful to him in the future. While performing his servant duties in the Waterman household, it was com-

mon practice for Roland to sing. On one occasion, Waterman heard singing and assumed that the young man was playing some of his prized
recordings without authorization. He rushed downstairs, expecting to
find Roland playing his phonograph, only to discover it was Roland singing. Hayes had no idea that he had been observed. Thereafter, Waterman
invited Roland to listen to his recordings but did not tell him he had
mistaken Roland's voice for a professional's until many years later.[71]

The relationship between Roland and Warren Waterman later developed into a genuine friendship. After moving to Evanston in the 1920s,
the chemist maintained regular communication with the singer. Hayes
later stayed as a guest in Waterman's home when performing in the Evanston area.

Roland's ability to sight-read notated music, pronounce and sing
English and other languages, and develop his overall musicianship was
dramatically enhanced under Jennie Robinson's watchful eye.[72] His
method of learning vocal repertoire under Arthur Calhoun had been
primarily through rote learning in which Calhoun played the notes for
Roland on the keyboard, who then memorized the music.[73] Through
study with Robinson, he learned several well-known arias and great sacred works such as "If with All Your Heart" and "Then Shall the Righ-
teous Shine Forth" from Mendelssohn's *Elijah,* pieces from Haydn's
Seven Last Words and Beethoven's *Christus am Olberge* (Christ on the
Mount of Olives), and various Schubert lieder.[74] Roland also sang solos
at area churches and in 1908 participated in the Negro Music Festival
in Louisville, Kentucky. Between 1908 and 1910, the tenor sang solos
in concerts given by the Fisk Mozart Society, which was, of course, a
Robinson-sanctioned outlet for his impressive talent.[75]

Some sources suggest that Hayes toured with the highly regarded Jubilee Singers, who were loosely affiliated with Fisk University,[76] but there
is no record of such travels.[77] In subsequent years, however, he received
communications from those who were either in the group with him or
saw him perform with the group.[78] His greatest involvement with the
Jubilee Singers seems to have been during his fourth year at Fisk, during
which time Roland continued his employment with Warren Waterman
but lived in a men's dormitory.

President Merrill, who had been so generous to the young student, left the university in 1908. During the 1908–09 academic year, George A. Gates assumed the helm of the growing university. Roland had made steady progress in the lower school, where he had one more year of study before seeking admission to the collegiate department.

In the spring of 1909, Roland was the victim of a racial attack, which made its way into the local African American weekly. Under an April 23 headline that read, "Row Over Beef Steak, Mr. Rowland [sic] W. Hayes Assaulted," the *Nashville Globe* detailed Roland's encounter with three white men:

> Mr. Rowland [sic] W. Hayes, a student at Fisk University, was brutally assaulted by three white men near the corner of Eighteenth avenue and Jefferson street one day last week, and was severely injured. It is said that two of the men held Mr. Hayes while the third man was doing the cowardly act. Mr. Hayes is slowly recovering from his injuries.
>
> The affair, it seems, was the result of a difference of opinion about a beefsteak. Mr. Hayes went into a grocery of one Burton to purchase a steak. He asked that he be given one to cost a certain price. When the grocer cut it the weight put the price in excess of what was asked for. Mr. Hayes told him that he could not accept it. Burton insisted and Mr. Hayes started out. He was followed to the door and across the street. Burton called him a s . . . of a b . . . and struck him a blow, felling him. Young Mr. Hayes rallied quickly and retaliated. He was giving a good account of himself until several other white men took Burton's part, preventing Hayes from defending himself, so that Burton could assault him.
>
> The citizens in the neighborhood are very indignant over the affair and are outspoken in their denunciation of the grocer-man. They entertain some fear as to the safety of this place.[79]

Such were the all-too-frequent affronts and injustices that southern African American men and women faced. Roland never mentioned this assault in any other biographical account, but defending himself as he did in a three-against-one fight was in line with his quick temper.

Having had some financial success with his Silver-Toned Quartet in Chattanooga a few years earlier, Roland put together another male quartet made up of Fisk students during the spring semester of 1910. The members included James Clarence Olden (who became a well-known Baptist minister and whose daughter, Sylvia Olden-Lee, was also a celebrated musician), second tenor; Leon Pulaski O'Hara, baritone; and

William Henry Patton, bass. Roland, of course, sang first tenor. The foursome initially advertised themselves as the "Fisk Quartette No. 2" and had placed notices in the *Globe* for an upcoming recital, but by the February 14, 1910, concert date, they staged a "Grand Concert" at Spruce Street Baptist Church at 8:00 PM as the "Apollo Quartet – Fisk University." However, by regulation of the school's music department (and no doubt the institution), they were forbidden to form such groups without written permission or to use the name of the university in their title. Specifically, "students in voice culture must consult the teacher of that department before joining any quartet, club, or other singing organization."[80]As the Apollo Quartet was a private for-profit organization with no official connection to the university, there was an obvious conflict of interest in using the university's name.

Thus, the stage was set for the drama that Roland later described as his second major epiphany. In early May, he was sent for by Miss Robinson and told that he must return all of his borrowed music to the library, to which he responded with an obligatory, "Yes ma'am," unaware of the implications of her demand. Robinson then explained that he was being dismissed from the university, an announcement that hit him like a thunderbolt.[81] When the totally bewildered Roland questioned Robinson about what offense he had committed to provoke such a dramatic action, she sternly told him to search his conscience and that it should tell him of his offense.[82]

The still-confused Roland immediately went to see his employer and mentor, Warren Waterman. The best the singer could discern from Waterman's inquiries was that Jennie Robinson was upset with him for spending too much time with the Jubilee Singers and not enough on his studies in the music department.[83] Waterman then told the young man that Jennie Robinson had been financing, through her personal funds or those solicited from friends, his very education. The seemingly forgetful Roland had not factored in that not only had he formed a quartet without permission, violating department and university policy, but also he had accepted money for it while representing it as an officially sanctioned group of the institution. His participation with these unauthorized groups, which were the antithesis of her musical direction, surely had outraged the strict instructor all the more.

At the time of his dismissal, Roland suspected that he was being told to leave because he had sometimes broken the rules that required students to receive permission before leaving campus. Admittedly, he had neglected to make such a request on several occasions. He understood that he had permission to take off-campus singing engagements, as this had been done with the faculty's implied, if not specific, approval.[84] Roland appealed his dismissal to the new president, George Gates, but was informed that Miss Robinson's action would stand.[85]

Had he been more contrite, Roland might have talked his way back into the institution, but his pride and anger, according to him, prevented him from admitting any fault. He eventually accepted the decision as fate and a part of some greater plan for him to leave Fisk University.[86] At Waterman's advice, Roland decided to leave quietly and be grateful for the four years of secondary education he had received. Before departing, however, he sang with the Jubilee Club at a university commencement exercise. When his solo was announced at the ceremony, his now-former teacher Jennie Robinson conspicuously stood up and left the chapel. This public snub was the final insult from his financier. It was also Roland's last performance as a student at the institution but not his final affiliation with Fisk.[87]

At twenty-three years old, Hayes acted on Warren Waterman's advice and traveled to Louisville, Kentucky, where he embarked on the next phase of his journey and joined a choral society, which was being directed at the time by a Fisk University trustee. He had performed in the city two years earlier in the Negro Music Festival, so it was not a totally unfamiliar location.

Roland's first nine months in Louisville were quite fruitful in terms of opportunities and social acquaintances. Early in his stay he met a white family, the Jordans, who showed him hospitality and friendship. After his experience with Jennie Robinson (and to a lesser extent with Warren Waterman, who Roland felt should have argued his case more vigorously) at Fisk, Roland had reason to be suspicious of European Americans, but he later said the Jordans helped to restore his faith in them collectively through their kindness.[88] The Jordans had a young son, Howard, who was about eight when Roland first met the family. Thirteen years later, Howard became Roland's personal secretary and assistant.

It was through his involvement with the choral society in Louisville that Roland was engaged to sing the tenor solo in Handel's *Messiah* at Howard University under the direction of Lulu Vere Childers.[89] As that university's music department chair, she was a major supporter of the young tenor's early career. Roland and Childers maintained a strong professional relationship for years.[90]

Roland's main job in Louisville, however, was as a waiter at the up-scale, all-men's Pendennis Club, founded in 1881. Of course in 1910, those of African ancestry held only servant roles at the club, as was the case with Roland.[91] His manners, waiting skills, and deportment were quite polished, and his newly cultivated speaking voice also placed him ahead of the other waitstaff.

After discovering his vocal talent, Pendennis Club management invited the singer to perform at several events, including dinners and "smokers." He was paid five dollars for solo engagements and was also given generous tips.[92] A performance at the Pendennis Club led to an offer from a local theater owner to sing opera arias from behind a screen while silent movies were being shown. Roland earned the tidy sum of forty dollars a week from such engagements.

In the spring of 1911, Roland sang at the Pendennis Club for a formal dinner held in honor of northern businessmen doing work in the region. Among the group was Henry H. Putnam, a top executive with the John Hancock Insurance Company in Boston. Putnam and Hayes did not formally meet at the dinner, but the Boston businessman spoke to the dinner's arranger after Hayes's performance at the social club. He was quite impressed with Roland's singing but felt the young tenor needed further vocal study to refine his talent and suggested that Roland come to Boston to do so.[93] The Pendennis manager eventually spoke to Roland about Putnam's comments.

On the heels of Henry Putnam's recommendation, Roland received a letter dated March 18, 1911:

My dear Mr. Hayes:

There is to be a great missionary exhibition in Boston in April and May. It is so large and comprehensive that it is called "The World in Boston." Fisk University has been asked to furnish a company of singers to represent the achievements in this line of Negro people as contrasted with conditions of those people in Africa and later in slavery. That puts upon us a grave responsibility. The judgment which probably more than a million of people will form concerning the ten millions of our people in this country is going to depend somewhat and somewhat largely upon the kind of spirit, as well as musical efficienty [*sic*], which this company of singers exhibits.

Realizing something of the importance of this undertaking I ventured to appoint a special committee, consisting of Prof. Work, Dean Wright, Miss Robinson, Mrs. Moore, Miss Spence and Miss Cook, which committee, with me, should select the members of this company to go North on this mission.

After several meetings and abundant discussion and earnest thought the following company has been chosen:

Sopranos: Mrs. Mari P. Merrill, Mrs. Hadley, Miss Lula Williams.
Altos: Mrs. J. W. Work, Miss Desrette Hodges.
Tenors: Mr. J. C. Olden, Mr. Roland W. Hayes.
Basses: Mr. N. W. Ryder, Mr. L. L. Foster.

Prof. Work expects to go along, at least to get the work started. . . .

The University will be put to large expense in this matter and it is hoped and really expected that the expense will be met from the proceeds of the exhibition.
. . .

In order to reach the high purpose with which these singers go North we hope that they will go with the same reverent and consecrated spirit as marked the outgoing of the original Jubilee Singers. As one learns more of the way those singers went out one wonders less that they touched the heart of the world. There is no reason in the nature of things why other companies of singers cannot accomplish something similar. In order to [accomplish] that two things are necessary. First, the spirit already mentioned; second, faithful and patient training with all accessible judgment brought to bear upon it. Therefore may we not ask you that nothing be neglected that can possibly add to the accomplishment of what we desire?

Sincerely yours,
George A. Gates[94]

This letter from the president of Fisk must have hit Roland with nearly the same force as his sudden dismissal from the university had ten months earlier, but this time in a positive way. Receiving this letter on the heels of Henry Putnam's suggestion that he come to Boston, of all places, to study was nothing short of an other-world sign.

Also of note is Jennie Robinson's participation in the selection committee that chose him to go north. Robinson most likely opposed Roland's inclusion in the group but was perhaps outvoted by a majority, most notably by John W. Work II, the director leading the ensemble. He

was well aware of the tenor's musical talent and likely insisted on including Roland based on the musical needs of the traveling choir.[95] In any
case, Roland looked upon Jennie Robinson more charitably in later years
when he considered her role in helping educate the barely literate young
man he was at the time.[96] The six-week engagement in Massachusetts's
most cosmopolitan city was to pay fifty dollars a month plus expenses.

Boston, with its large museums, libraries, concert halls, opera
houses, orchestras, plays, and many other trappings, was second only to
New York City in terms of its sophistication. A musical education in such
a setting, Roland opined, could facilitate his clear and determined career
goals more quickly than in any other location. Besides, he also had an
invitation to come to the city from an important Yankee businessman.

Seeing his Boston ambitions taking shape, Roland secured a letter
of introduction from his manager at the Pendennis Club to Henry Putnam of John Hancock Insurance Company and accepted the invitation
from President Gates to join the Fisk group, without revealing his real
intentions for wanting to participate in the "great missionary exhibition
in Boston."

Roland's return to the Nashville campus to attend rehearsals with
the Fisk group for its upcoming trip to Boston came exactly one year
after his inglorious dismissal. As he had performed for the commencement exercises of May 1910, he similarly performed for the graduating
class of 1911.

En route to Boston, however, Roland made an obligatory stop
through Chattanooga to see his mother, Fannie, who now was living
alone. By 1911, Robert had married and moved to the West Coast, and
"Baby" Jesse, who was at least twenty, had run away from home and
eventually joined the US Navy. When Roland informed his mother of
his plans to travel to Boston, she echoed her refrain that white people
would not accept black people singing their concert music. But Roland
had heard it all before. And as before, he was not easily discouraged. He
left Fannie with the promise of returning to bring her north. Roland
believed his move to Boston was the next step in his quest to become a
great artist. He was also certain that destiny was on his side.

TWO

Roland's World in Boston

1911–1920

THE GREAT MISSIONARY CONFERENCE "THE WORLD IN BOSTON" was staged in April and May 1911. It was from this important northern city that Roland launched his career and his new life. The city refined Roland even more and prepared him for the realities of the mostly European and American concert worlds.

"The World in Boston" was a showcase of global missionary activities that the *New York Times* claimed would "Give Vivid Reproductions of How Natives Live in Foreign Lands Where Church Work Is Carried On."[1] The event featured Muslims, Turks, continental Africans, Chinese missionaries (from the post–Boxer Movement of 1901), and others from the Far East. To demonstrate African American progress since the end of legal enslavement nearly fifty years prior, the missionary conference organizers invited the sophisticated Fisk University singers as well as other musical groups to perform. Fisk was an example of an African American university in a state that had once been the bastion of the Confederacy. The all-black school helped the state project a different image to the world. It was now educating a few of the sons and daughters of those it had once held captive. With this background, Roland's arrival in Boston in May 1911 had been many years in the making.

Roland reached the city in the dead of night and headed directly to the John Hancock Building, where he waited for Henry Putnam to arrive at his office.[2] As Roland recalled, Putnam was somewhat surprised to see the young man so soon. After reading the letter of introduction from the manager of the Pendennis Club, Putnam questioned Hayes:

"How much money have you got?"

"I have a hundred dollars," Roland answered.

"Where is it?"

"I have it on me," he replied.[3] Roland's naive and honest response to these basic questions demonstrated just how vulnerable and inexperienced he was in an urban cosmopolitan setting. Putnam took him to open a bank account.[4]

Roland had gambled everything on this meeting with a man whom he had never formally met. Putnam promised he would help develop Hayes's singing career by introducing him to the Boston musical community. When Hayes left Putnam that morning to join the singers at the missionary conference, he had already begun making plans to lay down roots in the city. He immediately started looking for service jobs.

Putnam arranged auditions for Roland with five area voice teachers. After Roland had sung for all of them, Putnam's report was not as encouraging as he would have liked, but his was not a lost cause, either: "Two of the five gentlemen who have heard you are willing to teach you . . . and one of them is ready to give you a scholarship. But I want to warn you that every man-Jack of them believes it is quite impossible for a Negro to be accepted as a serious artist."[5] Putnam's comments were sobering, but Roland had come too far to give up. Charles White, a voice professor at the New England Conservatory, and Arthur J. Hubbard, a voice instructor with a thriving private studio, were the two who provided favorable reports.[6]

White, like the others, saw limited possibilities for the young tenor as a serious concert artist in the exclusively European-derived concert world.[7] Yet he was impressed by Roland's potential and offered to get him a scholarship to the prestigious conservatory. But the tenor, while tempted by the opportunity, knew he could not attend school full time. He needed to work so that he could bring his mother to Boston as soon as he was able. Roland decided to study with Arthur Hubbard and pay for private lessons. He would begin formal study with Hubbard in the fall, after a summer of full-time work. In short order, he found a job as a bellhop at the Brunswick Hotel on Boylston Street.

At the conclusion of the missionary conference, Roland faced an inevitable confrontation with choir director John W. Work II. He had to inform Professor Work that he had decided to remain in Boston rather than return to Nashville with the Jubilee Singers. Caught completely by surprise, Work indignantly interrogated his defiant choir member:

"What would your mother say?"

"I have told my mother," Roland responded.

"You'll starve."

"No, I have a job at the Brunswick Hotel on Boylston Street."

"But suppose the job doesn't last?"

"I have a hundred dollars in the bank."[8]

Realizing in the brief but intense exchange that Roland had covered all of his bases, Work was indignant that Roland had found a job and begun employment without informing him. He warned the young man to be prepared for the severity of New England winters. Hayes would experience the Boston winter in due time, but he would not be deterred.[9]

Charles J. Harris, a fellow Georgian, had been in Boston teaching and studying piano for five years when Roland arrived with the Fisk group in 1911.[10] Harris attended one of the performances of the Jubilee Singers at the Mechanics Building and recalled being only moderately impressed when he heard Roland sing a solo for the first time. That impression changed dramatically when the two met at Harris's studio a few days later, at the pianist's invitation. Roland sang the aria "M'appari tutt'amor" (She appeared full of love) from Friedrich von Flotow's opera *Martha*.[11] The *messa di voce* demands of this aria made Harris appreciate the talent he was accompanying at the keyboard.[12] Not only did the two Georgia musicians become good friends, but Harris became Roland's first principal accompanist. In Hayes's first year in Boston, he and Harris presented several recitals, most of which were at African American churches and community centers, including those in the Boston Harbor, where Roland developed a loyal following.

About a month after starting his job emptying spittoons and performing other menial tasks, Hayes traveled to Atlantic City, where he met two former Fisk classmates who were working as waiters to support themselves. The threesome sang on the city's celebrated boardwalk in their spare time.

Roland recalled an incident around this time in which his temper emerged while he was serving a white patron a steak at the restaurant

where he worked. Intoxicated and obnoxious, the guest insulted Roland
when he presented the steak at the table: "Take that steak back to the
... kitchen, you nigger son-of-a-bitch!"[13] The insult, no doubt, triggered
memories of the assault that Roland had suffered in Nashville a few years
earlier. He dropped the plate on the table and promptly took up the carv-
ing knife, threatening to slice his rude customer instead of the steak. The
headwaiter and another assistant grabbed him to hold him back.[14] When
the incident was reported, the headwaiter sided with Roland to assert
that the customer had verbally abused him. Roland rarely displayed his
temper in public, but given the right provocation, it would surface. He
and his former school companions quit their jobs, finding they could do
better by singing as a group on the Atlantic City boardwalk. At the end
of the summer tourist season, Roland returned to Boston and began
working as a pageboy at the John Hancock Insurance Company. The
company's president, D. W. Sutherland, had offered him the job after
hearing him sing at the Boston City Club.[15]

Roland also began studying voice privately with his third and most
influential teacher, basso profundo Arthur J. Hubbard, as he had decided
to do back in May. Hubbard had enjoyed a moderately successful singing
career in the United States and in Europe, where he studied with the celebrated bel canto master Francesco Lamperti.[16] Lamperti had also been
the voice master of the great Polish soprano Marcella Sembrich, whose
recordings Roland had heard in the early part of the century. Hayes attended two private voice lessons a week, at five dollars per meeting,[17]
in Hubbard's home in order to avoid upsetting the white voice students
at Hubbard's studio. After Hayes became a successful artist, however,
Hubbard was more than proud to boast of his association with the singer.
Like Arthur Calhoun, Hubbard later mentioned his relationship with
Hayes in his advertisements and his summer teaching institutes.[18]

Roland occasionally took courses through Harvard University's ex-
tension school. He also learned he was eligible for discount tickets to the
Boston Symphony Orchestra concerts if he waited in line on Huntington
Avenue by Symphony Hall on the day of the performance. Gallery tickets
for Saturday engagements were fifty cents.[19] Roland's first symphony
orchestra experience, however, left him "bewildered." The myriad of
simultaneous sounds overwhelmed his senses. In subsequent symphony
concerts, he focused on specific sections of the ensemble (typically the

strings) and was able to apply the principles of legato string playing to his singing.

John Work returned to Nashville earlier that year without Roland but had not given up on the aspiring musician. He contacted Roland in the fall to tell him about a recording project scheduled for late December 1911 on the East Coast; it became Roland's first recording. The Edison recording of the Fisk University Jubilee Quartet featured Work as group leader and first tenor,[20] Roland as second tenor, Leon P. O'Hara (who was with Roland in Atlantic City and was now studying at Yale) as first bass, and Charles Wesley as second bass.[21] Hayes was the featured soloist in "My Soul Is a Witness," with the others in the quartet providing support.[22]

The new year would be even more promising than the previous one for Roland. His lessons with Arthur Hubbard were progressing smoothly, and after enduring the cold of his first winter in Boston, Roland journeyed south with Charles Harris, who had decided to travel home to Georgia for a visit. Their destination was Augusta, where Roland met and sang for the Harris family.

That spring, Roland also determined that it was time to bring his mother, Fannie, to live with him in the northeast, even though he had limited income. He went to Chattanooga and returned with her to Boston. Even though Fannie was around seventy years old, she was resolved to do her part and, being no stranger to hard work, took in washing jobs. After finding a church and making a few friends, Fannie began to settle down. Some financial relief also came to the Hayes family through the influence of Annie Cleveland Bridgman, who had served as the secretary of the American Missionary Association in Boston for thirty years.[23] She assisted Roland in finding engagements in mostly white area churches, which helped him cultivate a loyal following within those circles. Hayes reported one incident, however, in which Hubbard intervened on his behalf after he was turned down from a church job when it was discovered that he was African American. Hubbard shamed the church leaders for their overt un-Christianlike behavior. Hayes was then offered the job, which he accepted, and performed there for several years.[24]

Charles Harris proposed that he and Hayes do a recital that April at Boston's Steinert Hall, one of the smaller venues in the city.[25] The tenor was eager to participate, and he and Harris persuaded African American violinist Clarence Cameron White and William H. Richardson (also a singer who would later join Hayes in a vocal trio) to make it a quartet.[26] The performance was already sold out and fast approaching when news of the *Titanic* tragedy reached the United States. The musicians decided to postpone the concert out of respect for those who had perished. When the concert eventually took place before a packed house, the quartet's performance established solid reputations for each of its members. At Harris's invitation, Boston's most influential music critic, Philip Hale, attended the concert.[27] This would have been Hale's earliest exposure to Hayes's singing. In the years to come, he would become an enthusiastic supporter of the singer.

It was also in 1912 that Roland Hayes met celebrated baritone and composer Harry T. Burleigh.[28] Hayes routinely included in his programs the composer and arranger's vocal compositions. He was among the few vocalists who kept Burleigh's art songs and spiritual arrangements before the public for years to come.[29]

Burleigh accompanied Roland on occasion, and in the latter half of 1912 he was instrumental in establishing a prestigious vocal quartet, which featured Roland and himself and, as soprano and alto, Minnie Brown and Daisy Tapley.[30] The vocalists would become well-established singers of opera quartets and other special arrangements. Former president Theodore Roosevelt was at the quartet's Carnegie Hall performance that fall; it was Roosevelt's first public appearance after an attempt on his life earlier that year.

At the time, Harry Burleigh enjoyed greater name recognition than did Roland and the others in the quartet; however, Daisy Robinson Tapley was also a well-regarded musician. Her Columbia recording in 1910 made her, it is argued, the first African American woman to be captured on disc.[31] She had already traveled to Europe and had been a seasoned musician for some years. In addition to being an accomplished singer, Daisy was also a skilled keyboardist and accompanied Roland on several occasions throughout the 1910s.

Burleigh's relationship with Roland was longer lasting and considerably more extensive. Soon after meeting the young singer, he began to see the effect that Roland had on audiences and encouraged him to perform his (Burleigh's) vocal compositions, which he routinely accompanied.

It was good exposure for both of them. On January 13, 1913, the Samuel Coleridge-Taylor Choral Society staged a memorial concert in honor of the recently deceased Afro-British composer at Boston's Jordan Hall.[32] Hayes, Burleigh, and William Richardson (the baritone who had previously sung with Hayes) were among the singers participating in the concert. The speaker for the event was one of America's best-known black leaders, the respected educator Dr. W. E. B. Du Bois. Hayes and Du Bois would meet again in 1921 on the occasion of the Pan-African Congress outside of London.[33]

The following month Roland, Burleigh, Tapley, and Brown were featured soloists for a performance of Mendelssohn's masterpiece oratorio *Elijah* with the Peoples Choral Society in Philadelphia and received ecstatic reviews from local critics.[34] Among such a distinguished group, Roland increased his following up and down the Eastern Seaboard.

Sometime during the summer, Fannie received a letter telling her of illness in the family, so she made her first trip back to Chattanooga since moving to Boston the year before. Her oldest living son, John, had contracted smallpox, so Fannie went to Tennessee to help his wife, Ola, by looking after him and her grandson, Felton. Roland encouraged his mother to check on her land in Curryville while she was in the area. Since her departure from Curryville more than a decade before, it had been managed by a cousin, Obie Mann. Fannie had contemplated selling it off, but Roland discouraged any such idea.[35]

Despite the tug of maternal compassion, Fannie missed her life and friends in Boston and told Roland she was returning earlier than planned. Roland wired her money and asked that she delay her trip for a week. While Fannie was away, Roland had rented a larger apartment for them to live in and needed the extra time to set it up. Without notice, however, Fannie showed up at the train station in Boston.

The pleasant surprise of a larger place with her very own bed and rocking chair was tempered by a letter from her son Robert Brante, who was living in Los Angeles with his wife, Margaret.

> I am sorry to say that our baby died. She has been dead more than a month. She did not live very long. We did not have any pictures of her. People here say she was just like me. Doll [Margaret Hayes] says she was just like you with your

nose.... I forgot to say that baby Fannie Dorothea's grave cost $15. It is in a place
called "Mother's Heart." It is such a pretty place. Doll sends her love and regards
to you.

I remain your devoted son,
RB Hayes[36]

Fannie's response to the letter informing her of the death of her granddaughter, a child she never saw, is unknown. Unfortunately, it would not
be the last time that she would experience such grief.

In the spring of 1914, Roland and Charles Harris planned a tour of several
southern cities in Virginia, North Carolina, South Carolina, Georgia,
and Tennessee. They employed Roland's time-honored practice of con-
tacting African American ministers, as well as presidents at historically
black colleges and universities, to set up their engagements.[37] The tour
was self-arranged and managed by the duo, and Roland became quite
proficient at such details over the next several years. He also picked up
valuable contacts around the country that would serve him later as his
career continued to develop.

On May 8, 1914, Roland sang in Baltimore at the Bethel Church. The
Afro-American Ledger's review of the concert was flattering and mentioned other participants, including the local Peerless Quartette, and a
pianist, Louise Anderson, a music instructor at Morgan College.[38] Roland was accompanied by Beatrice Lewis, a professor of piano at Washington's Howard University.[39]

During this tour with Charles Harris, Roland met renowned educator, social leader, and president of Tuskegee Institute (later University)
Dr. Booker T. Washington.[40] By 1914, Washington was one of the most
powerful and influential African Americans in the country, but he was
not without detractors, the most prominent being Du Bois, whom Roland had met the year before and who had emerged prominently in the
Niagara Movement of 1905. That gathering led to the formation of the
NAACP, with Du Bois as the editor of the organization's news organ,
the *Crisis*. Du Bois had emerged as one of black America's intellectual
geniuses and Booker T. Washington's philosophical opposite. In Washington's consideration, the country's citizens of African ancestry were

making significant progress and simply needed to apply themselves more forcefully to reach their collective goal of economic and political independence. Du Bois questioned whether the United States even recognized the *citizenship* of the same group.[41]

Because of his background and personal struggles, there is little question that Roland found himself in agreement with Washington's ideology. He saw the dignity of physical labor as a character-building exercise for African Americans. It was only wealthier African Americans, according to the singer, who could afford to identify with Du Bois's program and philosophy, and there were not a substantial number of them.[42] In 1914, Washington's views carried considerably more weight among African Americans, as those views had produced more tangible results than any ideology that Du Bois had enunciated. At the time, Roland's only connection to Du Bois was that they were both Fiskites.

Washington conducted lecture tours of the northern states during the summer months, when Tuskegee Institute was out of session. His speaking engagements generally included a few musical selections from a prominent musician and a poetry reading or classical recitation, followed by Washington's keynote lecture on some topic of the day related to African Americans. Harry Burleigh invited Roland to participate in one of the Washington programs, with the two of them singing solos and duets.

Roland, Burleigh, and Washington did several lecture engagements in the Boston area in 1914, and in the summer of 1915, Hayes and Charles Harris spent a week in Tuskegee, Alabama, where they were invited to give a recital at Washington's institution. The concert was well received, and Washington, known to routinely get up and pace during such performances, sat through the entire recital. In appreciation of their presentation, Washington gave Hayes and Harris signed copies of his best-selling works *Up from Slavery* and *The Negro in Business*.[43]

In the fall of 1914, Roland had the opportunity to hear the celebrated African American tenor Sidney Woodward, accompanied by Charles Harris, in recital back in Boston.[44] Woodward had been the best-known black tenor in and around the city prior to Hayes's arrival. Woodward had also enjoyed a career in Europe after studying in Germany and had sung before many heads of state.[45] The two tenors knew of each other because of Charles Harris's previous association with Woodward, and Roland had sung for the older tenor when he and Harris were on tour in Atlanta earlier that year. By then, Woodward had scaled back his career and was a professor of music at Clark College in the city. By 1914, Woodward was in his mid-fifties, but as far as Roland was concerned, he had not lost the beauty of his voice.

Roland also gave a recital in Boston at Steinert Hall that fall, which Charles Harris accompanied. Participating in the recital were Wesley Howard, another Boston-based African American violinist, and Ruth Yeo, a pianist accompanying the string player. According to the review, Roland sang Wagner's "Winterstürme" (Winter Storm) from *Die Walküre* and "Ch'ella mi credea libero e lontano" (Let her believe I'm free and far away) from Puccini's *La fanciulla del West*.[46] This was not repertory that Roland was generally associated with, especially the Wagner, because it tended to require a more robust voice. The tenor also sang Burleigh's "The Hour Glass" and "Ahmed's Song of Farewell" from the newly published song cycle *Saracen Songs*.[47]

When Roland returned to Baltimore to perform on December 18, 1914, he was already known to many of the city's residents. For this occasion, instead of having his engagement at a church, he sang at the larger and more prestigious Albaugh's Theater on the corner of Druid Hill Avenue and Eutaw Street. The recital was a benefit for the NAACP and received a very favorable review. Once again, Beatrice Lewis of Howard University was his accompanist.[48]

Roland made an auspicious appearance in New York City in January of the new year when he was featured with the pioneering African American violinist and orchestra conductor Walter F. Craig.[49] By the time of Roland's debut with Craig, the orchestra leader was well known, especially on the Eastern Seaboard. He had introduced African American artists to the concert stage, and his spring concerts were renowned for premiering African American art music.[50]

Around this time Hayes also began receiving regular press attention outside of African American news organizations. A review of his concert in the February 9, 1915, edition of the Massachusetts-based *Fitchburg Daily Sentinel* was an early forecast of what would come. "Colored Tenor Sings – Roland W. Hayes Displays Splendid Voice at Choral Society Rehearsal" was the headline that informed local readers of Roland's appearance.[51] He offered arias, including "Celeste Aida" from the Verdi opera, "Che gelida manina" from Puccini's *La bohème,* as well as several African American folk songs, including "Why Adam Sinned" and "Since You Went Away," among other numbers. He was accompanied by Mabel Sheddon, one of Roland's many accompanists who have since disappeared into obscurity.

Roland then once again joined up with Burleigh, Tapley, and Brown to present Mendelssohn's *Elijah* in New York and Boston. Dr. W. O. Taylor, assisted by the "Elijah Chorus," led the Boston performance at Jordan Hall on April 15, 1915. Notably, the custom of listing pictures of the soloists in order by vocal range (soprano, alto, tenor, and bass, respectively) was not adhered to in the Boston performance. Instead, Roland's picture appeared first in the concert's program, which may have spoken to his growing celebrity, or perhaps he was privileged because he was regarded as the hometown singer.[52]

Apart from singing at Tuskegee Institute with Charles Harris in the summer of 1915, Roland teamed up with tenor and accompanist William Lawrence and baritone William Richardson to tour Pennsylvania's Chautauqua circuit for the lucrative salary of $175 per week. As Roland had bigger name recognition than either Lawrence or Richardson, the group was known as the Hayes Trio, with Roland receiving the lion's share of the fee.[53] The smartly dressed trio sang Western art music almost exclusively and paid little attention to African American art songs or folk music.

Roland returned to Boston in the fall, where he continued his lessons with Arthur Hubbard, but as a working musician he still sought performing opportunities. In his November 11 Jordan Hall recital, he teamed up, once more, with William Lawrence at the keyboard. William Richardson was also a part of the program. Another keyboardist, "Mr. Tibbs,"[54] a Fisk alum and, at the time, a music instructor at Howard University in Washington, participated as well. The program included Roland singing Burleigh art songs, "Onaway! Awake, Beloved!" from Coleridge-Taylor's *Hiawatha's Wedding Feast* (which Roland began adding with increasing frequency), and the well-known opera aria from Ponchielli's *La gioconda,* "Cielo e mar" (Heaven and sea). With William Richardson, Roland sang the hauntingly beautiful tenor/baritone duet from Verdi's *La forza del destino,* "Solenne in quest'ora" (In this solemn hour), which he recorded a few years later.[55] The concert was well received, and 1915 concluded as another impressive year for the tenor's growing career.

The year 1916 marked another level of development in Roland's goal as an artist and entrepreneur: he began receiving performance requests from around the country. Roland typically noted in his reply that his fee at that time was $100 plus travel expenses.[56] Not wanting to lose any momentum, Roland began advertising his availability in the *Crisis,* the NAACP's journal, which brought in even more requests for engagements. Roland was doing an adequate job of self-managing when he embarked on the first of what would be a series of cross-country concert tours, during which he performed up and down the East Coast for African American soldiers preparing to depart for the war in Europe.

Jesse Hayes briefly reemerged into the family picture about this time. After serving in the navy for several years, he was eligible for discharge. Roland attempted to persuade his youngest brother to come live with him in Boston so he could keep their mother company when Roland was away performing. Jesse, however, reenlisted in the navy – a decision that was absolutely heartbreaking for his mother.

In March 1916, Roland performed with William Lawrence at Industrial High School in West Palm Beach, Florida.[57] He and Lawrence alternated sets. Roland sang a Will Marion Cook song, "Morning," and a minstrel song, "The Little Pickaninny's Gone to Sleep," by J. Rosamond Johnson. He appropriately abandoned such works after a few years; they do not show up in his programs in the late 1910s.[58] As always, he included a Burleigh song, "The Young Warrior."[59]

Two weeks later, Roland did a benefit recital for the New-Century Club in Wilmington, Delaware, to aid the Tuberculosis Hospital for African American residents of the state. This recital centered on the life and works of Paul Lawrence Dunbar, especially those works that had been set to music, and also featured the poet's widow, Alice.[60]

Roland's reconciliation with his former voice teacher and secret benefactor, Jennie Robinson, had been some years in the making and culminated in a spring 1916 engagement at Fisk University, when Roland returned to sing in Mendelssohn's *Elijah* on the campus.[61] Robinson had written to him after hearing of his engagements with Burleigh and Booker T. Washington, but those activities had occurred nearly two years before.[62] Robinson then located Roland in Boston and proposed that they "bury the hatchet."[63] Roland responded that she could bury hers, but he had no hatchet to bury. Whatever transpired, Roland made the affirmative gesture of going back to the campus to perform.

There is a possibility that Robinson's motives in reconciling with Hayes were strategic. The intensity of her longstanding conflict with John Work II, classics professor and director of the Jubilee Singers at Fisk, had been increasing before he was removed by the newly installed (and Robinson-supporting) Fisk president, Fayette McKenzie. Robinson's idea to make up with Roland Hayes (whose star was clearly rising) in 1916 may have sprung from her desire to deflect any claims of racial animus and thereby to improve her appearance to McKenzie.[64]

Joining Hayes in the spring 1916 Fisk concert was Harry Burleigh, one of the reigning interpreters of *Elijah* in the country at the time. In a picture after the event with Roland and Burleigh, Jennie Robinson appears to be holding a score, so she may well have been the alto soloist.[65]

Even though Roland was nearly thirty, he was still very much in the building phase of his career and continued his voice lessons with Arthur Hubbard in Boston. Hubbard had grown very fond of Roland, and they communicated while Roland was away. Always appreciative of those who assisted him on his near-religious musical journey, Roland wrote his teacher in 1916 to thank him for the investment he had made in him and his talent. Hubbard responded with an equally appreciative message expressing to Roland how moving his letter was to him and that there were few people who meant as much to him as the singer.[66] Hubbard shared the sentiment with another colleague: "I have not a pupil in my classes for whom I have had a more genuine affection than for this lad nor have I one who possesses a keener intelligence or a surer musical feeling and taste."[67]

Roland was not interested in teaching voice himself at this point, but he seldom missed an opportunity to encourage younger singers who he thought had potential and ambition. He carried this attitude throughout his life. During a few of his performances in Philadelphia, he sang church recitals in which a local young contralto, Marian Anderson, also appeared. A full decade younger than Hayes, Anderson had the career-boosting opportunity to appear with Roland, singing the alto solo in Handel's *Messiah* in Philadelphia during the 1916 Easter season.[68] The "baby" (as she had been advertised) alto's actual age was nineteen. Anderson was known to have officially taken five years off her age, so Roland and the rest of the world thought he was performing with a fourteen-year-old girl. Of course the age discrepancy took nothing away from her phenomenal talent. Roland's mentorship with Marian Anderson was long lasting. Her admiration for him was also well known. Their paths would cross again in years to come.

Sometime in the late spring, Hayes and Harris performed their final recital. This performance at the Ebenezer Baptist Church in Boston was memorable to Harris, who admired the younger performer greatly.

Roland's November 1916 concert at Boston's Jordan Hall was carried out with the assistance, once again, of violinist Wesley Howard and Lawrence Brown at the keyboard. He programmed Rodolfo's aria from *La bohème* and Des Grieux's aria "Ah! Fuyez douce image" (Flee sweet image) from Massenet's *Manon*. With Howard playing the violin obbligato, Roland and William Lawrence also performed Liszt's liltingly beautiful "Du bist wie eine Blume" (You are like a flower) and Florence Spalding's "Liebestraum" (Dream of Love).[69] Roland concluded the recital with two Burleigh songs. He received increasingly favorable reviews for his concerts (especially in the African American press) but lost money during these early years after paying for the hall rental, his accompanist, and the other participating musicians.[70]

The management issue aside, Roland's steady progress continued into the following year. The increasing number of requests from around the country for his services resulted in another national tour. And in pursuit of his increasing career goals, he eventually entered the recording studio as a soloist in 1917, making him the first African American concert musician to record commercially.[71]

The year 1917 began routinely with Roland performing in the Boston area. He was featured, once again, in *Elijah* with Marian Anderson and Harry Burleigh singing the other solo parts during the Easter season.[72] The following month he appeared at a fund-raising benefit for the NAACP in Cleveland. His accompanist may have been William King, who became one of Anderson's accompanists and worked with her for many years. Roland then did what could be described as a mini-tour, with Daisy Tapley as his accompanist. They had several engagements in New York and traveled north for recitals in Canada.[73]

Roland sang in several African American churches in the South to finance what would be his boldest effort to date – to sing a solo concert at the prestigious Boston Symphony Hall. When he announced in the late spring of 1917 his intentions to rent and sing a concert at this elite venue, Arthur Hubbard, among others, wondered aloud about the wisdom of such a move. They attempted to dissuade Roland from performing in the hallowed venue for fear of a backlash against him, which could hurt other prospective African American performers.

Roland set the bar high for himself and immediately set out to attract influential backers for his proposed Symphony Hall recital. On his list was the wife of then Massachusetts governor Samuel W. McCall, but she turned him down with a somewhat dismissive, if not disdainful, comment: "I cannot let my name be attached to an enterprise which is bound to be a failure before it begins."[74] Even the well-known music critic Philip Hale, who seemed to have warmed up to Hayes, completely panned his intention of renting Symphony Hall. The critic's written commentary to that effect produced protest from the general public against Roland's course of action.[75] But never one to be dissuaded, the singer proceeded to the hall's rental office to pay his four hundred dollar deposit for a November engagement.

Roland's Symphony Hall recital was not the earliest manifestation of his business savvy, but it was his boldest. Demonstrating amazing creativity when it came to cultivating an audience for this recital, he hired a secretary to assist him with locating potential attendees. He even went to telephone directories, and when he came across a name that appealed to him, he placed it on a list for a follow-up call and invitation.[76] He also appealed to his former employers at the John Hancock Insurance Company to buy tickets, and the company responded by buying several hundred. Hayes printed the tickets at his expense, in addition to paying for all the related advertising.

In preparation for this recital, Roland pulled out all the stops. No doubt because of his name recognition, the tenor approached Harry Burleigh about accompanying the recital, as well as performing vocal duets.

Burleigh responded that his agent was not in favor of his accompanying the entire recital, as Roland should be the primary focus. Burleigh offered his services, however, to participate as a "special accompanist" at no charge, assisting Hayes in singing *his* compositions only.[77] In addition to the Burleigh-arranged spirituals, Roland programmed Schubert's "Du bist die Ruh" (You are calm) along with other Schubert lieder, a Mozart aria, and a Tchaikovsky song, among several other works.[78] William Lawrence was his accompanist for the other works.

By the November concert date, Roland had not only sold out the 2,600-seat house but had to turn away several hundred interested concertgoers. The success of the Symphony Hall concert placed Roland among Boston's elite musicians and made those who doubted his ability to draw a major audience take a second look.

To place Roland's 1917 Symphony Hall recital in context, it is important to note that within a mere six years of his arrival in Boston, he had ingratiated himself to several white power brokers and persuaded them to promote him. While many European Americans had found no reason to support Hayes (many thought that while he was talented, an African American succeeding on the American concert stage was an anomaly), they enthusiastically did so after he demonstrated his ability on such a grand scale.

Not willing to rest on his laurels, however, within days of his Symphony Hall success he was back at work. Roland made a Victor trial recording and had a few singing engagements to fulfill.[79] One of those engagements was in Baltimore, Maryland, on December 13, where Roland was scheduled to sing at Bethel AME Church under the sponsorship of the Cosmopolitan Choral Society. He was assisted by the up-and-coming Washington, D.C.–based soprano Lillian Evans (later billed as "Lillian Evanti") with Agnes Lewis at the keyboard.[80]

Also in December, Roland traveled to New York and entered Columbia Graphophone Company's recording studio.[81] Sometime earlier, he had inquired about the process and costs related to making personal recordings. His recording venture was more than a year in the making and was no doubt a response to commentaries that had begun appearing in black newspapers about the absence of recordings of worthy African American concert artists, including Hayes.[82]

The actual recording and production of the discs was a costly endeavor, but Roland saw it as an opportunity to spread his art and make a profit by selling the records privately. Columbia, at the same time, carried tremendous prestige, especially in the area of art music recordings. To support him in what would turn out to be a historic undertaking, he engaged the Boston-based African American entrepreneur George W. Broome, who had considerable business and social contacts, to assist him with promotion and sales.[83]

Accompanying Roland for his December New York recording was most likely Lawrence Benjamin Brown, a young keyboardist whom Roland had met and befriended the year before. Brown had come to Boston from Jacksonville, Florida, to further his keyboard studies.[84] Like Roland, Brown also came from a religious family and was a regular churchgoer, which put him in good standing with Roland's mother, Fannie.

Hayes and Brown recorded Burleigh's arrangement of "Swing Low, Sweet Chariot." Choral arrangements of the work had been available on record for some time, but Roland's was the first to be recorded by a solo artist.[85] The recording was subsequently made available for purchase at 130 Boylston Street in Boston at the A. J. Piano Store, George Broome's address, which also became Roland's official business address. Their letterhead read "Roland W. Hayes, Phonograph Records," listing "Roland W. Hayes, Sole Owner" on the left and "Geo. W. Broome, Sales Manager" on the right.[86] To assist in the success of the recording venture, Roland and Broome enlisted agents around the country to purchase and sell copies of the recordings to interested parties. They, in turn, earned a share of the enterprise as a premium for meeting sales targets.

Roland's growing profile, his advertisements in the *Crisis,* his very favorable reviews in the African American and mainstream press, and the availability of his new recording garnered him offers from around the country to perform. Letters from schools, churches, choral societies, private music clubs, and other social organizations invited him to Los Angeles; Salt Lake City; Detroit; Dayton, Ohio; Kansas City, Missouri; and Portland, Oregon.[87] The frequency of such requests made a more formal national tour obligatory, which he embarked on at the beginning of 1918. But it was one that Roland would self-manage, because even with his growing reputation, he could not attract a manager or booking agent. By 1917, Hayes's name and reputation were at least as prestigious as Burleigh's in the concert world, but the older artist had an agent while Roland did not.[88] It is possible that the absence of a booking agent for Hayes may have resulted from his not wanting to share his profits when he could handle arrangements just as easily on his own. On each letter of invitation he received, Roland hand-wrote some variation of "$100 plus expenses" – his fee per engagement at the time.[89]

On the January tour, Roland, Lawrence Brown, and Fannie Hayes set off across the country by train. Roland had promotional handbills printed, advertising himself as "Roland W. Hayes, Celebrated Negro Tenor." They traveled south to New York where he performed on January 30, then continued to Washington, D.C., and headed west from there. On a stop in Chattanooga for a recital, Fannie got the opportunity to see her sister Harriet and other family members. They proceeded to an engagement in Nashville, where Roland introduced Fannie to the now-friendly Jennie Robinson, who was in her thirty-first year as director of the music department at Fisk.[90] The group's ultimate destination was the West Coast, where Roland and Fannie were reunited with his brother Robert Brante in Los Angeles. They remained with him for a few months, as engagement requests continued to pour in for Roland.

Fan letters increasingly came as well, either asking him to perform a specific work from his growing repertory or complimenting him on some aspect of his performance. Flora Marguerite Bertelle, the secretary of the Louisville-based Kentucky Music Teachers' Association, praised Roland for his diction, especially in English and French. She also said that his singing voice reminded her of a "rich purplish red" quality, a comment that resonated with Roland as an appropriate metaphor for his vocal color.[91] The tour was successful in terms of exposure and additional performance requests, but, once again, it lost money after related expenses were settled.

By mid-April 1918, the travelers had made it back to the East Coast and were off to perform again regionally.[92] Based on the success of the cross-country tour, Roland increased his fee to $150 per engagement, which did not include his expenses or his accompanist's fee.[93]

On May 4, Roland returned to New York. This time it was for a more ambitious recording: the challenging but celebrated tenor aria

"Vesti la giubba" from Leoncavallo's *I Pagliacci,* made famous by Enrico Caruso – the very aria that had so mesmerized him nearly fifteen years earlier at the Stones' residence in Chattanooga. Many African American newspapers had begun comparing Hayes to the Italian dramatic tenor. Roland was even called the "Black Caruso" on occasion. But the analogy was not an appropriate one, because Caruso's career was primarily built around singing opera roles, whereas Roland had never appeared in an opera. Yet the "Black Caruso" marshaled his vocal resources and placed his stamp on the celebrated aria of the betrayed and heartbroken Canio. The results were impressive given the size of his voice, but it was not in the same league with the much larger and dramatic voice of the real Caruso.[94] In addition to being more vocally challenging, Roland's recording of the aria was also more expensive than his previous recording. According to the Columbia personal recording pricing schedule, a full orchestra, which accompanied Hayes for the session, fell into the three-hundred-dollar range.

After completing the New York session, Roland departed for Washington. During a stopover in Baltimore on May 6, he wrote Fannie a brief note in which he again expressed his profound gratitude to her. In the letter was a little poem titled "To my son," which said in part,

> Do you know that your soul is part of my soul
> such part, that you seem to be fiber and core
> of my heart; none other can pain me as you,
> son, can do; none other can praise me or please
> me as you.

To this sentiment, Roland concluded in his letter to Fannie, "I shall live as near to it as I can – Roland."[95]

In Washington, Roland met Charles Sumner Wormley, a prominent African American dentist and amateur singer. Wormley was also the Washington-based agent for Roland Hayes Records. They rehearsed for the next recording session back in New York, where Roland's even more ambitious (and costly) session took place.[96] He recorded another aria associated with Caruso, "Una furtiva lagrima" (A furtive tear) from Donizetti's *L'elisir d'amore,* and the spiritual "Steal Away." Then Roland and Wormley recorded a duet from *La forza del destino* with truly exceptional results. Supposedly an amateur singer, Wormley's recorded portrayal of

Verdi's vengeful Carlo came close to stealing the performance. Because of the length of the performance and the fact that it involved not only an orchestra but also another singer, the session was more expensive than recording the *I Pagliacci* or the *L'elisir d'amore* arias.[97]

Roland advertised the recording in the May 1918 issue of *Crisis* magazine – the very month he was back in New York making yet more recordings. In the advertisement, he marketed his recordings and made a not-so-subtle appeal to race pride in the process: "Roland W. Hayes, the acknowledged leading singer of the Negro race, has brought out his first record and he plans for many others in the very near future. Nothing else could so well introduce the series as the favorite and plaintive Negro melody, 'Swing Low, Sweet Chariot.' The record sells for $1.50 and can be used on any machine using disc records."[98] Roland's desired response was rather quickly achieved. After this session, whether through the actions of the tenor or of George Broome, the effort to get these recordings out to African Americans increased. Roland and Broome received several letters from individuals seeking to become agents for the sale and distribution of his recorded performances.[99]

The relationship with Broome, however, did not last. Letters from Roland from around late September sent out to prospective agents seeking to distribute his records or to those requesting his services stated that for "business reasons, Mr. Broome is no longer in my employ."[100] What brought about the break is not clear, but it may have resulted from the overall meager record sales.

With his new $150-plus-expenses fee structure per engagement in place, Roland continued to receive inquiries from around the country. Several organizations complained that his new fee was too high. Some clubs wanted him to come as part of fund-raising efforts and appealed to him to reduce his fee. One desperate woman pleaded with Roland to perform for a lower fee "for charity [*sic*] sake."[101] While Roland occasionally accommodated such special requests, he was decidedly not in business to perform "for charity sake."

As the winter of 1918–19 was in full swing, Roland, Lawrence Brown, and Fannie left Massachusetts on another cross-country tour. Following the path of their previous trip, they left Boston for New York, where Roland and Harry Burleigh did a recital on January 30, 1919, at the Aeolian Hall. Roland performed several of the composer's art songs as well as some of his arranged spirituals.[102] The group continued south, with stops in Baltimore, Washington, and several locations in Virginia before journeying through the Deep South. On February 20, the group had made it to the Midwest, where Roland and Brown performed at Chicago's Quinn Chapel. They proceeded to the West Coast, where they again stayed with Robert Brante. Roland and Lawrence Brown appeared at Liberty Hall Auditorium in San Diego on April 3. Roland performed several Burleigh works, including "By the Pool," "Benediction of Peace," and a few of his arranged spirituals. He also sang arias from *Manon* and *La Gioconda* and the Coleridge-Taylor song "Life and Death."[103]

During his extended stay in California, Roland had yet another epiphany about his purpose in life – "to understand the beauty of a black voice."[104] He reached this latest and possibly most crucial revelation as a result of a chance meeting with an elderly white fan after a recital in a white church in Santa Monica. The man approached Roland, complimenting him on mastering all the subtleties of any European or European American singer he had heard and further stating that he conveyed additional pathos in his performance. Initially Roland took umbrage at the comments and informed the man that he had the training of any of his white counterparts. Sensing that he might have offended the young singer, the man proposed that they have breakfast the following day; Roland agreed.

The man's comments stirred something deep within Roland and made him restless that night. He spoke to Fannie about his inner turmoil, asking her, "Do you suppose that I have been trying to turn myself into a white artist, instead of making the most of what I was born with?"

"I am glad you are finding yourself, son. I knowed what was what all the time, but I wasn't going to tell you. Now go ahead and work hard and be your own man," she said.[105]

Once again, Fannie's lack of "book learnin'" had not prevented her from being the most perceptive person in her son's life. She knew the inner struggle he was experiencing, but she was also wise enough to let him reach his own resolution. Roland met with the recital fan from the day before, which only seemed to confirm what Fannie had said earlier that day. His proper task, identifying and understanding "the beauty of the black voice" – his voice – would become his mission.

This artistic breakthrough for Roland was the sprouting of the seeds that had been sowed during his childhood in northwest Georgia. He now knew that he was "called" to discover his African origins and to explore those atavistic feelings.

In May, Roland returned to Boston. He attended a performance by James Reese Europe, the renowned African American bandleader and hero who had fought on the battlefields of Europe in World War I with the equally renowned Harlem Hell Fighters, so named because of their ferocity in combat.[106] Roland had just arrived in the great bandleader's dressing room with some members of the quartet the Harmony Kings when he witnessed a horrible scene. Disgruntled band member Herbert Wright, who many believed to be mentally unstable, had been quietly ushered out of the room moments before Roland and the others arrived but burst back in and screamed, "I'll kill anybody that takes advantage of me! Jim Europe, I'll kill you!" With that outburst, he attacked Europe and delivered what would turn out to be a fatal blow to the neck of the totally startled bandleader.[107] Europe died later that evening at a nearby hospital and was buried in Arlington National Cemetery.

By mid-1919, Roland's older brother John had left Chattanooga and moved to Boston with his wife, Ola, and their son, Felton.[108] No doubt they had come at the urging of Roland to be with Fannie, since Roland was frequently traveling. John answered a religious calling and was ordained as a Baptist minister. He began serving as a pastor at a local church.

Roland continued his recital appearances in the Midwest that October. The October 24 issue of Xenia, Ohio's *Evening Gazette* reviewed Roland's performance on the campus of Wilberforce College, where he had given a recital with William King.[109] According to the reviewer, the two also were scheduled to give concerts in Dayton, Detroit, Pittsburgh, and Philadelphia.

On November 19, 1919, not long after arriving back in Boston from being on the road, sad news came from Nashville: Jennie Robinson was dead. The sixty-two-year-old professor, director of music, and mentor to countless African American teachers and administrators around the country had been discovered in her room on campus that morning.[110] Fisk's campus went into mourning for the severe but beloved thirty-two-year veteran teacher. Her often bitter musical rival, John W. Work II, said that she had "studied with the best teachers almost yearly, so that her knowledge might be ever growing. . . . Through her efforts the musical department of Fisk University was brought to its splendid efficiency. . . . She was one of the pillars of Fisk."[111] Of course, the university also sought and received a note from its then most-famous alum:

> Roxbury, Mass., Nov 24.
>
> Words cannot express my great sorrow on hearing of the death of Miss Robinson. Personally, a very great friend. Also a friend of the race to which I belong . . .
>
> Roland W. Hayes.[112]

Jennie Robinson had obviously seen the true potential of her star pupil. Roland was genuinely sad about her death, because without her both accepting him into the music program at Fisk and later momentously kicking him out, he would not be on the path to what he believed was his destiny. In a final gesture of reconciliation and respect, Robinson had left her teaching materials to her former student.[113]

Roland was back in Boston on December 10, 1919, where he gave a recital at Steinert Hall, with Lawrence Brown as accompanist and Maria Baldwin as the reader of poetry. The performance was actually a benefit concert for Brown, presumably to raise money for his upcoming European trip that was just a few months away.[114] Eight days later, Roland and Brown were in Augusta, Georgia, at Paine College, where he was hosted by none other than Charles J. Harris, his friend and former accompanist from Boston. Harris had left Boston and was teaching at his alma mater.[115] As always, Roland did Burleigh songs and arranged spirituals but also performed spirituals arranged by Brown. Hayes also performed a spiritual with which he was credited, titled "Witness."[116] This performance was the last time that Harris shared the stage with Roland as a fellow artist.[117]

Sometime at the end of the year, Roland received a letter, forwarded from an acquaintance in Louisburg, Kentucky. The letter inquired into the whereabouts of Roland Hayes on behalf of a young British national, Angus Fletcher, who was living in the United States. He had recently heard Roland sing and was interested in assisting him when he traveled to London. Fletcher, who played a brief but pivotal role and subsequently disappeared into obscurity, seems to have been the link between Hayes and the British agents who would represent him throughout the British Isles.[118] A letter from Fletcher reached Roland in January 1920:

> My dear Mr. Hayes,
>
> I am much interested in your proposal to continue your studies of negro music in Europe and in Africa. There is no doubt that you would find a large mass of material in the British Museum in London and your investigations in Africa would almost certainly lead to most interesting results. It is only in London or Paris that you could obtain sufficient information as to the best locality in Africa to make your headquarters.
>
> You are capable of carrying on a work of great value in the field of music and folklore, and I trust that every opportunity will be provided you wherever you go.
>
> You are at liberty to use this letter for any official purpose. My address in London is 105 Piccadilly, W.[,] which will always find me.
>
> Very truly yours,
> Angus Fletcher[119]

When and under what circumstances exactly Roland and Fletcher met and interacted is lost to history, but it appears as though the meeting occurred after Roland decided to explore the resources of the African continent in search of a deeper understanding of the African people and the uniqueness of their vocal wealth.

In preparation for his trip to Africa via London, Roland began communicating in the early spring of 1920 with the British agents Robert Leigh Ibbs and John Tillett. The Ibbs and Tillett Agency, however, was not the only British firm Roland approached. He also had some dealings with Henry Bernhardt, the lead partner in H. Bernhardt Musical and Dramatic Agent of London. Likely because the Bernhardt agency specialized in big productions, Roland felt he would not be well handled as a solo artist on its roster.

In March, he wrote a letter to Tillett at 19 Hanover Square:

> Although personally unknown to you I am taking the liberty to write you at the suggestion of Mr. Angus Fletcher, of 105 Piccadilly W., who is now in America, and Messrs. Maxwell, of Ricordi and Co. Music Publishers, 14 W. 43rd St., N.Y.
>
> My purpose in writing is to say that I am sailing for London aboard the S.S. Mauretania, sailing East on April 17th. I am a concert artist and am anxious for an appearance in London some time during May at one of the best music halls. The above named gentlemen tell me that you are the agent I ought to secure to handle such a concert. Therefore I shall be much pleased if you will kindly tell me if it will be possible to handle a concert there for me and what would be your consideration in the matter. I enclose a few of my sample programs and some notices from some of the best music critics of the American press. If further data is necessary I am in a position to furnish you with as much as you desire whether it be in the form of letters or literature. In your communication please tell me if a hall can be secured (medium size) and what it would cost to run a concert there. In fact give me all the information you can.[120]

With that introductory letter was born a long-term relationship with the British agency. In his response to Roland, Tillett stated that he was impressed with what Roland had sent and quoted him the cost for a concert at Aeolian Hall and the larger and more prestigious Wigmore Hall, including Ibbs and Tillett's management fee and the cost of an accompanist. But because Lawrence Brown was also going on the trip, Roland would not need an accompanist in London. Tillett also told Hayes about London's Steinway Hall, which was a little smaller and less costly.

In the spring of 1920, there was no letup in Roland's performing schedule as he planned his first trip abroad. Roland netted $1,100 in a performance at Washington, D.C.'s Belasco Theater early in the year, earning the lion's share of what he would need for his European trip.[121] A February 9, 1920, program placed him and Lawrence Brown in Tulsa, Oklahoma. The same month, Roland's passport was issued, indicating that he intended to travel to Africa, London, and Belgium.[122]

Roland also had another major engagement at the American Academy of Music in Philadelphia, in which Harry Burleigh was also a guest participant. The tenor took the extra step of writing several distinguished Philadelphia patrons personal letters, inviting them to buy tickets for this concert: "As this will probably be my last appearance in your city before going abroad, I trust you will give me a favorable reply."[123]

On the home front, Robert Brante and his wife, Margaret, had moved to Boston to be with Fannie while Roland was in Europe. With John and his family already in the city, Fannie would have two of her sons with her by the time Roland was scheduled to depart that April. While he was out of the country, Roland made arrangements to leave the management and sale of his recordings to a Mrs. G. F. Shaw of Dorchester, Massachusetts. She had already assisted him with secretarial duties in the past.

On April 21, two days before he departed, Roland took care of an essential piece of family business. He signed a letter to the Massachusetts Trust Company authorizing Fannie to draw on his bank account at her discretion and giving her access to his safe deposit securities.[124] With all of the business details taken care of, Roland set sail for Africa with what he thought would be a relatively brief stay in England. Fate, however, would deal him another hand.

THREE

Roland Rules Britannia

1920–1921

ON FRIDAY, APRIL 23, 1920, ROLAND HAYES AND LAWRENCE Brown watched the New York skyline recede as the SS *Mauretania* set sail. Sister ship to the infamous *Lusitania,* the *Mauretania* served as a hospital ship during the war and had only recently been refitted as an exclusive cruise liner.[1] Roland's recent concert in Washington, D.C., had netted him what he needed in order to travel to Europe in first class passage with his accompanist. At the age of thirty-two, Roland's persona as a rising concert artist was well formed, and he enjoyed playing the part.

For the better part of 1919, he had been preparing himself for this day. His first passport made clear his plan. Issued in February 1920, it indicated he intended to travel to "Africa" (no particular country or region was specified), London, and Belgium. The United Kingdom and Belgium could also provide opportunities where he could raise more funds, make the necessary introductions and arrangements, and then move on.

His long-standing fascination with Africa was still largely unexplored, but in the last year it had become his most urgent and intriguing priority. He now believed, almost with religious certainty, that he was called to discover his African origins and explore the deep feelings drawing him there. The African songs he had learned as a child growing up in northwest Georgia from Jim Kirby (Uncle Nat) and Peter Vaughan gradually started coming back to him.

Roland also looked back to his time with the Jubilee Singers and the Apollo Quartet during his Fisk days as a prelude to his passion for the sound of black voices. He even reflected on his singing with the Silver-Toned Quartet in Chattanooga; with Leon O'Hara in Atlantic City;

with William Lawrence on the Chautauqua circuit; and with Professor
Work in Boston. Suddenly, it was beginning to make sense to Roland.
A common thread, which he had understood as a result of these many
performing experiences, was the ability of the black voice to stir deep
emotions within listeners – both black and white. It could employ subtle
shadings to communicate empathy, and it could also negotiate complex
vocal and rhythmic patterns, which Roland had been able to do since he
was a child singing in the Baptist church in Georgia. When he was young,
he had seen people "get happy" (an excited religious utterance) in church
in response to an affecting musical performance.

In spite of his remarkable success in singing spirituals on the concert
stage, for years he had labored privately to perfect the language and style
of the best European singers to further his concert ambitions. Now he
felt like a free man, liberated from the burden of that impossible and
sometime frustrating effort. Almost a year had passed since he realized
that as a black singer, he was already endowed with a uniquely beautiful
sound that he would do as well or better to understand and hone.

In this self-understanding and appreciation of the relevance of his
African heritage, Roland was very much a man of his times. A generation
of European and American intellectuals and artists were discovering a
font of personal inspiration in Africa's cultural achievements, as well as a
powerful argument against virulent racism on both sides of the Atlantic.
In the decade following World War I, from the studios of Paris to the
streets of London and New York, a torrent of artistic and political ideas
poured out, expressing the self-conscious blooming of the next generation. In a few years, contemporary black New Yorker and Puerto Rican
bibliophile Arthur A. Schomburg would put it this way: "The mind of the
Negro has leapt forward faster than the slow clearings of scholarship will
yet safely permit. But there is no doubt that here is a field full of the most
intriguing and inspiring possibilities. Already the Negro sees himself
against a reclaimed background, in a perspective that will give pride and
self-respect ample scope, and make history yield for him the same values
that the treasured past of any people affords."[2]

The "Harlem Renaissance," as it later came to be called, was known
by its artists and intellectuals as "the New Negro Renaissance." It grap-

pled with the issue of a new black identity and looked to "Mother Africa" as its inspiration. Whether it was literature, visual arts, or poetry, new young African American artists were all being inspired about the possibilities yet to be discovered on the African continent.

Musically, America was entering the Jazz Age, a genre toward which Roland had a decided antipathy. He saw much greater nobility in his "Negro" spirituals, as they had come from his people's hardship, struggle, and ultimate liberation. Jazz, as far as Roland was concerned, was frilly and superficial. He firmly believed it would be no more than "a passing fancy."[3]

Among the "New Negro" movement's leading chroniclers was Howard University professor Alain Locke, one of Roland's greatest admirers and friends. It is not clear when and how they met, but by the time that Roland and Lawrence Brown had left for Europe, Locke's mother, Mary Hawkins Locke, had befriended Roland's mother, Fannie.[4] Locke also admired Roland because he had similarly been inspired by the glories of the African experience, and the two had discussed these issues before Roland and Brown's intended sojourn to Africa.

Dubbed as the "unofficial father" of the Harlem Renaissance, Locke's 1925 anthology, *The New Negro: An Interpretation,* came to be considered as one of the definitive literary works of the movement.[5] In a letter to Roland, Locke spoke of how proud he was of the singer and his accomplishments and expressed how fortunate the tenor was to have a partner in pianist William Lawrence (who had previously accompanied Roland and would later became the tenor's official accompanist). Locke, who was gay, wrote that he wished that he had someone like Lawrence in his life. The implication here was that there was more than a professional relationship between Roland and Lawrence. While Roland was very private, professional, and careful about what he committed to paper up to that point, there is little to suggest that there was a sexual relationship between him and William Lawrence. The tenor did, on occasion, say in his written communications to very close personal friends that there was something that he did not want to write in a letter but would speak about when he met them in person. This was often the case with his dear friend Noël Sullivan. Roland Hayes clearly embodied, however, the Renaissance's spirit of race pride and self-confidence. Within a few short years he would be hailed as one of its most important icons by its brightest stars, including Alain Locke, Langston Hughes, and Paul Robeson.

Prior to leaving for Europe, Roland discussed his interest in "native" African music and traditions with his voice teacher Arthur Hubbard, his former accompanist Charles Harris, and, of course, his current accompanist, Lawrence Brown. Brown also shared Roland's interest in researching the roots of African American spirituals and would surely follow the singer to Africa in his quest.[6]

Roland's decision to embrace the black voice would drive his career for the next three years and beyond, changing the course of music history as he blazed a trail for brilliant young black concert artists on the brink of boundless careers, including Marian Anderson and Paul Robeson. African American concert stars had existed before Roland, notably soprano Sissieretta Jones (also known as the "the Black Patti") and the tenor Sidney Woodard, whom Roland had met and heard in recital. For Roland, the career of Ira Aldridge, the famous nineteenth-century black Shakespearean actor, also may have been an inspiration. Roland was already poised to become an icon among his contemporaries in this nascent, golden era.

For the duration of their passage to London, seasickness confined Roland and Brown to their cabins. It was probably just as well, since the presence of black men, regardless of how polite and well spoken they were, might have disturbed the other first-class passengers.[7] Disembarking in Southampton, England, they quickly recovered. They made a handsome duo, undoubtedly fastidious in their decorum and experienced as travelers after years of touring. They explained to officials that they were en route to Africa, obviating the need to supply additional documentation, and had no trouble getting through customs.[8]

At nearly thirty-three years old, the somewhat diminutive five-foot-four-inch Roland had a strikingly handsome, long dark brown face of mathematical precision. He had a comparatively narrow nose, which widened slightly at the nostrils, and full lips; he wore no beard. Already a few streaks of his trademark gray had begun to appear near the right side of his forehead. His upright posture and impeccable dress made him appear taller than his actual height. His demeanor was proud but not haughty. He was at all times gracious and polite, especially in public.

His younger accompanist had caramel colored skin with a pronounced forehead but possessed an equally handsome countenance. Slightly taller than Roland, Lawrence Brown had strong hands and long fingers for someone his height. Nearing thirty, Brown was as polished as the singer with whom he traveled. The always respectful Brown had impressed Roland's mother, Fannie, so much that she was convinced that her son was traveling with a fine churchgoing young man from a good family, which of course he was. One aspect of Lawrence Brown's life that Fannie most likely would not have approved of, however, was his homosexuality. He concealed his orientation from most but had more than one gay relationship during his time in Europe.

The young men hailed a taxi and set out to find a place to stay. For the past decade, London had been swelling with newly arrived West Indians and continental Africans, mostly from West Africa, flooding the black communities that had already been in the British Isles for generations.[9] London had become a hotbed of black organizations vociferously protesting human rights abuses in British colonial administrations as well as of vicious attacks on people of African ancestry in the United States.

Roland did not immediately realize how difficult it would be to find rooms. Approaching four and a half million people, the population of inner London had spilled over to the outer counties. Rooms everywhere were in short supply. Neither the Ibbs and Tillett Agency nor Roland's British contact from the United States, Angus Fletcher, had provided directions or housing information. After a while, the difficulty of the situation was evident. Roland and Brown abandoned the taxi to explore the city on foot.

In the St. John's Wood district, they stumbled onto a few Afro-British families. Welcoming these well-spoken, impressive young arrivals from the United States, the black Londoners directed them to Duse Mohammed Ali, who owned a boardinghouse in the neighborhood. Seemingly, fate itself had led the pair to his doorstep. Ali immediately offered Hayes and Brown rooms at his St. John's home for a minimal cost. Roland accepted readily the more than gracious accommodation offer.

Ali was of one of the central figures among London's Pan-African elite and had influential contacts across the social spectrum.[10] His long record of robust political activism frequently invited the condemnation of the British government. This reality, however, added to his celebrity among continental and diasporan Africans. It is hard to imagine a more unlikely pairing than the fiery Ali and the low-keyed Hayes, but over the years, even with Ali under British government surveillance, the American tenor continued his relationship with one of the world's foremost proponents of African nationalism.

Born in Alexandria, Egypt, in 1866 to an Egyptian father and a Sudanese mother, Duse Mohammed Ali grew up in a large family. According to various accounts, when he was a teenager, he was sent to study in Britain. But when his father and brothers died during the British occupation of Egypt in the 1880s, he could not afford to continue his education and turned to acting and playwriting to support himself. By 1920, Ali had traveled extensively, including a trip to the United States, and had made a name in British theater circles. His 1911 book, *In the Land of the Pharaoh,* was later exposed as being substantially plagiarized, but that seemed not to have hurt his reputation. He edited the London-based newspaper *African and Orient Review,* aimed at bringing about greater contact among continental Africans, Asians, and their descendants throughout the diaspora.[11] He routinely published accounts of British colonial atrocities on the African continent and throughout the 1910s was one of the empire's many vociferous black critics. While Ali's politics were viewed with alarm by the British establishment, the record shows the man himself to have been anything but a firebrand. He was as constructive and genial as he was progressive.

By the time he met Roland, Ali had already inspired a sense of higher purpose and confidence in many others, most notably his one-time protégé Marcus Garvey. The Jamaican, who came to make his presence known throughout the continental African and diasporan world, was an early apprentice of Ali in 1912, eight years before Roland Hayes arrived in London. It was from Duse Mohammed Ali that Garvey got the quote that he became known for around the black world, "Africa for the Africans."[12] Although he did not have the same level of zeal for the African continent as Garvey, Ali also inspired Roland to understand the

African continental experience as never before, and the tenor soaked the information up like a sponge.

A devout Muslim, Duse Mohammed Ali established Islamic support groups throughout London. In 1918, he had helped to found the African Progress Union (APU), a Pan-African organization whose members were made up of continental, British-born, and West Indian Africans.[13] The organization was dedicated to addressing human rights controversies as well as black representation issues on the continent and throughout the diaspora. A major effort of the APU was the call to restore indigenous control to those African colonies that Germany had lost after its defeat in World War I. It was to this organization that Roland would eventually lend his support.[14]

Roland was resolute in his goals of establishing himself as a serious artist and replenishing his earnings. The Ibbs and Tillett Agency proved to be ready and eager to work with him. In a letter dated April 1, John Tillett had quoted him the cost for a concert at Aeolian Hall and the larger, more prestigious Wigmore Hall, including the agency's 10 percent management fee. Barely twenty years old in 1920, Wigmore Hall had become one of London's premiere venues. Scoring a success at the hall could have a lasting impact on any singer's career.

Wigmore Hall, however, would have to wait. Instead, arrangements were concluded to present Roland and Brown in recital at the Aeolian Hall on May 31, 1920. Located in the affluent Mayfair section of east London, Aeolian Hall enjoyed a longer history than its competitors Wigmore and Steinway Halls. Because of its location, Aeolian Hall attracted many wealthy Londoners and catered to recitalists, chamber musicians, small choral groups, and other domestic music makers. It was, however, no match for the more prestigious Queen's Hall and the better-known Royal Opera House at Covent Garden.[15]

When Tillett pressed Roland on the financing, he responded decisively. On May 12, the agency asked Roland to put down a thirty-pound sterling deposit for the Aeolian Hall concert.[16] Roland sent a fifty-pound deposit instead; two days later it was acknowledged. To get a foothold in the British concert circuit, he was prepared to invest whatever it took. When booking an unknown artist (or one who lacked a London reputation), the hall required a deposit as insurance against low ticket sales. If the hall's costs were met, any excess would be paid to the artist. This also encouraged the artist to promote the concert among his or her associates.[17] A debut for an unknown artist could be pricey.

Roland's May 31 concert was not part of a subscription series or any other regularly scheduled performance. Because of the relative haste at which the concert was planned, the audience was relatively meager. The debut recital came and went, yielding mixed reviews. Roland registered the criticism but took it in stride. Decades later in a newspaper interview, he said, "I suppose most people came out of curiosity, but they stayed to cheer. One paper, however, called it a 'sacrilege that a black man should sing the love songs of white people.'"[18] John Tillett noted the nay-saying and may have expected as much, but he was more impressed by the crowd's enthusiasm. If he had doubts that his new black client would go over well with other British audiences, he showed no evidence of it. He immediately booked Roland and Brown into the Winter Gardens in Bournemouth for performances the following August and September at the moderate fee of fifteen guineas, minus the agency's commission.[19]

The Winter Gardens in the up-market seaside resort of Bournemouth had a three-decade-long history of presenting orchestral music under the guidance of Dan Godfrey and was subsidized by the city. The resort set out to attract the middle classes and in 1893 became the first British town to have a municipal orchestra. Dr. Godfrey was to become Sir Godfrey in 1922. He often picked new compositions and introduced new composers, and Bournemouth had heard some of the best, including Sir Edward Elgar, Jean Sibelius, and Samuel Coleridge-Taylor. The city had a fine reputation for fresh sea air mingled with the smell of pines and apparently also practiced racial tolerance. For more than twenty years it had been the home of Virginia-born Thomas Lewis Johnson, whose *Twenty-Eight Years a Slave* autobiography went into its eighth edition in 1909, published in Bournemouth.[20]

For Roland's Bournemouth debut, the initial proposal included an orchestral appearance directed by Godfrey. Wanting to take advantage of the orchestra's presence, Roland had prepared the celebrated aria from Verdi's *Aida*, "Celeste Aida," for the first performance and "Onaway! Awake, Beloved!" for the second in order to "show a side of his voice and art that the songs do not."[21] He wanted to make clear to British audiences and music directors that his repertory included many of the great tenor arias and extended well beyond African American spirituals. But Godfrey vetoed the idea, calling it impractical. Instead, he proposed that Roland stick to singing spirituals with Lawrence Brown at the keyboard.[22] Roland was forced to accept the premise that it would be safer to do the spirituals and save the orchestral appearance for another time. The number of American recitalists in London in the summer of 1920 was large – it was called the American invasion by *Hazell's Annual* – and Roland would appear more noteworthy with his distinct repertoire.[23]

Roland wrote to Fannie back in Boston and told her about his upcoming engagement in Bournemouth. He had already sent her several postcards with reassuring, affectionate letters following close behind. The letter dated July 12 took a prophetic turn: "I have been feeling for some days now that John is worse. Your last letter told me of his poor condition, but I hope he is better rather than worse."[24] John Hayes, Roland's oldest surviving brother, had died on July 6, six days before. An ordained pastor at the People's Baptist Church in Boston, he had left behind his widow and son. Roland, who would eventually assume responsibility for his sister-in-law and nephew, wrote his mother on July 26, now sadly aware of his brother's death:

My dear, dear Mother:

Again I write you to let you know that I am thinking of you and your well being. I have felt keenly the death of John and I have also felt for you. While you do not give evidence of your feelings outwardly, I know how deeply you feel everything where your own is concerned. I only wish that I might have been there through it all, not that I could have helped or hindered, but because there is something in me which told me that I ought to have been there.

I sang last night in a Baptist church here and I heard a fine sermon [from] the pastor of the church. His text taken from Obediah [*sic*] was a long one and I cannot remember all of it. His [illegible word] was on those who stand aloof of, or who stand neither for or against Christ.[25]

He continued writing solicitously and frequently to Fannie to ease her grief and most certainly his own. On August 5, he mentioned to his mother that he was under the weather. As it turned out, though, retreating to Ali's house gave him time to enjoy its revolving cast of characters.

"Last Sunday I did not feel my very best, so I stayed in all day. An African Chief, 'Oluwa,' who is visiting this country on behalf of African(s) in his part 'Lagos, Nigeria,' West Africa visited our house and we had a pleasant time. They took snapshots of us and I shall send you one as soon as I get them."[26] Chief Oluwa, whose given name was Amodu Tijani, had joined other renowned Nigerian nationalists like Herbert Macaulay in calling for the British government to restore land appropriated in the southwestern area of Nigeria. But Roland, despite his diffidence toward politics, got along with Oluwa and Ali's other continental African guests on cultural terms. He delighted in gathering information about African music as various continental visitors came through. Indeed, Oluwa may have provided the traditional Yoruba musical material that Roland added to his recital the following year. In addition to Oluwa, Roland told his mother, he had met other African royalty, such as Lagos chief Diuwa, who encouraged him to come to the continent to learn more about traditional African music firsthand.[27]

By early October Roland was quietly making headway on his African project. Responding to a query from a R. W. Wooding of Cape Town, South Africa, he wrote,

> Thank you for your letter of a few days ago and also for the one which Rev. East brought to me today . . . I have been thinking over the matter of coming to S. Africa very seriously for the past few days and have made up my mind to make the trip providing a few requirements which I must make before I can prepare for coming if I would make the trip. One is that owing to the great distance and big expense which the round trip passage for myself and pianist would entail I should have to be guaranteed my round trip expenses before I should start. The other is that necessary arrangements would have to be made there to assure my being able to land.[28]

If these requirements were met, he concluded, he would make the trip, but he needed to book the tickets soon. In the end, the trip fizzled, but the idea continued to burn brightly in his imagination.

While staying at Ali's residence, he regularly met and befriended politically connected continental Africans and Afro-Britons; Roland respectfully listened to their various political ideologies and justified grievances. But through it all, he remained fixed on his own agenda. If the dream of reaching Africa so far remained tantalizingly beyond his grasp, he was unwavering in its pursuit. He continued to consciously cultivate relationships with Africans in London and in doing so became known in his own right as a man of substance in Ali's circle.

On October 28, an impressive assemblage of London's best and brightest African men and their supporters, deeply impressed with the increasingly obvious convictions of the gifted American concert artist, honored him with their formal encouragement and acknowledgment.

Roland Hayes
The Negro Tenor

We, the undersigned, having closely observed your interesting rise to a pre-eminent and enviable position in the realm of music, and being members of the various races that go to make up the families who comprise the inhabitants of Africa as well as those who have descended from the same parent stock as yourself, beg to tender you our high felicitations and regard on this your visit to the seat of the British Empire.

We realize that your success is our success and that by proving that you are capable of the higher musical culture you are rendering incalculable benefits to your race. As blood of our blood, flesh of our flesh, and bone of our bone, we wish you continued success in all your undertakings praying that an All-Wise Creator will graciously grant you health and strength to complete the task you have so nobly undertaken which must indubitably redound to His Glory and to the amelioration and recognition of the undoubted mental capacities and endowments of your brothers of the Negro Race.

We, therefore, beg that you will accept this slight token of our undying admiration and esteem.

[Signatories]
London 28 October 1920[29]

The twenty-three signers to the proclamation were overwhelmingly continental Africans. Roland took home a laurel wreath and the scrolled tribute, which he treasured for the rest of his life. Although it was shaping up to be a lean year financially and none of his leads on getting to the African continent had panned out, Roland was greatly encouraged by the praise and acceptance he found among these distinguished men of color.

In addition to making his mark among the Pan-African Brahmins, Roland had entered the world of Anglo-London's intellectual elite. An enthusiastic buzz was building about him, and he was quietly becoming a sensation. Even American expat Ezra Pound was heard stating that the "celebrated negro tenor" and his accompanist were pleasing compatriots.[30]

Early on, Roland had caught the attention of the preeminent British composer Roger Quilter, who enthusiastically took him and Brown under his wing and introduced them to his circle of aristocratic friends, among whom were serious musicians. The gentle, soft-spoken only son of a baronet, Roger Quilter had been educated at Eton College and later studied composition at Hoch Conservatory in Frankfurt, Germany. By the time Roland and Brown arrived in London, Quilter's reputation as an accomplished composer of the English art song was solid. His place in the history of the genre was secured when several of his songs were premiered and recorded by Britain's beloved and best-known tenor, Gervaise Elwes, his collaborator.

Barely a decade older than Roland, Roger Quilter already commanded extraordinary respect among British musicians, and his patronage gave invaluable cachet. It was a matter of extraordinary consequence that Quilter recognized Roland's voice as a unique instrument. If he composed songs for Roland, as he did for the great Elwes, it would establish the tenor's career on a different plane. Roland recognized the value of his association with Quilter instantly, and ideas to engage Quilter as a guest artist began to germinate.

Roland and Brown made the best of their brush with the rich and famous. The tenor had not entirely depleted his funds, but growing public recognition was essential to the success of his European venture. By the end of 1920, the two Americans routinely dined with Quilter or accepted his financial assistance to subsidize their dwindling food budget. Quilter, however, seems to have had a deeper interest in Lawrence Brown. Brown was probably one of the brief and undocumented sexual encounters that Quilter had in the early 1920s.[31] The written communications between them indicate a very close and personal friendship that continued for more than thirty years.

New patrons spread the word about the duo's stirring performances and filled auditoriums, churches, concert halls, and drawing rooms throughout the British Isles. Even without an exclusive agreement, Ibbs and Tillett had no trouble securing concerts and arranging for test recordings with the British label His Master's Voice (HMV). Founded

around 1908, the label was a thriving vehicle for recording several classical artists, including Enrico Caruso, by the time Roland had arrived
in London. Roland was aware that by being recorded by such a major
label, his reputation throughout Europe could substantially increase. In
December, Roland went into the studio and made a test recording for
HMV, which was the first step in measuring the label's interest in him.

He mulled over his position as a cash-strapped, rising concert star;
his year of laboring to make a name for himself in England had shown
him that there was much more potential. He decided the time had come
to open his own negotiations with HMV to secure a formal contract. He
also informed Ibbs and Tillett that he wanted them to increase his asking
fee for future engagements. Tillett advised against it, claiming Roland's
demands were out of line with what their associated venues could afford.
Undeterred, Roland held out until the agency met his terms.

Contract talks with HMV continued into the following year but
broke down by February 1921 over the label's refusal to commit to a
promotional budget. After struggling with marketing and distributing
his recordings in the United States, Roland refused to settle for anything
less than the maximum from this prospective project. Unable to reach
an agreement with the label, he was eventually allowed to destroy the
HMV masters.

Roland's dealings with Ibbs and Tillett were audacious but smartly
timed. Roland never forgot that he potentially had another London-
based agent, Henry Bernhardt, waiting in the wings as he continued
negotiations with Ibbs and Tillett. Bernhardt had contacted Roland
the prior year in New York to offer his management services. Roland
reasoned that Bernhardt might be even more eager, now that he and
Brown had built a small following. After a few discreet inquiries, Roland determined that Bernhardt was more than agreeable to seeking
out and negotiating concert engagements that paid out at a higher rate
than the Ibbs and Tillett organization.[32] Starting with a performance in
Devon, England, in January 1921 in which Roland would sing excerpts
from Coleridge-Taylor's *Hiawatha's Wedding Feast* and several African
American spirituals,[33] Bernhardt began negotiating on Roland's behalf.
Thanks to Bernhardt, musical opportunities surfaced in Devonshire in
early April on Good Friday evening and the following month in London

at the Palladium Theater. Skillfully using the competition between Bernhardt and the Ibbs and Tillett agencies for leverage, Roland established a tactic that he would repeat successfully later in his career for even greater stakes.

On February 26, 1921, the London-based weekly *West Africa* breathlessly alerted its readers to Roland's impending concert at Wigmore Hall. Roland had decided it was time to step up to Wigmore. A success there could open up many more possibilities.

> I pass on to the West African colony in London the reminder that Mr. Roland Hayes, the American tenor, will give another recital today (Saturday) at Wigmore Hall, Wigmore Street, at 3 PM. It is the deliberate opinion of the music critic of *West Africa*, who has heard the best tenors of the last generation or so, that Mr. Hayes has a finer voice, and more ability in using his voice, than Caruso, or than Caruso's superior, the Belgian tenor, Razevet; that, in short, the African race has given to the world in Mr. Hayes the greatest tenor the world at present possesses.[34]

This flattering commentary by *West Africa*'s white editor, Albert Cartwright was just what Roland banked on to fill the seats at his concerts. Cartwright's review of the recital was even more enthusiastic than his announcement. In a later edition of the weekly, he devoted an entire page to praising the singer, in which he quoted similar accolades from the prestigious London *Times*. He even suggested that Roland should tour the African continent at the expense of one of the shipping lines, with appearances at unconventional venues like "stores and warehouses."[35] But Roland's Wigmore Hall concert, while impressive, did not carry the same prestige as it might have because it was an afternoon recital during the week. It did not attract the elite audience of an evening musical event.

Shortly afterward, the tenor found yet another reliable, high-profile outlet for his work through Stephen Graham, author of *Children of the Slaves*. Graham invited the tenor to a party where he introduced Roland to the Reverend Hugh B. Chapman. "Padre" Chapman, who had earned an international reputation for assisting impoverished souls in the slums of London, was the chaplain of the Royal Chapel of the Savoy when Roland arrived in England. As the chapel's principal leader, Chapman regularly hired musicians and was in a position to do Roland a lot of good.

Their meeting ignited deep mutual passions: the singer's spirituality and religiosity and the priest's enthusiasm for the art of song.

It was late in the Lenten season when Chapman first invited Roland to sing a series at the Royal Chapel with Brown at the keyboard. The initial performance on March 17 passed without incident. Roland's second performance a few days later on Palm Sunday, which featured an a cappella rendition of the spiritual "Were You There?," was such a phenomenon that a photo of it was later immortalized in a bust by Renée Vautier. It captured the tenor in a deep, almost transcendental pose with his head slightly raised and his eyes tightly closed as if he were internalizing the words that he had just sung about the crucified Christ dying on the cross: "Oh! Sometimes, it causes me to tremble, tremble, tremble . . ." As he delivered this line, Roland caused a few in his dispassionate British audience to drop their heads and shed tears. When he applied his well-developed *messa di voce* to the single word "Oh," with a stunning portamento, the listeners were totally enthralled. These were the deep feelings that the elusive black voice was capable of evoking, no matter the color of the listener.

But there was still grumbling from a few in the well-heeled congregation. Was it not a mistake, some sniffed, to offer the "Negro" spirituals on such a solemn occasion? Chapman counseled his new soloist to ignore such complaints and remain patient, because he was certain "something good" would occur.[36] What Chapman knew and Roland did not was that the Anglican minister had been working behind the scenes to get a representative of Buckingham Palace to attend that Palm Sunday service where Roland had delivered the stirring performance of "Were You There?" If the representative was not at the Palm Sunday performance, he would surely be at the tenor's scheduled Wigmore Hall recital the following month.

Chapman's counsel was undoubtedly a comfort to Roland, who had to prepare for his official evening debut on April 21 at Wigmore Hall. This recital would be in the evening and was expected to draw his biggest UK audience to date. It had great potential to attract important arts patrons and critics, particularly with Padre Chapman's support behind the scenes. Now that Roland had proved his ability to draw a sizable audience, Ibbs and Tillett put their reputation on the line by committing considerable resources to promote and stage the concert. Consistent with his occasional practice of presenting a well-known musician as part of his program, Roland took the additional step of inviting Roger Quilter to accompany him for part of the program, which in turn promoted ticket sales and drew attention from top music critics.

Increasing the pressure was a coal miner's strike that had begun in early April, forcing British prime minister David Lloyd George to shut down all nonessential buildings to conserve energy. The prime minister had taken a hard line with the strikers, whose heels were equally dug in for better conditions and wages. The governmental fiat had endangered not only the investment made by the Ibbs and Tillett Agency but, as Roland saw it, his future. A prolonged strike could cause the prime minister to cancel all unnecessary activities, such as a vocal recital. Seriously worried, Roland pushed himself by increasing his already grueling rehearsal schedule with Brown to the point of exhaustion. After a few grim weeks of this regimen (in which he was also neglecting his health), the singer developed pneumonia.[37]

On the Thursday of the performance, ill and suffering but determined to go onstage, Roland lay in bed. Duse Mohammed Ali helped him rise; he was still running a high temperature. The tenor's devoted supporter dressed his tenant and piled into a waiting car with him and Brown. Roland would recall the night as a matter of life and death:

> Wigmore Hall was full when we arrived. The manager was wringing his hands because I was late, but he grew hysterical when he saw what condition I was in. I had to be carried upstairs. I asked an attendant to place a chair between the piano and the door from the artist's room. Nearly unconscious when I made my entrance, I managed to reach out and grasp the back of the chair for support. I slid along the curve of the piano until I reached a point where I could stop to bow to my audience. Brown followed me, shaking with fear and momentarily awaiting my collapse. . . . I was resigned to any dreadful end. I only thought, "This may be the last act of my life." . . . When I returned to the stage for the second group [of songs], I had no feeling of sickness or infirmity. I reached out to my audience and gathered it into myself.[38]

He began with "Nimm mich dir zu eigen hin" (Take me to thee for thine own) from Bach's Cantata 65. He edged forward, taking on Handel's "Where'er You Walk" from *Semele,* then Beethoven's "Adelaïde," Debussy's "Romance," and Fauré's "Après un rêve" (After a dream). Having added several Roger Quilter songs to the program, including his arrangements of "Drink to Me Only with Thine Eyes," "Dream Valley," and "Over the Mountains," Roland had invited Quilter to join him onstage as accompanist. But, citing some indisposition, Quilter had bowed out at the last minute.[39] Roland soldiered on. He sang spirituals and even included a piece that he characterized as "a Native African Nigerian Folk Song in Yorùbá."[40]

By sheer will, Roland overcame his weakness to deliver a bravura performance under the most difficult circumstances imaginable for a singer. Neither audience nor reviewers suspected that the tenor, who had performed so wonderfully, had just risen from his sickbed. Years later, Roland was even more specific about his near-miraculous recovery: "As I sang, strength came. Perspiration fell from me almost like rain. But what happened is that I sweated out all the pneumonia. I was not sick another day."[41]

The following day, the *Times* reviewer led with the headline "A Fine Singer – Mr. Roland Hayes's Recital":

> Mr. Roland Hayes, who sang at Wigmore Hall last night, has been gradually making a reputation in London, and is now an exceptionally fine singer. His initial difficulties with the languages ... for he adds French, and pronounces it quite as clearly as he does English[,] have disappeared, and he has found his audience, and can sing straight to them.... He has a well sustained legato, and this is assisted by his way of singing on the *m*'s and *n*'s. He also sings throughout in perfect tune, thereby putting himself in a small class....
>
> But his more invaluable gift is that of personality, which came out most in the songs of his own country.... Incidentally, the harmonies, his own and his accompanist's Mr. Lawrence Brown's the barest imaginable, were an object lesson for all whom it may concern; the simple was treated simply. At the end of the recital a curious thing happened. Nobody moved or took his eyes off the platform. They had reality before them, and it had gone.[42]

London's April 23 issue of the *Daily Telegraph,* just as complimentary, focused on the Yoruba song:

> Nigerian folksongs do not often find their way to this country, and still less often are they found in the programme of a professional recital. Mr. Roland Hayes, the negro tenor who has so entranced London audiences of late with his singing, gave us, in the group of Negro Spirituals which were the most characteristic feature of his recital at Wigmore Hall on Thursday evening, a ballad recently

recorded in Lagos.... Mr. Hayes had his coadjutor Mr. Lawrence Brown, a
talented fellow-countryman, and between them they performed a programme of
fine music. The versatility of Mr. Hayes is remarkable, and few of our own singers could have carried through so exacting a programme.[43]

Fresh from their triumph, Roland and Lawrence Brown took tea
at Roger Quilter's home the following day, allowing Quilter to make
amends for his absence from the tenor's remarkable achievement. Feeling better, Roland was unwinding when he received a call from Robert
Tillbrook in the Ibbs and Tillett office. Roland later told the story most
effectively:

"Has Mrs. Fairfax told you the news?" he asked.
"No," said I, "what news?"
"I think I should wait for her to tell you," said he.
"Do tell me now," I pleaded.
"Well," said he, "if I tell you, you must not repeat it just yet. You have been com-
manded to sing before Their Majesties in Buckingham Palace." I fainted dead
away.[44]

The following day, in the late afternoon, Roland and Brown once
again dressed in their tuxedos and were ferried by limousine to Buckingham Palace for instruction on the proper etiquette for meeting Their
Majesties, King George and Queen Mary. When the moment arrived
for them to be presented, Roland and Brown stepped forward to bow,
but the king informed them that there would be no such formalities
and proposed that he and Roland meet "man to man."[45] Although the
performance was scheduled to last only thirty minutes, the visit lasted
for two hours.

The official court report in the *Times* on April 25 simply said, "Mr.
Roland Hayes had the honour of singing before Their Majesties this
evening." For the rest of the world, however, the news of Roland's royal
performance seemed to take on a life of its own. The journal *West Africa*
gave it glowing coverage in its April 30 edition:

The visit was to last half an hour, but it was extended longer.... Mr. Hayes sang
for 30 minutes, tea was served, and he was asked to sing again by his Majesty,
who chatted to his delighted guest for over a quarter of an hour. The King and
Queen expressed their pleasure over his singing, and warmly congratulated
him on his superb voice, which Londoners will again have the opportunity of

hearing, I believe, at a concert on May 27th. Before leaving the Palace, Mr. Hayes was presented with a beautiful tie pin by the King.[46]

The level of detail was obviously provided by Roland himself. On the way home from Buckingham Palace, he wired Fannie in Boston. Her predictably humble response was for him to remember who he was and that he should "give credit where it is due."[47] Questioned by Boston reporters, she was reported to be restrained, as if she were more interested in returning to her ironing than dwelling on her newly famous son.

But Roland appeared to be genuinely and unabashedly overwhelmed. He wrote to the London *Daily Telegraph* expressing his delight to the *Telegraph*'s readers. Having long ago learned the usefulness of positive press coverage in the United States, he carefully constructed remarks designed both to convey appreciation to his British audience and to inform them of his next recital the following month. The Wigmore Hall triumph was something he had gambled on and won. But the command performance exceeded even his most aggressive calculations. Coming together, the two performances so dramatically enhanced his standing that Roland could hardly believe it himself.

On May 13, he again wrote to Fannie. His tone was as matter-of-fact as he could manage:

Dear, dear Mother:

I was awfully glad to get your letter and it cheered me so very much . . .

By [this] time you received my letter telling all that has happened to me during the last 3 weeks. On Wednesday of this week Madame Nellie Melba, the famous singer of world wide fame, invited me to tea where I met other famous artists among whom was Fritz Kreisler, the greatest violinist in the world. Madame Melba gave her farewell recital on last Sunday. So she told people present at the tea that the king was there and asked her if she had heard me sing. She said "no." Well you want to hear him *at once* for he is a great artist.

Mme. Melba gave me her photograph signed, and with this inscription on it: *'Bravo! Mr. Hayes, you are a great artist.'* I am not telling you this because I am beside myself, but because I felt that you would like to know what is happening to me here. As far as I am concerned I am no different nor do I feel any different than I have always felt. I am just thanking God for all and dedicate all to his purpose. . . . I am your devoted son,

Roland Hayes
P.S. I expect to go to Paris for two weeks the 1st of June[48]

It is hard to imagine that Fannie fully appreciated what it meant to her son that on King George and Queen Mary's recommendation, the legendary Australian opera soprano Nellie Melba had invited him to a luncheon at her residence. Nearly twenty years earlier, Melba's magnificent recorded voice had touched him in the living room of William Stone in Chattanooga. He now found himself not only singing for her but having *her* pay the high compliment of recognizing him as a great artist. Perhaps making up for missing Roland's Wigmore Hall engagement, Roger Quilter accompanied the tenor at the keyboard. Renowned British composer Sir Edward Elgar was also among the distinguished guests at Melba's home.

When Roland's schedule began to fill up with dates at other prestigious venues, he told John Tillett to seek an even higher fee. Warned, once again, that his asking price was already too high for the British market, Roland persisted and, once again, received his requested fee. He sang to another full house at Wigmore Hall on May 27, 1921, and again received very strong reviews. At the home of the Virginia-born expatriate Lady Nancy Astor, he continued his conquest of the aristocracy, launching a friendship with her that lasted beyond the Second World War. Roland subsequently sang private recitals for British prime minister David Lloyd George, among others.

Understandably, the African diaspora in London was perfectly thrilled with these developments. After Hayes's triumph at Buckingham Palace, John Alcindor, a Trinidadian and signatory of the October 28, 1920, proclamation that had praised Roland, invited him to his home. Alcindor had completed his medical training in Britain and became president of the anticolonial African Progress Union sometime in 1921.[49] Among Alcindor's guests, Roland met Amanda Aldridge, daughter of the late African American tragedian Ira Aldridge, and Robert Broadhurst, the Afro-British amateur singer and secretary of the APU in 1919 who routinely communicated with W. E. B. Du Bois and attended the historic First Pan-African Congress in Paris.[50] That day at Alcindor's home, Aldridge and Broadhurst asked Hayes to give a benefit recital to support the work of the APU. Hayes, of course, accepted. The recital eventually took place in October 1921.[51] Roland also gave benefit recitals for several other Pan-African political organizations operating in the London area, including the nationalist National Congress of British West Africa. The members of these organizations became lasting fans of the tenor and continued to urge him to make a tour of Africa.

In the wake of these regular invitations to parties and the press's attention, Padre Chapman redoubled his efforts to help Roland stay grounded spiritually. Chapman gave Roland the kind of unconditional advice that he had always loved and needed from Fannie. Chapman's letters had a pastoral air. On June 17, 1921, he wrote:

> My dear Roland,
>
> I had intended to be present this afternoon at the Aeolian Hall but was prevented. . . . Remember that I love you in Jesus Christ and that shyness or pride should be impossible between us. What I want you to do is to sing here a couple of your sweetest things on Sunday evening before the meeting in Upper Grosvenor Street, so you must come to tea without fail at 5 PM and I am not going to allow it that an idealist singer whose aim is to glorify Christ should have to endure difficulties which he might evade in ten minutes if he took up a lower line. God bless you and Lawrence [Brown] from my heart and please ring up tomorrow morning to say that you are coming on Sunday.
>
> Your devoted,
> Padre[52]

The fatherly tone might suggest that Hugh Chapman was significantly older, but in fact the Anglican priest was fewer than five years Roland's senior. His loyalty and enthusiasm gave Roland not only work but also real emotional support, a soothing stream of messages affirming his worth and sympathizing with his struggle to prove that he was an admirable artist who could establish himself on the European continent.

The historic 1921 Second Pan-African Congress met in London late that summer. With parallel meetings held in Paris and Belgium, Roland and Lawrence Brown attended several sessions in London, out of which a number of important resolutions pertaining to colonized Africans on the continent and in the diaspora emerged. The most important work to come out of that trailblazing set of meetings was the well-known "London Manifesto."[53] The document affirmed Britain's leadership in terms of its independent courts and its overall progressive justice system, but it also accused the British crown of systematically "enslaving" continental

Africans and denying them the right of self-determination and self-government. It also stated that those "Natives" under British colonial rule were kept ignorant and were trained only to do menial jobs.[54]

The central driving force behind the second congress was Roland's acquaintance from Boston, W. E. B. Du Bois, who was instrumental in inviting the singer and his accompanist to the London meeting. There is no record of Roland and Brown performing at the congress, but because of the singer's growing reputation, Du Bois wanted Roland there with hopes of involving him in the goals of the congress in Europe, on the African continent, and back home in the United States.

Despite the vagueness of Roland's relationship to the politics of the congress and the Pan-African community, spanning both sides of the Atlantic, the tenor continued assiduously to promote his career. Responding to *West Africa* writer Albert Cartwright's suggestion that Roland journey to Africa, the Lagos Musical Association sent Roland a formal invitation to perform in Nigeria. The association's secretary, T. K. E. Phillips, a Nigerian organist and choirmaster, had received his musical training in London and returned to establish a strong Western art music tradition in his home country.[55] He invited Roland to perform a series of concerts in the Lagos area: "But perfect strangers though we are to each other, yet your illustrious career is the talk of us all in West Africa, as much as it is the great pride not only of us in this part of the world, but of the Negro race the world over."[56] In his response, Roland embraced the idea of traveling to Nigeria but said his current schedule made it difficult. He *was* willing, however, to adjust his plans, provided the necessary financial arrangements could be made. Roland's very gracious reply to Phillips's letter prompted the Lagos Musical Association's secretary to suggest they wait until a time more convenient for both parties. Phillips concluded the exchange by saying, "The association watch[es] your progress with the keenest interest and pray[s] that you may ever maintain your very high position in the World of Vocal music, thereby vindicating the cause of and uplifting the Negro race."[57]

Roland, too, had begun to envision himself attaining a major position in the world of vocal music. Engagement requests remained high. He appeared for the first time at Britain's traditional Promenade or "Prom"

Concert in early September. Founded in 1895, the musical festival spon-sored more than fifty performances throughout the greater London area as well as other parts of the British Isles. Roland returned to Wigmore Hall for yet another recital late that month. Reviews, routinely strong and supportive, poured in from around the United Kingdom, includ-ing stories or articles in the *Plymouth Herald,* the *Manchester Guardian,* London's *Daily Telegraph* and *Times,* the *New Age, Time and Tide,* and the *Halifax.* Though apparently still looking for a way to research the collec-tive black voice in Africa, Roland fully realized that he had positioned himself to become a first-rate international artist. The open question was what he would do about it.

By the end of 1921, Roland left Duse Mohammed Ali's boarding-house for a larger accommodation at 6 Finchley Road, N.W., in London. Lawrence Brown also moved on to attend Trinity College, taking a room in the boardinghouse of the African American singer John Payne while he studied keyboard, trained under the voice coach Amanda Aldridge, and worked on a volume of transcriptions.[58] It was at Payne's residence that Brown met Paul Robeson, whom he later accompanied. Apart from the likely relationship with Quilter, Lawrence Brown kept his personal relationships closely guarded.[59] Others have suggested that Brown de-clared himself a homosexual as a defense mechanism against any pos-sible accusation of a liaison with white women, as he was keenly aware of the consequences of such an illicit relationship. This claim was based in part on a lynching that Brown was said to have witnessed as a child in Florida.[60]

Roland, too, took the further step of engaging the services of Amanda Aldridge as his vocal coach. She had studied keyboard as a child and enrolled as a student at the Royal College of Music in London. Although she was primarily known as a keyboardist, she had studied voice with celebrated Swedish soprano Jenny Lind and Sir George Hen-schel. Amanda Aldridge also composed art songs under the pseudonym "Montague Ring" to separate her career as a pianist from her composing.

A significant outcome of his musical relationship with Aldridge was that Roland gained a sense of comfort with the quality of his voice and a greater insight into the uniqueness of the black voice. With Aldridge, he came to realize the special character of *his* voice and that seeking the roots of his instrument on the African continent was not really his mission, in the final analysis. Perfecting his art should, in fact, be his true goal. This reality caused Roland to approach studying music based on his personal insights as well as on the information about the life and times of the composers whose music he performed. It is clear that after Roland's work with Aldridge, his urgency to go to the African continent seems to have waned. Roland began adding her vocal compositions to his performances and always provided Aldridge with complimentary tickets when he appeared at Wigmore Hall and other London-area venues.[61]

Taking up the challenge of mastering German lieder, Roland began voice and coaching lessons with Sir George Henschel, most probably in the fall of 1921.[62] Helen Douglas, Roland's friend and supporter of many years, introduced them. This may have been the most telling indication that Roland intended to establish himself in the top rank among the tenors of his day. He was familiar with Henschel's name and reputation from his days in Boston. As the founding conductor of the Boston Symphony Orchestra in 1881, Henschel had established the ensemble, led it for three years, and then returned to England. Initially a singer and later a conductor and composer, Henschel had studied and performed with Johannes Brahms and, accordingly, had specialized in singing the art songs of Germany, the lieder. This was his claim to fame as a teacher, but he also taught and coached the repertoire of Mozart, Handel, and other great composers of earlier periods. George Henschel also had a very lucrative private studio in London.

Roland's decision to follow up with the introduction led to a seven-year musical relationship with "Sir George." Roland later credited the seasoned maestro with helping him to intensify and sustain his phrasing in a vocal line. Henschel referred to it as "proportioning" the phrase. Roland said that controlling the dynamics, even in the middle of a vocal phrase, had the effect of creating a nuance that could enliven a performance, without the audience consciously being aware of what was happening.[63] Roland studied the repertory of Brahms, Wolf, and Schumann and deepened his appreciation for Schubert's lieder, almost immediately emboldened by Henschel's instruction.

By the time Roland sang his October 8 Wigmore Hall benefit recital for the APU, his exploration into European musical styles and sources were discernible in his program selections. As the *Africa World* reviewer wrote: "A glorious voice is a magnet, but greater even than this endowment is that of the artist in song. And Mr. Roland Hayes' admirers realize this. They can never be satisfied, for his interpretations are of the essence of music."[64] The program included songs of Coleridge-Taylor, "Noontide Song" by Montague Ring, and several Roger Quilter songs (with the composer at the keyboard), in addition to several reliable spirituals.

The *Africa World* also reviewed Roland's Wigmore Hall recital the following month. The reviewer was struck by two Europeanized arrangements of traditional African folk songs from Nyasaland (modern day Malawi) arranged by Mrs. Ella Kidney. The reviewer ventured the opinion that they employed "too much Europe" and "too little Africa." Still, the reviewer, allowed, it "was another triumph" for Roland.[65]

Not every Briton with experience on the African continent and familiar with Roland's talent warmed up to the idea of him traveling there, however. A March 1922 letter that the tenor received from the famous (some would suggest infamous) explorer of the African continent Sir Harry Hamilton Johnston struck a dissonant chord when he addressed Roland's proposed trip. A former colonial administrator and scientist, Johnston had been involved in the well-known planning and execution of the "Scramble for Africa" in the mid-1880s. He had very specific advice for Roland regarding his proposed travels to Africa: "I am so glad that your talent has found appreciation on this side of the Atlantic and sincerely hope you have given up the intention of traveling in the wilds of West Africa! With such a voice of beauty you are a pledge to civilization, and we ought to keep you."[66]

Why Roland did not travel to the African continent when there was such intense interest in his performing there may have been a matter of finance; who would be responsible for his fees was not really made clear. Would there be a mechanism for ensuring his successful performances (that is, tuned pianos, appropriate venues, and the like)? How and under what circumstances would he perform for the indigenous population? These issues were real considerations. He had raised many of these very matters in his response to R. W. Wooding of Cape Town who had wanted him to travel to South Africa. Colonial Africa in the 1920s would have posed other challenges for the tenor, which he needed to weigh.

The other reality was the large number of elite and influential continental and diasporan Africans whom he had met and befriended during his stay in the British Isles. Perhaps he did not feel so compelled to go to the continent because he had access to those who taught and coached him in its languages and customs and traditional music. He continued to cultivate relationships with continental Africans throughout his adult life. In his interviews, writings, and correspondences, however, Roland continued to profess his desire to go to the continent, and continental Africans continued their efforts to get him there.

FOUR

"Le Rage de Paris"

1921–1922

FRESH FROM THEIR APRIL 1921 TRIUMPH AT WIGMORE HALL
and the completely unexpected command performance at Buckingham
Palace, Roland Hayes and Lawrence Brown took a much-needed break.
The following month, the two prepared to cross the English Channel
to France, where the tenor had hopes of advancing his career beyond
the British Isles. The trip was equal parts vacation and business. Roland
took a letter of introduction from Robert Leigh Ibbs and John Tillett to
their Parisian associate, Charles Kiesgen. In their letter, Ibbs and Tillett
told the French agent about Roland's recent successes in the United
Kingdom, including his unheralded yet impressive royal performance.[1]

Several people in France were anticipating Roland's first visit to
the country. Maud Christian Sherwood, one of Roland's supporters in
London, contacted the veteran French composer Vincent d'Indy asking him to be on the lookout for Roland and Brown and to assist them
if necessary.[2] Emma Koechlin, the wife of the equally respected French
composer Charles Koechlin, wrote to someone in London (possibly
someone at the Ibbs and Tillett Agency) about Roland's arrival:

> We're looking forward to receiving and hearing your "black angel." Tell him to
> inform us of his arrival so my husband can meet him in Paris to save him the trip
> to Valmondois – and that we have a terrible piano here. We have a friend in Paris
> who owns a studio where we will be better able to enjoy the music and chat....
>
> With all my heart, dear, dear, friend
> Koechlin[3]

As the French summer was underway at the beginning of June 1921,
the "black angel" and his accompanist, Lawrence Brown, landed in Paris

and checked into the chichi Mont Thabor Hotel, located at 4 Rue de Mont Thabor. Their hotel was ideally situated, as it was within walking distance of the Louvre, the Paris Opera House, and many other major tourist attractions. Seemingly unfazed by their dark-skinned visitors, the hotel staff received the Americans very cordially.[4]

Neither Roland nor Brown spoke French beyond basic simple courtesies, but they were not far from a growing community of African Americans who found the shores of France more welcoming than their homeland in the aftermath of World War I. While Brown took advantage of the many divertissements that the city had to offer in the vicinity of the hotel, Roland temporarily delayed such an indulgence and paid an immediate visit to one of the American expatriates who was also a familiar face from Boston. Wesley Howard, the African American violinist who had performed with Roland as early as 1914, had been studying in France and living in Paris with his wife when Roland called on him.

Roland received a very different reception from the hotel staff once he arrived back at the Mont Thabor. A white American couple had seen Lawrence Brown in the lobby and, after realizing he was a guest at the facility, demanded that the hotel management put him and Roland out.[5] Although the hotel complied with the request of the white Americans, the embarrassed staff assisted Roland and Brown in finding other accommodations. The Mont Thabor staff continued to receive and forward their mail for another several weeks. One of those forwarded letters came from Lady Astor, responding to a letter that Roland had sent her from Paris. In her response, she asked the singer to let her know when he expected to return to Britain as she was anxious to reengage him to sing at her Cliveden residence.[6]

Roland also received several informal invitations from various Parisians to dine and presumably perform at their private residences. In addition to composer Charles Koechlin, Roland met the more celebrated Venezuelan French composer Reynaldo Hahn, as a result of an introductory letter from Roger Quilter, and other distinguished Parisians during his three-week stay; one letter he received from a George Henry Manuel dated June 21, 1921, referred to the singer's initial meeting with a Francophone African who would play an important role in Roland's life during the early and mid-1920s: "Would you do me the pleasure of having lunch here next Monday? Also, [unclear passage] Prince Tovalou is supposed to be arriving tomorrow. Do you want to see if he'd like to join us? I'd love to see you both."[7] Prince Marc Kojo Tovalou Houenou of Dahomey (modern-day Benin Republic) was the nephew of the nineteenth-century deposed and exiled Dahomean ruler King Behanzin. Tovalou, a French-educated lawyer, became a well-known Pan-Africanist and was closely linked with Marcus Garvey's United Negro Improvement Association after he came to the United States.[8] Tovalou's cousin (King Behanzin's son) was Prince Oanilo, whom Roland also came to know. The singer credited Princes Oanilo and Tovalou with validating *his* claim to African royalty, based on the name of the singer's great-grandfather Abá 'Ougi.[9]

Apart from the racial incident at the Mont Thabor Hotel, Roland's first visit to the City of Lights was successful. He paid the city another visit two months later, and once again it was to see another familiar face from home. He told his mother, Fannie, about it in an August 21, 1921, letter:

Paris, France
Dear, dear Mother,

I was so happy to get your dear letter and to know that you are as well as usual, but I am also so sad that there is not more harmony between you and Robert, but I suppose you both know best.

I came here last Tuesday to see Mr. Hubbard who left on Saturday for Boston. I was glad to see him[;] we talked a long time each day . . .[10]

Roland also used his time in Paris with Arthur Hubbard to have a few voice lessons and to give Hubbard some idea of the repertory he was currently working on. When Roland returned to London, he temporarily moved to another address, 63 Bridge Lane, in the Hendon area of London, but by the end of the year he was back at his 6 Finchley Road address.

Roland's very busy autumn performing schedule included two more Wigmore Hall recitals, an engagement with the Samuel Coleridge-Taylor Choral Society, and a few private engagements for patrons like the Astors and British prime minister David Lloyd George. The frequency and high caliber of such performances meant one thing for Roland where his dealings with the Ibbs and Tillett Agency were concerned – he wanted a higher fee. Despite the agency's routine arguments to the contrary, Roland insisted that it should request no less than forty guineas (about $245 in U.S. dollars at the time), which was not inclusive of Brown's ac-

companying fee (typically between five and ten guineas). The requirement was a substantial increase over the previous twenty guineas for his
services. He sometime accepted a lower "special fee," but his contracts
qualified such as the exception.

The following year, 1922, saw Roland's climb up the European musical ladder continuing apace. He was frequently described as "Le Rage
de Paris" by the time he returned to the city in the spring of 1922. His
patrons' response to his performances led to his eventual recognition as
a celebrated artist throughout France as well as other major centers of
Western Europe. Roland's success there was ultimately tied to his relationship with the celebrated French cellist Joseph Salmon and his wife,
Madeleine Lily ("Maddie," for short), who supported and befriended the
singer for more than a decade. Roland and Joseph Salmon's meeting was
quite coincidental, yet it turned out to be a vital one for the tenor's career.

Among the private recitals that Roland sang in the London area
during the autumn of 1921 was the performance he gave at the home of
British composer Norman O'Neill, who was also an associate of Roger
Quilter. Among other works, the singer had delivered a particularly
soul-wrenching performance of "He Never Said a Mumberlin' Word."
His a cappella execution of the crucifixion song had sent the ordinarily
staid British guests from their seats to the corners of the room to hide
their emotions.[11] Equally moved, a tearful Joseph Salmon eventually
approached Roland to comment on his performance: "Mr. Hayes, I'm an
old man, and I cannot expect to live very long. You must come to France
while I am still alive. I shall introduce you to all Paris."[12] The renowned
cellist soon made good on his promise. In a January 15, 1922, letter to
Roland in London, he wrote:

Dear Mr. Hayes,

I've thought a lot about you ever since the great pleasure I had in hearing you in
London. I hope to see you in Paris and will do everything I can to meet you. I expect that the first house where you will sing [here] will be mine. . . . I'm expecting
a great success for you but it is not guaranteed. I wrote to Mr. [Gabriel] Pierné
and am awaiting his response. I'd like to know what pieces you can sing with an
orchestra. It is important to know this.

I am awaiting your response.
Joseph Salmon[13]

Gabriel Pierné was a highly respected composer who had gained fame by conducting the premiere of Igor Stravinsky's *L'oiseau de feu* for the Ballets Russes in 1910. When Roland had arrived in Europe, he was leading one of France's most prestigious musical organizations, the Collone Orchestra. Obviously, Salmon saw significant potential in having such an important advocate for the singer. Roland responded quickly, supplying his repertoire list; Salmon wrote him again a few days later, on January 25:

> I just received word from Mr. Pierné. He asked that I bring you to his house when you're in Paris. I spoke to him about the list you sent me and he is of the opinion that you [must not] sing pieces written for a woman's voice like "l'Enfant Prodigue" of Debussy, or "Chanson Triste" of Duparc, etc.
>
> I prefer works written for tenors – if you have any, remember to bring the orchestral parts.[14]

Although the details are not available, Roland sang with Maestro Pierné and the Collone Orchestra sometime in the spring of 1922. Pierné's reaction to what he heard, however, was enough to persuade him to contact his fellow countryman, the equally, if not more celebrated, conductor Pierre Monteux, who at the time was the head of the Boston Symphony Orchestra in Roland's adopted hometown.[15]

Always the pragmatist, Roland wanted a clear understanding of the financial arrangements regarding his performances. He was assured by the Salmons that he would receive no less than one thousand francs at minimum for most of his engagements. However, they informed him that he would need to do a certain number of "charity" performances as a means of promoting him in the area. Maddie Salmon was diligent in making hotel arrangements for him and seeing that his arrival was smooth.

The Salmon's Paris residence, 93 Rue Jouffroy, became ground zero for the launch of Roland's French career by March 1922. He had barely begun performing in France when the Salmons began receiving inquiries about Roland's availability outside of the country:

> March 29, 1922
> Rue Jouffroy 39 [sic]
> Mr. Joseph Salmon,
>
> Mr. Jacque Thibaud was nice enough to give us your address and we're taking the liberty of asking you if it will be possible for us to hire the singer, Mr. Roland Hayes for one or two concerts for the Kursale de Scheveningue.

Please let us know what are the terms and when he will be in Holland.

Hollandsche Concertdirectie
Dr. G. DeKoos, Manager[16]

In fact, Joseph and Maddie Salmon acted as a pseudo–management team for Roland as they responded to the many inquiries about his scheduling and availability.

A piece of business that Roland *did* see to that spring before going to France was to reach an agreement with the Ibbs and Tillett Agency to become his exclusive representatives throughout the British Isles and Ireland. The agreement was that they would be his sole agents for public and private singing engagements and gramophone recordings within that territory and that any engagements he accepted outside of the territory could not clash with previously booked dates within the United Kingdom. Either party could terminate the agreement with a three-month written notice to the other party.[17]

Meeting Roland and Lawrence Brown when they arrived in Paris around the third week of March 1922 was the singer's new friend Prince Tovalou. The two were received in the city under very different circumstances from what they had experienced when they first arrived nearly a year before.

Roland's initial performance at the Salmons' residence made a strong impression among their guests, because Joseph wrote right after the tenor's return to England, "It is necessary for me to express that your success has been enormous."[18] Maddie Salmon was equally complimentary of his work in her letter to Roland. But the congratulatory coup came from Prince Tovalou, who described the significance of the tenor's appearance in near Shakespearean, if not in glorified, Pan-African terms:

23 March 1922
My dear friend:

I hope you have been making advantageous journeys and that you have been justified in your round of concerts, always with the same success.

The impression which you made in Paris is magnificent. Your name runs out of their mouths like a train. The French whose custom it is [to] not manifest much sentiment and enthusiasm have adopted you as one of the most pure expressions of artistic beauty. The Parisians claim you with clamors and shouts. I do the same with tears and sobs because of the magic with which you completely overwhelm.

Paris is *your* capital. You reign supreme here because you have conquered all the hearts. Yours is an absolute power above which has no tyranny. You are making marvelous use of all your gifts. "It is the voice of the heart only which succeeds in reaching the hearts . . ."

Thanks for the hours you have made to pass so pleasantly. All Africa thanks you for my opportunity of listening to your voice which does her credit . . .

I await you with impatience for the End of April as it has been agreed. You will be sure to reserve May 3rd to be at my home. Will you please send to me the name of the publisher of "Go Down Moses" and "Sit Down." Mm. Dussaue, of the *Comedie Francaise* has asked me for it.

A million friendships to you and your faithful accompanist Lawrence Brown.

Sincerely,
Tovalou Houenou[19]

Roland returned to England to fulfill a few engagements, including yet another Wigmore Hall concert. The reviews of his performance were now routinely strong. He also received several personal congratulatory notes, including one from the well-known instrument collector Percy A. Bull, who became another Roland Hayes enthusiast. His comments regarding Roland's presentation of the "Crucifixion" at Wigmore Hall were that he should consider putting a note in the program asking the audience to refrain from applause at the conclusion of the selection, as such a response took away from the pathos and gravity of the performance.[20]

The Salmons in the meantime were making preparations for Roland's extended stay in Paris that summer. On some days, Maddie Salmon had him scheduled to sing multiple mini-recitals on a single day for a thousand francs per engagement.[21] This meant Roland could very easily earn five thousand or six thousand francs for a day's singing.

When Roland and Brown arrived back in Paris at the beginning of May, their official address was the Lavoisier Hotel, located at 21 Rue Lavoisier. In short order, Roland sang at soirees, mini-recitals, and a host of full recitals for the rich and famous of Parisian society. He was hosted by the likes of the Bourbons, the wealthy Jewish financiers the Rothschilds, the Baron d'Itajuba, the Marquis Boisguilbert, and Jacques Anthoine. The Duc and Duchess de La Rochefoucauld, one of the oldest and most prestigious families in France, engaged him to sing at their residence on May 30. Emmanuel de La Rochefoucauld wrote Roland a personal letter asking him to program some Italian and American pieces instead of the scheduled French works he had intended to perform. The duke's eight-year-old son, Charles-Emmanuel, remembered Roland's performance many years later.[22]

Roland had an initial annoying encounter with the Comtesse Anna de Noailles, who was also a wealthy arts patron and eventual supporter of Roland. Rather than listen to her attempt to speak over his singing at a soiree where he was performing, the tenor simply stopped singing, nodded apologies to his audience, and left the stage, holding his temper in abeyance. When the comtesse was informed that he had walked off because she had been interrupting his performance, she immediately rushed to apologize to him and thereafter threatened to "kill anyone who dared" cause a disturbance while he was singing.[23] Roland and the Comtesse de Noailles eventually became very good friends. As a talented poet, she supplied him with one of her poems, which was set to music by his future accompanist Reginald Boardman.[24]

Sometime in May or at the very beginning of June 1922, Roland met his lifelong friend, fellow American Noël Sullivan, at one of the private parties at which he performed in Paris. Sullivan was from a wealthy San Francisco family whose members had included prominent politicians, bankers, and other successful philanthropists. In what was perhaps his first letter to Roland (dated June 2, 1922), Sullivan invited the singer and Lawrence Brown to dine with him. He also wanted Roland to invite Prince Tovalou to join them.[25] Sullivan eventually became one of Roland's most trusted confidants and advisers. The publicly formal and always mannerly Roland revealed a vulnerable part of his personality to Sullivan that he appears not to have trusted to others.[26]

The summer of 1922 was an important period in Roland's professional life, as he met or worked with several celebrated contemporary French musical masters. Maddie Salmon proposed a plan to Roland vis-à-vis his operatic ambitions:

Dear Hayes –

Do you remember you told me one day that you would accept to sing an opera, which was written for you? Now listen. I have a friend who is [a] composer, a very good composer. His name is Tiarko Richepin, well known in Paris. This friend with whom I spoke a long time yesterday of you will write *for you*, only for you an opera which you would sing here in Paris in the "Opera [Comique]."

Would you accept it? He would take some old Negro songs, African songs, etc., and would write that for you – quite as you would like it. Write me quickly to tell me if it suits you.[27]

A similar offer of composing a dedicated opera for Roland came from the highly regarded French opera composer and conductor André Messager, for whom Roland sang during his time in Paris. Unlike those of Tiarko Richepin, Messager's operatic credentials were quite extensive, as he had composed and conducted his operas and those of others at major venues. He had also been the director of the Opéra Comique in Paris and had held a similar position at London's Covent Garden.[28] Mindful of his voice type as one that was usually typecast to play the romantic lead in an opera, Hayes discouraged the venture. Chances of success in the genre were quite limited, certainly in his home country, although they might have been greater in the more progressive France in the 1920s. Besides, as he explained to Messager, he had "long since" been discouraged by his teachers from pursuing such a career (presumably Jennie Robinson and Arthur Hubbard).[29] While Roland (for whatever reason) did not accept either Messager's or Richepin's offer to compose an opera for him, he no doubt was encouraged if not intrigued by such an idea. He later attempted to create an autobiographical music drama based on the same formula that Tiarko Richepin had proposed in 1922.

Roland also met the venerated British composer Frederick Delius, who by the 1920s was living in Fontainebleau and had adopted France as his permanent home. Roland said little about his interactions with Delius apart from the fact that the composer told him about his time spent in the United States as an orange grower and music teacher in Florida and Virginia.[30]

Roland had the opportunity to meet the crème de la crème of French composers, Gabriel Fauré, in 1922. Considered the foremost French composer of his generation, Fauré was within two years of his death when he met and also coached Roland in his music. Once again, it was through Roger Quilter (via an introductory letter) that their meeting took place, and Fauré invited the tenor to sing at his studio. Roland had produced Fauré's "Le secret," the very simple but elegant song that he had previously performed in concert; he was eager for the composer's reaction to his interpretation. The master told the younger musician *not* to overinterpret his songs. An understanding of his very carefully chosen texts, according to Fauré, was all that was necessary to communicate the needed sentiment to the audience.[31]

The seeds of Roland's history-making appearance with the Boston Symphony Orchestra (BSO) the following year were sewn in Paris in the spring of 1922, well over a year before he set foot on the stage at Symphony Hall. As a result of Joseph Salmon's advocacy for him with the Collone Orchestra director, Gabriel Pierné recommended Roland to his friend and BSO conductor Pierre Monteux, who came to Paris in the summer of 1922. Maestro Pierné and Salmon arranged for Roland to audition for Monteux that summer, and preliminary discussions began.[32] Monteux was undoubtedly aware of the historical significance of the path he was bravely embarking on by having Roland, the first of his race, sing with the orchestra.

Arthur J. Hubbard was also involved in the plan to have Roland mount the stage with the orchestra. He met with his student in Paris once again in August 1922, as he had the year before, to discuss, among other things, Roland's January recital at Symphony Hall. Hubbard had certainly played a role in helping keep Roland's name in the Boston press. He routinely reported on the tenor's enthusiastic reception on the European continent to local papers and to critics like Philip Hale of Boston. In a March 1922 note, Hale wrote in response to Hubbard:

> Thank you for the letter. I have made a note of Mr. Hayes' success for the *Herald* of next Sunday (as the WorldWays column).
>
> I hope the boy's head will not be turned. Also, that no Parisian Duchess or Princess will give him the bad disorder[33] in her enthusiasm.
>
> What a contrast between Paris and Boston in regard to the race question!
>
> Yours very truly,
> Philip Hale[34]

Realizing the prevailing prejudices of the period and that Roland's appearance with the symphony might upset white Boston concertgoers, Hubbard's plan to keep the singer's name before the public was a carefully considered strategic move.

When Maestro Monteux raised the idea of Roland appearing with the BSO, William Brennan, the symphony's general manager, initially opposed it, saying "the Hall will be full of Negroes" if the proposed concert took place. In lieu of such a symphony appearance, Brennan proposed that a "special" concert for Roland be staged at Symphony Hall. The maestro's calm and measured response to that suggestion was, "Then the hall *would* be full of Negroes."[35]

While Roland spent time in France during the summer of 1922, Lawrence Brown was not always at the keyboard as his accompanist. The beginnings of some apparent "detachment" between the two seemed to have begun manifesting themselves around this time. By late 1921, while Roland was staying on Finchley Road, Brown was living in the Maida Vale section of West London, not far from St. John's Wood. Roland kept in touch with his accompanist by sending him notes to set up rehearsal times or engagements.[36] Although Brown was formally studying in London, he went with Roland to Paris and accompanied him on many of those engagements. Roland continued to contact Brown sporadically throughout the summer, as the pianist had returned to London by late May or early June 1922.

Roland's September 19, 1922, note written to Lawrence Brown as the singer was vacationing with the Salmons and Prince Tovalou in France, however, signaled a clear strain between the two:

Dear Brown:

I am here with our friends [the] Salmons and Tovalou. They all send best wishes to you.

I enclose herewith my advance program for most of my autumn engagements.

Another matter I wish to speak of is this: you know we have many friends in common and there will no doubt be many questions asked of both of us with respect to your not playing my accompaniments at my next recital. Therefore to arrest misunderstanding and much talk which may not do either one of us any good, I ask that you write me a letter which will tell me the conclusion you came to with respect to this temporary detachment and an explanation as to why you feel it necessary.[37]

The tenor later commented on Brown's lack of response to the request. At the heart of the breach between Roland and Brown was money. The lack of appropriate recognition for Brown's role in the successful musical partnership was also an issue. Lawrence Brown had asked Roland for some sort of exclusive arrangement or contract, which the tenor was unwilling to do. In addition, there was the matter of Brown's accompanying salary. He was undoubtedly aware that Roland was receiving a higher fee because of his agency agreement with Ibbs and Tillett and felt that as he was a significant part of the musical duo, he was also entitled to more. Roland's reluctance (if not outright refusal) to agree to the terms caused Brown to pull away.

A lengthy letter from November 7, 1922, which Roland wrote to "Tova[lou]" after the tenor returned to England, all but confirmed a planned split between Roland and Brown. Tova had raised the issues of Brown's contract (probably at the instigation of the accompanist) and his continued musical relationship with Roland, to which the tenor responded:

> I am thinking much about our last conversation together concerning Mr. Brown, and my accompanist for the future. There are two or three things which I wish again to emphasize. One is that in your speaking to Mr. Brown with respect to his future and what he proposes to do with it must be quite distinct and apart from anything concerning me. He *must not* be persuaded to try and continue with me and this must not be your issue with him. . . .
>
> As for myself and my future. My present position in my profession is this: I am no longer to be tied to any one person or accompanist. I must, if possible, choose the accompanist suitable to my requirements each time I sing and if I cannot procure that one then I must do the best I can with whatever I can have. There will be times in future when I shall need someone like Mr. Brown and when that time comes I shall have him, if at all possible, and vice-versa. I am not at the present time making a contract with a living soul and I shall do *nothing* in this regard until I can see my way clear to do so. This is my definite program for the present and only this shall I follow until it is the right time to make a change. . . .
>
> Ever your friend,
> Roland[38]

Roland and Brown continued to communicate, and the talented pianist and arranger continued studying in London and even played for Roland the following year.

The year 1922, however, also turned out to be an eventful one for Lawrence Brown. While appearing in London in the play *Voodoo*, a twenty-four-year-old Paul Robeson became acquainted with Brown as they were staying in the same boardinghouse of a fellow African American singer.[39] Their initial exchange was friendly and congenial. When Brown returned to the United States a few years later, he met up with the now more prominent Paul Robeson and became his principal accompanist. Unlike the situation with Roland, however, Brown and Robeson had a contract drawn up in which Brown received an equal share of the fees for his work and joint billing. Robeson also credited Lawrence Brown with "guiding" him to the folk songs of African Americans as a result of the keyboardist's extensive research on spirituals, many of which he had had arranged.[40] In addition, Brown recorded extensively with Robeson (and often sang the tenor background in several of those recordings). In the final coup de grâce, Brown appeared in several Robeson movies as an extra or in small speaking roles.[41] All in all, he garnered far more recognition through his musical association with Paul Robeson than he could have ever hoped for with Roland Hayes.

Roland's schedule was fully booked in the United Kingdom in the fall of 1922, and he continued to receive praise in the press for his work. His appearance evoked the September 9, 1922, *Llandudno Advertiser* reviewer to say, "Not a sound whilst he was singing, and it is safe to assert he stirred the souls of many in the audience as they had not been stirred for many a long day." The *Times* comments on the same concert were even more complimentary when its reviewer proclaimed, "[Hayes] is one of the greatest living artists in the field he has chosen."

Roland secured the services of W. E. Beaumont as his secretary, and the Ibbs and Tillett Agency continued its unheeded pleas to him to lower his fee request. The management agency also negotiated a recording contract with Vocalion Records. Roland continued his lessons with Sir George Henschel, who was still active as a conductor, and he sang with the distinguished British conductor Sir Henry Wood, who led the tenor with the Queen's Hall Orchestra. His major orchestral appearance, however, took place back in Paris at the beginning of November when he sang with the Collone Orchestra under Gabriel Pierné's direction. Unlike his previous outing with the orchestra earlier in the year, this was Roland's first major orchestral appearance on the European continent, and on the day of the performance, he wrote the maestro a personal note:

November 4, 1922
Dear Maestro Pierné:

This note comes only to thank you *from the bottom of my heart* for the opportunity which you through the suggestion of my friend and great musician Joseph Salmon opened to me and my art today. The success I wish you to know in particular is not mine, but is that of many millions of black and many white people throughout the world who crave such opportunities as this you have given me. . . .

   May the *richest blessings* be on the heads of *you* and *yours* for *all time,* is my sincere and humble wish.

Yours gratefully,
Roland Hayes
6, Finchley Road, London[42]

Roland's appearance with the Collone Orchestra was so successful that the reviewer from the Paris newspaper *Comoedia* said, "[Hayes] showed a warmth of temperament, a power of making melody alive by softening the lines of it and modulating all the nuances." Maestro Pierné also related the success of Roland's performance to Pierre Monteux in Boston, who used the flattery about the singer from another celebrated conductor to support the case of having the tenor appear with the BSO.[43]

Before returning to the United States in December, Roland fulfilled an engagement singing a complete performance of his beloved Samuel Coleridge-Taylor's *Hiawatha's Wedding Feast* with the Liverpool Welsh Choral Union. Coleridge-Taylor's daughter, a soprano, sang one of the solo parts.

Back in Boston on December 6, 1922, Arthur J. Hubbard, Roland's former teacher, took another step to advance the stature of his student. He entered into an agreement on Roland's behalf with William Brennan and George Judd, assistant manager of the BSO, to give a major recital at Symphony Hall in Boston on January 7, 1923. Roland was to receive 50 percent of the gross receipts of the ticket sales.

With his reputation established and growing on the European continent, Roland sailed back across the ocean that winter much like the conquering hero he was. In the two years and seven months that he had been away from the United States, he had *ruled* the British Isles, and his reputation had, according to his friend the Comtesse de Noailles, spread around the greater French capital like the "measles."[44] Roland had been properly validated by the "culturally sophisticated" Europeans and was ready to return home to reap the fruits of his labor.

FIVE

"You're Tired, Chile"

1923

ROLAND RETURNED TO THE UNITED STATES DURING THE third week of December in 1922 apparently in response to a somewhat disturbing letter he had received from his mother, Fannie, now around eighty years old, a few months earlier.[1] Despite having been enslaved and denied a formal education, the mostly self-taught matriarch had little difficulty expressing her concerns.

By September 4 (the date of her letter), Fannie had moved to a larger apartment at 11 Arnold Street in the Roxbury area of Boston and was having domestic challenges with Roland's older brother Robert Brante. He had stopped attending church, and because of it she feared for his soul. Part of Fannie's letter bordered on the bizarre. She thought Robert Brante was afraid of her, because while he was in Chattanooga, he had heard rumors that she had killed his older brother John. Robert Brante had experienced a debilitating stroke that resulted in the paralysis of his left side and may also have left him with some mental deficiencies that would cause him to think such things. Fannie's letter was punctuated with a sense of her mortality: "I feel good because the lord let me have all the days he promised me. You ought to be glad for me and not feel sad when the lord comes to take me away. If I am who I say I am, I will be better off."[2] Despite the sobering and worrisome letter, Roland's performing schedule in Europe prevented him from returning to the United States any earlier than December.

Roland arrived in time to spend Christmas with his family. Robert Brante, his wife, Margaret (Maggie), John's widow, Ola, and their son, Felton, were all in Boston to meet the singer when he returned. Jesse had made brief visits to Boston to see Fannie but quickly returned to Atlantic City, where he resided. It is not likely that he saw his celebrated older brother when he returned from Europe in the winter of 1922.[3]

Much of the concertgoing population of Boston (especially the African Americans) eagerly anticipated the return of its hometown singer. His sold-out Sunday evening Symphony Hall recital was one of the hottest tickets in town, causing thousands to brave the city's bone-chilling weather that January 7, 1923. The event was billed as the tenor's "First Concert since returning to America after Two Seasons of Unprecedented Successes in Europe."[4] The playbill was also impressive. Under a striking frontal head shot of the singer in a formal evening tuxedo was ROLAND HAYES, in bold print. Just underneath his name, in much smaller print, was "The Great American Tenor."[5] When Roland walked out on the stage that evening, there was spontaneous cheering along with a standing ovation.[6] Following him onstage was the veteran Boston-based accompanist Margaret Kent Hubbard.

The program was ambitious and varied:

I.	Where'er you Walk from *Semele*	Handel
	Quando miro (Canzonetta)	Mozart
	Amarilli	Caccini
	Eviva rosa bella (La calamita de couri)	Galuppi
II.	L'invitation au voyage	Duparc
	Le thé	Koechlin
	Claire de lune	Fauré
	Chevauchée cosaque	Fourdrain
III.	In Waldeseinsamkeit	Brahms
	Botschaft	Brahms
	Verborgenheit	Wolf
	A Dream	Grieg
IV.	Steal Away	Arranged by Lawrence Brown
	Sit Down	Arranged by Roland Hayes
	I've Got a Robe	Arranged by Roland Hayes
	Go Down Moses	Arranged by H. T. Burleigh[7]

The reaction to the concert was uniformly enthusiastic, and Roland received adulation as the hometown boy who had conquered Europe. Philip Hale, the *Boston Herald* music critic who had been kept apprised of Roland's European successes by Arthur J. Hubbard, said the following:

"If nature gave this singer a superior voice, to his own hard and intelligent work alone does he owe – the neatness of his attack, his admirably smooth legato, and, above all else, his perfect diction, the like of which has not been heard in Boston for many a day."[8] Letters written to Hayes after the concert said that the tenor had grown in his musicality and vocal abilities. Some said that his time spent in Europe had refined the singer beyond measure.[9] Two days after the concert, Roland wrote to Lawrence Brown, who was still studying in London, to tell him about the standing ovation he received, even before he sang a note. He also told his former accompanist about his invitations to sing with both the Boston and New York orchestras the following fall.[10] Roland's comments about how well Margaret Kent Hubbard played surely did not sit well with Brown, who had only recently left the accompanist's chair.

Roland was not in the country very long, but he did take time to go to New York and Washington, D.C. Hardly a month after his arrival, he boarded a ship to return to Europe. This time, however, Roland departed with a personal assistant, Howard T. Jordan, who was the young son of the white family from Louisville who had befriended Roland after he had left Fisk University, disgraced, in 1910.

The morning of his departure, January 25, Roland, near tears, begged Fannie to come with him. She, of course, declined. He told her he would do whatever it took to make her comfortable in Europe, but she still refused. Fannie realized the burden that her decision was placing on her almost famous son, so she put her hands on his shoulders and said:

> I won't be here when you come again, son, but that ain't nothing. My days are over and yours are jest begun. I want *you* to promise *me* that when I fall down, you won't try to come back here and pick me up. You can't do me no good when I'm dead. Jes' remember this, you are a continuation of my desire. When I go, if you've been dutiful, all the best in me is going to double up in you and become a bulwark of strength. I never could do very much myself, and now I'm ol' I can't do nuthin' more – but I have always prayed the good Lord that I might do somethin' good through some of my children.[11]

A now openly weeping Roland begged his mother to tell him what she wanted of him. Stoic as ever, Fannie simply said:

> You are young, and can do anything. God said, "I call upon you, ye young men, 'cause you are strong." Now you go on, remember who you are and reverence yo'

heritage. You ain't got no cause to worry 'bout me. I'm all right. Jes' look what I
have aroun' me, the whole Church is roun' about my side.[12]

With the affirmation that he had nothing to worry about, Fannie bid her
son off on his next European conquest. Roland was nearly despondent
over leaving his mother in what he believed was a vulnerable, yet very
serene, state.

Part of Fannie's melancholy had been because she had not heard
from her youngest son, "Baby" Jesse, for some time. The youngest Hayes
brother had been away from the family for much of his adult life and was
most probably estranged from them. He had run off to join the U.S. Navy
while barely a teenager and for the most part had stayed away thereafter.
The few letters that he had written his mother established that, while he
would visit Fannie in Boston, he would not live there. Writing her from
Atlantic City, New Jersey, in late 1921, the youngest Hayes son said, "I
am writing you to let you know that I received your letter and I was very
glad to get it.... I promised I would not write you unless I could send you
some money. I told you before I left I was going to send you some money
but things didn't come my way. It is tight here now, but I think I can make
it alright."[13] Within two weeks of Roland's departure for London, fate
dealt Fannie Hayes another all-too-familiar blow:

> Mrs. Fannie Hayes of full age and being by me duly sworn according to law upon
> her oath deposes and says that she is a resident of Boston, Massachusetts, resid-
> ing at 11 Arnold Street.
> Deponent further avers that on or about February 6th, her son Jesse Hayes
> died in the City of Atlantic City, County of Atlantic and State of New Jersey and
> deponent did therefore employ Charles H. Donaway, funeral director, to take
> charge of his remains and to properly bury the body in Atlantic County.
> Affiant further avers that she is desirous that said Charles H. Donaway be paid
> the amount of One Hundred Forty One ($141.00) Dollars, the amount of the
> funeral expense for said Jesse Hayes. This sum to be paid from the proceeds of a
> check to be received from the Metropolitan Insurance Company.[14]

Having now lost five of the seven children to whom she had given
birth, Fannie seemed almost completely resigned to the fact that her days
were numbered and even welcomed her own death. Within a short time
of arriving back in Boston after Jesse's burial, she received some flowers
from her dear friend Ethel Jackson, whom she had often counseled on
various family matters. Fannie responded:

February 15, 1923
My Dear Mrs. Jackson,

I am writing to let you know I thank you so much that you even thought of
sending me a present. . . . I am glad you even thought of sending me a bunch of
flowers. I can't thank you, but the bible says in as much as yea [*sic*] do these thing
unto the least of these my little ones . . . Jesus say you do it unto me. . . . Now I am
old and I have got all the days the lord promise[d] me. Now I am living on borrowed days so I don't think I can live much longer. . . . You said you had an aged
father that lived with you. Tell him he is blessed to have his children to live with.
I haven't but two boys living. One is married and Roland is in Europe. I lived
with him before he went now I live alone.[15]

This is the closest that the ever stoic Fannie Hayes seemed to have come
to opening up in writing about the death of her "Baby" Jesse. She received condolence letters from relatives in Chattanooga and Curryville,
but whether she responded is unknown.

The impact Jesse's death had on Roland in London is not apparent.
After the death of his older brother John, who had died in 1920, Roland
attempted to console Fannie from afar. After Jesse's death, however, he
never mentioned his younger brother in any subsequent letters or personal writings.[16]

Nor did Roland slow his concertizing in Europe to mourn the tragic
event back home.[17] In early February, he was back in Paris to perform
at the celebrated Salle Gaveau and nearly sold out the house.[18] Robert
Leigh Ibbs and John Tillett, his agents, fully understood what his salary
requirements were and negotiated his engagements accordingly.

Sometime in mid-February, Roland entered the Aeolian (Vocalion)
Records studio in London to lay a group of six spirituals on disk, four
of which were released the following year in the United States on the
Vocalion label. As in his previous recording attempt two years before,
Lawrence Brown would accompany the singer.[19] Roland re-recorded
Harry Burleigh's "Swing Low, Sweet Chariot" with remarkable results.
In his 1917 recording of the same work, his sound was brighter and his
diction was precise (for example, his "ing"s, as in "coming for to carry
me home," are very clearly articulated). The 1923 recording of the work
is far more plaintive, his voice is a little darker, and his "ing"s are less
pronounced. Roland also projected an emotive character lacking in the
earlier version. In addition, he recorded Burleigh's arrangements of "By

an' By," "Deep River," and "Go Down Moses." Filling out the session, Roland recorded Brown's arrangement of "Steal Away" and his own arrangement of "Sit Down."[20]

"Sit Down" captured Hayes's voice at its height. He delivered the performance with conviction, passion, and pathos. The subtle vocal turns that he employed on words and phrases like "child" and "Oh sit down" are both haunting and paralyzing. The final phrase in the work, "in your kingdom," was delivered with near total serenity. This was the collective black voice at its most sublime. Without setting foot on the African continent, Roland had achieved his goal.

Shortly after completing the session, Roland had Ibbs and Tillett contact the Aeolian label about rerecording "Sit Down" because he was unsatisfied with the performance. His determination to reproduce the recording probably stemmed from more than his artistic temperament. This particular spiritual held emotional significance for the tenor.

The song told of an enslaved, pre–Civil War black woman, whom Roland seemed to have likened to Fannie (who had taught him the song when he was a child). As it was important to her, it also held an artistic and emotional significance for him. The woman in Fannie's version had reached the age of eighty and knew her end was near. Sitting in her rocking chair, angels ask about her restlessness. She responds, "I'm waiting for my mother, I want to tell her howdy." The angels in turn respond, "Sit down and rest a little while."[21] He dedicated the performance to his elderly mother, perhaps mindful of her most recent loss and the toll it surely must have taken on her.

After recording, Roland shuttled between Paris and London for engagements. When he was in England, Prince Tovalou communicated with the French booking agents Kiesgen and Daneloit to set up dates for him at the Salle Gaveau, among other great Paris venues.[22] Roland wanted Tova to join him in Vienna, as he had come to rely on his counsel, but the prince was unable to do so.

After another successful April 10 recital in London, Roland began preparing for his trip to Vienna. He arrived there on April 16, as spring was blossoming throughout the musical capital of Europe. Roland believed that the beautiful atmosphere of the city alone lent itself to his work. He began preparing for his recital, but more troubling news came from home in a forwarded letter from Fannie. She and Robert Brante apparently had had another falling out (probably over his straying away from the church), and he had left Boston for Chattanooga. Based on Roland's response, Fannie must have written to him again that her death was imminent, and she wanted him to have several of her personal items afterward.[23] Once again, he attempted to persuade her to join him in Europe, because, he said, the earliest he would be able to return to the United States would be in the fall of the year.

Roland's April 26 concert in Vienna was enthusiastically received by his public and was reviewed with a similar vigor by the critics. Roland commented that this audience *really* knew art. His ambitious agenda to sing Schubert, Schuman, and Brahms to an audience of lieder connoisseurs garnered their complete approval. He was called "exotic" in the press, but several of the reviewers expressed their amazement at his ability, as an African American, to capture and communicate the spirit of their great composers.[24] There was no information on who accompanied Roland at the keyboard; however, it was most probably not Lawrence Brown. Although Hayes's April appearance in Vienna was brief, he was quickly engaged to reappear in the city later that year for a series of concerts. Roland returned to England to continue his work.

As the new architects and builders of Roland's concert career in the United States and Canada, William Brennan and his assistant George Judd of the Boston Symphony Orchestra were steadily fielding inquiries and assembling the fall tour schedule. Despite Brennan's initial resistance to Roland appearing with the BSO, he embraced the idea of representing the tenor and worked diligently to advance his stature. The BSO's Orchestra Hall became Roland's official address for professional engagements and inquiries. Brennan and Judd were exceptionally careful about putting together Roland's "first American professional tour," as it was billed. When inquiry letters came to them expecting to engage the tenor at his old fee, before he had made a name in Europe, Brennan politely reminded solicitors that the singer had been artistically affirmed "all over Europe" and was being sought after at a minimal fee of $750 per engagement. He also gently replied that their client's schedule was filling up and available dates were quickly disappearing.[25]

Brennan communicated with Roland in the United Kingdom to keep him apprised of the developments surrounding his concert schedule that fall. Roland was also well aware of the financial aspects of anything concerning his career. In London, his now-standard fee for performing for the British elite was fifty guineas, and he made occasional trips across the channel to appear in Paris.[26]

Roland was in Paris performing in June when he heard from his older brother, Robert Brante, about a serious domestic situation between him and his wife, Maggie. Roland laid the blame for the situation squarely on the shoulders of his sister-in-law, commenting to Fannie that Maggie needed to be mindful of his brother's delicate health and that Robert Brante needed to *"stand firm as a man* and as *head of his house"* in dealing with his wayward wife. Failing that, he should leave her. If Robert needed anything, he, Roland, was there to provide for him.[27] The quarreling couple eventually split up and divorced.

Fannie wrote Roland in London at the end of August and once again informed her son that her death was near and, as before, she wanted him to have several of her personal belongings. Unlike in any other letter she had previously sent him, Fannie *thanked* her son for bringing her north and taking her across the country with him. She also said that she had only "three" sons, and they could do whatever they pleased with her ten acres in Georgia. In closing, Fannie warned Roland to "stay in bound of reason and don't let the folks cheer you to death."[28]

For his part, Roland was active as ever that summer between the British Isles and France. He gave a well-received performance at Dublin's Mansion House, where he was partnered with Gerald Moore at the keyboard. The other participant on the program was violinist Renée Chemet. Among other works, Roland sang the well-known mezzo-soprano aria "When I Am Laid in Earth" from Purcell's *Dido and Aeneas.* (Roland's routine practice of singing songs and arias that were specifically not intended for the tenor voice, or even for a man, such as the Purcell aria, was discouraged by conductor Gabriel Pierné.) He also included a work, "Japanese Love Song," by Yoshinori Matsuyama.

Putting the finishing touches on Roland's concert tour back in the United States, Brennan and Judd had to resolve the issue of who would accompany their client at the keyboard. The tenor had expressed an interest in working with William Lawrence, whom he had known since the early 1910s when they had performed together in the Hayes Trio on the Chautauqua circuit. He also gave Brennan and Judd the name of Richard Percival Parham, who was less well known but whose reputation as a very good keyboardist was growing. Roland also suggested the name of his former teacher Arthur Calhoun. As Roland's first choice, Brennan and Judd offered William Lawrence the fee of fifty dollars per concert to accompany the tenor for the entire 1923–24 American tour. Lawrence wrote back saying he would accept seventy-five dollars per concert. They quickly sent another letter indicating that fifty dollars was the best they could do, and he needed to let them know in short order.

As a backup, Brennan also wrote Parham, asking him about his availability to play for Roland. Parham was more than happy to accept the fifty dollars per concert terms and communicated as much to Roland's managers. Realizing that Brennan's fee offer was intractable, William Lawrence reconsidered his stance and decided to accept the fifty dollars per concert terms.[29] Brennan had to then write Parham back and rescind his offer to accompany Roland. In this letter, he held out the possibility that they might end up working together, but his services would need to be declined for the upcoming season.[30]

Brennan and Judd also ran into challenges when informing potential promoters and booking agents of Roland's new fee structure. In one dispute, the tenor agreed to perform at the Hampton Institute in Virginia for a special, lower fee of five hundred dollars, but only after a protracted negotiation between his managers and the Afro-Canadian choir director and composer R. Nathaniel Dett. Perhaps as a slight to Dett, who negotiated the recital terms, Hayes neglected to perform any of Dett's arrangements of African American spirituals at his recitals.

By early fall, the news of Roland's pending debut with the Boston Symphony Orchestra was spreading among the city's concertgoing public. Although Fannie was in the city without either of her sons, she received heightened press attention because of Roland's forthcoming BSO appearance. In a letter at the end of August, she told Robert Brante that she had not heard from Roland for some time but that he had sent her his recording of "Deep River" (made earlier that year) and a Victrola to play it on for her birthday. Robert Brante and his wife (not yet divorced) returned to Boston apparently at the urging of Fannie, because they were with her in mid-September.

In Europe, Roland had returned to Vienna for a series of concerts during the third week of September. He arrived there on the fifteenth so that the Polish baritone Dr. Theodore Lierhammer, now living in Vienna, could coach him in his lieder repertoire.[31] Fannie had written Roland, again mentioning her approaching death; Roland had received her letter before departing London but had been unable to reply until September 22, after settling in Vienna.[32] He said that he would carry out her final wishes according to her directives,[33] but having heard her speak about her imminent death several times in recent months, he minimized such talk. Fannie apparently said something in her letter to Roland about looking for a house, and he encouraged her in that undertaking, thinking that it would give her something to do other than discuss her death, and he wanted to have her new address, if she moved before his arrival. He also told her that he planned to be back in the Unites States in just a few weeks.

On Sunday, September 23, a lengthy article, "Roland Hayes, Colored Singer, First of Race to Sing in Symphony," appeared in the *Boston Sunday Post*. The article, which was the formal announcement of the upcoming debut of the tenor with the BSO, had been written by music critic Olin Downes, Roland's sometimes-reluctant supporter. Fannie, Robert, and Maggie were interviewed and quoted extensively. Fannie made many of the same statements that she had been making to her sons and her friends in several letters about her tentative health, saying she was not feeling so "awful good" lately and pointing out how "Rollin [*sic*] is always asking about my well-being." She said the only thing wrong with her health was "old age" and that she would accept her end when it came.[34]

Roland had already given one performance in Vienna and was scheduled to give his second on the evening of September 26.[35] The well-known scholar and writer Dr. Alain Locke, his friend from the United States, was in Vienna at the time and met Roland at his hotel and was with him for the day. For some unexplainable reason, Roland was troubled throughout that day. Locke encouraged him to come out of that mood and rise to the occasion, because Roland would be competing that night with the renowned soprano Maria Jeritza (known as the "Moravian Thunderbolt"), who was also performing in the city that evening.[36]

Locke was unable to lift Roland out of his mysterious depression, and the tenor carried his disturbed mood into his recital that night.[37] Roland believed that because he sang so introspectively and closed out his audience, he had performed poorly. As a result, Roland was visibly upset to the point of tears. He was met backstage by the British conductor Simeon Rumschiski, which exacerbated his depressed mood and embarrassment at having given what he believed to have been a substandard performance. The British conductor then soberly spoke to Roland:

> "My poor Roland, my poor Roland," the conductor said. "I have something to
> tell you. I am afraid your mother is very ill."
> "She is dead," Roland instinctively knew.
> "Yes, your mother is dead."[38]

The actual news had come from Boston earlier that day in a telegram from his sister-in-law, Maggie: "your mother passed away five o'clock this morning."[39] Because Austria was at least six hours ahead of U.S. Eastern Standard Time, the telegram would have been received in Europe by the afternoon at the very latest. Fannie's death had been intentionally withheld from Roland until after his performance, probably by the concert managers, who were fearful that he might have rightfully canceled his engagement had he received the news before going onstage. Totally devastated, Roland comforted himself with the words that his mother had said to him before his departure that January, "Son, you are a continuation of me."[40] Although his relationship with Lawrence Brown had become distant at that point, he wrote his former accompanist a brief note, "Mother is no more."[41]

In one of her final letters to Roland, Fannie had said he was not to worry, because her church was surrounding her. And it did. Her grand funeral procession was at least two blocks long. Unable to attend the funeral, Roland cabled instructions to the Reverend Cassius Ward of Ebenezer Baptist Church (who conducted the funeral service and who had occasionally communicated with Roland while he was in Europe) that he wanted his recent London recording of "Sit Down" played at the service.

It was Fannie, after all, who had taught the song to her son when they lived in northwest Georgia, and Roland, in turn, had made it known around the world.[42] Knowing of his mother's enslaved background combined with her personal sacrifices, struggles, and losses, Roland saw the repeated phrase throughout the spiritual, "Sit down and rest a little while," as a metaphor for her life. The final phrase of the work, "Sit down, sit down, yes, my Lord. Oh, Hallelujah, in my kingdom," was an equally meaningful metaphor for Fannie Hayes's death.

SIT DOWN

I'm going up to heaven and sit down.
Going up to heaven and sit down.
Oh! Sit down, sit down, sit down, child,
Sit down rest a little while.

I'll see my Lord, he'll say sit down.
See my Lord he'll say sit down.
Oh! Sit down, sit down, sit down, child.
Sit down rest a little while.

Your back is bent from burdens borne,
There are furrows on'-a your brow.
Oh come, my child, you will come home,
Your troubles are over now.

Oh! Sit down, sit down, oh sit down sister,
Sit down, oh sit down, sit down child,
Sit down rest a little while.

Sit down, sit down, yes, my Lord.

Oh, Hallelujah, in my kingdom.

The Hayes Conquest

1923–1924

ROLAND CRISSCROSSED EUROPE LIKE AN EVANGELIST proselytizing among the unconverted. With Howard Jordan, his personal assistant, and Leo Rosenek, his accompanist, who was an up-and-coming pianist and later a conductor, Roland traveled from Vienna to Graz and from Budapest to Karlsbad, channeling his mourning into exquisite performances. Countess Marguerite Hoyos, daughter of Austro-Hungarian nobility, had heard and met Roland in Vienna. She was so moved by his performance she wrote a letter to her friend Countess Bertha Henriette Katharina Nadine Colloredo-Mansfeld enthusiastically suggesting that she call on this new tenor sensation when he debuted in Prague.[1]

The thirty-six-year-old tenor arrived in Prague in October 1923. He retreated to a comfortable hotel suite, unaware of the social currents eddying in the capital of the five-year-old Czechoslovak Republic. Politics permeated the city, and the art scene was no exception. Concertgoers from all levels of society flocked to music halls, each group wary, if not suspicious, of others in attendance. The tension was as palpable as the situation was complex. Industrialized Czechs holding economic advantage over rural Slovaks vigorously championed the unifying virtues of the common language they shared.[2] The German minority, despite the downfall of the Hapsburg Empire, kept a tight grip on their economic interests by closely guarding what remained of their old cultural influence.[3]

Roland was oblivious to the politics of the region, but his patrons were another matter. On the evening of his Prague debut, October 11, 1923, when he found the fashionably dressed Countess Bertha standing in his hotel parlor unannounced and unexpected, he kept his poise and dignity. The strikingly beautiful thirty-three-year-old had a regal, commanding presence. The shocked hotel staff had directed her to his room on her request.[4]

As she recalled, "Roland came out of his bathroom and said, 'Oh, excuse me, I haven't quite finished dressing.' He was just knotting his bow tie. I thought that was so charming, so nice. I noticed he had a delicate figure, perfectly formed in black. We sat down and talked as if we had known each other always."[5]

Roland, at five feet four inches, was not particularly diminutive for a man of that era, but the countess, at six feet one inch, was extraordinarily tall by any standard. He recounted, "She introduced herself charmingly, as though she were asking instead of conferring a favor. 'The Countess Hoyos has most kindly made it possible for me to meet you,' she said. 'My friends and I are delighted when we can come to know the visiting artists. It helps us to enter into their art.' I told her a good deal about myself – in fact, I am afraid I poured out most of the story of my life into her sympathetic ears – and then I described the program I was to sing in Prague."[6] Countess Bertha eventually departed for City Hall, where the concert was scheduled to take place, leaving Roland to his thoughts.

When Hayes and Rosenek strode onstage shortly afterward, the accompanist stepped forward to announce a small change in the program. It would have been an unremarkable occurrence, except for one thing: Rosenek spoke in German, as he anticipated was customary.[7] In the audience, a smattering of booing and hissing instantly erupted among the Czech-speaking contingent, apparently encouraged by Prague's anti-German and very popular mayor Karel Baxa.[8] Roland was stunned, clueless as to what had triggered the uproar.[9] Was the audience attacking him because of his race? It was not out of the question. In any event, he, too, stepped forward and called out to his hecklers, "If you don't want to listen to my songs, go out!"[10] The crowd grew even rowdier.

Hayes and Rosenek headed to Roland's dressing room, preparing to leave, but a lone woman intercepted them backstage and explained the problem. Leo Rosenek had spoken to the audience in the detested language of the former Austro-Hungarian oppressors. Roland's retort in English had set off a nationalist firestorm. The people were demanding that something be said in the Czech language.[11] Roland eventually grasped the delicacy of the situation and his unwitting complicity in it. He returned to the stage with Rosenek and the woman who had interceded. While she explained in Czech to the audience what had taken place earlier, Roland beckoned to the mayor to join them and apologized to him for the mishap.[12] Baxa, apparently appeased, shook the tenor's hand, which cleared the way for Roland to sing. The mayor even rallied the crowd to carry the tenor out on their shoulders when the recital had ended.[13]

For the countess, the recital was unforgettable. She noticed that Roland had knelt down on the platform to give someone a little pat on the shoulder and muttered, "All right, all right, I can begin my concert now."[14] "And that gave it such an intimate atmosphere, a feeling that everything was going to be perfect," she said. "Roland always had wonderful programs. He sang the classics, then at the end, spirituals, which I had never heard before. When they came, I had the feeling that all my life had been rolled back to the beginning of time, and there he stood and I stood and we belonged together."[15]

Roland riveted her with his humility, graceful manners, and virtuosity. The countess was not only intrigued but also astonished to find these qualities in a handsome black man. Her ancestors had held high political and military posts in the Hapsburg Empire for centuries. Her father, Count Leopold Philip Kolowrat-Krakowsky, had survived the last fatal duel fought in the Austro-Hungarian Empire, and her mother, Baroness Nadine von Huppmann-Valbella, was from a family that owned cigarette factories in Germany and Russia.[16] One of Bertha's three brothers, Alexander (known as "Sascha"), was a pioneer in Europe's automobile industry as a financial backer of the Porsche company; the first Porsche automobile, Saschawagen, was named after him. Sascha was also a major force in the nascent film industry, having been credited with discovering Marlene Dietrich.[17] In short, Bertha was not easily impressed, but in Roland Hayes, she immediately recognized a great artist.

By early November Roland had returned to Boston, with his next major American concert merely weeks away: on November 17, 1923, Roland was scheduled to make his American orchestral debut with the Boston Symphony Orchestra.[18] In fact there were three BSO concerts. The first was on November 15 at 8:00 PM at the Sanders Theatre at Harvard University's campus in Cambridge. The following afternoon the same program was repeated at the same location. On November 17 Maestro Monteux and Roland repeated the same program at Symphony Hall in a benefit concert for the orchestra's pension fund.

But first, Roland had personal business to do. He had not been home since his mother's death two months earlier. His only surviving brother, Robert Brante, had already packed up her house, leaving Roland the task of visiting Fannie's church friends and thanking people who had helped her in her final days.[19]

Going through his mother's bank statements and the receipts for her ten acres in Georgia (including those for payments that Robert Brante made after her death), Roland discovered that she had not withdrawn a cent from the joint bank account he had set up for her.[20] He read her plainly stated will, dated April 13, 1916, handwritten on his stationery and tucked inside an envelope at a time when she had four sons alive and the family resided at 3 Warwick Street in Boston. It was a testament to her simple values.

> I, Fannie Hayes is writing my will. When I die I have four boys. I have ten acres of land in Georgia I want my boys to have it and do what they like with it. I have a dollar or two in the bank here in Boston. At my death, if I don't spend it before I die, I want my boys to divide the money among themselves. Now my personal things I have three quilts for the baby,[21] one silk quilt, two cotton ones. If I stay with Roland till I die, all the other things I have is Roland's. He can do as he likes with them. This is Fannie Hayes will – written 13 day of April 1916[22]

Roland gathered his mother's treasures together for safekeeping. Among them was a lock of her hair tied with a piece of string.[23]

It was during this season of mourning and reflection that Roland began to correspond with the countess from Prague. Even though the initial letters were friendly and respectful, the two were beginning to very quickly connect at a much deeper level than either of them had anticipated.[24]

The BSO performances had been in the works since the BSO's maestro Pierre Monteux heard Roland in Paris in 1922. From that point it was a matter of quiet preparation by the BSO's general manager, William

Brennan, and Roland's former teacher, Arthur Hubbard. Roland's continental "stamp of approval" (soloing with renowned European orchestras and conductors) had more than prepared him to stand in front of the prestigious BSO.

On the evening of November 17, Maestro Monteux opened the program with Jean Sibelius's Symphony no. 1 in E minor, op. 39.[25] After a ten-minute intermission, the lights dimmed and Roland walked onstage to thunderous applause, followed by the smiling maestro who had fought for this moment in history. For the first time an African American soloist was performing with a major symphony orchestra in the United States.

It was an exhilarating yet nervous evening for all onstage, but Roland performed with complete authority, putting everyone at ease with his ability to handle such an event. His first offering was the romantic aria from Mozart's *Così fan tutte*, "Un'aura amorosa," followed by the tender aria "Le repos de la sainte famille" (The repose of the holy family) from Berlioz's oratorio *La fuite en Egypte* (The flight into Egypt), which would later be known as *L'enfance du Christ* (The infancy of Christ).[26] Roland had picked it up at the suggestion of Maestro Gabriel Pierné and had worked on it with Pierre Monteux, whose interpretation Roland felt surpassed even that of the eminent Maestro Pierné.[27]

Monteux then led the BSO in Mussorgsky's orchestral fantasy *Une nuit sur Mont Chauve* (A night on Bald Mountain), and Roland returned with two spirituals, "Go Down Moses," and "Bye and Bye," arranged for orchestra by Harry T. Burleigh and Lawrence Brown, respectively. And as Monteux expected, admiring reviews poured in:

> Certainly no better singer now traverses our concert halls. Slender, straight laced graceful of movement, Mr. Hayes is pleasing to the eye.... In the use of his voice, Mr. Hayes now does the work of both skill and imagination....
>
> Dame Nature gave Hayes a beautiful voice. She also gave him singing brains. Not content with nature's gift, he has studied intelligently. He has learned also by observation, pondering his art and by experience.[28]

For the next fifty years of his performing career, *this* concert was Roland's calling card. On the basis of this event, he was credible as a featured soloist with any orchestra in the world. The tenor was especially grateful to Maestro Monteux, realizing more than most the risk the maestro had taken to present an African American in America. Monteux left his position as music director of the BSO at the end of 1924. He had probably scheduled Hayes's concert as a farewell gesture, just in case the Boston public rejected the progressive stance of an African American performing with the elite orchestra.

As far as Roland was concerned, the only thing marring his debut with the BSO was the relative absence of African Americans at Symphony Hall, as there were relatively few rush tickets available for non-subscribers on the day of the performance.[29] This was not a problem on December 1, 1923, when Hayes performed in New York City's Town Hall. One of the major promoters was the NAACP assistant secretary, Walter White. Roland had befriended White while he was visiting London in 1921, when they both had attended the historic Pan-African Congress in London.[30]

Born in Atlanta in 1893, Walter Francis White was a music aficionado who reveled in his fellow Georgian's successes in Europe. He had seen Roland's continental triumphs firsthand and realized the social value of duplicating them at home. At five feet six inches (two inches taller than Roland), the blond-haired, blue-eyed African American, who could easily pass for white, had often gone south to investigate African American lynchings, mixing in with redneck groups and employing his natural Georgian accent without drawing attention to himself.[31]

As a professional journalist, Walter White used his extensive media contacts to call reviewers' attention to the up-and-coming tenor, including the powerful *New York World* columnist Heywood Broun. At his New York concert, Roland sang his standard Handel, Purcell, Schubert, Schumann, and Bach selections, but Broun was enraptured by the spirituals: "Roland Hayes sang of Jesus. . . . I saw a miracle in Town Hall. Half of the people who heard Hayes were black and half white, and while the mood of the song ["He Never Said a Mumberlin' Word"] held they were all the same. They shared together the close silence. One emotion wrapped them. And in the end it was a single sob."[32]

To Roland's delight, one of the African American concertgoers was his first cousin, Helen Alzada Mann. Born in 1893, Alzada was thirty years old, unmarried, and working as a seamstress in New York City. Roland was impressed by her and knew that he wanted to see her again.

But within a day, he had to get back to Boston. His reunion with Alzada would have to wait.

Roland found to his satisfaction that African Americans filled many of the seats in Boston for his next concert there. He repeated his Town Hall program and then boarded a train for Michigan, where, on December 9, he soloed with the Detroit Symphony Orchestra, led by its assistant conductor, Victor Kolar.[33] The Detroit musical organizations did not have the same prestige of the BSO, nor was Victor Kolar in the same league as Maestro Monteux. But it was satisfying, nonetheless, to win over another major audience before his official tour got underway.

Roland's first professionally managed national tour was in the able hands of William Brennan and his assistant George Judd. A stop in Chattanooga in December was a real homecoming. William Stone, still the editor of the *Chattanooga Times*, intended for the concert to be packed. He published a flattering article in the December 12 issue of the *Times* quoting the Boston papers' praise of the tenor's recent performances and promoting the December 17 local appearance.[34] It was so heavily attended and well received that Roland was obliged to give a second, sold-out performance.

In the South, segregated seating was still the norm. A few cities, such as Atlanta, had a different policy: the race that bought the most tickets occupied the main auditorium. As Roland's reputation grew, more African American concertgoers were allowed this modicum of respect.

William Lawrence was his official accompanist that season. Roland and Lawrence had been old friends since the mid-1910s when they had toured the Pennsylvania and Chautauqua circuit as part of the Hayes Trio. Lawrence was also a skilled accompanist and arranger.

When Roland returned to Carnegie Hall in 1924 for a February 5 concert, Daisy Tapley and Harry Burleigh, his old friends from the *Elijah* quartet, attended. Daisy wrote a letter a few days after the concert to her old friend "Ro" offering mostly praise. She was not as impressed with his inclusion of an indigenous African song, claiming it was not "native" enough; the accompaniment was too European for her taste. But the meatiest topic of her letter was Harry Burleigh. She warned Roland that

"Har" had become jealous of his newfound celebrity. She felt that the way Burleigh had opened and closed doors for Roland after the concert was somehow disingenuous. Her letter also suggested that there was some breach between her and Burleigh and that Daisy was no longer on good terms with him. Although Hayes continued to include Burleigh's spirituals in his programs, there appeared to be few communications between the two after this point.[35] Now that Roland had become an internationally acclaimed artist, he had long since surpassed Burleigh's rather limited exposure. This was all the more difficult for the older singer, because it was *he* who had given Roland a significant boost to his career from the tenor's early days in Boston. Not attending any of Roland's previous New York concerts made Burleigh's deferential gesture at Carnegie Hall suspect, in Daisy's eyes.[36]

Just after the Carnegie Hall engagement, Walter White, Heywood Broun, and Roland met in New York for lunch and traded favors. White suggested that Roland write to Broun's supervisor, the executive editor of the *New York World,* praising Broun for his journalistic professionalism. A letter dated January 21, 1924, confirmed that Roland complied.

At the same lunch, Roland asked Walter White to be his personal manager and official biographer.[37] White thought others could do a better job as his personal manager, yet he wrote Roland a note later, accepting the job as biographer. That he never wrote the biography seemed to have no ill effect on their relationship. For many years, Walter White continued promoting Hayes.[38]

By mid-February 1924, Roland was back at his residence in London. He had a letter waiting for him from Maddie Salmon confirming his engagement with the Collone Orchestra and Maestro Pierné the following month. The maestro had agreed to include Berlioz's *La fuite en Egypte* but not Franck's "La procession," as it was composed for a woman's voice and Pierné did not support this practice.[39] At the end of February, Roland was featured in an orchestra appearance at Queen's Hall with Sir Henry Wood conducting. The concert included William Lawrence–arranged spirituals for strings and piano accompaniment.[40] While his teacher Sir George Henschel was unable to attend the concert, his wife was present and informed him of the tenor's success. Sir George called to Roland's attention that he had recently completed a composition, "Morning Hymn," which was scored for voice and orchestra. He suggested that his former student consider performing it.[41]

Before his engagement at the Berlioz festival with the Collone, Roland did a solo concert at the Salle Gaveau. Clarence Lucas, the French correspondent for the New York–based *Musical Courier*, complimented him on his ability to sing "ah" without it being somehow distorted – an achievement that he felt was beyond the abilities of many French singers.[42]

For reasons that are not apparent, Roland had departed for Europe this particular time without Howard Jordan, his secretary and personal assistant. But by March, he had William Lawrence write Jordan outlining his duties as the personal assistant to the singer. The position paid twenty-five dollars a week, in addition to travel expenses (second-class train travel). It required that Jordan be proficient in stenography and typing. He was advised to take courses in business English and French.[43]

Roland and Lawrence returned to London briefly and then departed for Vienna, as spring bloomed again in Europe. Roland wrote his friend Alain Locke, whom he had not seen since they were both in Vienna when Roland had received the news of Fannie's death. Locke was still teaching at Howard University when the tenor wrote him from Prague in early April about his blissful life:

> We are filling 10 concert dates in Czechoslovakia, one in Budapest, and two in Berlin. I shall be in Berlin on the 10th of May. My London and Paris concerts have been one triumph after another. I sang in Paris with the Collone Orchestra on March 22nd. Dear boy, my life is so beautiful and satisfying now that my cup of joy remains perpetually at a state of overflow. I never expected to have been so happy in this life as the success of my work (which is my meat and drink) has brought me. My darling Mother passed on to bring all of this to me and I recognize her individuality and her great Love in it all. My heart is daily lifted up in thanksgiving to this all Divine Deity for the rich benefits afforded me here during my days and hours of endeavor and sojourn.[44]

Returning to Prague by early April, Roland had reunited with Countess Bertha. The towering beauty who had charmed him with her impromptu visit to his hotel room in October 1923 had become a fixture in his life. The timing of the above letter to Locke made it crystal clear that *she* was, in part, responsible for his life being "so beautiful and satisfying." Only weeks after Fannie's death, Bertha had appeared in the vulnerable Roland's life and captivated him. Roland's very revealing letter to Locke also intimated that he believed there was some other worldly connection between the two events. It was as if he were crediting his late mother for the gift of the countess ("My darling Mother passed on to bring all of this to me and I recognize her individuality and her great Love in it all").

For the past six months, Roland and the countess had been exchanging increasingly passionate letters in which the tenor surrendered his natural guardedness and confessed his total delight in her friendship.[45] Roland's initial communications had been polite, but as Bertha revealed more of herself to him, the tenor's letters to her were like a man expressing his most closely guarded secrets from the bottom of his heart to his one and only soul mate.[46]

In his biographical narrative, however, Hayes carefully shielded her identity, discreetly referring to a "high born lady from Prague" who was crucial to his artistic success.[47] In *Angel Mo' and Her Son, Roland Hayes*, the references to Countess Colloredo-Mansfeld are unmistakable but could easily be overlooked because no name is attached to the description given to her. In that context, the relationship was communicated as a platonic one in which she inspired his artistry for altruistic reasons. To further blur even the possibility of a physical relationship between them in his sanitized narrative, Roland also credited the countess's son in their interactions, although there is no evidence to suggest that any of her four sons was even remotely a factor in their dealings with each other. In truth, before the year was out, Bertha would prove to be a godsend for Roland.

Born as Bertha Henriette Katharina Nadine Kolowrat-Krakowsky on June 21, 1890, in Tynec u Klatov (also known as Teinitzl), site of one of the several castles and palaces her family owned in what was called Bohemia before the Czechoslovak Republic, she was reared under the watchful eye of the widowed aunt after whom she had been named. As was customary in her social class, the countess was formally trained in literature, languages, music, and fine arts. She was steeped in centuries of European history and culture and brought that level of understanding to Roland as he was absorbing and interpreting the great composers of the European continent. Incorrigibly curious, Bertha would eventually be nicknamed "Issten" by her grandchildren because she would repeat-edly inquire, "Was ist denn, was ist denn?" (What's going on, what's going on?)[48]

She was compassionate. With empathy beyond her years, Bertha had read Harriet Beecher Stowe's *Uncle Tom's Cabin* and was stung by the in-justice of American enslavement.[49] "It made such an impression on me," she recalled. "I thought, 'How is this possible?'"[50] So, characteristically direct, she took action and signed up with a European-based missionary program to feed a child in Africa.[51] From that point on, she abhorred racial prejudice. By the time she was thirteen, Bertha was determined to set the world – including her own – right.

One day, she impulsively packed her things and ran away from her aunt's home. Her parents were appalled when she showed up at their castle in Teinitzl complaining that life with her aunt was oppressive. But Bertha's adolescent rebellion was easily squashed. The parents were as decisive as their willful child and immediately sent her to a convent to be tutored by nuns.[52] It would become the job of a mother superior and an order of religious women to rein Bertha in for her future role as a wife and mother. Bertha eventually succumbed to her obligations. Her formal education concluded with a year at a private English school in Paris. Her English and French were impeccable.[53]

By nineteen, she appeared to have learned her parents' lesson. She had suitors in France and Bohemia. As a result of her brother Sascha's connections, eligible bachelors throughout Austria clamored for her at-tention. She chose a naval officer, Count Hieronymus Colloredo-Man-sfeld, from the family that was formerly the musical patron of Leopold and Wolfgang Amadeus Mozart. A favorite of Bertha's mother and scion of an aristocratic family with vast landholdings, spectacular castles, and centuries of connections to the Hapsburg dynasty, he would put Bertha at the center of a very important family.[54] Bertha, known for her pas-sionate temperament, at last had found a worthy purpose for her life: "to give new life to a family that would otherwise be extinguished."[55] They had four sons in quick succession. Hieronymus never failed to support her in public, despite her irrepressible tendency to disregard protocol.[56]

On the surface she had an enviable, almost fairy-tale life, but it led to frustration as the years passed and the children grew up. The fact that

Hieronymus, true to his social class and nineteenth-century upbringing, rarely, if ever, expressed deep feelings created a difficult situation for his emotional wife: "All he knew was ships, ships, ships. He had not the imagination to think that he could make me happy."[57] She remembered that he thought that "women have some time in their lives when they get crazy."[58] With a typically Prussian attitude, he dismissed her complaints, as if to say, "Ach, you think too much. You need to have stockings to knit. If you had knitting, you wouldn't have all these ideas."[59]

She was devastated when the Hapsburg Austro-Hungarian Empire collapsed in 1918. "I thought that I would never be able to laugh again," she reflected later.[60] But the public and private disaster that she feared did not materialize. The privileges of her social class went on much as before, but she personally struggled to carry on as usual. With the end of the empire had come women's liberation. As far as Hieronymus was concerned, that meant losing even more control over his naturally independent wife. Confining Bertha more tightly inside their rigid society, he puzzled over how to keep her in check. She refused to cooperate. Her friendship with Hayes was evidence, if any were ever needed, that she had a different vision of how to live her life. In Roland, she had found a more flattering self-image and a noble commitment that reached beyond that to her family.

She came to focus on the tenor, whom she believed to be a genius and a representation of the very best of the black race. As such, she established a "cause" to which they would both commit. For her, having a child with the tenor meant bringing about the blending of the two races, which would enhance, and perhaps save, humanity. As usual, in the face of her headstrong behavior, Hieronymus seems to have shrugged his shoulders and accepted her unusual relationship with the tenor, which he did not fully grasp at the time.

Meanwhile, Bertha became the best thing that could have happened to Roland. He was overwhelmed with gratitude for her tutelage. On April 29, 1924, as his train pushed across Central Europe, the tenor started a stream-of-consciousness letter to her; he poured out his swelling emotions, finishing the correspondence several days later when he seemed satisfied that he had left no doubt in her mind that the experience of working with her had fundamentally transformed him as an artist – and as a man.

29th Morning   Budapest April 29th <u>1924</u>

What a great revelation! And you, my revealer of wonders, have caused a great illumination in my Heaven sky. I see endless reaches, and as I behold all the *matchless* beauty I am overcome with its all enveloping sweetness.

How we have advanced since the 18th. Does it not sometimes awaken astonishment in *you* as it does in myself, when you can see with clear eyes this advancement that has taken on such enormous dimensions and which also has rung in so much else of sheer beauty and loveliness?

It is a revelation of which *no part* must be lost on us, because in order that we reach the next advanced point, we most need [to] understand and cram our storehouses of knowledge with *all* the wisdom it reveals.

My revealer, what great aid do you render me as I pass on [the] way to the place to which my guiding Star continually beckons and urges me forward. I am filled with an added great delight when I realize that sometime and somewhere we together shall be rejoicing in the calmness of sweet tranquility over all the marvels that we now know and also those that are surely in store for us when we shall have advanced along the *whole* of the distance to the abode of the blessed.

And now, dear, dear revealer of revelations, I shall back to rest and dreams for a time gazing all the while on the wonders you have made in my Heaven sky.

Akorin, da re, da re
[the master sings]
pronounced: A – as in, <u>Father</u>.
ko – as in English word <u>Caution</u>.
rin – as in the French word pele<u>rin</u>.

29th Evening

A good rest amid tranquility and quiet dream – thoughts. The illumination continues *now,* and *shall always!* I have been with the "gardener" the while, and he has wanted *us* to know in his song – 52nd, that, "By giving we gain, by holding we lose." We both know this already but he wishes us to keep our thoughts steadfastly upon it "the while." As it is now, we cannot lose because the silken cord that binds is not taxed to its utmost capacity and it shall be to our interest and to our infinite joy and future happiness not to over press through eager anxious desire. You are quite right! We must always give and *happily!*

Akorin!

Morning [April] 30th

T'is not beautiful and clear out of doors, but it *is* within the chamber of my soul, and, *mach nichts!* The other, because with the heavenly light within one quickly forgets all the other conditions. The night passed as usual and the morning brings fresh hopes and inspirations anew for the tasks set before me. I don't mind the inconveniences and hazardous travail. At the end there awaits that which rewards bountifully and completely satisfactory all honest and unselfish strivings. If this be so, why should we mind the *nothings* which inevitably one encounters? T'will not be long, my dear, "we are nearing the place."

Akorin!

Evening 30th After the work: 12 PM

It has been so splendid and my message so well understood. Besides, I have been in splendid condition. The best since in these parts. The academie was quite crowded and the people nearly mobbed me with their emotions and enthusiasm. After the music I went with my comrade and managers to a coffee house where we had light supper. At this coffee house I saw someone so much like yourself that for an instant I was quite startled, but t'was not long before I realized I was "quite" mistaken. I am very very weary and must try and rest a little as I travel early in the morning, but I just had to spend a moment with my revealer of all things sweet and beautiful. Good night my *divine!*

Akorin, da re, da re ("da re
da re, – means the *best*)

Morning May 1st, En route:

My Comfort, everywhere I gaze is the freshness of May offerings of flowers [unintelligible], and green foliage. It all turns my thoughts to the time of May existing in our innermost souls where our planted flowers bloom. The four seasons are one mass of all exquisite loveliness, we are the workers in this flower garden of May, and, oh! what bliss as we work side by side in *one* purpose. I am indeed most fortunate to be given such an *altogether satisfactory* fellow-mate.

I need you *so* this morning because I am still weary of last night's task, and my being cries out for the safe pillow of your presence that it might find the comfort for which it longs and sorely needs. The spirit is quite intact, but the material calls for support and recuperation from arduous travail. Just now, we are passing an interesting chain of hills and they give me *strength as do all things* that suggests loftiness. Can you see, my comfort and my strength, why I never can bear to be without you and your presence there in the chambers of my stirring soul? I am not complaining dear one, it is only that I am a little fatigued and this little communication with your spirit gives the soothing effect necessary to rapid restoration to a natural state of being.

Yesterday I rehearse these daily messages that you may have what you have already felt concerning my thoughts of you verified.

Au revoir, a bientot.
Akorin, da re, da re.[61]

While rambling and poetically incoherent, Roland no doubt made his emotions plain. He was nearly thirty-seven years old; these were hardly the written utterances of an infatuated schoolboy. In the remaining fifty-two years of his life, Roland never again declared himself in writing to anyone in such a way as this or even came close to doing so. The vulnerability and sheer delight that he expressed in this early communication provides more than a glimpse into his soul and into the spirit of the man and the artist that Countess Bertha was fast creating. With complete abandon, he refers to her as "my divine," "my strength," and "my comfort" and makes other unambiguous declarations such as "you, my revealer of wonders, have caused a great illumination in my Heaven sky" and "I never can bear to be without you and your presence."

Roland's ecstasy in this letter is akin to religious excitement. His reference to having been with "the gardener" suggests some sort of communion with God (or the spirit that drove him) and was also telling. It insinuates that by giving of his art through the spirit (as he believed he was called to do), he, in return, would reap ever greater rewards ("By giving we gain, by holding we lose"). At some deeper level the singer seems to be implying that cultivating his own beautiful voice represented some mastery of the spirit placed in his care by the "gardener." Here religious ecstasy had the same symptoms as romance. When this letter was written in April and May 1924, Roland and Bertha had not yet consummated their relationship, but there was little question that it was quickly moving in that direction.

As secretive as Roland was about this relationship, he acknowledged the phenomenal impact that the countess had had on his artistic and intellectual development. As he explained years later:

> To this lady . . . I owe the real beginning of my intellectual life and my musical maturity. In preparation for my visits she would assemble a bibliography of whatever composer we had nominated for study. We read the definitive biographies and sang and played the music in chronological sequence. . . . Whenever I appeared, from America or England, from Paris or Germany, my friend would be waiting to plunge with me into new problems, with shelves of books and stacks of music ready for research and study[62]

This was as public as he could get in acknowledging Bertha's influence in front of an often intolerant world. Countess Bertha, however, wanted more.

As Roland's communications indicated, he was busy concertizing in Central Europe in April 1924. As a seasoned artist, Roland paid very close attention to those who were representing him, and as he had in England, he did not hesitate to play one agency against another when it came to seeking the best financial deal. His Czechoslovakian dates were under the auspices of Jaromir Zid of the Bel Canto Management Agency. With this round of European engagements, Roland enforced his new policy of wanting half of his fee in U.S. dollars deposited in his bank account before he performed. This might have had something to do with the political instability of the new republic.

Trouble of another sort was brewing in the German capital before Roland even arrived. An April 2, 1924, letter set the stage for another defining experience for Roland that would raise him to near legendary stature. T. C. White[63] wrote to the Bel Canto Management Agency:

> I am in receipt of your letter of April 2nd requesting the "protectorship" of this Legation for a concert to be given under your auspices in Aussig, Reichenberg, and Teplitz [Teplice] by Mr. Roland Hayes on the grounds that two German papers of North Bohemia have written articles hostile to this gentleman.
>
> It is not the custom for diplomatic offices of the United States to give special recommendations of this nature. Further in this present instance I feel that no statement of this sort is needed. The comments in the newspaper articles to which you bring [to] my attention, reflect a political atmosphere with which the American negroes have no connection.
>
> Moreover, the people of Bohemia are renowned the world over for their appreciation of good music and I have no reason to suppose that the inhabitants of Reichenberg, and Teplitz and Aussig constitute any exception. To insinuate therefore that they would fail to give a [unintelligible] reception to a well-known artist such as Mr. Roland Hayes would seem to me to be doing the musical public of these cities scant justice.[64]

Roland, or the Bel Canto Management Agency on his behalf, had contacted the United States embassy in Prague. He was anticipating trouble in Berlin based on negative commentaries in German papers and other disparaging actions. Roland was informed by a U.S. embassy official that the minister of the U.S. embassy in the Czechoslovakian capital could not express an opinion but would refer the matter to Ambassador Alanson B. Houghton in Berlin for guidance.[65]

The Weimar Republic presented a complex period in German history, and it was in this climate in which Roland was about to make his Berlin debut. Having suffered defeat at the hands of the Allied Forces, including Great Britain, France, and the United States, Germany had also been stripped of its colonial possessions in Africa under the terms of the Treaty of Versailles. The final humiliation as far as the Germans were concerned was the presence of Francophone Africans throughout the Rhineland as a policing force, with the authority to arrest and detain. Germany had repeatedly appealed the imposition of continental African troops within its borders but with little consequence.[66] There was fear

Check-Out Receipt

Alameda Free Library
Main Branch
1550 Oak Street
Alameda, CA
Tel: 510-747-7777
www.alamedafree.org

Checkout Date: 08-5 -2015 - 13:47:18

Patron ID.: xxxxxxxxxx5385

---

1 Roland Hayes : the legacy of an
33341007842247   Due Date: 08/26/15

---

al Items: 1

Balance Due: $ 3.60

Effective July 8: Main Branch will open
at 10 AM on Wed

among the German population that the Africans and their Afro-German children would lead to the "bastardization" of the German race.[67] In his infamous work *Mein Kampf,* Adolf Hitler even accused the Jews of bringing the Africans into the Rhineland for the purpose of corrupting the purity of the German people.[68]

What Roland referred to as one of his "greatest triumphs over hatred" was a well- advertised and scheduled appearance at the German capital's celebrated Beethoven-Saal in May 1924.[69] In Berlin, he was primarily represented by the Russian impresario J. Borkon, who under the best circumstances had a complex relationship with the tenor. Hoping to capitalize on Roland's success in other parts of Europe, Borkon had begun advertising the singer's recital in major German papers, which included a six-inch head-shot. In addition to promoting the concert as Roland's first Berlin appearance, the ad stated that he would sing the lieder of Beethoven, Schubert, Schumann, Brahms, Strauss, and Wolf. Although it also said that Roland would sing the music of Handel and Mozart, as well as African American spirituals, it was the announcement of the first group of great German song composers that was distasteful to many concertgoing Berliners. They had primarily associated African American musicians with jazz and what they regarded as lesser forms of popular music. Open letters began appearing in German newspapers denouncing Roland's appearance as a sacrilege.

Roland stayed in Prague until two days before his scheduled appearance in Berlin. He crossed the German border inconspicuously with Lawrence and traveled to the city. On the morning before his May 10 concert, Roland received a copy of an American newspaper published in the capital, which once again called his appearance at the Beethoven-Saal scandalous, saying that the best he could do would be to remind the German public of "the cotton fields of Georgia."[70] Roland consulted Ambassador Houghton about the matter. Hoping that the presence of the American ambassador at the recital that evening would stave off any unpleasant situation, the tenor offered him tickets to the concert. The ambassador declined the invitation and gave the tickets to his staff.

The night of the concert was tense for Roland and Lawrence. The Berlin house was filled to its 1,000-seat capacity. Backstage, Roland braced himself for what he suspected would be an intractable audience. Unlike in previous performances, where the custom was to dim the lights as the performers walked onstage, Roland and Lawrence walked into near total darkness and took their respective positions in a single spotlight aimed at where the tenor was to stand, as if he were somehow a target. When he made it to the bend of the piano, he began hearing faint hisses. Over the course of a minute, they grew louder and louder. The "barrage" of protest continued for close to ten minutes while Roland stood perfectly still with his eyes closed and his head upright. He felt a calm come over him as the audience continued its demonstration.[71] In his mind he uttered his standard prayer while facing an audience before a performance, "God, please blot out Roland Hayes so that the people will see only thee."[72] After some time, the audience calmed down to a deadening silence. It was so quiet, according to Roland, "that the hush began to hurt."[73] He opened his eyes and, with only the slightest nod of his head, signaled William Lawrence at the keyboard to begin.

Following the indicated tempo marking, *langsam* (slowly), Lawrence began Schubert's familiar song with a text by Rückert in E-flat major at a barely audible pianissimo. Schubert took seven measures in the introductory accompaniment to paint a scene of absolute, peaceful repose. With gripped hands and closed eyes, the consummate singer began as if he were almost in a transcendental state as the spirit took over:

> Du bist die Ruh' der Friede mild
> (You are calm, the mild peace)
> Die Sehnsucht du, und was sie stillt.
> (You are longing and what stills it.)

Allowing only his raised eyebrows and altered facial gestures to communicate the dissonant harmonies of the next phrase, he delivered with a sense of longing,

> Ich weihe dir, voll Lust und Schmerz
> (I consecrate to you full of pleasure and pain)
> Zur Wohnung hier mein Aug und Herz.
> (As a dwelling here, my eyes and heart.)

The final phrase, "mein Aug und Herz," returned to the warmer original E-flat major and was then repeated as an affirmation. After a brief piano interlude, the tonic E-flat major opening returned to establish, once again, the peaceful mood heard at the beginning of the composition. The next verse is nearly identical harmonically to the first, so Roland gradually opened his eyes and was left to emote and communicate the different text:

> Kehr ein bei mir, und schließe du
> (Come live with me, and close)
> Still hinter dir die Pforten zu.
> (Quietly behind you, the gates.)
> Treib andern Schmerz aus dieser Brust!
> (Drive other pain out of this breast!)
> Voll sei dies Herz von deiner Lust.
> (That my heart may be full, with your pleasure. [last phrase repeated])

Only in the final climactic section of the song did Roland give more volume to his otherwise pianissimo singing. He gradually crescendoed in the vocal line, while Lawrence played the complementary harmonies on the keyboard, which included several accidentals. Roland's voice simply soared above the accompaniment:

> Dies Augenzelt von deinem Glanz,
> (The tabernacle of my eyes by your radiance)
> Allein erhellt. O füll es ganz!
> (Alone is illumined. Oh fill it completely!)[74]

The gradual urgency in this musical passage climaxed on the word "erhellt," sung on a forte G-natural over a dramatic secondary dominant E-flat seventh chord and resolved to a simple A-flat in the voice and piano. This was where Roland sang full voice for the first time. As his voice rang throughout the concert hall, he gave his listeners a moment to absorb the forte singing that had just taken place, adhering to Schubert's one measure rest. He then peacefully returned to the restful and calm E-flat original with "O füll es ganz." The composer then repeated the same passage, but the second time, Roland, following the dynamic markings, sang "erhellt" in a stunningly effective pianissimo. He then finished the song by repeating the passage, "O *füll* es ganz, O füll es ganz."

Once Roland had completed the vocal line, he remained perfectly still and calm as he had at the beginning of the song, allowing Lawrence to complete the last few chords at the keyboard. At the close of the performance, there was total silence throughout the house. In his heart and psyche, Roland knew that the performance had transformed the audience's disdain into respect, if not admiration, for him and his artistry. Only then did he slowly open his eyes. The spirit *had* done its work.

Still stunned by what it had just experienced, the audience was jolted back into reality by the sound of a lone sustained clap, followed by a few sparsely isolated claps, which quickly turned into cheers and stomping. The audience members, one thousand strong, hastily rose to their feet in loud applause. Not four minutes earlier, the majority of the highbrow Berliners were convinced that the best this black man could do was to sing jazz or songs from the Georgia cotton fields. Instead, he had convincingly demonstrated his mastery of one of their most revered lieder composers. Roland gave a faint smile of acknowledgment (as if to say to his doubting Berliners, "Now, what do you think of that?"), but it was far from the grin that he might have otherwise displayed. And the applause continued. There was little question about who was in control of the theater for the rest of the evening. If the tenor had elected to end the recital at that point, the Berlin audience would have considered his task done. But he gave them more.

After an intermission, Roland took his daring strategy one step further: he sang French repertoire to the post–World War I German audience. This was a risk, considering that the French were the very people who had introduced the continental African troops into the Rhineland and as such were reviled throughout the country.[75] Singing French to *this* audience was not unlike Leo Rosenek having spoken German to the Czech audience at Roland's Prague debut the year before.

By the end of his concert, his detractors-turned-ardent-admirers greeted him onstage. Among the well-wishers was a white American music student studying in Berlin. He shook the tenor's hand with an enthusiastic "Goddam it, put it there! This is the first time I have seen the Germans admit that good art can come out of America!"[76] The concert was not reviewed until two days later in the May 12 edition of the city's prestigious *Berliner Montag Post*. There was no ambiguity on the part of the reviewer about how the tenor had fared:

> Roland Hayes, the negro tenor who had been announced with such a flourish of trumpets, made his appearance on Saturday in Beethoven Hall. Mr. Hayes shamed his managers, for without exaggeration one can say that their sensational claims were not of a sufficiently high order. The method of Mr. Hayes is very unusual. His tenor voice has the sweetness of the great Romantic singers. His special facility for languages is remarkable.[77]

While Roland's May 10 debut achieved the adoration of the Berlin public as he had hoped, there is the very strong possibility that his choice of song, and the execution of it, was planned. After his experience the year before in Prague, where he was booed because his accompanist had addressed the audience in German and he had spoken to them in English as opposed to Czech, it is more than likely that the savvy tenor had anticipated some kind of demonstration in Berlin. In light of the mean-spirited editorials that had circulated before his arrival, he may even have planned on such an action. If starting his program with the demanding Schubert work to demonstrate his ability was, in fact, a gamble that Roland took, it paid off big. Borkon engaged Roland for another concert in the city at the beginning of the following month, based on the demand of the audience and organizers.

Some years later, Roland made clear that he believed that the Beethoven-Saal protest was inspired, if not staged, by the Nationalsozialistische Deutsche Arbeiterpartei, more commonly known as the German Nationalist Party or the all-too-familiar Nazi Party.[78] His deduction would have been consistent with the well-documented racist ideologies of Nazism.

Roland and Lawrence traveled back to London with a slew of positive reviews of his Berlin debut following them. Shortly after their arrival, they were scheduled for a May 22 performance at Queen's Hall with the Philharmonic String Quartet; Lawrence was at the piano accompanying his spirituals arranged for orchestra. While Roland had been away from London, his dear friend Robert Broadhurst had been taking care of his personal affairs. Broadhurst also became Roland's scout and promoter throughout the British Isles.

As an ardent Pan-Africanist, Robert Broadhurst also reported Roland's successes to the African serials in the London area and on the continent. Several of them were especially overjoyed at how Roland had put the culturally snobbish Germans in their place with his Berlin debut. Many of the Pan-Africanists in London were well aware of the abuses that their continental brethren had received patrolling the Rhineland in Germany. Several of the Pan-Africanists in London and Paris began referring to Roland Hayes as the "African tenor."[79]

Roland and William Lawrence fulfilled their June 3 return engagement in Berlin (which also happened to be the tenor's thirty-seventh birthday) with a very different reception from what they had received before. Borkon and his assistant Conrad Dwerthon rolled out the red carpet for the singer, and once again, his converted public flocked to see him.

That same month, Roland was named the tenth recipient of the NAACP's prestigious Spingarn Award. After his Berlin triumph had been reported internationally, there was little question that he was one of the most famous African Americans in the world. The specific reason cited for his receipt of the award and the accompanying medal, however, was his historic Boston Symphony Orchestra debut. As a Spingarn winner, Roland was in the company of his one-time colleague and occasional accompanist Harry Burleigh and was only the second musician to be so honored. The immediate past recipient of the award was his friend and father figure George Washington Carver, the biologist. The NAACP's annual conference award ceremony in Philadelphia at the First African Church fell on the calendar at the beginning of July. Roland had already accepted an engagement to sing at the Viscountess Harcourt's English summer home on July 1, so he sent his acceptance and recognition of the honor as well as his apology for not being there by telegram, adding pointedly that King George of England was expected at his July 1 performance. His Spingarn Medal was accepted in absentia by Harry Burleigh, who spoke on his behalf.[80] Marian Anderson, the contralto whom Roland had been mentoring for years, sang at the ceremony. Roland formally received the medal the following year aboard the SS *Aquitania* as he was about to depart for Europe.[81]

Ultimately, however, it was another announcement that made 1924 a pivotal year in Roland's career. In early July, Walter Brennan, Roland's U.S. manager, wrote him in England to tell him that he had booked him for three separate engagements at Boston's Symphony Hall as well as at Carnegie Hall. This meant that the singer would have to prepare three separate programs. Fortunately, to help him measure up to this challenge, there was Countess Bertha.[82] She was "the only friend I had in the world who could help me in such an ambitious undertaking."[83]

SEVEN

Roland and the Countess

1924-1926

OFF AND ON FOR THE REST OF THE SUMMER OF 1924, ROLAND and Countess Bertha worked on the three programs Roland needed for his 1924–25 season. Bertha made Roland's life easier in small ways – for example, by receiving his mail when he was on the road performing. But it was his repertory that mattered most to them both. Roland devoured her library. He took extensive notes on her suggestions and studied the composers' styles, including those of Brahms, Bach, Beethoven, Schubert, Schumann, and Hugo Wolf. They also studied the styles of great Italian masters such as Claudio Monteverdi and Baldassare Galuppi. Roland had a particular fondness for reading with the countess about George Frideric Handel and Joseph Haydn. He absorbed the stories about the composers' lives and the contexts in which they produced their bodies of work, and in later years he required of his voice students the same type of study of composers' backgrounds.

Bertha suggested small but effective performance practice devices, such as elongating or doubling the consonants on certain words – for example, the L in *Liebe* (love) in German lieder – to heighten the dramatic impact of the song.[1] Day by day, Bertha helped Roland expand his musical knowledge and opened avenues for him to approach his singing authoritatively.[2]

Sometime in July, they took a break. At Bertha's invitation, Roland joined her for tea at the Colloredo castle in Zbiroh, a town some twenty miles outside of Prague. Her husband, Count Hieronymus, received him cordially, giving him a tour of the grand salons and the surrounding woods. After tea, with the couple and their friends and neighbors,

Roland sang for the gathering. Hieronymus warmly congratulated him on the performance, but Roland coolly insisted that it was not he who deserved the credit but the spirit within him. An awkward standoff between the two followed as Hieronymus retorted that Roland was just being modest, and the tenor with equal persistence held to his position that any praise should go to that spirit. Bertha's circumspect recollection of the exchange was simply, "He really thought that God could occupy him personally so that he could do that. . . . Roland really considered himself to be a sort of vibrating column."[3]

Bertha was not put off by his mysticism. In the black race, specifically in Roland, she found an exceptional sincerity and spiritual capacity that, in her view, white people lacked.[4] Might the blending of the "old aristocracy of one race and the innate genius of the other create a new and better society?" she wondered.[5] For Bertha, the notion slowly ripened into an obsession to forge that blend. "The purpose was to bring a new light to humanity," she would say later.[6]

When she and Roland parted for the summer, she could not imagine their relationship ending. Not only had they completed the arduous task of preparing and polishing the three programs, but also they had blended at a deeper, more spiritual level. Later, she remembered declaring, "We must do something together."[7]

On August 9, 1924, with his ambitious fall programs prepared, Roland returned to the United States, departing from Le Havre on the SS *Paris*. Prince Tovalou had joined him for the voyage. Roland expected Tovalou to continue traveling with him on tour, giving occasional lectures arranged with the help of the NAACP. Earlier in the year, Roland had written to Alain Locke that the prince would be coming with him to the United States when he returned and that Tovalou was interested in lecturing about the African continent. Locke replied to Roland's letter while he was performing in Berlin and said that he was prepared to assist Prince Tovalou with securing lecture engagements, to the extent they could be arranged.[8]

Arriving in New York on August 15, Roland and Tovalou parted, with Roland expecting that they would reconnect soon. But he didn't hear from Tova., And what he heard of him from friends was vaguely disconcerting.[9] Word was that Tova had formed an alliance with Marcus

Garvey and the United Negro Improvement Association (UNIA). In fact, he was the "star attraction" at the UNIA's 1924 convention, where he proposed a formal alliance between the Garvey movement and his organization, la Ligue universelle pour la defense de la race noire.[10] Writing to Joseph Salmon, among others, Roland implied that he felt used by the prince, because in addition to Locke, Roland had also written to W. E. B. Du Bois soliciting engagements for the prince.[11] Ultimately, this now committed and dedicated Pan-Africanist prince may have become too political for the tenor's comfort. Roland had a clear following among white America, and the perception of him being openly affiliated with black nationalists like Garvey or Prince Tovalou would have hurt his image among his core supporters.[12] Roland was finding that it was one thing to be linked to someone as outspoken and radical as Tovalou in Europe and quite another in America. Nonetheless, Roland continued to admire Robert Broadhurst and W. E. B. Du Bois, who, in contrast to Prince Tovalou, were more acceptable cohorts.

Roland had little time to dwell on the matter. He retreated to Nantucket Island, where he had an extended stay. Howard Jordan, his personal assistant, joined him to take care of the pending business. It was from there that Roland wrote to Russian impresario J. Borkon in Berlin to inform him that in the future he required no less than eight hundred dollars (and up to one thousand dollars) per European concert. Borkon immediately responded that the price was too high for that market, but Roland had already been through that exercise with his agents Robert Leigh Ibbs and John Tillett a few years earlier and was not ready to compromise.[13] William Brennan and George Judd also contacted Roland on the island regarding William Lawrence's fee for the upcoming season. The experienced accompanist, validated by having performed with Roland throughout Europe (including the pivotal Berlin recital), argued that he should be receiving one hundred dollars per concert, but Brennan was not prepared to go that high and instead offered him seventy-five dollars per concert. Once again, he sent Lawrence a "take the offer or we will find someone else" letter, and once again, Lawrence conceded at the eleventh hour, although not without some bitterness.[14]

Roland was heading out for the tour season when he learned that his former accompanist Daisy Tapley was seriously ill. Her domestic partner, Minnie Brown, had written to him on Daisy's behalf, telling him that Daisy was in St. Luke's Hospital in Harlem. Her condition prevented her from all but signing her name, so the letters to Roland were being dictated to Minnie. Roland was so fond of Daisy that for some time he had been sending her a monthly allowance.[15] He assumed complete financial responsibility for her hospital stay as her condition worsened. In a letter that Daisy dictated to Minnie from the hospital, she asked Roland if he would continue to "help" Minnie if Daisy should "pass on." Roland eventually visited her at St. Luke's Hospital late in November while he was performing in New York.[16]

In addition to Daisy's troubles, other nagging problems persisted. Borkon, who was still dealing with issues back in Europe, was constantly bickering with Roland to lower his fee. Roland began communicating with Jaromir Zid about taking over his future German and possibly other European concert appearances.[17] Borkon discovered the communications between the two and complained to Roland that it was *he* who had introduced the tenor to the Berlin public with such spectacular results.[18] Somehow, Roland got the word out that he was not under the exclusive representation of any continental European management, because other promoters and agencies began approaching him about continental representation. At least five concert promoters sought the opportunity to handle Roland's career in Europe, and he seemed not to have discouraged any of it. He was content to let them all fight it out to see who emerged as the victor – which meant the one who could present him with the most lucrative terms. Even Borkon's assistant, Conrad Dwerthon, broke from his employer and set up his own agency with the aim of poaching Roland from Borkon.[19]

Throughout December 1924, Roland continued providing for Daisy, who was still in the hospital. Dictating to Minnie and calling him by the nickname she had given him, "Ro," Daisy told the tenor that she would need a little more for the month of December because of gas and telephone expenses. She also reminded him that he had once told her to "pass [her] worries" to him. In her own unsteady handwriting, she scribbled, "Yours lovingly – Daisy."[20]

Also in December, Roland was immersed in a family drama with his cousins Alzada Mann and her younger sister Alma, who had developed a crush on Roland. Alma Mann turned nineteen in 1924 when she began communicating with her celebrated cousin. Having completed public school in Detroit, Alma returned to Chattanooga with the hope of attending Fisk University. She was initially wait-listed with a possible admission the following fall, but Roland used his connections with the president to facilitate her fall 1924 admission.[21] Her early letters depict a young lady smitten with the celebrity of an older family member. Arriving at Fisk, Alma began to appreciate the significance of Roland's reputation at the institution and became all the more intrigued with his fame. The fact that they were related seemed to have enhanced *her* reputation at the school. A letter from Alma to Roland dated December 26, 1924, provides the strongest evidence that she had romantic feelings for him. Roland had given a Christmas concert on the campus and afterward paid a visit to Alma, who had elected not to go home that year for the holiday. In part she said, "I felt so badly over the thought of you leaving me so soon I could not say anything when you left. I went upstairs and cried until about 2 'o clock." Alma asked Roland for his photograph and signed her letter with an unambiguous "I love you – Alma."[22] The other Mann sisters, including Alzada, were definitely aware of Alma's feelings for Roland and wrote to tell him so. Roland, the financier of Alma's university education, and Alma kept communicating with one another for the next two years, but none of the letters were quite as intense as the one of December. Roland eventually sent his wayward nephew Felton to Fisk, and he and Alma became acquainted with each other, though in the end, neither of them graduated.

Early in January 1925, Daisy was expecting to get a call from Roland, which did not come. He was immersed in work. By the middle of the month, he had presented his three separate programs that he and Bertha had prepared in Europe. The third program was probably the least demanding, vocally:

I.	Nimm mich dir zu eigen hin (Take me to thee for thine own)	Bach
	"Cara selve," from *Atalanta*	Handel
II.	Die Mainacht (That May Night)	Brahms
	Erhebung (Exaltation)	Schoenberg
	Für Musik (For Music)	Franz

III.	In a Myrtle Shade	Griffes
	I Know a Hill	Whelpley
	In the Silence of Night	Rachmaninoff

IV.   NEGRO SPIRITUALS

The "spirituals," like no other songs in form and content, shine as pure gold, bearing a strange kinship to old masters like Bach, as though they were merely repeating a familiar message in new words.

I've Got a Home in That Rock	Arranged by Roland Hayes
Hail the Crown	Arranged by Avery Robinson
New Born Again	Arranged by Heilman
You Hear de Lambs a-Cryin'?	Arranged by Roland Hayes

Although the third recital was announced as his last in the city for the season, New York wanted more of Roland Hayes.[23] *Musical America*'s review of his January 16 recital described his style and singing with the usual flattering adjectives, making special note of his effective employment of *messa di voce* and pianissimo singing, even though the reviewer felt he could improve the "quality of his full-voice upper tones which had a touch of forcing and throatiness."[24] The positive comments about his portrayal of Brahms's achingly beautiful yet pensive "Die Mainacht" were especially meaningful to Roland. It was among the lieder that he had worked on with Bertha the summer before. Accompanying him at the keyboard, she had been profoundly touched by Roland's interpretation of the wrenching final phrase, "Und die einsame Thräne Bebt mir heißer die Wang' herab!" (The lonely tear flows trembling, burning, down my cheek). It turned out that Brennan's three-program scenario was a brilliant stroke.

A few weeks after his solo recital in January 1925, Roland returned to New York as the featured soloist with the visiting Boston Symphony Orchestra. Pierre Monteux had ended his tenure with the elite organization in 1924, and the orchestra's new music director, Serge Koussevitzky, was now in command of the podium and holding the conductor's baton.

In the audience to see her old friend and colleague on the New York stage was Minnie Brown. Backstage after the concert, Minnie and Roland reminisced about how far he had come since the two of them and Daisy and Harry Burleigh had performed as the "*Elijah* quartet" a decade earlier. Weakened and still bedridden at St. Luke's Hospital, Daisy sent her congratulations to Roland in a letter dated January 30, 1925.

My Dear Ro:

To think that after all my hopes of what you would do in N.Y. with the Boston Symphony, I wasn't able to see you. That hurts worse than anything for it has always been my ambition to see you walk out there and do your best. But Minnie told me all about it and I feel that I know just about what happened. So all I can do is to congratulate you. I'm sorry for your cold and hope that you will recover soon. I feel just a little bit sad to know that you were right in our midst and yet I cannot see you. Today was such a beautiful day. I felt that with your car and the beautiful sunshine that you would surely be induced to come out and get a little fresh air. And that meant you would step up in this way, however you know best. I received your letter and check last night after Minnie came from the concert. Many many thanks, my dear. You know how I appreciate it. I don't know what in the world I would have done if God hadn't raised you up to look after me. [Unintelligible] for I am, as you know, absolutely dependent upon you. I can only say Thank God, for such a friend. Be good, take care of yourself until I can see you.

Continued success,
With all my love,
Daisy[25]

Six days later on February 5, 1925, Daisy Robinson Tapley died at age forty-two of ovarian cancer.[26] As Daisy was "absolutely dependent" on Roland financially, he also paid for her funeral, which was well attended by many of New York's musical elite, including her estranged husband.

Roland managed to reach out to those who had assisted or befriended him in the past. In addition to Daisy Tapley, he also assisted his first voice teacher from Chattanooga, Arthur Calhoun. Calhoun had moved to New York and set up a moderately successful music studio on Seventh Avenue. He advertised himself as "Concert Pianist, Organist and Choir Master of Union Baptist Church" as well as the "Musical Director of the S. Coleridge-Taylor Society." In early 1925 Calhoun had consistent nosebleeds, which required minor surgery. Roland paid the bill, and Calhoun expressed his eternal gratitude to his former student and wished him well with his upcoming recital, which the tenor was scheduled to give at Calhoun's alma mater, Oberlin.[27]

Roland's generosity stopped abruptly, however, when it came to his performance fees. Asked by Howard University's president, Dr. J. Stanley Durkee, to do a regional tour of Coleridge-Taylor's *Hiawatha's Wedding Feast* with the school's choir, directed by his early advocate and one-time supporter Lulu Vere Childers, he declined, claiming a scheduling conflict.[28] Plainly, the enterprise was not expected to raise large sums of money, which translated to Roland as a low fee. He also turned down a similar benefit request from his friend Walter White of the NAACP by saying that he would be out of the country or by giving some other evasive reason for not being available.

However gratifying, these types of engagements paid little or nothing. And Roland Hayes had moved on. The February 27 issue of the Northern California–based weekly the *San Francisco Call* published an extensive interview in which he stated that while he was of African descent, his art transcended race.[29] In the same interview, he also dismissed the idea of appearing in an opera because "the scenery, the competition of many voices, the orchestra, the mixture of so many mediums of expression" got in the way of what Roland called "pure art."[30] Although opera roles were suggested to the tenor, he may have still been influenced by the advice of his teachers Jennie Robinson and Arthur Hubbard, who had discouraged him from following such a path. At this point in his career, his annual salary rivaled, if not surpassed, many of the great singers appearing at the Metropolitan and other international companies.

On March 26, Roland appeared at Carnegie Hall with the New York Symphony Orchestra to perform Bach's *St. Matthew Passion* and several orchestrated spirituals. At the helm was the legendary Maestro Bruno Walter. Walter had an even bigger name than Pierre Monteux and was generally recognized as one of the greatest living conductors at the time. Not only had Walter been a colleague of Richard Strauss, he had also assisted Gustav Mahler. The preeminent maestro was so touched by Roland's performance of the Bach that he proposed future orchestral performances to Roland. No further proof was needed that Roland Hayes had arrived.

In early April, Roland boarded the SS *Aquitania* once more with Howard Jordan. William Lawrence was missing, most probably over a contract dispute. In any event, Eduardo Gendron, the principal accompanist of the celebrated Spanish cellist Pablo Casals, had stepped in for the tenor. Gendron was affable, based in Paris, and, most important, available and able to play whatever the tenor put before him at the keyboard. The fact that Gendron was fluent in Spanish proved to be an advantage in Spain, their immediate destination.[31]

Borkon had not given in to the competition in Europe. The seasoned impresario had pleaded with Roland to consider the European economic climate and accept that it was too difficult to meet the eight hundred dollars per concert fee demand. But for the dates in Spain, Borkon had thrown up his hands, leaving Roland to finalize the arrangements himself for appearances in Madrid, Barcelona, and Toledo.[32] There, Roland had begun enforcing his new policy – his fee in U.S. currency in advance of his appearance. His initial engagement was with the Sociedad Filarmonica de Madrid in late April. The highlight was a private recital for the Queen Mother, Maria Christina, the sexagenarian descendant of the Hapsburg dynasty who had heard about Roland from Britain's Queen Mary.[33] With great courtesy, the Queen Mother presented him with a diamond stickpin. She said she was especially impressed with his interpretation of Bach and Schubert and with his African American spirituals.[34] Roland was somewhat embarrassed to discover that his rigid fee stipulation for his appearance with the Sociedad Filarmonica had been required of an organization under the direct sponsorship of the Queen Mother.

For close to a month after his Madrid performance, Roland stayed on in the Spanish countryside, where Countess Bertha joined him.[35] They had planned the rendezvous after he received an alarming letter from her while he was touring. "We must have a child together," she declared. Not waiting for a response, she burst into his room in the concert hall to confirm that he had gotten the letter and understood what she was proposing. To say that he was overwhelmed would have been an understatement.[36] In fact, it is hard to imagine that he was not terrified. If the public knew of the countess's intentions, it could destroy his career.[37] Yet, Bertha had been his artistic muse, his "revealer of wonders," and "his comfort." Apart from that, he had become totally enthralled, if not enchanted, by her. Bertha had fulfilled her commitment to him by helping him to reach his "intellectual and musical maturity."[38] The proof of her impact on his artistic development was undeniable. He had sung with major orchestras and with some of the world's most renowned conductors. Her rationale for what she proposed was that by taking on the immense sacrifice implicit in having a child together, she would be sanctifying their relationship, not to mention fulfilling her destiny in bringing about a new world order by "blending the races."[39] Certainly, no one understood better than Roland the implicit risk in what the countess proposed. The idea of an African American man having a child with a married woman of the old European aristocracy in 1924 was daunting, to say the least.[40] The implications for his carefully crafted career, which was nearing its peak, were obvious. Yet, he felt helpless to deny her wish, to say nothing of his own desire.

"It wasn't something rash that a silly young girl might do," Bertha explained.

> I was almost forty. Nusl [her pet name for Hieronymus] and I hadn't been living as man and wife for some time, though he still loved me very much. I had married him because I didn't want his great family line to die out. I was certain he wouldn't have another chance with somebody else. . . . But now our sons were grown up. I was ready for something more than having teas with old ladies and playing bridge . . . yes, a new mission, a new sacrifice.[41]

She escaped to meet Roland in Spain on the pretext of attending a special performance of Wagner's *Tristan und Isolde* in Berlin. "[Nusl] didn't mind my going," Bertha explained. "He didn't want to hear Wagner. When I came back, there was no enormous emotion."[42] A few months later, she told her husband that she had conceived Roland's child. Count Hieronymus was furious but perhaps not altogether surprised. Acting through a family intermediary, he offered the following arrangement: a divorce during her pregnancy and then a quick remarriage after the birth of the child to ensure that he or she would not be able to make claims on the vast Colloredo-Mansfeld estate. There was a good reason for the legal position – one of Hieronymus's grandchildren remains today the largest single landholder in the Czech Republic as well as owner of vast tracts of forests in Austria. For a dreamer like Bertha, however, the offer was unacceptable. She insisted that her husband maintain the public facade of their union at all costs. In the end, Hieronymus agreed. He had no desire to ever permanently separate from his wife.

After completing his time in Spain with Bertha, Roland returned to Germany, where Borkon had tentatively conceded and agreed to his fee requirement. Roland was also hopeful that his interlude with the countess would never be exposed. But he ran right into trouble of a different kind, once more with Borkon.[43] Roland, accompanist Leo Rosenek, and valet Howard Jordan arrived at the Philharmoniesaal in Berlin for that evening's performance, but there was no Borkon – and no advance fee. Roland had by this time decided how to deal with situations like this. He simply waited in his dressing room, well past the start time of his recital. Borkon eventually arrived and angrily said, "So? You keep the public waiting, do you?"

"It is you who are keeping them waiting," Roland protested. "I will give you five minutes to pay me my money. After that time I shall go back to my hotel."[44]

After some more heated words, Borkon realized that Roland would not budge on this issue. Roland made good on his threat. He had Howard Jordan gather their things, and he and Rosenek returned to their hotel rooms.

Borkon went before the audience to tell them that the tenor had refused to appear because he had not been paid in advance.[45] Hoping to deflect the audience's frustration, the impresario blamed Roland for the delay in the concert. But it was a miscalculation. An audience member demanded that Borkon immediately pay the singer what he was due and bring him back to the theater. Others began hissing and hooting at Borkon to bring Roland back, which, a few hours later, he did. Roland took note of the headlines the following day: "The Naughty Negro Who Would Not Sing until He Heard the Money Ringing in the Till"[46] was one of the least flattering, but there were also editorials supporting his action, saying that he had good reason to stand up for his rights.[47] He had no intention of backing down on his business style.

Riding on the momentum of the successful season, Roland toured Italy for the first time and returned to England for several engagements, including one that he had attempted to cancel in Oxford before winding down in France. He spent the rest of the summer there, enjoying friends, as far as the public record was concerned. But privately he was preparing himself for the news of Bertha's pregnancy with his child and the possible fallout that might come from his situation, if it became public. In August he bought a chateau in the Seine-et-Oise section of Paris, once owned by Henry IV and the former residence of Gabrielle d'Estrées, the king's mistress and political adviser.[48] The chateau fit his grand plan for cultivating other singers once he retired. It also placed him strategically near the countess, where they could meet privately.

While Roland was spreading his message in Europe, his business interests in America were being looked after by Henry Putnam, among others, and his official address was still his mother Fannie's 8 Arnold Street, Boston. Roland had attempted to buy an apartment in New York, but he was persuaded by Putnam (as well as by the all-white co-op board) to look elsewhere. Putnam scouted in Framingham and other locations in the greater Boston area and finally came up with a prospect in Brookline. The house in question had been owned by a Civil War hero, General Russell. His daughter, Mary Russell, was all too pleased to sell the house at 58 Allerton Street to Roland.[49] It would be his primary residence for the rest of his life.

By mid-September, Roland could see that William Brennan had put the finishing touches on the next tour. Once again, William Lawrence's fee was going to be an issue. Finally it was agreed that Lawrence be paid one hundred dollars per concert. Further, he would be compensated if there was any break longer than two weeks. That way he was guaranteed a steady income.[50] Beyond Lawrence's compensation, there had been other contractual shifts. For the first time, Roland agreed to accept a percentage of the house's take for certain recitals. In some cases, he was guaranteed a minimum of one thousand dollars (of a 60/40 split, for example). Brennan and Judd sent Roland a list of the fees for the various concerts, including those that had some percentage arrangement attached to them. Most significant, two important orchestral appearances were scheduled in the United States, an appearance with the Philadelphia Symphony Orchestra with the legendary maestro Leopold Stokowski and a return performance with the BSO with its new conductor, Serge Koussevitzky.

Roland returned to the United States in October. By early November, he was on the road again with William Lawrence and Howard Jordan. They made stops in the major markets like Boston, New York, Washington, Baltimore, Chicago, and Philadelphia and in places like Lynchburg, Virginia; Worcester, Massachusetts; Wichita, Kansas; and Evanston, Illinois.[51] The year culminated with Stokowski and the Philadelphia Symphony Orchestra. The performances on December 26 and 28 were familiar repertory for Roland. He sang the Mozart concert aria K. 209, "Si mostra la sorte," which had become something of his signature aria with orchestra, and the three spirituals "Sit Down," "Heaven," and "Deep River." The reviews of his appearance with the orchestra were spectacular.[52]

Stokowski was at ease with Roland, who had now performed with several of the world's greatest living conductors, including Bruno Walter, Gabriel Pierné, and Pierre Monteux. He would perform with several others in short order, although never again with the legendary "Stoki." It is not clear why.

Riding on the tide of his Philadelphia triumph, Roland moved north to New York's Carnegie Hall for another solo recital with predictable results: "Roland Hayes, the gifted colored tenor, gave his second recital of the season in Carnegie Hall last night and again packed the house to the doors."[53] Triumph after triumph, Roland Hayes's work was being heralded. His final engagement of the year was at the home of his former employer Walton L. Crocker, the president of John Hancock Insurance Company. Hayes agreed to give the concert for the special fee of one thousand dollars, half of his usual fee, in recognition of the support that he had once received from the president.[54] By the end of 1925, he was recognized as one of the greatest tenors in the world.

Roland and Bertha's daughter, Maria Dolores Franzyska Kolowrat-Krakowsky, soon to be known as "Maya," was born at 2:00 AM on February 12, 1926, in a private clinic in Basel, Switzerland. Roland was in Boston awaiting the news.[55] He felt no less overwhelmed than he had been since Bertha's proposal. At the height of his emotional turmoil, he had even intimated to Bertha that the child might not be his. His response to Bertha's telegram announcing their daughter's birth was more resigned than paternal. "Truth is supreme, am going on in silence and solitude," was her recollection of his responding telegram.[56]

The birth also left Bertha ambivalent. "I only wanted to bring that child into the world to prove one can have perfection just as well in black as any other way," she explained.[57] She had been certain that she would have yet another son after having already produced four for Hieronymus.

With the birth of a girl, she had to modify her expectations. "Of course, it ought to have been a boy, not a girl," she openly admitted. "I wanted to give it to [Mahatma] Gandhi to be properly raised so he could make his mark on the world. But a girl? Impossible! Not in those days."[58]

Three months later, a birth registration document was issued in Switzerland that declared that by judgment of a civil tribunal in Prague on May 5, 1926, the daughter of Bertha Henriette Katharina Nadine, born the Countess Kolowrat-Krakowsky, was illegitimate.[59] Despite his initial misgivings, Roland accepted that Maya was his daughter and began making plans to adopt her and bring her back to the United States to be raised.[60] Roland's European lawyer and confidant, Dr. Edward Coumont, assisted him in having affidavits and other legal instruments drawn up to facilitate the "adoption." Roland also gave Bertha three thousand dollars before returning to the United States, where he then obtained the necessary declarations and instruments from the Commonwealth of Massachusetts to implement a foreign adoption.[61]

"Bring me a queen!" Fannie used to admonish Roland (and her other sons). "If you marry a white girl, boy, bring me a queen. Otherwise, stay in your own race."[62] With the highborn Countess Colloredo-Mansfeld, Roland found himself at a crossroads that Fannie could not have anticipated or imagined. By the early fall of 1926, as he was preparing to return to the United States for his 1926–27 touring season, newspapers in Europe (and eventually in the United States) had begun printing stories about the "engagement" of Roland and the countess. German and Austrian papers like *Stünde* and *Die Präger Tagblatt* were among the European periodicals that published such stories. In the United States, well-established news organizations such as the *Chicago Tribune,* the *New York Times, Time* magazine, and, not surprisingly, several African American papers, including the Baltimore *Afro-American,* began reporting on the sensational affair between Roland Hayes and the countess.

This raised the ante on Bertha and Roland. He had an international musical career that could be irrevocably damaged. Bertha's reputation was already compromised, and she now stood the real possibility of losing any future contact with her sons.

Attempting damage control, Bertha asked Roland's lawyer, Edward Coumont, to intervene:

Zuoz, Engadin
Villa Alpina
10 November 1926.
Dear Dr. Coumont,

The article published on November 7th in the "Stünde" and on the same day in
the "Präger Tagblatt" about the projected marriage of Mr. Roland Hayes with me
forces me to apply to you as his legal advisor with the request to rectify [deny]
this news at once and I think the following text the most suitable in its brevity
and avoidance of names.

> My client, Mr. Roland Hayes, requests me contradict most emphatically
> the news spread with sensational comments by the different Viennese and
> foreign newspapers, of this forthcoming marriage with a lady of the former
> Austrian aristocracy.

signed Dr. Eduard Coumont

I should ask you to insert the following article in the most widely circulated
trash newspapers such as the "Stünde" and the "Präger Tagblatt" too.

The forthcoming or proposed marriage of Mr. Roland Hayes.

We are specially informed as follows: The news which reaches us from
different newspapers of the forthcoming marriage of the Negro Tenor,
Roland Hayes, well known in Europe, with a lady of the former Austrian
aristocracy who presumably for this reason recently got her divorce, does
not at all correspond with the facts and is most emphatically denied from
well informed quarters.

In the same article Roland Hayes is said to be descended from an
Abyssinian emperor.

He stands in no need of such sensational advertisement. Whoever knows
Mr. Roland Hayes as a man and as an artist knows that he without this
unfounded imperial descent belongs to that company of noble mind and
heart which is alas only too rare both in the white and coloured race.

I beg you to do your utmost to remove the point[ed] and hateful sensa-
tionalism from the matter [and] as far as possible to do [so] today.

He [Roland] cabled me yesterday before I had the Viennese article in my
hands, that an article dated November 7th Vienna, had already been published
in America. What these people over there are doing is boundless in its consequences. White people as well as black will be indignant at this attempt to break
through the "colour-line," and we can do nothing else than deny. I telegraphed
Mr. Hayes today that I had placed the matter in your hands and I would beg you
to keep me informed as to the course of things, likewise if you should require my
information or a stronger dementi [denial]. Above all things, his position and

mission must be protected. Could not the Viennese dementi be published in the American papers too?

I would beg you to treat my letter in the strictest confidence.

I am with my highest esteem,
Gfin. Colloredo-Mansfeld m.p.[63]

The countess also asked Coumont to run interference with her mother, the elder Countess Kolowrat-Krakowsky:

Zuoz
28th November 1926
Dear Dr. Coumont,

If my mother, Countess Kolowrat, or any other member of my family should apply to you in order to get the address of Mr. Hayes in America I beg you on no account to publish [send] it.

With my highest esteem
Gfin. Colloredo-Mansfeld m.p.[64]

Edward Coumont (and perhaps Roland as well) suggested that the countess write a denial of a pending marriage, but in a November 20 letter she concluded:

1) I do not wish my name to be published in anyway whatever in the newspapers again as I have already expressed in the form of dementi and,
2) I do not bind myself by any written or printed word.
As you will without difficulty understand my family, along with whom I am fighting a hard struggle to keep my children in some way or other would take such a public declaration on my part as a binding word and of that there can be no question.[65]

Despite struggling to keep all her children, Bertha refused to make a public statement, which her family might interpret as binding, that she would leave Roland. In her private comments to Coumont, Bertha was unequivocal that there was not even the slightest chance of that happening.

Yet gossip about the affair persisted. In the January 8, 1927, Baltimore *Afro-American,* a cartoon strip parodied Roland and the countess's relationship. In the first panel, white women fight in the streets of Vienna to get in a concert hall where the tenor is to sing. In the second, they swoon over Roland onstage.[66] The third displays the countess with a love arrow in her heart, totally smitten with the tenor. The caption below the image reported that she sat at Hayes's feet while he sang in her castle. In the fourth, Roland and the countess walk arm in arm with a beaten and dejected Hieronymus seated at the top of a staircase. The final panel has Roland imagining himself in a crown as emperor.

Time magazine and other journals eventually retracted their reports of the engagement. Meanwhile, Roland and Bertha tried to make the best of their new reality: "As tired as I was after an exacting tour at home or abroad on the Continent, I found it so exciting to spend long weeks working with my friend, during the late months of summer and early fall, that I was able each winter, from 1924 to 1930, [to] take up my work in America as fresh as a cucumber."[67] That was Roland's public pronouncement in his biographical narrative. While the truth was not as simple or rosy, life could have been much harder for the lovers.

Actually, Roland and Bertha had spent long weeks working together in Prague during the summer of 1924. Now they met at Roland's St. Germain villa or traveled together on the Continent. Despite his humiliation, Hieronymus continued to provide for Bertha. As part of the agreement for their quiet separation, he bought her an impressive chateau in southern France in the village of St. Lary, not far from the Spanish border at the foot of the Pyrenees, and paid for its extensive renovations. He also provided Bertha with a generous lifelong monthly stipend, continued by their eldest son after Hieronymus's death during World War II.

Each year after Maya's birth, Bertha reunited with Hieronymus for a week or so at their eldest son's Austrian country retreat, and the two never spoke of what had transpired between them. They acted as if they were a normal, long-married couple sleeping apart in front of the household help.[68] This annual charade continued until 1938, when the political tensions leading up to World War II made international travel increasingly difficult. As for Bertha's mother, the elder Countess Kolowrat-Krakowsky, she visited St. Lary several times and likewise never broached the subject of her daughter's scandalous involvement with the African American singer. But she could not entirely hide her feelings. "Your mother doesn't love me," the three-year-old Maya confided to Bertha in a brooding voice reminiscent of Roland's on the first such visit. "I can see it in her eyes," the young girl said.[69]

Despite Roland's assertion that his summer weeks with the countess left him "as fresh as a cucumber," their relationship was not without tensions or even high drama. Bertha's view of their time together was hardly as one-dimensional as Roland's. She had entered into the relationship with the readiness to sacrifice for a higher cause, and while she had expected the rift with her family and the resulting public scandal, she had not bargained for the additional trauma resulting from trying to merge the lives of these two strong-minded individuals from vastly different backgrounds.

As part of her cause to remove racial barriers, the countess was eager to travel openly with Roland and withstand being "humiliated even in the advanced countries . . . [that] looked upon us as a pair of curious beasts."[70] She organized her life around their "cause," retaining a Swiss governess for Maya so that she would be free to join Roland whenever he might need her. Roland, however, was not quite so committed. He continued to harbor fears about how *their* "cause" might affect *his* career. He pointed out to Bertha that she had come from a milieu where she had always had everything and could not understand what it meant to have had nothing. On their trips together, he preferred that they eat alone in their hotel room. "Roland also had this tremendous jealousy, a tremendous jealousy of everything I did, of everybody I spoke to, against every newspaper I read," Bertha explained. In exasperation, she concluded that "the cause" seemed to be for her "to be locked up in a closet while everybody comes to see him and talk to him."[71]

According to Bertha, Roland "didn't think that it was possible that a woman of my standing, of my capacity, of my beauty at that time, could submit to him and his ideas."[72] The only way he could rationalize their physical relationship was that the countess was no less easy in bestowing her favors on others. He suspected her intentions with every man she spotted with her curious, roving eye. He had at one point even expressed his suspicion that she might have had an affair with his accompanist William Lawrence.[73]

Roland's jealousy, or more probably his insecurity, about this relationship produced situations that could sometimes be comical. On one occasion when the countess accompanied Roland to a tailor shop in Paris, she became intrigued by another customer, an Indian officer in uniform who happened to be picking his nose. "It was astonishing that he could have a finger in his nose," Bertha recounted. As soon as they left the shop and got into a taxi, Roland flew into a rage. "You were looking at that Indian with wide eyes," Bertha recalled his ranting. "You're so unconscious. You don't know yourself what you are doing. That drives me mad."[74] His uncontrollable temper occasionally resulted in physical violence, and he once gave Bertha a black eye. Stoically, she had herself photographed in that condition as a reminder of her commitment to their cause.

"I was the last person who would deceive him," Bertha explained. "It was such an awful struggle never to know whether he believed me. Sitting there for hours, not speaking a word, only ruminating in this awful, awful jealousy. . . . On the other hand, he was so extremely cultivated that one couldn't imagine he could be as silly as that. It was something like a cancer on his mind." But no matter how punishing Roland's rage, Bertha never held such behavior against him, explaining, "I knew I was only paying the price for what our race had done to the blacks."[75]

Bertha would have represented a formidable challenge for any man, not just for one of Roland's incomparably modest background. Her noble peers would have been no less liable to have misgivings or even cower at the prospect of what this striking, uninhibited woman might say or do next.[76] No matter how much she tried to accommodate Roland and subjugate herself to his will, Bertha's commanding presence left no doubt as to who was in charge. Indeed, she was willing to sacrifice, yet in the most important decision of all – to have a child – it was Bertha who had totally prevailed. In a way, she had used Roland for her own goals, which may have contributed to – or even been the underlying cause of – Roland's fury.[77]

During those summers between 1924 and 1930, Roland and the countess nevertheless continued to have a vibrant physical relationship. She loved the feel of his skin and "often watched him when he slept, those delicate hands covering his face." Moreover, through the sharing of their daily endeavors, she transformed Roland's life in some of the most fundamental ways. She formed his taste in furniture and food and introduced him even to such esoteric practices as astrology, numerology, and alchemy. With her, he embraced an intellectual companionship that he had never before experienced and probably never would again.[78]

EIGHT

The Conquest Slows

1926–1930

BY EARLY 1926, ROLAND'S SEASON WAS COMFORTABLY underway, and he was enjoying, once again, phenomenal reviews for his engagements. But the December 7, 1925, issue of *Time* magazine, a journal that had been favorably disposed to him in the past, questioned his artistry, implying his tremendous success was mostly due to the country's interest in African American music and asking whether Hayes would have achieved his current level of celebrity had he been white instead of a "Negro." The answer: it was "doubtful."[1] This reviewer, however, overlooked the fact that it was *Europe* that had propelled Roland to international stardom. Only after his conquest of Europe was he recognized as a great artist in his own country. But even after proving his musical skills in Western art music and scoring celebrity and fame throughout the Continent, Roland was still subjected to the greatest scrutiny and criticism in his home country.

Even though Roland was not the first African American to have had a notable career in art music in Europe, in the mid-1920s he was ahead of a relatively small group of prominent African American concert artists, including Marian Anderson and Paul Robeson. As such, Roland was expected by many to be a political symbol in matters involving race. The tenor had instinctively avoided political involvement in the United States before leaving for Europe. Even though he was befriended by several of the celebrated Pan-Africanists in the United Kingdom and France, had attended the historic Second Pan-African Congress in London in 1921, and had made friends with many NAACP leaders, most notably W. E. B. Du Bois and Walter White, he maintained a low political profile, especially at home. Events that took place in Baltimore in January 1926, however, shook him off of his apolitical fence and forced him to take a stand.

One of the most important civil rights issues of the period was confronting the wicked Jim Crow segregation laws. Such statutes required separate seating accommodations for whites and blacks. Born and raised a southerner, Roland had understood and accepted such arrangements as "just the way things were," going all the way back to his childhood. By 1926, however, Roland had been exposed to another way as a result of his international travels and high-profile contacts. His Pan-African friends in Europe, specifically, had enlightened him on the greatness of his continental African ancestors and the possibilities yet to come from that continent. Furthermore, Roland's receipt of the prestigious NAACP Spingarn Medal in 1924 had established his credentials as one of black America's leading race men. He had also moved north and made his home in Boston, where he found less overt racial animus. Yet, when it came to southern America (as well as certain midwestern and northern locations), segregation laws were not only entrenched but were rigorously enforced. With this reality, the publicly reserved Roland was generally not inclined to "rock" the segregation boat. Even with his recent celebrity, he still did not have the leverage – especially not in the South – to challenge the ironclad segregation rules of the 1920s, even if he were disposed to. Nonetheless, his artistic influence and integrity were put to the test in Maryland's most populated and racially diverse city.

On January 5, Roland had been booked by Mrs. Kate Wilson-Green, a highly respected concert promoter, to sing in the nation's capital at the Washington Auditorium, to be followed two days later by a concert in Baltimore's Lyric Theater.[2] She had presented the likes of Jascha Heifetz and Sergei Rachmaninoff, among other A-list artists, so she was quite capable of producing someone of Roland's caliber.

Wilson-Green had booked Roland in the respective venues at least six months prior to the scheduled concerts. It had been agreed that his Washington Auditorium concert would be integrated, but no such arrangement had been sanctioned, secured, or anticipated for his Lyric Theater engagement on January 7. That perceived slight was enough to attract the attention of the Baltimore *Afro-American*, which took up the issue and ran with it. Like other news outlets that primarily catered to

African American communities around the country, the *Afro-American* was in the forefront of challenging Jim Crow segregation wherever and whenever it could.

Roland's January 5 Washington recital was reviewed in the *Washington Daily American* the following day with the headline "Roland Hayes Given Ovation at Washington Auditorium: Colored People Scattered throughout Orchestra as Result of the Strenuous Protests against Attempted Segregation."[3] The January 6 edition of the *Washington Tribune* and *Daily Washington American* reported more enthusiastic reactions to the tenor's recital:

> Roland Hayes . . . delighted his hearers by his artistry, his dramatic expression and fine restraint in tone effects. . . . Throughout the evening the audience was most enthusiastic, and the applause at times amounted to an ovation.

> Roland Hayes Given Ovation at Washington Auditorium – Famous Tenor Stirs vast audience almost to point of frenzy with Wonderful Rendition of Negro Spirituals.

The reporter from the *Daily Washington American,* however, was less generous in discussing Roland's participation in Jim Crow segregation activity. When the *Tribune's* reporter attempted to seek Roland's opinion about his integrated Washington recital on the evening of the concert, the reporter said the tenor "feigned fatigue and referred him to his secretary – without results."[4] The singer obviously knew of the land mines that lay in wait were he to answer any questions related to his integrated audience in Washington, especially with the Baltimore engagement coming two days later. Anything said in Washington would easily be heard in Baltimore, just forty miles north. While in Washington, Roland and his accompanist, William Lawrence, chose to stay in a private residence as opposed to a hotel. This underscored his determination to avoid the press and any unwanted questions about his Washington concert.[5]

News of the "integrated" recital in the nation's capital of course reached Baltimore. Ominously, the city's black ministers and anti–Jim Crow demonstrators found Roland's dual standard outrageous. News of his refusal to speak with reporters also did not play well in the African American press. The Washington *Afro-American* (a branch of the Baltimore-based paper) ran a story confirming the incident.

Roland arrived at Baltimore's Penn Station and encountered a vociferous protest. There were calls for him to cancel his concert if it remained segregated, and demeaning names appeared on signs that read "Roland 'Uncle Tom' Hayes" and "Jim Crow Roland."[6] From their pulpits the Sunday before, several prominent African American Baltimore ministers denounced Roland's apparent willingness to sing before a Jim Crow audience in the city.[7] Rev. Dr. Ernest Lyons had said that no "self-respecting colored person" would pay to be "Jim Crowed."[8] Some ministers cited the lesser-known Hampton University conductor – and Canadian – R. Nathaniel Dett, who had refused to perform at a segregated auditorium in Washington, as an appropriate example.

Roland, his secretary,[9] and William Lawrence were once again lodging at a private residence, that of Baltimore physician Dr. Edward Wheatley and his wife, Laura, president of the Colored Parents Teachers Association and aspiring arts and concert promoter, but their stay at the Wheatleys' was anything but peaceful. The deluge of calls from reporters and anti–Jim Crow protesters led the family to temporarily disconnect their telephone. After some orchestrated delays, Roland agreed to meet with several area ministers, an *Afro-American* representative, and other prominent equal rights advocates at the Wheatleys' home the afternoon of his recital. Out of this meeting, it was agreed that he would wire his managers, William Brennan and George Judd, in Boston and ask them to cancel that evening's concert.

For reasons that are not fully clear, however, Roland dressed and readied himself to perform at the Lyric Theater that evening, where yet another obstreperous group of protesting African Americans were in wait. He endured a barrage of insults that made the protest at Penn Station the day before appear mild. Some who had withstood the bone chilling January weather for hours anticipating the tenor's arrival turned mean-spirited and spat at him while he entered the backstage entrance of the Lyric. As always, Roland was publicly dignified, even in the face of such treatment.

Waiting in the tenor's dressing room was the very nervous concert promoter, Kate Wilson-Green, who had arranged both the Washington and Baltimore recitals. When Roland refused to go through with the performance, describing what he had just endured in order to enter the concert hall, her desperate pleas quickly turned into tears as she begged the singer to go onstage. Roland was guaranteed at least one thousand dollars whether he performed or not, but she and the theater stood to lose much more if he canceled at the eleventh hour. The standoff took more than half an hour to resolve. Calmly, Roland walked onstage, followed by an anxious William Lawrence, and made an announcement with a quavering voice and shaking hands: "I may not be able to finish my program. And if I do not finish it, you will know why."[10]

Roland began his concert with the unscheduled arrangement of the "Crucifixion," for which he was well known. When he completed the work, the applause made clear he had the audience, with a few exceptions, on his side. He also sang Schubert's "Du bist die Ruh," which had once worked for him when he confronted the hostile Berlin audience nearly two years earlier.[11] But Baltimore in January 1926 was no Berlin. Roland had transformed those irate Germans' hisses and boos into adulation when he handily demonstrated his artistry and ability to master the music of *their* great composers. But the tenor's primary detractors that wintry Thursday night at Baltimore's Lyric Theater were his own people.

From an artistic standpoint, the concert was an unqualified success. However, various Baltimore readers and opinion makers who wrote to the *Afro-American* would not let the issue go away. Beginning with the January 9 edition of the weekly, the editorials and commentaries poured in. "Flay Roland Hayes for Jim Crow" was the headline of the early edition of the paper. Predictably, there were calls for him to return his Spingarn Medal, saying he had failed to stand up for the race on this crucial issue. An editorial in the January 9 *Afro-American* said African American restaurants should refuse to serve the singer, and if he wanted to eat, he could go to "Mrs. Wilson Green's kitchen for a meal."[12] An editorial one week later titled "'Rolling' Hayes" said that, despite his education at Fisk University in Tennessee as well as in New England, Roland was ultimately from rural Georgia, thus proving the old adage that it was easier to "take the man out of the country than it was to take the country out of the man."[13] The same editorial also decried Kate Wilson-Green, who had "ignorantly" declared that one part of the theater was as good as the other.[14] Some of Roland's white supporters who had attended his concert praised his bravery for singing under such difficult conditions and denounced his critics as unsophisticated troublemakers. Such callous remarks from whites (however well-meaning) only fueled this very volatile issue.

Eventually, the average *Afro-American* readers began weighing in. With the simple heading "'Afro' Readers Blame Roland Hayes for Lyric Jim Crow," more than twenty individual views were expressed, starting with Laura Wheatley, who had hosted Roland and his small entourage when they were in the city:

> Mr. Hayes was my house guest while in the city. The circumstance at the theater was most unfortunate. Mr. Hayes seemed really not to know that there was going to be any separation in the audience until he got to the theater. Had he known before, I believe he would not have sung. However, as matters stand his singing here has softened many of our enemies, has gained new friends for us and bound many of our old friends closer to us.
> Mrs. Laura D. Wheatley, 1230 Druid Hill Avenue[15]

> I think that Roland Hayes should not have sung before a segregated audience.
> Mrs. Mary Brown, 226 W. Chase Str.

> It is unfortunate for the colored people of the city that Roland Hayes performed before a separate audience.
> Mrs. Lula Richardson, 216 Dolphin Street

> Personally I feel Mr. Hayes committed no imposition upon his race in performing for a segregated audience inasmuch as he was engaged by the whites.
> Rev. J. J. Barnes, 553 W. Biddle Street

> Mr. Hayes was right in performing before a separate audience as his concerts are for monetary gain.
> David H. Parham, musician, 229 W. Hamburg Street

> Mr. Hayes should not have violated the integrity of his race for gold.
> William H. Brown, musician, 278 S. Mary Street

> Mr. Hayes committed a serious infringement against the integrity of his race in singing before a segregated audience.
> Milton Green, 1406 Myrtle Avenue[16]

An article in the following issue of the *Afro-American* stated that Roland heroically gave Kate Wilson-Green a piece of his mind while he delayed the concert. But many African American Baltimoreans believed that Roland in the end had taken his thirty pieces of silver and *sung.* The debate over Roland's performance that January continued in the *Afro-American* off and on for another three years.

Roland received several personal letters of support from his Fisk classmates as well as letters from those who did not know him express-ing their solidarity with his decision to perform. Stung by what he felt was totally unjust criticism, Roland refused to perform in the city for another seven years.

The Baltimore incident aside, Roland's overall reputation had not suffered greatly. He was still highly respected among Europeans and European Americans and remained the darling of the African American elite. Perhaps in response to the turmoil he had experienced in the press, he received an invitation from A'lelia Walker to rest at her estate outside of New York City, which she had inherited from her celebrated mother, Madam C. J. Walker. A'lelia had opened her home as a refuge for other artists such as Langston Hughes. Roland, however, had his secretary, Howard Jordan, politely decline the offer, with the excuse that the de-mands of his schedule would not permit such a luxury.[17]

In February 1926, Roland appeared again with the New York Sym-phony Orchestra with yet another celebrated European-born conduc-tor, Otto Klemperer, a Jewish maestro whose distinguished career as an opera and orchestral conductor in Germany had been cut short after the rise of the Nazi Party in Germany. Roland sang to a capacity audience of four thousand people.[18] The Rosenek-arranged spirituals were accompa-nied at the keyboard by William Lawrence. Following the accolades he received from the likes of the *New York Times,* Roland raised his base fee to $2,500 per engagement. The complaints that he, Brennan, and Judd received from such a fee request seem not to have fazed him. However, given Roland's reputation for delivering well-reviewed performances, concert managers and booking agents who wanted to engage him paid it.

As Roland neared the end of his 1925–26 tour, one of his last stops was in his hometown, Curryville. Now at the height of his career, the singer reflected on those who had played a role in his rise to fame. He contacted his former employer William Waterman about purchasing the Victrola Talking Machine, which had so inspired him in Nashville. Roland offered to buy Waterman a new machine in exchange for the original. In addition, Hayes had been contacted by the Georgia lawyer A. L. Henson, who had wanted the singer to establish a school for African American children in the Curryville area. He and Roland had discussed the possibility of the singer purchasing land for such a project, and it finally got underway later in 1926.

After several unqualified successes, Roland departed, once again, for Europe at the end of April. Prior to leaving, he was contacted by a familiar voice from his past, Duse Mohammed Ali – his friend, protector, concert promoter, and landlord from his early days in London. Ali had moved to the United States, had a brief but ultimately failed involvement with Marcus Garvey's UNIA, and had subsequently moved to Detroit, where he became president of the newly established Universal Islamic Society.[19] By April 1926, Duse Mohammed Ali and the Islamic Society were in financial stress. He appealed to Roland for immediate aid: "I require 50 pounds [two hundred and fifty dollars at the time] and I need it NOW!"[20] In his letter to the tenor, he bluntly reminded Roland of the times when he had been in need during his early London days and that it had been he, Ali, who came to his assistance. Now that their fortunes had dramatically reversed and Roland was at the height of his success, Ali expected reciprocity. Roland no doubt fulfilled the request, but after Duse Mohammed Ali's unashamedly demanding letter to the tenor, there was no further communication between the two men. Ali eventually returned to Africa. He was primarily based in Nigeria, where he edited another paper and continued staging and producing plays. He died in the country in 1945.

While on board the SS *Paris* out of New York for the port of Le Havre, France, Roland met the celebrated Metropolitan Opera soprano Frieda Hempel, who was at the height of her opera career. The singers dined with the Russian composer Sergei Rachmaninoff, who was also a passenger.[21]

When Roland arrived in France, spring was in full bloom and flowers seemed to be everywhere. It was his favorite time to visit in the country. He stayed for more than a week with his friends Edgar Raoul-Duval and his wife, Renée Vautier, the sculptor who had produced a well-known bust of him.[22] Hayes and the Duvals discussed their mutual yet wayward friend Prince Tovalou. Roland had advanced the prince some money for his U.S. tour, and Tovalou had apparently absconded with the funds and made no further communication. Edgar promised to write Tovalou's brother to see if Roland could recover his money.[23] After resting, Roland performed at the Salle de Conservatoire, but according to him the venue was too small for the number of people who showed up to hear him. His French manager, Charles Kiesgen, then informed him that there was a request for him to perform in Barcelona early in June. As usual, Roland held out until his fee request was met.[24]

He and French accompanist Eugene Wagner traveled to Barcelona, where they performed a recital on June 6. He also heard the Spanish singer Conchita Badia de Agusti, one of the great sopranos of the country and a celebrated interpreter of twentieth-century Spanish song. Roland then left Barcelona for Switzerland, where he found a little villa on the lake to rest for the summer.

Roland reported the Spanish engagement and his other social activities to William Brennan late in the summer. What he did not tell his American manager was that his time in Switzerland was no accident. There, back in February, Countess Bertha had given birth to his baby daughter, Maya, in a private clinic in the country. She was still there when Roland arrived. The three spent the summer in Switzerland as a family. Bertha helped Roland choose antique furniture for his recently purchased Brookline residence on Allerton Street. The two moved around quite openly in and near the Swiss capital. From every outward appearance, they were happy together. It was not surprising when news reports began surfacing of the couple being engaged. It was naive of both of them to think that they would not attract such attention.

In early September, however, Roland had to begin his fall season in Europe. He did a brief tour with the Tivoli Symphony Orchestra in Copenhagen under the direction of Frederik Schnedler-Petersen. He essayed for the first time the plaintive aria "Voglio dire al mio tesoro" (I would like to tell my beloved) from Handel's little-known opera *Partenope,* and the rest were standards that he had already performed, such as works by Berlioz and Mozart and the orchestral-arranged spirituals.[25] Roland had to reluctantly decline the opportunity to perform, once again, with Maestro Pierre Monteux in Amsterdam because he was already booked for several engagements in Germany.[26] The German dates were relatively close together, starting with Hamburg on September 17 and from there proceeding to Munich, Berlin, Leipzig, Vienna, and finally Zurich on October 13. He arranged for his final concert to be in Zurich so he would be with Bertha and baby Maya before leaving again.[27]

While in Vienna, a few papers made disparaging remarks about Roland and warned that the Viennese public should not be surprised to see black babies being rolled around in their strollers after the singer's departure.[28] While most of the public took such statements as gossip, the editorialist may have had specific knowledge of Roland, Bertha, and their child.

Three days after his final fall concert in Zurich, Roland boarded a ship to return home for his 1926–27 American season. The season got underway routinely, but as Roland worked his way south, there was a concert in his home state with heightened significance.

On December 20 he sang at the Municipal Auditorium in Rome, Georgia, sponsored by the Floyd Medical Dental and Pharmaceutical Association. The concert was booked as "'Roland Hayes' World Famous Negro Tenor." The advertising bill also stated, "Half of the auditorium is reserved for white people and the other half for colored people."[29] Roland received an affirmation for his concert from the Rome Chamber of Commission as well as from the city manager, S. S. King.[30] The city fathers rolled out the red carpet for their returning son, and the sponsors' payment of Roland's $2,500 fee most certainly made him feel good about this particular engagement.

During this trip, Roland traveled back to his mother Fannie's ten acres and to the ancestral home where she had been enslaved in the previous century. There he met once more with the elderly Joe Mann, the former owner of his ancestors, who at the time was poverty-stricken and in failing health. Mann's second wife's condition was more severe than his. In addition to meeting Mann and filling in the gaps of his personal family history, Roland informed the old man that he had purchased the land where his mother had once lived against her will and welcomed Mann and his sickly wife to stay on *his* land as nonpaying residents.

The irony of the proposed living situation for Mann and his wife could not have escaped the tenor. He was intending to maintain the enslaver of his beloved mother on the land where she, her immediate family, and her ancestors had once been held in bondage. The son of the once-enslaved Fannie would become, in a very real sense, the "master" of her former captor. Fate, however, intervened. Before Roland could formally take possession of the land, Joe Mann and his wife died. But Mann had not passed on before giving the singer the much-desired information he needed to start Angelmo (a contraction of "Angel Mother") Farm as a legacy and tribute to his late mother on the very land where she had been in servitude.

According to the tenor, Angelmo Farm was a place where "inspiration and talent and ambition of any kind among my own people (and yours, too, if any of them choose to come; the doors will never be closed), will be trained and given an outlet. . . . I do not aim at impressiveness in the buildings or equipment. All must be secondary to the quality or instruction dispensed. . . . It will not be done in a hurry. Such ideals as I have in mind are necessarily matters of slow growth."[31] When he was not touring, Roland increasingly spent time in Calhoun, Georgia, developing Angelmo Farm. His surviving brother, Robert Brante, moved to the area and managed the land and the necessary staff to work the six hundred acres.

The tenor envisioned Angelmo not only as a functioning farm but as a formal artists' colony. His good friend from the United Kingdom Robert Broadhurst (who had given Roland the "African" name "Cunjah") submitted a detailed architectural design of the proposed Georgia colony to Roland, including dormitories, a performing venue, and an elaborate garden for reflection and solitude.[32] In Broadhurst's letter to Roland, he asked him to send some kind of write-up about the purchase and establishment of Angelmo Farm so that he could have it mentioned in *West Africa Magazine* and broadcast over the radio in several African colonies on the continent. This, Broadhurst said, "would demonstrate what the race was capable of doing."[33]

Roland also called on an architect, Barry,[34] whom he had met on one of his transatlantic crossings, to consider designing a school on his newly acquired land and to provide plans for an Egyptian-style building to be erected in memory of Fannie. Roland also asked Barry (who had extensive knowledge of Europe) if he could help him to locate a small house near the Swiss border but with easy access to the south of France.[35] The place, according to Roland, should allow for maximum privacy "quite away from the crowd."[36] Unbeknownst to Barry, of course, Roland's very specific geographical requirements were to facilitate his contact with Bertha and their daughter. The countess would eventually locate to the south of France, where her estranged husband, Count Hieronymus Colloredo-Mansfeld, had bought and renovated a castle for her.

Angelmo Farm was to have been the first phase of a three-part educational and learning experience. There, talented students would receive their basic education as well as a fundamental musical exposure. Students who displayed outstanding musical skills would then have the opportunity to study with Roland Hayes at his Brookline residence or with one of the many talented voice teachers with whom he had come in contact at Villa Saint Pierre in Paris. It was a grand plan, which Roland had discussed at length with friends like Robert Broadhurst, among others.

After several successful professionally planned and executed national tours, Roland's trust in the Brennan and Judd management team at Symphony Hall in Boston was sufficient enough for him to authorize the two to be his exclusive representatives for the next three years (1927–30) in the United States and Canada.[37] They were apt at handling negative news accounts similar to those coming from Europe about Roland's "engagement" to the countess. These rumors had begun circulating in respected American news outlets like *Time* magazine, the *Chicago Tribune,* and the *New York Times.* The African American papers like the Baltimore *Afro-American* also played up the story with information that was unflattering or at the very least distorted the relationship.[38] Roland instantly had Brennan and Judd write each news outlet that published anything about him and the countess and labeled such stories as complete fabrication and a "brazen" attempt to harm the respectable singer's sterling career.[39] Given his penchant for maintaining secrecy about this entire relationship, it is likely that neither Brennan nor Judd knew the truth about the situation with Roland and Countess Bertha. Even if they had, it is likely that they would have taken the same actions to protect their investment.

As his spring 1927 tour worked its way around the country, Roland received some good news. On March 7, the Roland Hayes Parent Teacher

Association in Saint Alban, West Virginia, politely informed him that, "after careful consideration," they had decided to rename their school the Roland Hayes Grade School. They asked for his endorsement of their decision, and the tenor quickly complied.[40]

Around the same time, Roland got another opportunity to counter some of his recent bad press. He had agreed to meet the writer, civil rights activist, and founding member of the NAACP Mary White Ovington in New York in mid-April for an interview. The result of their meeting was published in Ovington's *Portraits in Color,* a compilation of biographical sketches of several prominent African Americans, including Roland, Marcus Garvey, Booker T. Washington, W. E. B. Du Bois, and James Weldon Johnson, among others.[41] Ovington's portrait of Roland emphasized the tenor's rags-to-riches story with the claim that both of his parents had been enslaved, although the record indicates that it was only his mother who had been enslaved. The essay also established the importance of Roland's ambitions in continental Africa, where he had intended to study "the music of his race at its source."[42] The chapter ended with a lengthy quote from Roland verifying his spiritual essence: "We all have the same divine spark, whether our skin is white or black or yellow or brown. I want to show that in my singing. . . . Only by keeping my purpose firmly before me, only by feeling that I am the instrument of a great idea, shall I be able to give real art, that art that goes to people's hearts, that leads to my life's goal: the end of race hatred with no difference between the colors of the skin, Peace and Brotherhood all over the world."[43]

As Roland prepared to leave for Europe in early May, he made several trial recordings for the Victor label.[44] He recorded "Crucifixion," "Lit'l David," "It's Me, O Lord," "Du bist die Ruh," and "Der Jüngling an der Quelle" (The youth by the spring) (the latter two both Schubert lieder). Beatrice Lewis was listed as the accompanist on the "Crucifixion" and probably played for the remaining works. These recordings were eventually released but not until years later.

Later in the month, with Howard Jordan as his valet/personal assistant, Roland sailed to Europe. This trip was different because he remained there longer than usual and did not begin another American tour until the following year. Initially, Roland was at his residence in Paris, and it is not clear if Bertha joined him there or even if Jordan was aware of Hayes's relationship with Bertha. The singer's decision to remain in Europe longer may have been his attempt to absent himself from the "engagement" rumors circulating in the United States, but it was more likely that he wanted to be with Bertha and his child.

Roland was eventually joined in Europe by William Lawrence and his wife, Lillian. They traveled to Italy in November for the tenor's first appearance in that country. He was hosted by Giulia Cora in Siena and Conte Chigi Saracini.[45]

The Florence portion of the trip was memorable, but not for the reason that Roland would have preferred. He was dining with William and Lillian Lawrence and his Russian friends the Count and Countess Boutourline, whom he had known as patrons from his early days in Paris. The count and countess had told Roland and Lawrence that they needed to have plenty of warm clothes for their upcoming tour of the Soviet Union the following February. With no prior notice at all to Roland, William Lawrence announced that he would not be going with the tenor on that tour. Roland was totally taken aback by his accompanist's surprise declaration, given that the fees and schedule were already in place and the programs had already been printed.

In a letter to William Brennan, Roland bitterly complained about Lawrence's unexpected announcement at the dinner: "Lawrence up and said, 'I am sorry, but I am not going to Russia.'" According to the letter, Lawrence had calmly continued, "Oh, it is not worthwhile. I'd have to take my wife, and buy her furs for the journey and prepare myself for going too and there is not enough in it."[46] Lawrence may have calculated that, if he embarrassed Roland in front of his aristocratic friends, Hayes would concede to his salary requirements. If so, the plan did not work.

The seeds of this strain between Roland and Lawrence, however, were sown some years before, in the mid-1920s. When the singer was requiring upwards of $1,500 per concert, William Lawrence was being offered $50 per concert by Brennan and Judd.[47] On those occasions when Lawrence had asked for an increase in his fee, he was routinely informed by the managers that it was the best they could do and that they had other accompanists, like Percival Parham, ready and waiting if Lawrence would not accept the offer.[48] By 1927, however, William Lawrence was earning $150 per concert for Roland's U.S. dates, which, according to Roland, "is more than I have paid any accompanist in Europe or at home."[49] Still, that fee was less than one-tenth of what the singer was earning at the time. William Lawrence also harbored singing ambitions, but his singing career did not match the fame of his accompanying and arranging. In any case, Roland had had "too much."[50] He and Lawrence had a few more dates in Paris and London but ended their musical partnership, which had dated back to the 1910s, on an acrimonious note.

Roland immediately wired Percival Parham to join him in Paris to take over as his partner at the keyboard. Parham had been waiting in the wings for such an opportunity. Before Roland had left for Europe the previous May, Parham had even offered to serve as the tenor's valet in order to get a chance to travel overseas to study.[51]

Parham was nothing short of the tenor's dream. He could not have asked for anyone better. Humble but extremely talented, Richard Percival Parham needed just this opportunity to demonstrate his amazing ability at the keyboard and on the stage. Not only did Parham play expertly, but his arranging skills easily rivaled, if not surpassed, those of William Lawrence and Lawrence Brown. Most important for Roland, Parham had not sought equal billing with the tenor, nor was he insistent about his fees. Parham wanted the opportunity to play for the celebrated singer and gain exposure for his compositions and arrangements. He did both for the next decade that he and Roland shared the stage.

As Roland had remained in Europe for the late fall months, when he would have ordinarily been back in the United States concertizing, he asked his U.S. manager, William Brennan, for U.S. dollars to purchase furniture for his home in Paris. After Parham arrived in Paris in late December, he and Roland began rehearsing the programs he would sing in the USSR. Before their trip to the Soviet Union, however, Parham accompanied the singer for several dates in Holland and Germany where he, Jordan, and Roland had to wait while Roland's manager, and occasional vocal coach, Dr. Ernst Pieta, worked out arrangements with his Russian counterpart for the upcoming trip.[52]

Roland kept a very detailed journal of his trip to the Soviet Union in which he was quite critical of the conditions he found there.[53] They waited until the end of January to collect visas to travel by train from

Berlin. Spartan conditions on the train, however, made the journey to the country somewhat difficult. Roland was scheduled to perform in Moscow on January 31 and February 7, in Kiev on February 11, in Kharkiv on February 13, in Rostov on February 16, back in Moscow on February 19, in Leningrad on February 21, in Moscow again on February 27 and 28, and in Leningrad, to wrap it up, on March 1.[54]

The tour started out on the wrong foot. Roland had to argue with his Russian manager, Kolischer, over his policy of being paid up front in U.S. currency before walking out onstage. His assistant, Howard Jordan, took up the argument and attempted to impress on the Russian the seriousness of this policy while Roland rested for his first concert. Kolischer tried to explain that it was against official policy for hard foreign currency to be handled in such a manner. After some time, the singer broke the impasse, simply saying that if he were not paid up front, he would not perform that evening.[55] That seemed to resolve the issue, as Kolischer eventually yielded on this account.

Roland's introductory concert for the Russian people on January 31 was an event. When he walked on the stage, he and Parham heard a murmur from the audience. For many Russians, this was the first time that they had seen a person of African descent. Roland believed that the audience was somehow expecting to see an African savage, a "stupendous giant with huge, bulging neck muscles, and stride."[56] Instead they saw the five-foot-four-inch, impeccably dressed, graying singer. As Roland put it, the audience expected a great trumpet and received only a pitch pipe.[57]

At first, the audience members were politely respectful. Gradually they warmed up, and by the end of the program, they were enthusiastic. Once the concertgoers realized the extent of the tenor's artistry, they began to yell, "Bis, bis, bis," asking him to repeat the just-completed work. Translations of his spirituals were given political or struggle-related interpretations, due to the official ban on organized religion within the Soviet state. When he performed the works of Russian composers like Rachmaninoff, the Muscovite audience really became worked up.

After his very successful introduction to the Soviet people, he returned to his hotel and met up with a young East Indian poet who was in the USSR and who had attended the tenor's concert, where he had introduced himself to Roland afterward. The poet, Harindranath[58] (called "Herin" for short), approached the tenor and reintroduced himself, saying, "You see, here I am again, I come not to weary you, but I have come, because I love you."[59] Roland described him as a "wanderer and seeker of and for the verities."[60] In any case, he joined the singer's small entourage and kept him company throughout the month-long visit to the Soviet Union.[61]

The reviews of Roland's first appearance in the country were characteristically unambiguous. The official organ of the Communist Party, *Pravda* (Truth), set the tone in its February 3, 1928, issue, which said: "We have every reason to say with the appearance of Hayes, the Moscow public received a great quality of artistic impression which cannot be forgotten, and the Soviet vocal art has received an impetus for its further development."[62] Also notable was the review from *Virchirniaya* (Evening) of the same date: "A large and noisy advertisement spreading around the name of this famous Negro Tenor did not disappoint anyone. Roland Hayes is a singer of tremendous vocal beauty and culture and great inborn musical talent."[63] The February 7 edition of *Issvestya* (Message) was similarly flattering: "Hayes is a phenomenal combination of voice, talent and culture. It is not necessary to lessen the demands upon this great to appreciate him. We must say that his coming is an exceptionally artistic event."[64]

Much of the trip, however, was filled with frustration for Roland, who, as an internationally renowned singer, was accustomed to getting things done with a different level of speed and efficiency.[65] Roland did have rest days in which he, Herin, or the others attended operas or plays, participated in other cultural activities, or visited old churches to admire their artwork.[66]

Another interesting aspect about Roland's day-by-day journal is that he often referred to himself in the third person when writing. On certain days he referred to himself as the "artist," on other occasions as "one." For example, his entry on February 11, 1928, after delivering a grueling performance in Kiev, details his return to his hotel room for the night. Some audience members located him and called on him to sing. In his description of the event, he said: "The Artist is furious, 'You ask that when I have sung to you for two hours? No, not tonight.' He nearly slams the door when the pathetic voices begin again saying, 'We don't mean tonight. We want you to come to our music school tomorrow.'"[67] Regretful that he had displayed his well-known temper to his Soviet fans for such an innocent request, "the artist" complied and sang for the school the following day. Many fan letters followed Roland out of the Soviet Union. Most praised his singing and his art and begged him to return as soon as possible.[68]

Despite being moved by the enthusiasm of his audiences, the opera productions, and many physical structures in the Soviet state, Roland was less than impressed with the Communist experience. In addition to being critical of the room service in the hotels, Roland decried the poverty and dullness of the everyday Soviet people he saw on the street. He likened the overall condition of privations that he found to that of African Americans.

Roland's one-month association with Harindranath resulted in an invitation from Mahatma Gandhi to regard his "little Ashram" as his home should he visit the country.[69] Roland intended to visit India, but he said that Gandhi's subsequent arrest and imprisonment stopped him from making the trip.

When he would have ordinarily been touring in the United States, Roland elected to stay in Europe, remaining in Paris with Parham and Jordan nearby. One of his engagements in early April was in Amsterdam, where he also had the opportunity to hear a performance of Bach's *St. Matthew Passion* conducted by Willem Mengelberg. Roland was so moved by the offering that he wrote Mengelberg a note about how deeply he had been touched by his interpretation.[70] Roland made a brief trip back to the United States in mid April to deal with some issue in New York.[71] Before returning to Europe, he performed a recital at Symphony Hall in Boston, his only concert in the United States during the 1927–28 season.

After arriving back in Europe, his good friend from London Robert Broadhurst brought up the idea once again of keeping the singer connected to his African ancestry. Broadhurst's hopes of getting the tenor to perform on the African continent had not completely faded, although given the economic considerations and Roland's fee schedule, it appeared it would be a tougher sell. To that end, however, Broadhurst introduced Roland to several important continental Africans, including Nana Sir Ofori Atta, the paramount chief and member of the executive council of the Gold Coast (later modern day Ghana).[72] Either through Broadhurst or through other contacts, Roland met other continental Africans with whom he maintained long-term associations.

Christine and Kamba Simango were friends of Roland whom he had met in London while they were training for mission posts in Africa. Christine was from the Gold Coast and Kamba was from Southern Rhodesia (now Zimbabwe) near the modern Mozambican border. By the spring of 1928, they had married and been posted to the Mount Silinda Mission in Southern Rhodesia where Christine had given birth to their first child. While in Paris in the summer of 1928, Roland responded to a letter she had recently written. Roland spoke eloquently of Africa and its greatness and said how connected he felt to the continent, so much so that he identified himself as an African. Roland also suggested that he might someday launch his Angelmo school project there and still held out the possibility to Broadhurst of his touring the African continent.[73]

Christine's response was as inspiring as the letter Roland had sent to her. In it, she encouraged him to visit the area, said the largest urban area was Salisbury (now Harare in Zimbabwe), and suggested a route for him to get there. She said that she and Kamba could promise him "fine scenery, ample wild game hunting and really primitive Africa."[74] She also noted that in that particular district, "the people are practically untouched by western civilization so . . . it would be an ideal situation for a study of the people and their customs."[75] This had once been Roland's goal for going to the African continent. Christine Simango also informed Roland about some of the social realities that she dealt with on a daily basis as a missionary. For example, she noted the customary second-class status of women and the reality of working-age men being forced, of necessity, to go away and labor in the mines of Natal (in eastern South Africa).[76]

Christine's information about her husband, Kamba, completely captured the tenor's attention. Roland learned that C. Kamba Simango was the same person who had collaborated with the distinguished German American anthropologist Franz Boas in *Tales and Proverbs of the Vandau of Portuguese South Africa* and had assisted the ethnomusicologist and folklorist Natalie Curtis Burlin with the collection of songs and proverbs *Songs and Tales from the Dark Continent.* Simango also had musical stage credentials from his time in the United States, playing the role of the Beze in the 1922 Broadway production of the drama *Taboo,* which also starred Paul Robeson. By the late 1920s, Kamba Simango had committed himself to the life of a missionary, but it was his musical skills and knowledge of the continent that had seized Roland's attention. Roland wanted Kamba to collect some indigenous musical instruments from the region, as he had developed an interest in crafts and curios from different parts of the continent.

Most important, Christine stressed to the tenor that as an ambassador of the continent (even though he was a de facto one), Roland's international profile would let people know that "good things can come out of Africa."[77] After a few more exchanges between Roland and Christine, Kamba wrote the tenor from the Mount Silinda Mission. He reinforced what his wife had said about the seriousness of their work and that the uplift of the African race was the ultimate goal. He also requested that Roland send him a motorcycle so that he could get around to the various locations more efficiently.[78] Although it took a few months to work out the details, Roland had a motorcycle sent to Kamba from India. Unfortunately, however, Roland did not get to see his friends in southern Africa or any other part of the continent.[79]

As the time neared for Roland to return to the United States in the fall of 1928, he was in communication with loved ones back home. His Boston voice teacher, Arthur Hubbard, had taken sick and was being cared for by his sister Emma. Roland offered to shoulder the financial responsibility of Hubbard's studio, but Emma politely declined, saying that it was already taken care of.[80] The tenor arrived back in the United States in late October, and his concert season got underway in November. Practically all the reviews commented on the excellent playing of his new accompanist, Percival Parham. Roland's programs also included several of Parham's spiritual arrangements, which received special attention.[81]

His return to Carnegie Hall on November 15 drew a capacity audience. The *New York Times'* review the following day commented on the opening of the tenor's fifth American tour and that he had recently debuted in Italy, Holland, and Russia.[82]

The remainder of the 1928 concert season was spent in the northeast part of the country, but with the winter months of 1929 approached a chill in one of Roland's most important early relationships. By 1929, Henry Putnam had been an adviser, supporter, and a financial consultant for the singer for nearly twenty years. A January 26 note from Putnam to Roland's manager William Brennan unequivocally altered that relationship. Henry Putnam had asked his former protégé for a personal loan, and Roland, in consultation with Brennan, stipulated that there be some sort of promissory note attached to such a loan. Putnam was unwilling to meet those conditions "at that time," but they eventually came to terms.[83] In Putnam's note to Brennan, he expressed "surprise" at the steps that Roland's manager was requiring, as the situation with Roland was a "personal and friendly matter."[84] This situation seems to have caused a significant if not permanent breach between the two, because there was no further communication between Roland and Putnam after the latter's terse note to Brennan. Almost a year later (January 21, 1930), William Brennan wrote Roland a brief letter, saying, "Here is a paper I was supposed to give to you to sign. It is a release in the Putnam matter. ... And my lawyer wants it." This confirmed that it was a financial matter that caused the relationship between Putnam and Roland to come to an abrupt and unhappy end.[85]

As the friendship with Henry Putnam seemed to have ended so unceremoniously, the tenor's ties with the San Francisco–based arts patron and amateur musician Noël Sullivan grew closer.[86] Roland and Sullivan had met in Paris in 1922 as the tenor was conquering the city, and over the next several years they became good friends. In fact, Roland revealed more personal information to Sullivan than he did to most people (although there is nothing to indicate that he ever informed Sullivan of his relationship with Bertha). Sullivan and Roland were rarely out of touch for more than a few months. Because of his musical background, Sullivan commented on Roland's programming choices and was a major influence in his performing on the West Coast. The tenor sent Sullivan copies of the three programs for his 1928–29 national tour and had informed him of his Russian tour, including translations of his glowing reviews.[87]

Sullivan was also one of the few whom Roland kept apprised of his tour dates and schedules. The two friends met up again in early March when Roland's spring 1929 tour included several California dates.

Born on Christmas Day in 1891 (hence he was named Noël, and it was pronounced as the French term for "Christmas"), Sullivan was from a wealthy Irish Catholic family whose lineage included a U.S. senator, among other high-profile political and philanthropic types. He was also an amateur singer and had a deep musical empathy with Roland and several other professional musicians. Noël Sullivan was an enthusiastic opera lover and regularly attended performances in the United States and Europe. Financially, Sullivan supported many artistic endeavors throughout his adult life, and his largesse had extended to African American artists like Langston Hughes, Marian Anderson, and William Lawrence, among others. When he and Roland met up in the spring of 1929, they both agreed to support a young African American singer, Marcus Hall, in his desire to study voice with Sir George Henschel in London. Sullivan and Roland sent young Hall to Sir George in England for an introduction and an assessment of his potential for a musical career.

Roland returned to Europe sometime in early May but apparently had a light schedule that summer. He did attempt to sort out arrangements for a tour the following year with Pieta that would have taken him back to Russia and Italy and included dates in Hungary and Romania.[88] Because of a fee disagreement (and possibly a looming financial situation), the tour did not take place.

Although Roland was in France with Bertha and now three-year-old Maya, he maintained his contact with Broadhurst in London, who also took on the task of following the progress of Roland and Noël Sullivan's protégé, Marcus Hall. Sir George also informed Roland of the young man's development. He liked Hall's voice but was not sure if he was tenor or a baritone with good high notes.[89] Roland wanted Sir George to give Hall an honest assessment of his talent, and if he felt Hall was not good enough, he should say so. Broadhurst was less encouraging in his letter to Roland; after the youth sang for him, he reported to his friend that the young man had a "long, long way to go."[90]

Roland was in France on the fateful "Black Monday," September 29, 1929, when the New York Stock Market crashed and began the economic decline that was felt around the world, but there was no immediate impact discernible in Roland's communications with those in contact with him. He returned to the United States at the end of October and began his tour on November 7 in Chicago and then traveled back east. In November, William Brennan sent a telegram to a physician in Rome, Georgia, agreeing to lower Roland's fee to one thousand dollars for a hospital benefit, which appears to be the earliest manifestation of the impact of the national economic slump on the singer and his fee structure. While in the region, he did a benefit concert for Fisk University for expenses only (estimated at three hundred dollars).[91]

In January the following year, Roland left the South and returned to New York to sing, once again, at Carnegie Hall. Whenever he had such major engagements (like at Carnegie or at other A-list venues like Boston's Symphony Hall), Roland could reliably expect to receive an encouraging or congratulatory telegram from Noël Sullivan. He and Roland continued their financial commitment to young Marcus Hall in London, but by the spring of 1930, Roland advised Sullivan that his other financial demands were beginning to make his continued support of Hall more challenging.[92]

February 18, 1930, marked the eightieth birthday of Sir George Henschel. The organizers of his birthday celebration had contacted Roland from the United Kingdom and asked for a small contribution toward celebrating the event. On the actual day, Roland had a major engagement at Town Hall in New York. He read a prepared statement before the start of his concert and dedicated his performance to his former teacher and friend:

> On the occasion of your 80th birthday we, fellow-members of the musical profession, wish to express the deep admiration we feel for your art and our gratitude for the exceptionally long services you have given to Music in this country and abroad.
>
> We believe that we are voicing the feelings of that vast audience to whom your music has given delight in sending you a message of warm affection and in saying that we hope you may have many more years of happiness and fruitful work before you.[93]

Roland's return to Europe in the spring of 1930 was relatively uneventful. He heard from the Ibbs and Tillett Agency while he was in

France; his agents raised the possibility of his performing in England but admitted that musical activities countrywide had slowed as a result of the world economic situation. The highest fee they could possibly get for him would be seventy-five guineas per concert. Still not willing to concede to the new economic reality, Roland wrote that it would not be practical for him to consider a tour of England for less than one hundred guineas per engagement. Similarly, in the summer of 1930, Roland told his French manager, Charles Kiesgen, that the current fee of $750, for which he was performing, was too low, and he should not be expected to sing for that fee in the future. Kiesgen informed his client that the financial situation in much of Europe was unfavorable, but once again, Roland did not comprehend the severity of the oncoming worldwide depression.

The tenor returned to the United States and began his fall and winter season with far fewer dates than what he had played during the last several years. When he was in the South, he made a surprise visit to Calhoun, Georgia, to pay a visit to Angelmo Farm and was not pleased with what he found. He wrote a letter to someone identified only as "My dearest,"[94] telling her that he was very distressed at the conditions he had met at Angelmo Farm under his brother's supervision. He complained that Robert's new wife, Margaret,[95] had let the place go into decline. He generally kept his opinions of Margaret quiet, but initially, it was clear that he did not approve of her because of her social status.

While he was in the area, Roland made a brief trip north to Chattanooga. He also heard from Edgar L. Scott Jr., a young medical student at Meharry Medical School in Nashville and his cousin Alma's new husband. Scott asked Roland for a loan of three hundred dollars, which would be repaid after his internship.[96] As 1930 ended, the impact of the coming depression was felt by the once unstoppable Hayes. His conquest had definitely slowed. Like the gracefully aging tenor, however, it continued to endure.

1–2. Hayes with Joseph Mann, 1926.
Courtesy of Afrika Hayes Lambe.

3. Mother Fannie Hayes, c. 1913.
Courtesy of Afrika Hayes Lambe.

4. Hayes family home in Chattanooga in the early 1900s.
Courtesy of the E. Azalia Hackley Collection, Detroit Public Library.

5. Hayes as a student at Fisk University, c. 1910.
Courtesy of the E. Azalia Hackley Collection, Detroit Public Library.

FISK JUBILEE SINGERS
"WORLD IN BOSTON"

6. Fisk Jubilee Singers in Boston, May 1911. Hayes is fourth from the left. *Courtesy of Afrika Hayes Lambe.*

7. Hayes with Charles J. Harris in Boston, 1915. *Courtesy of Patricia A. Murray.*

8. Arthur Hubbard, Hayes's Boston voice teacher. *Courtesy of Afrika Hayes Lambe.*

9. Hayes's publicity photo from the early 1910s. *Courtesy of Afrika Hayes Lambe.*

10. Hayes Trio, 1915: William Richardson (*left*), Roland Hayes (*center*), and William Lawrence (*right*). *Courtesy of the E. Azalia Hackley Collection, Detroit Public Library.*

11. Harry T. Burleigh, Jennie Robinson, and Hayes preparing to perform *Elijah* at Fisk, 1916. *Courtesy of the E. Azalia Hackley Collection, Detroit Public Library.*

12. Accompanist Lawrence Brown and Hayes, late 1910s. *Courtesy of the E. Azalia Hackley Collection, Detroit Public Library.*

13. John Hayes with his wife, Ola, and son, Felton, c. 1918. *Courtesy of the E. Azalia Hackley Collection, Detroit Public Library.*

14. The "Elijah quartet," April 15, 1915, at Boston's Jordan Hall. *Courtesy of the Azalia Hackley Collection, Detroit Public Library.*

15. African nationalist Duse Mohammed Ali, 1911.

16. Hayes with British composer Roger Quilter, early 1920s. *Courtesy of the E. Azalia Hackley Collection, Detroit Public Library.*

17. Hayes wearing his diamond tie pin presented by King George V and Queen Mary in London, 1921. *Courtesy of the E. Azalia Hackley Collection, Detroit Public Library.*

18. Hayes's January 7, 1923, Symphony Hall recital playbill. *Courtesy of the Azalia Hackley Collection, Detroit Public Library.*

19. Hayes with vocal coach and composer Sir George Henschel in London, 1924. *Courtesy of the E. Azalia Hackley Collection, Detroit Public Library.*

20. Pierre Monteux.
*Courtesy of Alfred Brown,
Brooklyn, N.Y.*

21. Hayes, the 1924 Spingarn
Medal recipient, with
conductor Walter Damrosch
and James Weldon Johnson.
The medal was received by
Hayes in the spring of 1925.
*Courtesy of the E. Azalia
Hackley Collection, Detroit
Public Library.*

22. Hayes's Spingarn Medal. *Courtesy of Afrika Hayes Lambe.*

23. Hayes with accompanist Leo Rosenek in Austria, 1924. *Courtesy of Afrika Hayes Lambe.*

24. Hayes in a recording studio in Europe, c. 1930s. *Courtesy of Afrika Hayes Lambe.*

25. Hayes with British accompanist Dame Myra Hess, c. 1930s. *Courtesy of Afrika Hayes Lambe.*

26. Fannie Hayes's burial site.
Courtesy of Robert Sims.

27. Countess Bertha Colloredo-
Mansfeld as a young woman, c. 1920.
Courtesy of Ernest Kolowrat.

28. Hayes as proclaimed "king of song" (*Akorin dare dare*), c. 1927.
Courtesy of the E. Azalia Hackley Collection, Detroit Public Library.

29. January 8, 1927, cartoon in the Baltimore *Afro-American*.
Courtesy of Afro-American Newspapers Archives and Research Center.

30. Maya, c. 1935.
Courtesy of Ernest Kolowrat.

31. Hayes (*left*) with brother Robert
Brante at Angelmo Farm, c. 1940.
Courtesy of Afrika Hayes Lambe.

32. Hayes family: Roland,
Africa (later Afrika), and Alzada, 1936.
Courtesy of Afrika Hayes Lambe.

33. Africa, late 1930s.
Courtesy of Afrika Hayes Lambe.

34. Africa, c. 1940. *Courtesy of the E. Azalia Hackley Collection, Detroit Public Library.*

35. Colonel Thrasher, conductor Hugo Weisgall, and Hayes in London, 1943. *Courtesy of Afrika Hayes Lambe.*

36. Noël Sullivan and
Hayes in Carmel,
California, 1946. *Courtesy
of the E. Azalia Hackley
Collection, Detroit Public
Library.*

37. Hayes publicity
photo, 1940s. *Courtesy
of the E. Azalia Hackley
Collection, Detroit Public
Library.*

38. Maya, late 1940s. *Courtesy of Ernest Kolowrat.*

39. Countess Bertha and twins Igor and Grichka, 1950. *Courtesy of Ernest Kolowrat.*

40. Hayes, Alzada, and Afrika, late 1950s. *Courtesy of Afrika Hayes Lambe.*

41. Countess Bertha, 1960s. *Courtesy of Ernest Kolowrat.*

42. Alzada and Hayes, late 1960s. *Courtesy of Afrika Hayes Lambe.*

43. Maya with five of her six children in southern France, c. 1966. *Courtesy of Ernest Kolowrat.*

44. Hayes with granddaughters Zaida and Erika, 1968. *Courtesy of Afrika Hayes Lambe.*

45. Roland Hayes, 1975. *Courtesy of Afrika Hayes Lambe.*

46. Hayes's burial site.
Courtesy of Robert Sims.

47. Erika Lambe-Holland with husband Karl (*left*) and Ernest Kolowrat, nephew of the countess, c. 2005. *Courtesy of Ernest Kolowrat.*

48. Twelve of Hayes's sixteen living descendants in France with Ernest Kolowrat, c. 2010. *Courtesy of Ernest Kolowrat.*

"Hard Trials, Great Tribulations"

1930–1935

ROLAND'S DREAM OF NURTURING TALENT CENTERED UPON four hundred acres at Angelmo Farm. His London friend Robert Broadhurst had sketched a design that included an education center with living quarters for staff and students, classrooms, a museum, and even a small hospital. However, most of the plans came to naught, as financial realities dashed Hayes's idealism. In July 1930, writing from Paris, Roland complained to his brother Robert Brante about the farm's mismanagement, saying that there needed to be tighter restrictions on spending and certain land practices. It was micromanagement at its worst:

> You may remember that I said to you and to Youngblood [an assistant manager at the farm] as well that I wished to sell the gasoline to Angelmo Farm as well as to the public, but that the farm was to pay two cents less for the gas than the public pays. . . . Don't sell gas on credit to anyone, unless it be to the Angelmo workers from whose monthly salaries you shall be able to deduct their indebtedness.
>
> FROM NOW ON PLEASE DO NOT ALLOW ANYTHING NEW OR OTHERWISE TO BE BOUGHT EXCEPT SPECIFICALLY UPON MY ORDER. THE FARM IS COSTING ME ENTIRELY TOO MUCH MONEY AND EXPENSES MUST ABSOLUTELY BE KEPT DOWN TO THE PARAMOUNT NEED OF THE ANGLEMO FARM. ALSO, THE MOTOR TRUCK, THE TRACTOR, AND THE ELECTRIC PUMP MUST BE USED ONLY WHEN THERE IS ABSOLUTE NEED FOR THE SAME, AND WHENEVER USED IT MUST BE UPON THE MOST ECONOMIC BASIS. PLEASE DEFINITELY IMPRESS THIS FACT UPON THE MINDS OF RUFUS AND ALL OF THE OTHER MEN. FINANCE IS SCARCE AND WE MUST HEW CLOSELY TO THE LINE OF ECONOMY.
>
> I note with interest that you have exchanged your old car for a new one which I certainly feel was necessary but not at this time.[1]

Hayes's remarkable condescension makes him sound as if he were addressing a field hand from his farm rather than his older brother. In any case, Roland's admonition concluded with instructions to reach him at his Paris address. The Angelmo Farm experiment was quickly becoming an expensive burden, and Hayes's attempt to handle the farm from afar did not improve matters.

But Roland *did* have help with Angelmo Farm the following year from the preeminent African American scientist George Washington Carver, with whom Roland met at Tuskegee when he performed there in February 1931. Hayes's time on campus was brief, but he did get the opportunity to speak with Carver about the Angelmo experiment. He explained some of the challenges he had experienced and wrote a very gracious letter after their meeting, saying that "Angelmo is cheerfully awaiting your honored visit."[2] Carver immediately responded to the singer in equally inspirational terms, saying how Roland's "rare gift had inspired *him!*"[3] Roland's communications with Carver about his aspirations of how Angelmo Farm could develop a new generation of young "Negro minds" resonated with Carver and elicited an even more inspiring response than the previous one:

My wonderful friend, Mr. Hayes,

What a joy to get your splendid message. This is simply to acknowledge receipt of it. I can appreciate how very very busy you are compelled to be with so gifted a talent which allows you to do God's work for humanity.

What you are doing, my beloved friend, is bigger than one race. It is a contribution to all mankind. Of course it helps us particularly because you belong to us.

When you return we must try to get a few days together. How I would love to just sit, talk and ramble around with you.

My prayers will follow you all the way wherever you go. I am so glad you took the liberty to send me the sample of water and the [unintelligible] you did was exactly right. I shall be greatly interested in them and shall make my report to your Paris address. May God ever bless, help, guide and prosper you my great friend.

Yours with genuine love and admiration,
G. W. Carver[4]

If ever there was anyone whom Roland truly admired and looked upon as a father figure, it was the elder scientist, and he treasured the communications from him. But inspiration and encouragement did not pay the bills, and Roland was eventually forced to abandon his dreams for the Angelmo experiment.

Five years after Roland's 1926 dramatic appearance at the Lyric Theater in Baltimore, he went another round with the infamous Jim Crow policy at Constitution Hall in Washington, D.C.. The hall, built by the Daughters of the American Revolution (DAR), had been opened only a few years prior to Hayes's appearance. Once again, Mrs. Kate Wilson-Green, the concert manager who had booked Roland in Washington and Baltimore (and who had presented the tenor in the nation's capital at least twice since 1926), was at the center of the drama that took place at the end of January. Roland's January 1931 appearance at Constitution Hall had been announced in the *Washington Post* nine months earlier and at least twice more before the concert.[5] By custom, African Americans were segregated when they were allowed to attend an event in the theater, but tickets could be sold in blocks through a surrogate organization or society. The theater's general manager, Fred Hand, had apparently allowed limited use of the facility by African American groups or individuals prior to the Roland's concert.[6]

When Hayes walked onstage followed by Percival Parham that Saturday evening, he immediately noticed a block of African Americans sitting together in the orchestra left. Roland recognized it as a classic hallmark of a Jim Crow–style segregated group sell, which he had seen on countless occasions. Although there were a few African Americans scattered in other parts of the theater, Roland announced to the audience that he would not sing to a segregated gathering. After a pause of a minute or so, he motioned to Parham, and the pair walked off the stage.

Roland insisted that he would not return until the audience was desegregated.[7] The singer remained backstage for more than thirty minutes, while no one in the audience, black or white, budged from their seats. Unbeknownst to Roland, Fred Hand, the hall's manager, had walked down the aisle and stood with folded arms where African Americans were segregated, as if to intimidate them into staying in their seats.[8] Kate Wilson-Green's role in this scenario is a mystery, but in light of the Baltimore incident, it is certain that she would have been mindful of Roland's sensitivities concerning the Jim Crow issue. Roland eventually returned to the stage and sang, ignoring his earlier demand. Fred Hand, in the meantime, was so "infuriated" with the tenor's "petulant" demonstration that he vowed no other African American would perform at Constitution Hall while he was manager.[9]

The Washington Post's review the next day, "Negro Spirituals Win Hayes Praise," focused on the "scope of the [tenor's] genius" and described how artistically he delivered the works of the great art music composers. As the headline implies, his interpretation of spirituals was the most noteworthy.[10] The review said nothing of Roland's protest before the concert.[11] Although Roland had made yet another gallant attempt at standing up to segregation in the Constitution Hall concert, after the battle was over and the dust had settled, the score was Jim Crow–2, Roland Hayes–0.

A year after the Constitution Hall protest, Fred Hand and the board of the DAR formally adopted a "white artists only" policy for the use of the facility. Apparently there had previously been a tacit agreement between a few board members of the DAR and a major donor to exclude all but white artists once the hall was completed. After Roland's brief protest, Fred Hand simply invoked that policy.[12] It took the highly publicized 1939 Marian Anderson incident, which denied her use of the venue, and the subsequent international controversy (including First Lady Eleanor Roosevelt resigning her membership in the DAR) to focus attention on Constitution Hall's discriminatory practices.[13]

After the Constitution Hall incident, Roland and Parham continued their recital tour in the South and the Midwest, areas where Roland knew better than to attempt a demonstration. Their April 23 concert at Boston Symphony Hall was their final U.S. date before they boarded a ship for Europe for the summer season. As he had in the past, Roland disembarked in France and visited his friends Renée Vautier and Edgar Raoul-Duval.

Despite the stresses and secrecy of their relationship, Roland wrote Bertha in the spring of 1931 to inform her of when he would be in Europe to sing there and prepare for his 1931–32 tour of the United States. He hoped they would be able to have a quiet summer together. He also made it clear to her in advance that he wanted "no complications, no scenes, [and] no catastrophes."[14]

Bertha agreed and wrote that, as before, she and five-year-old Maya would come up from her chateau in St. Lary to his house in St. Germain outside of Paris. On previous visits, when she arrived from southern France, Bertha would typically check into a hotel in Paris and then go to St. Germain to see Roland. However, when she arrived at the house this time, which she had helped Roland to furnish over the years, she was met at the gate by the gardener's wife, who confirmed that "monsieur" (Roland) had arrived the previous evening but with "une madame comme vous" (a lady like you). Bertha stood at the gate, momentarily at a loss as to what to do. When she composed herself, she decided to take a taxi back to her Paris hotel, where she wrote a twenty-page letter to the singer. She then returned to St. Germain and went up to the house, where she found the doors locked. Noticing an open window, she knocked on its shutters. "They could see out but I couldn't see inside. So when I knocked, he came to the shutters, and I said, 'I brought you a letter,' and I pushed the letter through the shutters and he took the letter and I heard that he took it, and that he tore the envelope open. . . . I heard one sheet after the other fall to the floor as he read. Once he finished, I waited, and waited, and waited. Then he said, 'Now, you can go!'"[15] In the letter the countess had written to Roland, she spoke of their child, Maya, and their "cause" of reaching a higher goal by creating a new race. She also spoke of the sacrifices that she had made to be with him at the cost of her prestige, family, and reputation.[16]

Devastated by the unexpected and heartbreaking encounter with her paramour of the last eight years, Countess Bertha left the St. Germain house for what was probably the final time. Roland had also refused to pay the bill (as he had in the past) at the Hotel Continental where Bertha was staying. She had to borrow money from a contact in Paris before returning to St. Lary in southern France with their daughter, Maya.[17]

Before embarking for the United States late in the summer, Roland gave a final recital in Paris. Madeleine "Maddie" Salmon, the wife of the cellist, Joseph, had come to know and befriend Bertha and Maya. Maddie informed the countess of Roland's Paris recital, and Bertha decided to go to attempt contact with the tenor once more. She also brought their daughter with her to the concert. She sent a note backstage to Roland, explaining that she wanted to see him before he left for home. According to her note, if he sang a specific spiritual during his program or among his encores, it would signal that he would see her and his daughter.[18] But the specified spiritual was not sung by Roland, and the message was unmistakable for the countess – and their child. There would be no meeting before his departure. The next time Bertha laid eyes on Roland, it would also be on a Parisian concert stage, but it would not be until some years later and under very different circumstances.[19]

What could have driven the tenor to break off his relationship with the woman he had been totally enamored with, the mother of his child, whom he had once called his comfort and artistic muse, in such a callous manner? Their five-year-old daughter, Maya, may have been at the heart of the situation. When she was three, in 1929, Roland had made yet another attempt at "adopting" Maya and raising her in the United States. He believed that his biracial child (whom he was prepared to say was an orphan whom he adopted in Europe) would fare much better in the States than in provincial southern France. But, once again, Bertha had refused to give up their little girl.[20] According to her, Maya, although a female child with limited possibilities and prospects, was still the result of their shared cause (at least her cause). If she gave her up, Bertha believed, she would have no one (as her relationship with Roland was seasonal at best and carried off in secret for the most part) and nothing to show for the sacrifice she had made and the loss she had sustained. No doubt, along with the other complications of their sometimes-turbulent relationship, her steadfast position where the child was concerned had led to considerable enmity between them.

Yet does the disagreement over the child explain Roland's apparent cruelty toward Bertha? Since he had written to her to say when he would be at St. Germain and had every reason to expect her arrival, why would he have the gardener (or his wife) prevent Bertha from entering the premises with the harsh announcement that another "madame" was there? Moreover, why would he have had another woman present, knowing that Bertha was expected at a specific time? It is more likely that Roland staged the entire scene to precipitate a permanent break.[21]

Bertha did not enter the premises or see anyone inside, and her account does not suggest that she saw this other woman but knew only what the help told her. She knew Roland was inside (as he received her lengthy letter) but nothing else.

A likely explanation for the reason that Roland sent the countess and their child off in such an inelegant and unceremonious manner was that by the spring of 1931, Roland had become romantically involved with his first cousin Alzada, who by that time was staying at his home in Brookline, Massachusetts. Earlier that year, he had found her ill in New York and took her to his home outside of Boston to recuperate.[22] She had become somewhat of a household manager of the residence and "transformed" 58 Allerton Street into a real home, including terminating the household staff, as she believed they overcharged for their services.[23] In any case, a love relationship developed. Yet, there was the unresolved issue of Roland's relationship with the countess in France. His first order of business after returning to Europe was to "take care" of that situation with the mother of his child.

After having witnessed the fickleness of the public toward celebrated African American "heroes" and seeing how easily they could be excoriated by the press, Roland was not willing to risk his career at home by making his relationship with Bertha public. The singer had seen how white America had turned against the renowned boxer Jack Johnson, who had brazenly flaunted his relationship with several white women. He quickly moved from being beloved to being reviled by a public that held him in total disdain.[24] Roland feared exposure of his affair with a married white woman. Even worse, this woman was of the Austro-Hungarian aristocracy. Had Roland dared to reveal this relationship, he believed his carefully cultivated career would go down in flames in an atmosphere of racial intolerance.[25]

But in walking away from the countess, Roland also walked out of the life of his five-year-old daughter. She was the unintended victim of the soured relationship between her strong-willed parents. Other than occasional letters – more often written by her to him – and a brief late-1930s meeting, Roland had little contact with Maya until she was an adult, married with children of her own. A January 1942 letter written by Maya to Hayes established a line of communication between the two.

The countess, however, recalled not seeing Hayes again until their meeting in Paris in 1954.[26] Roland kept this part of his life from the woman whom he would subsequently marry. He was prepared to reveal it to her only *after* his death.[27]

Another difficult event, which he apparently kept secret for some time, was that he gave up his St. Germain house outside Paris. The reality of the depression had made it impossible for the singer to hold on to the property while maintaining Angelmo Farm in Georgia and his primary residence in Brookline. He informed Noël Sullivan of the reality of the situation only at the end of the summer. In his August 1 letter to his friend, Roland said in a somewhat matter-of-fact tone, "I had to give up my abode at Villa St. Pierre this summer. I don't know where I shall stay when I go back for next year's season."[28] The singer eventually had his furniture and other belongings (including six trunks of music and personal correspondence) moved into storage or placed with friends, where they would eventually be lost to him and to history.

Roland's performances on the European continent in the spring of 1931 lacked the drama of his personal life, but as before, his concerts were enthusiastically reviewed in the press. Major news vehicles like *Monde Musical, Excelsior, Débats,* and *Figaro* in France, as well as the London *Times* and the *Oxford Mail* in Great Britain, hailed his artistry and musicianship. William Brennan contacted Roland in Europe to tell him of plans for his upcoming eighth national U.S. tour. Brennan informed him that dates in the Midwest for October and November were completely booked, but at a fee considerably reduced from the $2,500 that he had been getting just a few years earlier.[29]

Roland returned to the United States in late August, earlier than he had anticipated. Several engagements that he was expecting to fill on the Continent either fell through or simply did not materialize. The worldwide depression had begun to severely hurt the concert business in Europe.

Even though he had "ended" his relationship with Bertha, her influence continued. Led by Bertha's example, Roland had begun consulting astrologers and the like. He continued this practice for the rest of his life.[30] He began a multiyear relationship with Blanche Watson, a

New York–based numerologist and character analyst specialist, whom he consulted about his career, his business dealings, and, of course, his relationship with Alzada, including the advisability of marriage to her.[31] After Watson placed her name, "Helen Alzada Mann," in a numerical grid, she gave the tenor a written assessment of her character and her suitability as a mate.

The affirming answer from the numerologist seemed to have motivated Roland in this relationship. By the late fall of 1931, he was greeting Alzada in his letters to her as "Tootsie, Wootsie – How is my child today? So glad to get your letter, dear. I just love you, my little darling!" He concluded this particular letter with "Much love, my little 'Brown doll' from Rolly."[32] This was obviously a very different relationship from that with Bertha – one without the unnecessary drama. In his letters to Alzada, he never used flowery and transcendental language like "my revealer of wonders" or "my comfort" or "I need you so," yet there was no question that he deeply loved her and, perhaps more important, appreciated Alzada's value to his life. She represented to the tenor the familiar, the continuity of his African American heritage, and she obviously had more in common with his direct lineage (literally as his uncle's daughter) than the cultured and polished, yet unpredictable Bertha. While he had been deeply mesmerized by the countess, the distance between his humble beginnings and her aristocratic background proved to be too great. When Roland reflected on his relationship with Alzada, he quoted from the conclusion of Goethe's epic legend *Faust:*

> "The eternal woman lifts us up." I had leaned
> heavily upon women in my time. Now, uniquely
> since my mother's death, I was to find myself
> raised up by woman's undistracted love.[33]

In his biographical account, Roland gave the impression that there was a gap between his mother Fannie's "undistracted love" and the arrival of Alzada's. In fact, there was a multiyear bridge. Literally within weeks of his mother's death, Countess Colloredo-Mansfeld appeared in his life, and over the following eight years, it had been Roland's central relationship. As that bond gradually drifted into troubled waters, the relationship with Alzada emerged. So Roland's reference to the Faustian legend and the role of the "eternal woman" was more than appropriate. It could even be seen as a lifelong theme. A woman had given him birth and inculcated the values that he applied in his early youth and into adulthood. Another woman raised him to a higher level as an artist and as a man (not to mention made him a father, one of the ultimate manifestations of manhood). And yet another woman became his life partner and companion. Alzada was his quiet but steady supporter for the balance of the singer's life.[34]

Roland's eighth tour of America was underway by October. He spent part of the Christmas season at Angelmo Farm in Georgia, where he visited with his brother, Robert Brante, and his newborn daughter, Winell. Roland also played Santa Claus for several mothers in the area who, as the effects of the national depression deepened, were unable to afford Christmas presents for their young children.[35] On Christmas Day, he was comfortably settled in his Brookline home with Alzada. Two days later the tenor had an engagement with the Boston Symphony Orchestra to raise money for the symphony's pension fund.

As he prepared for a performance in the South in January 1932, he received a letter dated December 24, 1931, from Thomas E. Jones, the fifth president of Fisk University. The board of trustees, meeting earlier in the month in New York, had voted unanimously (against previous institutional practices) to award him the honorary doctor of music degree.[36] The president proposed that Roland come to campus during the annual musical festival at the university in April, and the event would culminate in the degree convocation.[37] The proposed April date, however, conflicted with an appearance Roland was scheduled to make in Havana, Cuba, with the Philharmonic Society. He discussed the conflict with William Brennan, who thought the public relations value of Roland receiving the honorary doctorate from his home institution outweighed the Cuban symphonic appearance.[38] Brennan suggested that he could reschedule the Cuban engagement, and in late January, Roland graciously accepted the invitation issued by President Jones.[39]

A few weeks later, Roland and Alzada secretly married in Los Angeles on February 16, 1932, although it is not clear why they were in that city. They kept the news from the public for several years.[40]

In April, a special commission in Washington, D.C., was created to celebrate the bicentennial of George Washington's birth. Among the per-

formers invited to participate were the Fisk Jubilee Singers, and the chair
of the Washington commission wanted Roland to participate in the celebration as well. There was one caveat, however – the commission could
defray only the costs of travel and accommodation, and there would be
no fee attached. Roland briefly considered the proposal and then turned
it down (via Brennan). The reason offered was that the proposed venue
for the performance was the Washington Auditorium (where Roland
had already sung on numerous occasions), where the acoustics were
"unsuitable" for singers.[41] In addition, according to Brennan's explanation, the tenor's season would have ended, and he would be resting at his
farm in Georgia.

On the same day in April that Roland received his honorary degree from
Fisk, he received a letter from his friend Christine Simango, who was still
working as a missionary in southern Africa. She remarked on the severe
race prejudice she and her husband, Kamba, had experienced over the
four years that they had been missionaries in that part of the African
continent.[42] She wanted Roland to come and do a concert tour in the
area to "show the white community what a negro has achieved." She even
acknowledged that someone of his stature might have to initially endure
some racial animus, but she was "certain that it would not last long after
your opening concert."[43]

Simango's heartfelt letter only hinted at the racial oppression that
she and Kamba must have experienced in southern Africa's tripartite system, which had manifested itself well before the formal introduction of
apartheid in the late 1940s. Roland had been approached about performing in South Africa shortly after arriving in London in 1920, but even
then he cautioned his proposed sponsors that, were he to come there,
they would have to assure that he would experience no racially motivated
unpleasantness. It is unlikely that the Simangos, as black missionaries,
would have been able to exercise the necessary influence to bring about
a concert tour of the caliber that Roland would have required.

For nearly a decade, Roland had ended his spring concert tour of
the United States and returned to Europe by late April or early May.
The spring of 1932 was an exception to that. With the world economy
worsening, the European concert circuit had dried up, and in any case,

few concert bookers were willing to pay Roland's substantial fee. Instead, he remained in the United States over the summer and went to Angelmo Farm. He worked his way west for a short time, but by early June he was back in Georgia.[44] He wrote Noël Sullivan that Angelmo Farm had been hard-hit like the rest of the country but acknowledged that it could have been "a thousand times worse."[45]

William Brennan and George Judd were working on a deal with the Concert Bureau of the National Broadcasting Corporation (NBC) to feature Roland in smaller markets, where he had not performed. The fee was to be not less than $875 per performance, which was a considerable compromise, given the tenor's former fee. To put the offer in perspective, Brennan and Judd informed their client that NBC had also been negotiating with other celebrated musicians like Fritz Kreisler, Sergei Rachmaninoff, and the celebrated opera singer Beniamino Gigli (also a tenor).[46] Just a few years before, Roland would have scoffed at such a fee, but times being what they were, he was forced to agree. However, he stipulated that he not be required to "broadcast greetings."[47] When Roland wrote his managers with his requirements, he also raised the issue of the next season and future prospects, informing them that he needed to concertize in order to meet overhead and other expenses. Ultimately, however, the NBC negotiations fell through over the issue of radio broadcasting. Roland held fast to the notion that his art was not intended for mass distribution in that medium.

Roland performed very little, if any, throughout the summer of 1932 but was still attempting to assist with the activities of Angelmo Farm. He and Alzada returned to the West Coast by September, where he made an appearance at the Symphony under the Stars Series in Los Angeles.

Despite a relatively slim fall schedule, on November 25 and 27 Roland made an important orchestral debut with Maestro Eugene Ormandy and the Minneapolis Symphony. Having stood in for an ailing Arturo Toscanini, who was scheduled to conduct the Philadelphia Symphony Orchestra, Ormandy quickly made a name for himself and was eventually engaged as the principal conductor of the Minnesota-based music organization. He had built up a significant reputation and recorded repertory when Roland sang with the conductor in the fall of 1932.[48] In addition to the arias from Mozart's *Così fan tutte* and Berlioz's *L'enfance du Christ,* Roland sang "Wohin, Wohin?" (Where, Where?) from Tchai-kovsky's *Eugene Onegin.* He also sang orchestral-arranged spirituals on both evenings.[49]

By the fall, William Brennan's health was tentative and George Judd was carrying on the day-to-day activities of managing the BSO and Ro-land's concert affairs, diminished as they were. There were also person-nel issues at Angelmo Farm. One of his senior employees, R. G. Gardner, wrote him that he was leaving the farm because of ongoing disputes with Robert Brante and his management style.[50] Still more challenges lay ahead for the artists' colony. By the end of 1932, the farm, like Roland's career in some aspects, faced uncertainty, but it could have been "a thou-sand times worse."[51]

Attempting to bolster his sagging finances, Roland wrote to his Lon-don managers, Robert Leigh Ibbs and John Tillett, casting about to see if there were performance prospects that might allow for him to return to the British Isles. To his dismay, little was available.[52]

As 1933 came in, Roland was back in the New England area with a reduced concert season. He wrote to the distinguished NAACP founder, W. E. B. Du Bois, asking him if he still wanted him to write an article for the *Crisis.* Du Bois had approached Roland about this at least two years prior. Roland, ever mindful of good public relations, saw this as an op-portunity to get his name back into the widely circulated magazine.[53] Du Bois was a visiting professor at Spellman College when he received Roland's letter but quickly responded that the singer was free to write about whatever topic suited him. It is unclear whether Hayes ever pub-lished with the magazine.[54]

Whether it was the disappointing showing of his 1932–33 season, personal frustration, or a worsening financial situation, Roland felt com-pelled to push the envelope with his managers Brennan and Judd when he wrote them a letter dated February 4, 1933. In part it said:

> Things have come to a place now where I need to know something definite concerning what I am to expect from you as managers of my Artistic interests during the next year – which I wish to begin with June 1st, 1933.
> That you may have a clear understanding of the foregoing, I beg to give a general outline of a few paramount requirements. I do so because – as exclusive managers in the U.S.A. and Canada for the last eight seasons – of my Artistic

successes and otherwise (mutually shared) I feel that you can hardly be of less concern than myself.[55]

Hayes's requirements included four main points: an extended period of "rest, work, and study"; the commission of a biography by a literary master of the stature of Emil Ludwig, who had already produced acclaimed biographies of Napoleon, Otto von Bismarck, Goethe, and Jesus Christ;[56] the commission of a musical work specifically for Hayes by a preeminent composer like Ravel, Stravinsky, or Prokofiev; and, finally, financial backing to the tune of six thousand dollars in order that the above be achievable.[57]

This was nothing short of a bold effort by Roland to withdraw from public view and reinvent himself as an artistic personality of the first caliber. A biography would keep his name before the public, and a dedicated composition would highlight his artistic worthiness when he resumed performing. This was a plan that, as he saw it, could have assured his name among the celebrated musicians of the foreseeable future.

At face value, the strategy was a good one. Had it been offered a few years earlier, when Roland and the United States were in a different economic situation, the plan might have succeeded. However, the country (and much of the world) was deep into the most severe economic depression in generations, and there was especially tremendous uncertainty among arts organizations. Added to that, William Brennan was not well, and George Judd was managing the day-to-day affairs of the office. There was also the issue of the advance Roland was asking for against future earnings. While Brennan and Judd had done an excellent job in managing, producing, promoting, and protecting their client because he was generating a steady stream of income (from which they received 10 percent), in this time of economic uncertainty he was not bringing in the kinds of fees to justify such an action. Further, they might have felt that Roland's public appeal was waning, and he was simply not worth the investment that he was asking them to make in his future.

In the midst of Roland's dramatic proposal to his managers, more drama occurred at Angelmo Farm in Georgia when a fire destroyed one of the barns not far from the main house.[58] Roland's response was to simply not deal with it. Sometime in mid-April, Roland contacted his brother, who answered, "Your long expected letter came the day before 2 PM. Thought you was never going to write me anymore."[59] Robert Brante continued that he had dealt with a significant struggle on the farm (with little support from Roland), but things were looking "brighter."

Roland's despair at his entire situation and the stress he was under in the United States was shared with his friend Renée Vautier (sculptress and wife of Edgar Raoul-Duval) in France. He thanked her for allowing him to keep some of his belongings at their house. He was hoping to send Howard Jordan, his former secretary who still lived in France, to retrieve some of them and make shipping arrangements. He also told her how much he missed his "dear France."[60]

Roland also reached out to one of his true and unconditional friends, Noël Sullivan. He wrote Sullivan a letter full of anguish, entreating his friend to allow him and his "cousin" (Alzada) to stay at his home in Carmel, California, for a few months because he found it necessary to "get away from Boston and the East into a quarter where [he] could concentrate and prepare for the new era."[61] He also said there was another reason that he needed to be away (most probably a situation with him and Alzada) but would wait to tell Sullivan about it when he saw him. In addition, Roland raised the possibility of Sullivan taking over the management of his career on the West Coast, which would be done strictly on a business basis, and mentioned a management scenario that he had previously employed in Europe (that is, having separate managements in various European countries). In Roland's scheme, he would have someone managing him on the West Coast, someone else in the Northeast and South, and yet someone different in the Midwest.

In the meantime, he awaited a reply from Brennan and Judd concerning his letter from February. Their response was polite and professional, yet they unequivocally declined their client's proposal.[62] The result was an unspoken but strained relationship between Roland and his managers, but Brennan and Judd continued to handle the little concert work open to him (including recitals in Washington, D.C., a Symphony Hall concert in Boston, and a concert at Finney Chapel on the campus of Oberlin College, among a few others).

The situation ultimately came to a head during a May 1 meeting of the three principals in Boston. In a press-statement-like letter afterward, Roland announced that the three had met and that "owing that this last

... (1932–33) concert season having been such a failure – Mr. Brennan being ill and Mr. Judd not being in position to take the initiative in [his] concert affairs – that I should handle my own concert bookings, where and whenever found in the future."[63] The letter stated that Judd could continue to accept future engagements for the singer, as long as the fee was over one thousand dollars (and Brennan and Judd would still be entitled to their standard commission on such engagements). They would be required to turn over to him (or to any other representative of his) anything below that amount for handling and execution and would have no financial claim on such an offer. Further, there would be no press release or any other formal statement of dissociation among the parties so as not to hurt the singer's career and future prospects. This decision marked the beginning of Roland's managerial flux, as well as uncertainty in his career for another several years.

Also on May 1, Roland wrote Ruth Cowan of the NBC Artists Services in Los Angeles, whom he had met on one of his recent trips to California, about the possibility of her handling certain upcoming engagements on the West Coast. Roland emphasized in his letter to Cowan that his request of her should not be interpreted that he was looking after his own management. Instead, he wanted to tap into her unique geographical location and her skills in that region.[64] Ruth Cowan, in turn, wrote to "George Brennon" (that is, William Brennan) seeking clarification of this arrangement and asking how far she could go in arranging such concerts on the tenor's behalf.[65] She immediately began working to secure several engagements for him in California. In addition to live engagements, Cowan raised the possibility of Roland appearing in a Hollywood-produced musical, an idea that the tenor seemed to embrace.

Sometime in mid-May, Roland and Alzada journeyed to California and settled at 10 Eucalyptus Lane in Santa Barbara. Ruth Cowan had taken the idea of telling Roland's story on the big screen and to production people at RKO Pictures; this idea had received a good reception.[66]

Roland had come to California with the sketch of an autobiographical script, which he had tentatively titled "Spirituals," and was eager to shop it. He met Beth Wendell, presumably an aspiring Hollywood agent, who became interested in his plan to move his script and began approaching studios. After soliciting and receiving interest from a few studios, Wendell wanted a more formal deal for her efforts and requested two hundred dollars a week from the tenor. Even if Roland had been in a position to pay such a fee (which he was not at the time), he would have balked at the idea without a firm commitment from a studio in place. Perhaps the salary demand from Wendell is what caused Roland to clarify the arrangement. He agreed to pay her a sum of six hundred dollars if and when any portion of his story were to be employed in a movie.[67]

Roland did have another major engagement that Ruth Cowan set up at the Hollywood Bowl in Los Angeles. On August 3 he sang with the British conductor Sir Hamilton Harty sponsored by the Symphony under the Stars Series.[68] His performance was so well received that there was an effort to bring the tenor back under the baton of Maestro Stokowski later that summer.[69]

As challenging as it was for Roland during that period, it was far worse for his loyal accompanist, Percival Parham, who was in New York struggling to stay afloat. Roland attempted to assure him in an August letter that he had not forgotten him but pointed out that he was appearing with orchestras and, at the moment, not in need of his services.[70] He said that although he wanted Parham with him in California, he simply could not afford to bring and maintain him there. Roland, of course, had given a few recitals but found it more feasible to use local accompanists. That September, Parham contacted Roland once again out west and received yet another promise from the tenor that he was still working to make a way for him to join him on the coast.[71]

Roland approached Fox Films and then entered preliminary discussions with Warner Brothers about a possible biographical movie scenario, but nothing firm was agreed upon. He did not, however, abandon his concert activities, and when Ruth Cowan did not move fast enough with concrete plans for his autumn schedule, he returned to George Judd to set up a few engagements on the East Coast. On September 25, one day after her fortieth birthday, Alzada gave birth to her and Roland's only child, and the tenor's second daughter, Africa (pronounced "A-FREE-ka" and later changed to "Afrika") Fanzada Hayes in Hollywood, California.[72] For some months, her parents did not take her back to the East Coast.

Roland ended the year on December 29 with the San Francisco Symphony Orchestra. He had sent letters to prospective venues in Denver,

Colorado, and Omaha, Nebraska, informing booking agents that he would be traveling back east at the end of January and would be available for engagements.[73]

The year 1934 started with greater promise, as Roland had several concert bookings, all in the West and Pacific Northwest: January featured dates in Carmel, California; Tacoma, Bellingham, Eugene, and Seattle, Washington; and Portland, Oregon.[74] No one received the news of this schedule with more jubilation and relief than Percival Parham, who quickly made his way west to be reunited with the tenor on the concert stage.

While Roland was a guest at Noël Sullivan's residence in Carmel, his friend Langston Hughes reviewed the tenor's January 7 concert for the ANP wire service with the heading "Hayes Wins Artist Colony." The overflow audience had also welcomed the presence of the well-known poet Robinson Jeffers.[75]

After his recital in Tacoma, Roland was involved in a car accident in Seattle on January 15. He suffered a dislocated shoulder, but it was not properly diagnosed until he returned to Santa Barbara to enter a clinic.[76] He left Parham in Washington and wrote him there in early February in order to reschedule the rest of the tour. When Roland was released from the clinic in mid-February, he and Parham traveled to Winnipeg, Canada, to perform.

On January 20, 1934, an article appeared in the *Boston Chronicle* with the headline "Noted Tenor Cancels Race Libel Film" with the subheading "Refuses to Accept Hollywood's Version of his Life's Story."[77] The article started off by denying rumors that the tenor had separated from his Boston Symphony Hall Concert management, William Brennan and George Judd. The rumor was "emphatically" denied by Judd, who was quoted in the article as saying that only the "most amicable relations existed" between the tenor and the Boston management. And technically, Judd's denials were accurate. Although he and Brennan had altered their exclusive arrangement, Judd was still accepting engagements for the singer.[78]

The other section of the *Chronicle* story had come from California and stated that "Mr. Hayes['s] fondest dreams has [*sic*] come to an abrupt and unhappy awakening. . . . Hayes and the producers could not agree upon what was . . . not to be in the picture, and the whole matter was formally brought to a close."[79] The article also mentioned Roland's distaste for jazz and his advocacy of the spiritual as the true African American ("Negro") art form.

On the same date, an article appeared in the *Pittsburgh Courier* with similar information. Its heading and subheading read "Roland Hayes, Despite Success, Turns Back on Fame to Join Hands with His Own People; White Management No Longer Directs Singer's Concerts; Will Try to Build New Contacts after Movie Failure."[80] The *Chronicle* and *Courier* articles both mention that the tenor did not approve of some of the content of a movie project, and rather than betray his race for money, he had simply walked away from the project. No other specifics were mentioned.

The validity of these stories is suspect at best. Roland was the only source of these accounts, and it is probable that he was seeking the publicity from such sensational news stories. In neither account are there any relevant details about the studios involved or the substance of the conversation, not to mention any Hollywood denials to such charges. None of the existing written communications with the various studios that he approached suggested that Roland had made it beyond preliminary discussions by the time the newspaper articles appeared. For Roland to have walked away from such a scenario would have indicated that some formal agreement had been reached and that there was some production schedule pending, or at least serious discussions. The *Courier* story also said that Roland had separated from his Boston management and that he was taking control of his career himself, which was, in various ways, closer to the reality of his situation.

As he had mentioned to Noël Sullivan the year before, Roland did act on the plan to have several managers handle his career in different regions of the country. On March 19, Aaron Richmond, who had once worked with Brennan and Judd and who had known Roland for years, sent him an agreement of understanding regarding his services as the tenor's exclusive representative in the New England area, New York, and Pennsylvania for the 1934–35 season.[81] Roland immediately replied that he wanted a more limited arrangement and that he was free to make certain negotiations independent of Richmond.[82] Richmond's response was that to avoid any "awkwardness," the tenor should let him know what cities he was authorized to book in and what ones he should avoid. Richmond also wanted to move Roland from performing in Boston's Symphony Hall to the smaller Jordan Hall, where he had personal contacts.

Even while the negotiations between Roland and Richmond were taking place, George Judd was still scouting to find suitable engagements for the tenor. At the time of the exchange between Hayes and Richmond, Judd had made contacts in New York for a radio broadcast. Roland was on record opposing any radio broadcast because he felt that it cheapened his art, even though Paul Robeson, among others, had successfully sung on the radio. But while Roland recognized Robeson's "natural vocal talent," he did not view him as an artist who was of his caliber.[83]

The apparent haughtiness of Roland's position hurt him in the long run. Had he broadcast routinely, he would have reached and cultivated a much larger audience. Roland had taken a similar position, although a less strident one, when it came to recording. Because of his avoidance of the studio in his prime vocal years, there are relatively few recordings of the tenor at the height his career.

Roland also communicated with Frank Andrews of the Ellison-White Agency about representing him on the West Coast and in the northwest part of the country. As with Aaron Richmond, the asking price per concert was to be between $1,000 and $1,500, but Roland could accept a fee as low as $750.[84] On certain occasions, a "special fee" of $500 could be entertained, but was certainly not to be encouraged.

Roland and Parham continued their spring schedule. They had an engagement at the historically African American West Virginia State College in Bluefield at the end of April, but after his performance, Roland complained that the organizers did not take in enough money to pay the first $250 of the agreement. He wrote Alzada, saying, "The affair here bears the ear mark of the usual C.P. ["Colored People"] inaccuracy, sloppiness, and lack of good taste and judgment."[85] Only a few more engagements remained before Roland and Parham finished their spring 1934 season. It had been better than the 1933 season but was still disappointing by previous years' standards.

While Roland had been out west attempting to resuscitate his floundering career, in spite of the nationwide depression, he had neglected all but the essential activities on Angelmo Farm. Robert Brante had been left to handle affairs as best he could. Against considerable odds, Robert was struggling to keep the farm afloat, even though he was married with a growing family. Needing to do some fence mending, Roland wrote his brother in August, acknowledging his importance and indispensability when it came to the important issues surrounding Angelmo Farm.[86] Roland realized that they had agreed that Robert Brante's management of the farm was worth at least two hundred dollars a month, but the tenor was unable to pay that. In lieu of such compensation, Roland offered his brother the following:

1. All the farm tools and equipment
2. All livestock
3. Electric Kohler Motors and all their equipment, including the underground cable
4. The house-to-house telephone system and all extra wire
5. His share of the year's revenue from farm products and the amount of the contract with Brewster Keys for the two mules, Dick and Nell
6. All his share of the year's crop production of every description
7. A little less than an acre of land[87]

Roland concluded that if the terms were acceptable to Robert Brante, he should indicate it accordingly. This letter was a far cry from the one he had sent his brother a few years earlier, where he addressed him less like a brother and more like a low-ranking hired hand. Roland signed the letter "Devotedly Yours, Buddie," a term of endearment that the two used in their respective letters. Some weeks later, Robert Brante responded positively to his brother's proposal, and the deal between the siblings was sealed in a very gentlemanly manner.

The impact of the national economic depression was evident once again when Roland politely asked the Buffalo, New York–based businesswoman and concert promoter Bessie Bellanca for her patience for the money he owed her for some antique furniture he had purchased from her some four years earlier.[88] According to Roland, he and the Colonial Flower Shop of Buffalo had an understanding that payment for goods would be made over a period of time. Bessie Bellanca's prompt response to his letter dismissed any such notion, and she demanded payment in full. She proposed, however, that he could give a recital in Buffalo, which she would promote on a percentage basis. After the house's take was satisfied, he would then have enough to settle his debt with her. Failing that, she was prepared to "make trouble" for him.[89] Reluctantly, Roland agreed to her terms and informed her of his availability to perform the proposed concert in late January or the beginning of February 1935.[90]

As 1934 was ending, Roland received an analysis from Blanche Watson, his New York–based numerologist.[91] In it, she commented on his and Alzada's new child, Africa, predicting that she was likely to be known by her middle name, "Franzada" [sic], and describing the baby's personality and other characteristics. Watson also commented positively on the merits of Roland's biographical script and felt that if it was presented in the right way, it could make a contribution to the "White problem" – she believed the phrase "Negro problem" to be a misnomer.[92] Tellingly, the analyst made no mention of Roland having had disagreements with any Hollywood studios or the like; she simply referenced the work. This supports the idea that Roland had been attempting to garner positive press with the news stories that had appeared at the beginning of the year.

Roland was invited to spend the Christmas holidays in Daytona Beach, Florida, by celebrated African American leader Mary McLeod Bethune, president of Bethune-Cookman College. She and Roland had met a few years prior, and Roland had since performed on the campus. They eventually became good friends, and she wanted to use his eminent position to boost an effort to build a music complex that would carry his name on her growing campus.

As a result of his agents, the supporting work of others, and his personal efforts, the fall portion of Roland's 1934–35 season was more promising than it had been in the last several years.[93] Although he was singing at mostly B-level venues he would have disdained only a few years earlier, he was at least performing with a full schedule once again, thanks to his adjustment of his fee structure so that it was in line with the new economic reality.

Roland and Parham's engagements in January 1935 were mainly in New York and New Jersey, but they also had dates in Toronto, Kentucky, Ohio, and Michigan. While in the New York area, Roland stayed at the International House on Riverside Drive. Better known as "I House," it had hosted students and professionals from hundreds of countries world-wide and was where Roland met South African composer and musician Reuben T. Caluza.[94] Caluza had recently completed an undergraduate degree from Hampton University and was studying further in the New York area. When he met Roland in January 1935, he was well aware of the tenor's name and reputation. The ostensible reason for the meeting between the two was so that Roland could get the address of Kamba Simango, with whom he had been out of touch for some time. Roland also wanted Caluza to assist him in acquiring some traditional African instruments. As it turned out, however, Roland was more interested in Caluza's skill as a traditional African music specialist and wanted to tap his expertise for a creative project.[95] Caluza told Roland in a follow-up letter when he would be available to consult with him on the music of his biographical project in Brookline. Caluza was also interested in having Roland use his influence to assist him in studying orchestration at the New England Conservatory of Music. But, above all, he realized that Roland "required *strict* confidence" about the entire biographical endeavor.[96]

Receipts fell short for Roland's February 2 Buffalo engagement, but Roland told Bessie Bellanca he would have his debt settled by the following April. As his concert activity had increased, he found it necessary to hire someone to assist him with the logistics and engaged Katherine Brock, based in Evanston, Illinois, for this task.[97] Brock was so enthusiastic about her duties that she had stationery printed up that read "Tour Manager for Roland Hayes." Although he initially resisted her promoting herself as such, she more than earned his respect with her ability to wrangle his affairs.

While on tour in California in late March, Roland had a meeting with Jessie Lasky of the Fox Film Corporation Studio in Hollywood. He made yet another pitch for his autobiographical film, during which he explained that he had all the necessary personnel to complete such a production, including African ballet music, plantation melodies, and conventional music combined with the "action to the end that [there] can be no lack to the effectiveness of the production."[98] Hoping for a positive response, he provided Fox his itinerary as he traveled back to the East Coast, but he left without the slightest formal commitment.

After years of being out of communication, Roland heard from his friend Robert Broadhurst, who chided him for not responding to his many letters and asked about the latest developments at Angelmo Farm.[99] Roland was very apologetic in his immediate response and told him that the depression weighed heavily and had given him "a few more grey hairs, since [they] had last seen each other."[100] He told Broadhurst about his film project, which set forth four generations of his ancestral line, beginning in the Ivory Coast. He even suggested that it deserved operatic treatment. The singer concluded his letter with "I know my great work has just begun."

At about the time Broadhurst's letter arrived, Roland received news that William Brennan, his first professional manager and tour director, had died in Boston. He had been ill for at least two years. George Judd, who had been the de facto manager of the B S O throughout Brennan's illness and had continued to work with Roland in setting up engagements, became the symphony's new principal manager.

Roland's good friend and longtime supporter Walter White (who had succeeded James Weldon Johnson as the secretary of the N A A C P) approached Hayes about performing at the White House for First Lady Eleanor Roosevelt. Roland agreed to do so, provided the performance could be arranged under the "correct circumstances."[101] White had been in contact with the First Lady and proposed the idea to her. After several communications among White (as an intermediary), Hayes, and eventually with the White House, it was proposed that Roland be paired on a program with a jazz singer to demonstrate the musical versatility of African Americans. But Roland found such an arrangement inappropriate and declined the White House invitation. The secretary of the N A A C P asked him to reconsider his position, but Roland would not yield on this point.

TEN

Return to Europe

1936–1942

ROLAND OPENED HIS 1936 SEASON WITH A BENEFIT RECITAL AT Howard University for his friend and supporter of more than twenty-five years, Lulu Vere Childers, the well-known and influential music director at the university. She had wanted Roland to come and teach at Howard as a guest lecturer for the 1935–36 academic year, but he told her he was free only during the summer but needed that time to rest and prepare for the next season.[1] He agreed however, to do a recital at the "special fee" of five hundred dollars, which included Percival Parham's accompanying compensation. Shortly after the Howard engagement, Roland wrote to his former benefactor from the BSO, Maestro Pierre Monteux, who was in San Francisco, to propose they work together again. Monteux said he hoped they would in fact perform together soon and gradually moved in that direction.[2]

Blanche Watson remained in regular contact with Roland and eventually began predicting for Alzada. Once the numerologist completed her forecast for 1936, she sent it to him. She foretold the importance of the year in the tenor's career, but her remaining comments were vague, as they had been in the past.[3] The following month, Roland wrote Alzada a "happy anniversary" letter, marking their fourth year as a married couple:

February 12, 1936
Dearest:

I am reminded that this is the happiest anniversary that we have had. Peace is with us and our offspring, and I feel the future has ever greater joys and happiness for us. So let's keep close to God and each other and husband abiding faith and confidence.

Your "Buddie"
Roland[4]

They continued to keep their marriage secret, but their personal communications were loving and tender. Even with the secrecy, information and misinformation began showing up in print. The February 4, 1936, edition of the *Washington Tribune* reported, "Roland Hayes' wife said to be his Cousin." It referred to Alzada as "Franzata Mann of Georgia . . . who devotes a great deal of time to their charming two-year old daughter Afreca [sic]."[5] A few months later, the *Afro-American* published a picture of the couple with the caption "FLASH!!! HERE IS THE FIRST PHOTO OF MR. AND MRS. ROLAND HAYES."[6] The picture displayed Roland and Alzada sitting with a little girl standing in front of them. The caption clearly stated that the child was not their daughter.

Lacking work, Roland's financial situation steadily worsened. A new crisis arose in February when he was warned of pending default on the mortgage on Angelmo Farm, held by the Federal Land Bank of Columbia. Roland managed to settle the debt before any foreclosure proceedings formally started.

Meanwhile, he explored the possible collaboration on the biographical project with Reuben Caluza, who had returned to South Africa. Caluza had begun speaking to people there about bringing the tenor to the area for a tour, banking on Hayes's international celebrity to persuade the racially polarized South African government officials to endorse his appearance in the country. Once again, however, nothing materialized.

Political tensions in Europe contributed to his financial woes. Roland wrote a contact in London, a Mr. Bradby, informing him that he had intended to concertize in Spain, France, Italy, and Egypt in March of the year, "but the war between Italy and Ethiopia, and the general European war scare" caused his agents to ask for "a postponement of a year."[7] Hayes referred to Italy's invasion of Ethiopia in 1935, commonly known in the United States as the "Abyssinian Affair," especially among African Americans. In response to Italy's attack on Ethiopia – one of the only uncolonized African countries at that time – African Americans were especially incensed. Collectively, they boycotted Italian goods and staged other forms of protests. It is not clear if Roland's postponed concert was in any way connected to such an action, but had he performed in Italy at the time, he was sure to generate more negative press, especially among African Americans. He informed Bradby that he had not traveled outside the United States since 1931, which was the longest time he had been away from the Continent since first going to Europe in 1920.[8]

For much of the spring of 1936, Roland and Parham were on the road throughout the East Coast and Upper South. At the historically African American Delaware State College in Dover on March 14, however, he was accompanied by Marc Dalbert. Although Parham did not play for Roland on this concert, his composition "Life for Me Ain't Been No Crystal Stair," with the text of Langston Hughes, was included on the program.[9] The reviewer of the concert referred to Parham as Roland's "former accompanist," but there was certainly no truth to this characterization. They had their annual fall engagement at Symphony Hall in Boston in October and had another major engagement on the West Coast at the War Memorial Opera House in San Francisco.

By late 1936, young Africa was three years old, and a father/daughter relationship began to emerge through the letters that he wrote her while on the road. From Seattle in November, he wrote, "Sweetest Baby Mine: Daddy has not forgotten his little darling. He thinks of her all the time and wonders if she is being good and if she goes to sleep every day and every night at bed time."[10] He closed this very affectionate and tender message to young Africa with "Be good, sleep, sing, and be sweet to Mother every hour in the day and night. Daddy sends Baby an arm full of [unintelligible] xxxxxxxxx umph! Good day, darling from Daddy."[11]

As 1937 arrived, Roland wrote to his friend of many years, British composer Roger Quilter, announcing his return to Europe. Quilter hoped they would be able to see each other while Roland was in the United Kingdom.[12]

Roland had not given up on his ambition of producing his autobiographical work, which he had begun referring to as a "music-drama" (in the Wagnerian tradition of the word). In early 1937, he wrote to a man associated with the Hibernia Bank in San Francisco, asking him to intervene on his behalf to help him to stage his "American Negro Music

Drama." Roland would write, direct, and produce it as an exhibition at the forthcoming 1939 World Exposition opening in San Francisco.[13] The show would be between "an hour to an hour and a quarter" from beginning to end and would require as many as forty participants.[14] His request bordered on a desperate plea regarding this "tremendous" and worthy undertaking.

The idea for the proposed work was, in large part, the same he had unsuccessfully pitched to several Hollywood studios. The drama's characters included Olin (Roland's character as a child and then as an adult); Pony (the name by which his mother, Fannie, was known when she had been enslaved); Unca Nat (the formerly enslaved African who in Roland's youth had taught him the spiritual "Po' Pilgrim"); Abawiggi (Abá 'Ougi, Roland's continental African forebear); Calhoun (Arthur Calhoun, Roland's first voice teacher); Zadie (presumably Alzada, or possibly Alzada's sister Alma, as this character marries someone else in the drama); Peter (another of Roland's paternal forebears and the son of Abá 'Ougi); Dr. Wiltsie (presumably an elderly version of Roland); Maria (Peter's wife); and Bobby (a minstrel-like character).[15] In an earlier version of the work (perhaps the Hollywood version), the mythical Yoruba deity Oluwa (which would have been played by Roland in the drama) appeared as a character but was apparently removed in later versions of the drama.

As of the late 1930s, this romanticized version of his life was divided into thirty-three chronological scenes, which included descriptions and often the song or spiritual that accompanied a specific scene. For example, scene 2 featured a slave ship and the dramatically depicted capture and enslavement of Abawiggi, the African king, and his resistance to bondage. This is the point where Roland had intended to utilize the services of Reuben Caluza or some other continental African to provide indigenous music. The finale was a choral procession in a performance of the spiritual "Done Made my Vow to the Lord."[16] In a slightly altered version of the music drama (presumably for a European production), Roland's work was to have been accompanied by the Collone Orchestra at the Chattellets Theatre in Paris with the eminent Maestro Gabriel Pierné.[17] But to Roland's chagrin, neither the San Francisco nor the European version of the music drama took place. Roland had not advanced the idea beyond conceptualizing the scenes.[18]

In January 1937, Roland received sad news from Europe that his former voice teacher and coach Dr. Theo Lierhammer, had died. The bearer of this news had been Dr. Ernst Pieta, who was preparing for Roland's return to Europe. The two had been out of contact with each other for some years, but Pieta was eager to have the tenor back on the Continent and began ambitious negotiations for him to do another tour in the Soviet Union.[19]

Roland and Parham had a major engagement at New York's Town Hall on February 21, and the accompanist played so well that Roland was motivated to compliment him on this particular performance in a letter. He passed along a comment that he had received from a fan: "The sympathetic accompaniment by Mr. Parham called to mind the drums in other African motifs," to which Roland added his own flattering comments about Parham's effective arrangement of "Sit Down."[20]

Excitement at the Hayes household in Brookline was building in March on the cusp of their first family trip to Europe. It would be Roland's first trip back to the Continent since 1931 and the first time out of the country for Alzada and Africa. Quilter wrote Roland again telling him how much he was looking forward to seeing him in the United Kingdom. Before going, however, Roland and Parham had a few engagements in the South. The Hayes family also had to return Robert Brante's daughter, who had been staying with them as an older companion to little Africa.

While in the area, Roland, Alzada, and Africa passed through Chattanooga to see their cousins. Alzada's oldest brother, Jesse (Roland's cousin and brother-in-law), had a private conversation with the tenor about the latter's support of the recently deposed and exiled Ethiopian monarch Haile Selassie. At the beginning of April, Jesse felt compelled to write his brother-in-law and sister to say, "As you well know Hallie Selasse [sic] is in England so be very careful with Africa. We shall treat the little matter you mentioned as advised – mum."[21] The admonition from Jesse suggested that he was aware of the controversy surrounding the outcast Ethiopian leader (because of his involvement in the collective African American boycott of Italian American goods as a result of Italy's 1935 invasion of the country) and warned Roland to take precautions where the young girl was concerned.

On April 28, the entire Hayes family along with Percival Parham boarded the SS *Normandie* out of New York for Europe.[22] Roland and Parham gave a concert on board with Alzada and Africa in attendance. Much later in life, Africa recalled the trip. Approaching the age of four, she recalled being offered wine aboard the ship (an apparent French custom), but her parents objected and insisted that she have milk. They arrived at Port South Hampton in the British Isles in early May and were met there by none other than Robert Broadhurst. After making their way to London's Fernshaw House, where the family was based, Roland paid calls on old friends like Roger Quilter, whom he had not seen for some years.

In a meeting with Broadhurst on May 15, Roland spoke about his support and deep commitment to the deposed "Conquering Lion of the Tribe of Judah," one of the several honorific titles of Haile Selassie I, and his wish to meet Selassie while he was in England. Broadhurst referred to the exiled leader as "our emperor, His Majesty," and told Roland that he would facilitate the meeting. Roland would perform a private recital at the deposed ruler's Bath residence through the London-based Ethiopian resistance movement, the Friends of Abyssinia.[23] As this recital was kept secret, there is no conclusive date as to when they made the journey. Roland left no notes or reflections about his meeting with the Ethiopian ruler.

Roland's first major public engagement on the European continent was at the Salle Gaveau in Paris on May 20, 1937. His accompanist was Erich Itor Kahn, who incidentally was not paid as late as October 1937.[24] It remains unclear why Parham did not accompany the tenor at this performance, which was hailed by the press as Hayes's return to the French public. The reviewer bemoaned that he had been away from the country for such a long period.

Knowing full well that her former paramour was in France, Countess Bertha also attended the concert with their eleven-year-old daughter, Maya. The countess apparently arranged for the father and daughter to see each other, if only briefly. This concert at the Salle Gaveau would have been the only occasion on which the two Hayes daughters would have been in the vicinity of each other; the same is true of Alzada and Bertha.[25]

The Salle Gaveau performance was, no doubt, a dramatic and tense experience for Roland with both familial contingents in the same audience. Knowing the sophisticated Bertha as he did, Roland was surely more concerned for the welfare of his wife if the two were to meet. Bertha, who was fully aware of Alzada, could have easily approached and intimidated her, but there is nothing to suggest that the two women encountered each other. When, how, and under what circumstances Roland met with Bertha and their daughter cannot be determined, but a letter from Maya to her father years later made clear that such a meeting took place in Paris in 1937.

Also in attendance at the Salle Gaveau concert was Roland's old friend Joseph Salmon, the renowned cellist who had almost single-handedly made Roland "Le Rage de Paris" in the early 1920s. Although Salmon complimented the tenor for his performance in a personal written note, the communication was anything but friendly. Roland had been out of touch with Salmon and his wife, Maddie, for some time, in spite of their close personal and professional relationship during the 1920s. An unmistakable breach had occurred in their relationship, and the chastising tone of the elder cellist's letter to Roland left little question about the seriousness of his resolve and who he believed was at fault for their estrangement:

24 May 1937
93 rue Jouffroy
My dear Roland,

I must absolutely tell you that with a [unintelligible] incomparable – you sang better than ever. However, I must also tell you that you are wrong for not sending the slightest word during your stay in Paris, and for not coming to see me. I am placing the entire responsibility for this unjustified act with you. I assume that you are angry with me because I returned to you a Christmas card, some years ago, that you addressed to me only. I was right to return it and you were wrong for sending it; I will never accept something addressed to me only when I have a wife and a daughter! I also assume that you are angry with Maddy [sic] for not kicking out the Countess and your child. You are again in the wrong because it was you who introduced us to the Countess and besides, since having met her, we have only seen her maybe 2 or 3 times and that's it.

That is all that I want to say to you today. I am not happy with how you have treated me. I admire and like you just the same.

Joseph Salmon[26]

If Roland responded to this unambiguous letter from Salmon, it is unknown. What is unmistakable, however, is that he had wanted his friends
the Salmons to side with him in some apparent dispute with Bertha,
and apparently Maddie had not done what he wanted. This is one of the
few documents that both confirms the relationship between Hayes and
Bertha and acknowledges their child, Maya. The letter suggests that the
countess and Maya had been hosted by the Salmons at some point (probably the summer of 1931, when Roland had ended their relationship) and
that Hayes became disturbed at this apparent betrayal.

On May 31, Roland sang, once more, at his beloved Wigmore Hall
in London. He had debuted in the city on the exact date seventeen years
earlier under very different circumstances. By 1937, of course, he was an
internationally renowned musician and a well-known name to the concertgoing British public. His old management agency, Ibbs and Tillett,
facilitated other smaller engagements for him throughout the British
Isles. Among those were a few performances at the home of his friends
Lord and Lady Astor.

Dr. Pieta had made good on his promise to arrange for Roland to
make another tour to the Soviet Union. He had begun communicating
with the tenor before his departure for Europe in late April and wanted
to arrange several USSR dates for the following year.[27] Unlike before,
however, Soviet government officials were quite fixed in their position
that the American singer would have to be paid in rubles and could not
export it out of the country. The Soviet cultural official suggested that
Roland could do what other artists of his caliber (for example, Jascha
Heifetz) did and buy antiques or other indigenous curios, which the
government would have to approve before they could be released from
the country. Although Roland informed Pieta of his 1928 arrangement
and how his salary requirements were met at that time, the official simply
replied that that was a different time. There would be no such arrangement for a proposed second visit. After that, there was little motivation
for the second Soviet trip, which never materialized.

The Hayes family returned to the United States in June, where they
spent time at the farm in Georgia. Roland also prepared for the upcoming season, which began with a fall recital at New York's Town Hall, a
fund-raiser for the New York Committee to Aid the Southern Negro
Youth Congress.[28] Formed in Richmond, Virginia, the conference took

positions on a variety of issues facing African American communities, such as poverty and empowerment. Present at that October 9 engagement was Roland's first voice teacher, W. Arthur Calhoun.[29] He and Roland had not seen each other for some years.

Calhoun continued his contact with Roland, who, on more than one occasion, assisted his early mentor/teacher financially. The depth of their relationship, however, was revealed in a remarkably moving letter written by Calhoun days after his now-celebrated student's recital in New York City. It spoke to their days as teacher and student in Chattanooga dating back to the early 1900s:

> I can not describe so that you could understand me exactly how I felt as I sat there in Town Hall spell bound listening to your matchless singing. My mind rushed ... back through the years to the city auditorium ... when in the role of "David the shepherd boy," you electrified that vast audience of those who had worked with you, worshipped at church and had gone to both day and Sunday school with you. And they *loved* you.
>
> I had visions that night of what I hoped you would someday be and I prayed to Almighty God to direct me that I could give you guidance and inspiration to make you an artist. In those days the world was little known and understood to us simple everyday folk in Chattanooga which at the time was little more than a thriving little city.
>
> I had vivid recollections of Chickamauga Park and Warner City Park where Negroes were not allowed but your voice was sweet music to the thousands of the South's best whites every Sunday. ... I thought of all those throngs of white people, old, middle-aged and young ones of every description who listened breathlessly, and never once offered an insult. And of course I had a vivid vision of that big hearted Southern-born and reared gentleman Mr. Will Stone. I have always thought that God directed me to have you go there and sing for him and his family because ever after that, you were esteemed as one of their most cherished and desired acquaintances. Just think of such a thing happening in the heart of the South!
>
> When ever we visited them, it was as welcomed guests. Never did they try to hide us, but they seemed always eager to display their appreciation of us in the presence of their white friends. We always ate at the same table and receiving all considerations and treatment on terms of absolute equality. ... Those were wonderful days Roland and I lived them all over again while listening to you at Town Hall Saturday last. ... Don't forget me when you are on your knees and in touch with God. In closing, I beg to be remembered as one whose inspiration has been greatly quickened.[30]

Calhoun's very moving and reflective October 12 letter went on to say that he was not well and had been able to attend Roland's recital only because of the assistance of one of his daughters, who had to help him prepare for the concert. Calhoun and Roland did see each other after the recital, and Roland noted in response to Calhoun's letter some weeks later that he was "pained" to find his former teacher in such "feeble" condition.[31] As Calhoun had relied on Roland's largesse in the past, he no doubt was hoping that the tenor would make a similar offer after seeing him in such a debilitated state. However, Roland ruled out such assistance on this occasion because of the country's "depressed" condition. The tenor also subtly informed his teacher that, unlike before, when he was a single man, he now had a family to support.

As in years past, Roland received his end-of-year prediction and forecast for the year to come (1937 to 1938) from Blanche Watson. Alzada was also a part of the consultation. Watson had predicted (in writing after the fact) that 1937 would be a good year for Roland.[32] Given that he had already had several successful engagements in Europe (although nothing comparable to his earlier years there), he continued to be persuaded by her forecasting abilities, as was Alzada.

The new year marked yet another career milestone for the tenor as he and Parham traveled south out of the country to Mexico, with the plan of continuing to South America. It was a first for both of them. The tour had been arranged by Roland's latest manager, Richard Copley.[33] Their first engagement was in Mexico City on January 28, and a diplomat from the U.S. embassy, Joseph Daniels, was present for the performance. In a letter to his host, Señor Ernesto de Quesada, Daniels said, "As a Southerner I rejoice in the reputation which this gifted singer has made and am glad that the Mexican public is having the opportunity to hear him."[34]

The Mexican tour, however, was abruptly interrupted during the third week of February because Parham took ill and had to return home for treatment in New York. Because there was no one available locally to play for Roland, he too returned. Parham's physician, Dr. May Chin, wrote Roland on February 23 reporting that Parham was suffering from "hypertension with kidney complications and cardiac embarrassment" (that is, some impairment).[35] Roland responded to Dr. Chin at the beginning of March inquiring about his friend and accompanist's condition. He also asked if he needed to make arrangements to retain someone else for upcoming engagements, including one at Williams College in Massachusetts. At the time he had written Chin, he was in Milwaukee and had to use a local person to play for him. Chin assured Roland that Parham "should" be able to meet those engagements. However, Parham himself contacted Roland to tell him that he did not feel up to playing the recital. The Williams College performance was handled by another accompanist, Reginald Boardman, with Parham's endorsement and blessings.[36]

While Roland and Parham were in Mexico, Roland had met Oliver Kisich, yet another contact in his effort to produce his music drama (which he started referring to as a "pageant") at the 1939 World Exposition in San Francisco.[37] In outlining the project for Kisich, who was favorably impressed with what he heard from the singer, Roland said he needed a financial commitment of three thousand dollars to move the work forward. Roland now spoke of a collaboration with a Viennese playwright (unnamed) who would assist him with crafting the spoken text in the work, but the music was "WHOLLY" his with the help of a "coadjutor" (that is, an assistant, who was also unnamed) at his elbow for orchestral instrumentation.[38]

The latest version of the work opened with a scene on the African continent with a Mother Nature/Mother Africa figure. He had borrowed this idea from the "eternal woman" theme found in the conclusion of Goethe's epic *Faust*. The African mother then transformed into the human mother, and the "pageant" proceeded as described earlier.

To stress the urgency of this project, Roland pointed out to Oliver Kisich in his letter that he had *just* that day received a letter from his unnamed Viennese playwright who said that for the "meager sum" of one thousand dollars he would spend three months exclusively on the work and drop everything else until it was complete. Once again, Roland appeared to have concocted the entire scenario, a ploy he had attempted in the past to exaggerate the musical drama's importance. But being vague about several aspects of the production and claiming he had attracted the services of an "important Viennese playwright" for a "meager sum" didn't work when making a pitch to prospective financial backers. If there had been an important Viennese playwright, Roland would have strengthened his case by naming the person. There was nothing to be gained from secrecy.

It is more plausible that he was attempting to give the project a European, high-brow touch so that it would not be perceived as exclusively African American–derived. Roland had not been above such tactics in the past, given the news stories he had most certainly planted in 1934 about refusing to "sell out" his race by conceding to Hollywood demands that he alter his work. He had not named any studio then and was unwilling to name his European "writer" at this point because it is likely neither existed.

But Roland continued to cultivate interest from continental Africans about such an undertaking. After the planned collaboration with Reuben Caluza evaporated, the next continental citizens who captured the tenor's attention were Africanus and Victoria Schaak of Liberia. The letter and accompanying brochure they sent to Roland read, "Liberia Revealed . . . An hour spent with the Schaaks and Liberia is never forgotten."[39] According to their publicity material, both Schaaks were educated on the African continent as well as in the West. In addition to having mastered several Liberian indigenous languages, Victoria was fluent in all of the major European languages. At this time, Roland's primary interest in the Schaaks was their knowledge of indigenous African songs, which he wanted for his fall recital.

Roland and his family spent the summer of 1938 at Angelmo Farm in Georgia, where he allowed a white Canadian student to come study voice with him.[40] The student wasn't there long before one of Roland's white tenant farmers reported that he had "heard threats" made against Roland and the boy by white locals if the young man continued to stay in the same living quarters with the Hayes family. Roland's relationship with the Canadian man violated norms of the separation of blacks and whites. Although the locals' threats seemed hypocritical and selective – after all, Roland had white tenants working on his farm as field hands; should he run them off also? – Roland conceded to local segregation customs and sent the young man away. The experience left him a little jaded but did not dissuade him from his goal of bringing the races closer together.[41]

Despite what he had written to Roland in his March 1938 letter about feeling "good in places I never remember feeling before," Percival Parham's situation had not gotten appreciably better throughout the summer.[42] He convalesced at the Long Island residence of a Mrs. Griffin, although he expected to return to Boston. When his financial resources were depleted, Roland stepped in. However, on September 20, Parham passed

away. The *New York Times* noted: "Richard Percival Parham, Negro pianist who for the last twelve years had accompanied Roland Hayes, Negro
tenor, died here this evening at the home of a friend after a long illness.
A native of Cambridge, Mass., Mr. Parham studied music in Boston and
abroad, and before becoming associated with Mr. Hayes served as an
organist in Boston."[43] When the end came, the tenor assisted with the
arrangements for him to be funeralized back in his native Cambridge,
and Roland mourned his longtime accompanist and friend. Roland and
Alzada's daughter remembered going to the funeral of Percival Parham
as a five-year-old child and seeing a young boy (whom she understood to
be Parham's son) crying at his father's funeral. She also remembered it as
one of the few times that she saw her father cry.[44] Hayes received condolence notes from several who knew of his long association with Parham,
including Howard Jordan, who had traveled with him and Parham in
Europe and throughout the Soviet Union, among other places. But it was
Roland's response to a sympathy note that he had received from Noël
Sullivan where the singer expressed the depth of his grief:

> I am sure that no one knows as well as yourself what a tremendous loss, both as
> friend and musician, the passing of Parham has brought me. I had constantly
> feared the worse from January when we were in Mexico City, but I kept hoping
> against hope up to the last minute that he might pull through. Yes, he was and
> is a great friend and loyal to the last degree. His going has left me groping for
> another spirit . . . whose musical point of view and equipment may blend in with
> my own. For the present, I have a member of your race, Mr. Reginald Boardman,
> who will be with me for my Autumn concerts.[45]

Parham was, by Roland's estimation, his strongest accompanist. He
never spoke so flatteringly of any of his previous pianists (although he
had a clear affinity for the long-deceased Daisy Tapley). Percival Parham
had never sought parity with the singer (as had been the case with Lawrence Brown) but merely wanted the opportunity to prove himself as a
world-class musician. Roland, unquestionably, provided him with the
vehicle to demonstrate his skill as a first-rate keyboardist as well as an
ultra-talented composer and arranger. As a show of loyalty, Roland sang
more of Percival Parham's spiritual arrangements and compositions than
those of Lawrence Brown and William Lawrence combined.

The tenor's "temporary" accompanist, Reginald Boardman, wound
up enjoying an even longer tenure with Roland. Having had his musi-

cianship endorsed by Percival Parham, Boardman's skills were better than adequate, even if his arranging abilities did not fall in the same league as Parham's, Lawrence's, or Brown's. Yet he had the unique distinction of being with Roland longer than any of his previous accompanists combined. Although Roland occasionally performed with local accompanists, between 1938 and 1973, Reginald Boardman's thirty-five-year musical relationship with him was steadfast.

After their major engagement at Symphony Hall in Boston, the 1938 fall schedule took Roland and Boardman south to Charlotte, North Carolina; Baton Rouge, Louisiana; Jackson, Mississippi; and Tallahassee, Florida. A black artist and white artist sharing the same stage in concert in the Deep South could have caused a racial disturbance in certain places, but it seemed that he and Boardman encountered little or no resistance in their travel and living accommodations, apart from the accustomed segregation practices.

Maestro Monteux eventually responded to Roland's earlier inquiry, proposing a joint appearance, from his Paris home in mid-December; the maestro was more than willing to entertain such a proposal. Monteux unsuccessfully attempted to locate an aria of the celebrated eighteenth-century French baroque composer Jean-Philippe Rameau in Paris for him and Roland and suggested that Roland use the manuscript that the maestro had found in a London library and have someone in Boston score it for strings and a few other instruments.[46] However, the record of such a performance has not materialized. Maestro Monteux led the San Francisco Orchestra between 1935 and 1952; perhaps such a performance took place with that ensemble. Roland's spring 1939 schedule started where the December one left off, in the South. He and Boardman performed on the campus of the University of Texas at Austin, went north to Kentucky, and then proceeded west.

Roland had yet another shift in his dizzying series of management changes. Richard Copley, who was with the tenor for a short time, had also died; his surviving associate, Ray Halmans, established the Ray Halmans Concert Management Agency (also in New York) and took over as Roland's personal manager. She was just as professional as Copley yet a little too detached for Roland's taste. Nevertheless, by the time she took over managing his career, he had had dealings with more than ten different people with more to come.

The relationship between Roland and Alzada had grown since their marriage seven years earlier. He often wrote to her when he was traveling, expressing his deep feelings for her. He understood that his touring placed stresses on her; she had to hold the household together with young Africa. In a March letter, he told her that they would be together in the summer.[47] Eventually, Roland and Boardman made it to the West Coast, where he was reunited with his friend Noël Sullivan at his Hollow Hills Farm in Carmel, California.

Around this time Roland was contacted by yet another continental African, whom he had met a few years before, who had the ambition of getting the singer to visit the continent. The latest in a series was Duke Kwesi Kuntu of the Gold Coast. He had had some discussion with Roland about activities on Angelmo Farm and wanted to see something of that experiment duplicated in his country.

As the tenor had promised Alzada, the entire Hayes family spent the summer in Georgia at Angelmo Farm. Roland was a dutiful father, husband, and part-time farm hand. He was photographed harvesting the crops in the fields and caring for the farm animals. As an added bonus for Alzada and Africa, they accompanied him to Ohio, where on June 13 he received another honorary doctor of musical arts degree from Ohio Wesleyan University. Roland was honored once again at the end of the summer when the Hamilton County Department of Education in Tennessee informed him that another school was to bear his name in Chattanooga. The entire family was invited to attend the dedication on August 30, and he gave brief remarks and sang a mini-recital.[48]

At the end of September 1939, Roland and Boardman began several recording sessions for the Columbia label in New York, which were not completed until mid-November.[49] In the four sessions, they recorded only a small sample of Roland's vast repertory. Among them were several spirituals, including a few of Percival Parham's arrangements. He recorded Beethoven's very romantic "Adelaïde" (parts 1 and 2) on two separate occasions in those sessions.[50] The project was released to the public the following year as *A Song Recital by Roland Hayes,* which featured ten of the roughly twenty works that were recorded. At fifty-two years old, however, he was no longer at his vocal zenith.

Based on the catastrophic economic events that had so affected his career and prestige during the 1930s, Roland was happy to wave good-bye to the decade. Blanche Watson had predicted more prosperous times for Roland and the country, but not even her forecasting skills could foresee another devastating world war on the horizon. It would take such a dramatic event to facilitate an economic resurgence in the United States.

In February 1940, Roland and Boardman traveled to Daytona Beach, Florida, at the request of Dr. Mary McLeod Bethune, president of Bethune-Cookman College, to perform at a building dedication on the campus. He and the highly distinguished African American educator, presidential adviser, and social activist had known each other for some time and had become close friends. When she wrote him at the end of February to thank him for singing at the college, she signed the letter "Sister Mary," as he had come to know her.[51]

Roland received another letter from "Sister" Mary in April, this time from Johns Hopkins Hospital in Baltimore, where she had been admitted for medical testing. She wanted Roland to go to Bethune-Cookman College and spend three or four months of the year there to establish the Roland Hayes Music Center on the campus. She saw it as an opportunity to draw attention to the work of the institution, have someone of his prestige to help train the voice students, and offer him a formidable base of operation in the South. She cited the example of R. Nathaniel Dett (formerly of Hampton University) and his relationship with Bennett College.[52] Roland politely declined the invitation after giving it much thought. In the end, he informed Dr. Bethune he was not inclined to take on a full-time teaching position.

Also in April, Roland participated in a radio broadcast honoring the late Booker T. Washington and marking the issuance of a stamp honoring the African American pioneer through the U.S. postal service. The current president of Tuskegee Institute, F. D. Patterson, had invited Roland to participate, as had Roland's longtime friend Walter White, secretary of the NAACP. White also informed the singer that he had been in communication with the legendary conductor Leopold Stokowski, who had vowed to feature more African American musicians in his concerts as a concession to the organization and to better integrate the performing arts.[53] At the event, Roland sang a musical setting of the Langston Hughes poem "Alabama Earth," set to music by Reginald Boardman. The ceremony was attended by the U.S. postmaster general and other prominent officials. Roland later wrote Noël Sullivan saying that the radio performance was just "okay," as he could not "muster" much enthusiasm to sing before the radio microphone.[54]

At the end of the year, on December 21, Roland sang at the Library of Congress in Washington, D.C., at an event commemorating the seventy-fifth anniversary of the U.S. Constitutional amendment abolishing African enslavement in the United States. The series of public events was under the auspices of the Gertrude Clarke Whittall Foundation. Also singing on the program with Roland was a youthful but up-and-coming soprano from Virginia, Dorothy Maynor. This seems to be the only time they appeared on a program together. The theme of the event focused on African American cultural contributions through a series of art exhibitions, manuscript displays, and books. Other participants included Dr. Alain Locke, Roland's old friend from Howard University, and Sterling Brown. Among those who served on the blue ribbon advisory committee were Dr. Carter G. Woodson, Harry T. Burleigh, R. Nathaniel Dett, and Lulu Vere Childers, all (but Dett) acquaintances of Hayes.

In February 1941, Roland and Boardman entered the Columbia Records Studio once again, where they recorded another seven works, including "Steal Away" (again), "Micheu Banjo" (a Creole folk song), and "Xango" by Villa-Lobos.[55] Roland also recorded "I Wanna Go Home" (a cappella) and "You're Tired, Chile" (with piano accompaniment). The contrast between the 1923 version of "Sit Down" and the 1941 "You're Tired, Chile" is noticeable. Much had taken place in the tenor's life in the intervening eighteen years, or perhaps it was just "water under the bridge," a phrase Roland was fond of using when he wanted to avoid the specifics of a topic.

In December 1941, when the Pearl Harbor attack ushered the United States promptly into World War II, the country and the world braced for conflict and battles as never before. In the comfort and safety of their suburban home, Alzada and Africa wrote Roland while he was on the road participating in the war effort through singing benefit concerts and encouraging support among African Americans. In January 1942, at the urging of his manager, Ray Halmans, he sang for the National Republican Club.[56]

While Roland continued his annual tour, Alzada and eight-year-old "Baby" (Hayes's pet name for Africa) frequently sent letters to him while he was on the road. The young girl wrote things like, "How are you? . . . I am getting along fine with my arithmetic. . . . I would cook your breakfast for you if you had let me come with you. . . . Nova [the dog] still runs the cat, and I am sorry I did not write you sooner."[57]

In stark contrast to the relationship that Roland enjoyed with Africa, a far more toned down and furtive, if not clandestine, relationship emerged in a war-braced Europe between Roland and his older daughter, Maya. By early January 1942, the fifteen-year-old adolescent (about to turn sixteen) was experiencing normal teenage angst. She had grown up in an environment where many questions about her personal circumstances and history were not asked. And if questions were asked, they were not answered, at least not initially. Her friends knew there were certain topics that they needed to avoid, yet she knew she was different in appearance when her beautiful light-caramel-colored skin was compared to that of her paler playmates. Her light brown hair (with more than a few blond streaks) was also of a thicker texture than theirs. She had fuller lips and other distinctive physical characteristics that made her stand out in the otherwise homogeneous southern French province. Because of her mother's aristocratic status (even in the provincial St. Lary), the girl was somewhat shielded from what might have otherwise been a more troubled existence.

She had grown up in a household where she was not allowed to call her mother "Mammi" or "Maman," as did the other children, or anything similar to that until she was about ten years old. She had been told by her mother, Bertha, that she had been brought by fairies and found in a shoebox and raised accordingly. She had endured the disdain, if not the hostility, of Bertha's mother, the elder Countess Kolowrat-Krakowsky, and her relationship with her half-brothers (that is, Bertha's sons from her marriage to Count Hieronymus) could be best described as marginal.

Maya's education, on the other hand, was extensive. Bertha had hired governesses when Maya was young and private tutors to assist her as she reached school age. She was perfectly fluent in French and German and could also read and write in both languages. Eventually she came to have facility with Russian. She spoke perfect English without the hint of an accent. Her written command of the language demonstrated her European upbringing and training.[58]

Maya also had extensive musical training. She played the keyboard and had an interest in singing for some time. When she was eight or nine years old, little Maya had wanted to run away, join a circus, and become a lion tamer. After seeing a performance of Bizet's *Carmen,* she wanted to be an opera singer.[59]

With such lofty ambitions, there were times when Maya must have seemed literally sequestered in her seemingly remote world in the southern Pyrenees Mountains on the Spanish border. But even there, the European conflict could not be escaped.

In World War II France, Bertha, the Countess Colloredo-Mansfeld, had received from her husband, Count Hieronymus, a somewhat spacious chateau in southern France and a substantial stipend on which she and her daughter could survive. But because of her generous spirit, she was constantly assisting others whose economic situations were more severe than hers. She had managed to harbor Jewish refugees (whom Maya referred to in her letters as "cronies") in the castle and, amazingly, without detection.

Where her father was concerned, Maya steadfastly held on to the hope of a relationship and that she would one day join him in the United States. Her January 1942 communication written to him at Angelmo Farm spoke to the hope of such a relationship coming about as well as to a number of the complex emotions of a fifteen-year-old girl making the transition into womanhood.[60] The letter also reminded him that she had had contact with him earlier. When Roland gave his May 20, 1937, concert at Salle Gaveau, an eleven-year-old Maya and her mother had been in the audience. She recalled it years later when she wrote him, "I would so like to see you again, to hear your wonderful concert. I'll never forget the last one in Paris six [sic] years ago. It was so beautiful."[61]

It was Bertha who sent Maya's letter to Roland at his Georgia farm with her own letter as a preface. Begun on December 25, 1941 (and continued early into the new year), Bertha opened her letter to Roland by saying, "My dear, I am sending you Maya's letter fully aware of the importance or non-importance it might have for you." She continued, "You cannot say that you have been bothered by either of us and I have quite deliberately kept silent for years after three or four messages . . . have remained unanswered by you."[62] Bertha explained to the father of her daughter that their child was "slowly approaching the turning point in her existence." She wanted to get out of Europe (which, like the United States, was in the midst of World War II). She spoke about respecting Roland's right to privacy, but she said that she would make any "sacrifice" to help and protect her daughter – *their* daughter. If it meant her having contact with her father, she was willing to facilitate it in any way she could. Her primary concern was to see the rudderless Maya have some path to happiness. Bertha pleaded that if Roland were to communicate with their daughter now and then and give her at least the hope of seeing Angelmo Farm someday, it would also give her life the purpose that, at that specific time, she sorely needed. As always, Bertha wished her former soul mate and the father of her daughter "all the happiness and success [he] deserved."[63]

Maya opened her letter to her father with the pseudonym that she had used when writing him for the last several years: "Dear Mario . . ." All of the letters had been sent to Angelmo Farm (per the instructions of Roland). When referring to her mother, Bertha, in the letter, she used yet another pseudonym, "Lady Fair." She continued:

> It is already such a long [time] since . . . I have written to you. I have so many things to tell you. . . . I have lived through the war with relative patience until the summer 1940. Till then, I had little companions and still used to play Indian and cowboys with them, but they went away and I stayed alone with myself. I love to be alone, but the result was that I began to think and to think much too much, because I am getting intolerable of everybody with my peculiar ideas.[64]

Maya then told "Mario" about her fascination with Native American culture, which stemmed from an Indian doll he had given her some years before (probably when he saw her in 1937). According to her, "It has got all my respect, and is the only doll I didn't break. I secretly called him 'Red Cloud,' after the great war chief."[65]

This letter provides a glimpse of the adolescent Maya. These are the expressed feelings of a melancholy young woman reaching out for some acceptance from an absent father whom she admired from afar. So as not to raise any suspicions among the Nazi mail censors (the envelope had an inspector's clearance sticker on it), she shifted to typewritten pages.

Maya's latest dream was to see the Native American prairies, where the war chiefs whom she had read about had once lived. Although she had once been attracted to their face paint, costumes, and colorful features, of late, she loved them because they "were a very free people, great liberty-lovers, because of their curious . . . and individual customs."[66] Maya's extensive reading on African Americans vis-à-vis their situation with Native Americans led her to some very prophetic observations. She had read about the tragedies of Little Big Horn and Wounded Knee and concluded that these battles marked the beginning of the end of the indigenous inhabitants of North America.

In contrast, Maya saw a very different trajectory for African Americans: "For the Negroes, it is quite different. They are a growing race. They are growing into Glory. The Indian is growing too, but into Death . . ." She had also familiarized herself (through her gramophone recordings) of celebrated African American singers such as Marian Anderson and Paul Robeson. She had heard their recorded performances of spirituals like "City Called Heaven," "Deep River," and "Go Down Moses." The latter was her favorite, and she had memorized all the words.

Above all, Maya urged her father to write her back because her overwhelming desire was to come to the United States and see Angelmo Farm. Whatever limited communications Roland had had with his daughter, Maya latched onto even the slimmest of hopes with the fervency of a child believing in Santa Claus. Her letter included a drawing of an Indian scene from the American Wild West with the imaginary Chief Winnetou (of the Karl May stories) mounted on a horse shooting arrows at buffalos. Her artistic skills were considerable for a fifteen-year-old.

This is the only letter from Maya's teen years that has survived. She did not emerge in Roland Hayes's life (through letters or other measurable contact) again until she was an adult another twelve years later. Roland missed out on *this* daughter's childhood and young adulthood. In fact, he missed out on most of her life.

ELEVEN

Rome, Georgia

1942

YOUNG AFRICA NEEDED NEW TENNIS SHOES, SO ON SATURDAY morning, July 11, 1942, Roland and Alzada took her to Rome, Georgia, to buy them. Rome was like many midsize and larger southern urban areas; African Americans had access to certain stores but had to be inconspicuous and move about with the requisite deference for the town's white residents. This was standard practice in the South. Recently, however, there had been two incidents in Rome involving blacks' asserting their rights against standard southern traditions. In the first incident, a young African American man sat in the white section of a bus, which caused a disruption. The second involved an African American preacher in Rome who had allegedly said from the pulpit that with white men and boys away fighting the war, it would be the right time for African Americans to stand up for themselves.[1]

The oppressive July heat of Georgia got the better of Alzada when the Hayes family went shopping. Alzada entered Higgins Shoe Store in downtown Rome with Africa. It was her first time in the store, and not seeing a sign directing African American patrons to a particular section, she and her daughter sat under a ceiling fan to cool themselves – which happened to be where white patrons were assisted.[2] When Alzada was spotted by a clerk, she was told aggressively that she had to be served in the area reserved for African American customers.[3] Alzada responded that she did not see a sign to that effect. When the clerk became a little more threatening, Alzada said, "This is not the time to talk about racial prejudice and segregation. [Adolf] Hitler ought to have you."[4] The clerk demanded that she leave the store and threatened to call the police if she didn't do so immediately. Alzada and Africa left. Africa began whining because she hadn't gotten her shoes, but her mother calmly told her that the store didn't want them there.

The mother and daughter went into another nearby shoe store to purchase the tennis shoes. Roland found them as they were leaving it and asked how things had gone. When Alzada told him about the incident in Higgins Shoe Store, he told his wife that they needed to return there, as he was sure there had been some misunderstanding. When they walked in, they encountered the owner, Fred Higgins. Once Roland identified himself and made the owner aware that he had patronized the store in the past without incident, Higgins was very apologetic about the earlier episode and offered to personally wait on Alzada at that very moment. She politely declined the offer, pointing out that she had gone elsewhere to find shoes for her daughter.

Believing the matter had been resolved amicably, the Hayes family left the store. Alzada went into another shop and left Africa with her father, walking down the sidewalk. Within minutes, Alzada heard her daughter's distinctive scream and ran out, terrified that some accident had taken place. She saw Africa standing on the street crying, "Don't take him! Don't take him!" as a crowd had begun to assemble around a police car in front of Higgins Shoe Store. She ran to her daughter to ask where Roland was. Not being able to see through the crowd, Alzada instinctively knew that her husband was somehow involved in this altercation; she ran to the police car and jumped in the front seat, only to see her husband being beaten by several policemen in the back seat of the patrol car. She screamed when she saw an officer, with the full force of his clenched fist, strike her husband in the jaw. Pinning Roland in the back seat of the car, the officers sat on him while they forcefully handcuffed him. Alzada's protests of the brutal treatment being meted out to her husband only seemed to anger the police all the more, and they continued to punch him violently in the mouth and on his head. Even though his already bruised face was pressed up against the back seat, Roland managed to tell his wife not to say anymore and just take their child and leave. The policemen beat him some more, telling him to "shut the hell up!"

Alzada got out of the car and grabbed her hysterical daughter. But another police officer ordered her to get back into the car as *she* was the apparent cause of all the "trouble."[5] So with little Africa in tow, the Hayes family and the Rome, Georgia, police all drove off to the county courthouse, which was in city hall, with the tenor suffering from his "beat down" in the back seat of the police car.[6] When Alzada continued to protest against her husband being struck repeatedly, even though he was completely subdued, the policeman driving the car told her again to "shut up" or they would give her some of what they were giving him.[7]

When they arrived at the courthouse, Roland and Alzada were led inside and placed together in a jail cell. The child was left crying in the jailhouse lobby. After a short while, two officers came to the cell and entered. They asked Alzada her name, and she defiantly responded, *"Mrs. Hayes."* One of the policemen drew back his fist as if to punch her and said, "God dammit! Don't ch'u say no 'Mrs.' to me."[8] They were in the cell about an hour and a half before the tenor was allowed to post the fifty-dollar bond.

As the incident occurred on a Saturday morning, it took a few days before the general public came to know of the Hayes family's ordeal in Rome. The African American newspaper the *Atlanta Daily Word,* in its July 15, 1942, issue, seems to have been one of the earliest to report on it. Two days after that, the *New York Times'* July 17 headline (and bylines) read:

BEATEN IN GEORGIA
SAYS Roland HAYES

Negro Singer Asserts He and
Wife Were Put in Cell After
a Store Dispute

POLICE MAKE A DENIAL

Charges of Being Slugged and
Dragged Into Patrol Car Are
Not True, Says Chief[9]

The *Times* account incorporated input from Roland; the store owner, Fred Higgins; and hearsay remarks from the Rome chief of police, Charles I. Harris.[10] According to the *Times,* Alzada had been verbally abusive to the store clerk. The store owner, Higgins, then came along and reminded her that as a "Negro" who had been "born and reared" in the South, she was well aware of the region's segregation rules regarding African Americans. (In the account offered by Alzada, Higgins was not present when the initial encounter took place.) When Roland returned with Alzada, Higgins had offered to assist the family on the spot. However, he appeared to change his account for the *Times* story, saying he had been present when Alzada was initially in the store. Roland acknowledged to the *Times* reporter that Alzada had indeed made a remark about racial prejudice and that the clerk should be with Hitler. He also briefly related his initial encounter with the Nazi Party, describing their interruption of his Berlin recital in 1924. Roland's concluding comments were that he was not embittered by the incident and that the "humiliation [was] on the other side." He said that he was ashamed that such an action should have occurred in his home state but that he would continue to come back, as he had land there.[11]

The reaction to the *Times* story was swift and sustained. One day after the July 17 article appeared, Roland began receiving letters and telegrams of condolence and support. One of the first came from his New York manager, Ray Halmans, who, having read the story in the *Herald-Tribune,* wrote to him that she "ached" that he would be subjected to such "indignities and vile treatment."[12] Other communications from around the country came pouring in to Roland at Angelmo Farm. "Sister Mary" McLeod Bethune wrote:

> Not until last night did the distressing news of the outrage upon you and your family reach me. I have failed to sleep. My wails and prayers have been loud to a God who must hear and understand why should such treatment come to you and yours. All America is distressed – white and black. All that can be done will be done. Our souls are stirred. WE are suffering with you. If I am needed in person, let me know.[13]

Roland received official communications from several organizations like the Department of Race Relations of the Federal Council of the Churches of Christ in America; the United Christian Youth Movement; the Boston Symphony Orchestra; the president and alumni of Fisk University (encouraging all Fiskites to rally to the side of their famous alum); the Haines Normal and Industrial Institute in Augusta, Georgia; African American (and white) Freemason lodges from around the country; the Workers Defense League; and various boards of education throughout the United States. Numerous lawyers from around the country offered their services pro bono to sue the guilty parties.[14] The National Association for Improving Negro Country Life, based at Georgia State College, invited Roland to sit on its board of directors. He received letters of solidarity and support from the composer William Grant Still, who was in Los Angeles, and Charles Harris (not to be confused with the Rome chief of police by the same name), his good friend and fraternity brother from his early days in Boston, who was still teaching at South Carolina State in Orangeburg.

Roland also heard from many lesser-known well-wishers, black and white. Such letters came from concerned individuals like Mrs. Valeno Costello and her family in Biloxi, Mississippi, who said, in part:

> I want to say this to you. This thing happened to you, true enough, but, just be thankful to our God that they did not take away your life completely. I imagine, that really was what they were trying to do.
>
> They are jealous of you because you have climbed your ladder to success in your singing. Now they want to destroy you because your skin is dark.
>
> It seems to us, that God is taking his own time in giving our race a brake [*sic*].
> ... What has been done to you will never be forgotten, but, try to be strong and courageous.[15]

An even larger number of well-meaning European Americans wrote Roland from different parts of the country. When the incident was reported in *Time* magazine,[16] it brought another round of letters, like those from H. L. Smith of Madison, Wisconsin:

> You will probably receive many crackpot letters after the article in TIME magazine, but there must be hundreds who are thoroughly indignant at the way you and Mrs. Hayes were treated. It may make some of us wonder what we are fighting for, when such a large section of the country doesn't even know the meaning of the word Democracy.
>
> One thing is clear, and that is that every time an intelligent, useful member of your race reacts with dignity and largeness of spirit, you put us one step nearer to the ultimate brotherhood of man, for which we are really fighting. In the encounter you came out second best, but because you acted with restraint, you arouse the sympathy of thousands who believe in fair play and democracy.[17]

To the majority of these well-wishers, Roland sent a generic response – that is, he was grateful for their concern and support; the assault was an outrageous and shameful act; while his head had been bloodied, it was not bowed; the unfortunate policemen of Rome, Georgia, brutalized and manhandled him and threw him and his wife in a dingy cell and exposed his young child to such indecencies. But ultimately, he had confidence in *all* people who worked for justice and decency throughout the land.[18]

That was Roland's official and public position. Behind the scenes, however, the tenor was totally degraded and outraged. He wanted certain and swift redress for the dastardly behavior of all of those who had carried off this humiliation against him and his family. Whether it was due to the influence of "Sister Mary" or his fellow Georgian, Walter White, the Roland Hayes case resonated at the highest levels of the state and federal government and even spread beyond the shores of the country.

The *New York Times* and *Time* magazine articles both intimated that when Chief Harris realized whom his officers had assaulted and imprisoned in his town, he called Georgia's controversial and arch-segregationist governor, Eugene Talmadge, to consult on how to proceed with their high-profile prisoner. Talmadge was running for another term as governor, and this case could be potentially explosive for his campaign. Talmadge was not fearful of an African American reaction because black citizens were mostly disenfranchised through generations of having been denied the right to vote. However, he was concerned that his open involvement in this case could negatively affect him among those white voters who were favorably disposed to the beloved singer. Word from the governor's office varied, depending on which news account was more credible. One news source indicated that the governor's office told Chief Harris to handle the situation himself. Another account said that the governor's office gave word to Harris that *it* would handle the matter.[19] In any case, Roland had been allowed to make bail, and he and Alzada were released.

The evening of the assault, some of Rome's concerned white citizens (several of whom had been friends and supporters of the tenor) paid the Hayes family a visit at Angelmo Farm to offer their sincere apologies and sympathies for the shameful actions that had been taken against him, his wife, and their young child earlier that day. Even though he had obviously been beaten about the face and his eyes were nearly swollen shut from having been repeatedly punched, Roland received his guests graciously. As always, he was impeccably dressed, but he made no attempt to conceal his injuries. The Rome delegation made clear that nothing would be gained by the tenor pursuing the case legally and that innocent people could get hurt (a veiled threat that other African Americans in the area could suffer as the result of a backlash if he moved forward with such an action). According to the visitors, even Chief Harris was "anxious" to have this case dismissed, and they assured him there would be no follow-up to the incident in the courts. They asked the tenor if he would be "amenable" to their suggestions, to which Roland diplomatically responded, "I'll think about it."[20]

True to the concerned delegation's word, when the case was called in court the following Monday, no one appeared to prosecute it. When Roland and Alzada showed up for the hearing, his uncashed fifty-dollar bond check was returned to him. The city fathers of Rome wanted the assault on *this* particular African American man, who had willingly given benefit recitals in behalf of the town and who, by all accounts, had been a model neighbor and a good steward of the land (which included employing several white seasonal workers), swept under the rug.

What made the citizens of Rome even more nervous was that not even the most ardent conservative or rabid segregationist could claim that Roland had been anything other than respectful and tolerant of southern racial customs. He was a far cry from the northern "outsiders" attempting to agitate for African American rights.[21] But sweeping the assault under the rug was the very last thing that would happen in this case.

When Walter White received a telegram from Roland about the assault, the NAACP secretary began by reaching out to his contacts at the Justice Department and asked for the intervention of the Federal Bureau of Investigation and other high-level government officials. This had been an all-too-familiar scenario for the secretary, but this time it involved a high-profile individual as well as a personal friend. There may have even been behind-the-scenes White House intervention, because after hearing about the Hayes attack, First Lady Eleanor Roosevelt had expressed sympathy for the tenor in a closed-door speech at New York's International House.[22] The U.S. attorney general, Francis Biddle, assigned his assistant AG, Wendell Berge, and Victor Rotnem, chief of the Civil Liberties Section of the Justice Department, to direct the case. He also had the Atlanta Bureau of the FBI involved to determine if a federal criminal case could be pursued against the perpetrators.[23] The NAACP special counsel, Thurgood Marshall (later to be appointed as the first African American Supreme Court justice), was among those monitoring the case for the civil rights organization.

At issue, at least initially, was whether the case against the policemen who had physically beaten Roland needed to be pursued criminally in the state courts (making it a state's rights issue) or at the federal level. The Justice Department was tentative about filing a case under the federal Conspiracy Statute of the U.S. Criminal Code (Title 18, sections 51 and 52), fearing that the state of Georgia (specifically the governor) might decry such an action as federal intervention into its state's rights.

Talmadge was running for another term as governor of Georgia in the summer of 1942, and Justice Department officials (as well as Walter White) believed, with good reason, that if cornered, Talmadge would not be above using the Hayes attack to his political advantage by claiming that the federal government had meddled in Georgia's affairs regarding its "Negro problem" (the popularly used expression of the day) and that he needed voter support to fight off the federal government. Although Talmadge belonged to the same political party as the U.S. president, he was no fan of Franklin D. Roosevelt, especially when it came to increased civil rights for African Americans, and the governor had previously suffered negative publicity when he became involved in the removal of Walter Cocking, the law school dean at the University of Georgia, claiming Cocking was too liberal on racial integration issues.[24]

So the Department of Justice and the NAACP proceeded carefully, waiting until after the gubernatorial primary before initiating action. They began building their case with official statements from Roland and Alzada. In addition to what had already been reported on the record, Alzada's official account (dated August 4, 1942) stated that while she was in Higgins Shoe Store having the negative encounter with the clerk who had ordered her out of the white section of the store, another employee had approached her waving an artificial foot and, threatening to strike her with it, ordered her out of the store. When she warned the clerk not to hit her, he said that he would call the police and apparently left the store to do so. When she had returned with Roland and spoke to the owner, she believed that her husband's intervention had settled the situation, especially after the proprietor, Mr. Higgins, had offered her immediate service. After her daughter's scream drew her outside of a subsequent store, she described the ensuing ruckus as presented earlier, including her brief jailing.

Roland's official account (also dated August 4, 1942) was necessarily more detailed, as he realized that as the target of the physical attack, he suffered more physical and psychological torment than his wife or child. And it was, after all, his name recognition that had drawn attention to what might have otherwise been an unremarkable case of an uppity "n – " being put in his place for "sassin'" white people.

Roland's typewritten statement began: "Re – the assault upon my person by Rome, Ga, Policemen." He said that he, Alzada, and their daughter had been driven to the city by his hired man and arrived around 10:00 AM. While he went to the bank, Alzada went to buy their child some shoes. When he met up with them later, Alzada told him what had happened in Higgins Shoe Store. He took her back to the store because, unlike his wife, he had traded there before and had never encountered any negative behavior. In fact, he had experienced only polite and courteous treatment there. When they entered, they found the clerk ("front man") who had earlier ordered Alzada out of the store, and Roland asked him what she had done to provoke such a reaction. The clerk told him that Alzada had cursed him. When Roland informed him that Alzada did not curse, the clerk said, "Well she was throwing Hitler in my face!" Roland informed the clerk who he was and stated that he simply wanted to have an understanding of the matter. The owner then arrived and explained that although he had not been there when the incident took place, it was the policy for the races to be separated, but he would be happy to serve them at that moment. According to Roland, he declined the offer and the family left.

After Alzada went into another store, Africa stayed with her father, walking up and down the street. Shortly afterward, a policeman came up to Roland and, according to Africa's later account, said, "There's been a charge made against you, boy!"[25] When Roland inquired about it, the policeman grabbed him by the front of his belt and dragged him to Higgins Shoe Store, with Africa holding tightly to him. Just before entering the store, Roland asked the officer to let him hand over his daughter to her mother, but the officer refused with the comment, "Your wife will be here soon enough." When they went in the store, the "front man" reiterated his version of his earlier encounter with Alzada. When Roland again came to her defense, the initial policeman and a second one grabbed him and lifted him off the floor. When he said that they had no right to lay hands on him in such a way, a person in a white shirt (presumably a white bystander) clenched his fist and struck Roland in the jaw. The blow cut his lip and bruised his jaw, and he began to bleed. Africa began screaming at the top of her lungs. Although the policemen tried, they could not pull her away from her father. In the scuffle, they knocked off his Panama hat. Someone grabbed it and pulled it over his face so he could not see. Roland then recalled being dragged across the sidewalk and tossed in a car. Someone sat on him while he was handcuffed from behind. When Roland protested this brutality, telling the officers that he was no criminal, it only intensified the brutality and cruelty of their assault. In his recollection, Alzada then arrived and climbed into the police vehicle. All the while, she pleaded with them to stop the abuse. After heeding Roland's instruction to be quiet and get the child, she got out of the car and collected her daughter but was quickly ordered back in. They all drove off to the courthouse with the tenor being totally dazed by the beating.

When they arrived, he was searched and stripped of his belongings. At no time was he told that he was under arrest, fingerprinted, or photographed (which would have obviously documented the brutal beating that he had just received). He and Alzada were placed in a cell with a drunk and disorderly African American detainee (whom young Africa recalled as having "red eyes").[26]

At some point after the Hayes family was unloaded at the courthouse, Chief Harris arrived. Roland was eventually taken to Harris, who explained that he had made a "thorough" investigation (within one hour of the incident) of the unfortunate experience, and it did not amount to much. He also said that he had checked with the FBI, and because Alzada had used the name of Hitler, she might be accused of sedition and could get into serious trouble. Roland kept quiet while the chief spoke and afterward asked for permission to speak. When he began explaining how his officers had brutalized him, the chief made clear that he did not want to hear about it, so Roland stopped. Roland then inquired about the bond and was informed by the chief that it would be fifty dollars for the two of them and that they would have to appear in court the following Monday to formally answer the "charge" (which was still unspecified). The chief accepted the check from Roland and assured him that his case would turn out all right. They were released. In his statement, Roland then described the previously mentioned visit of the white delegation from Rome that evening at his farm. Roland and Alzada returned to the Rome courthouse the following Monday, and his uncashed check was returned. No one showed up to prosecute the case, and it was consequently dismissed. This was Roland's recollection of the experience a little over three weeks after it had occurred.[27]

A few weeks after Roland had sent his and Alzada's official statements to Walter White (who in turn had them delivered to Assistant Attorney General Burge), he received a late August visit from Special Agent Lee Hancock of the FBI's Atlanta Division. Agent Hancock said that he had been directed by the Justice Department to get an official statement about the incident from him and Alzada. Even after examining the agent's credentials, Roland became suspicious of Agent Hancock, fearing that he might be a "plant" sent by the "Rome people" to get a statement from him contradicting what had already been said in his and Alzada's official statements. After all, if Hancock had been legitimate, how could he not know that their official statements had already been submitted weeks earlier? When questioned by Roland, Agent Hancock indicated that the purpose of the statement was to determine if his case should be pursued as a criminal matter (that is, under the Justice Department's mechanisms) or as a civil matter. He said further that because the singer was world-renowned, the department wanted to handle this case very sensitively. Roland feigned some excuse for not providing a statement and did not reveal to Agent Hancock that he and Alzada had already given official accounts of the events in question.[28]

In the meantime, the assault had become an international cause cé-lèbre. Roland received a letter from a Señor M. A. Contreras of Havana, Cuba, who described himself as "100% white," expressing outrage at the attack that he had suffered and solidarity with him in the tenor's conciliatory statement that "the humiliation [was] on the other side." An even stronger and more personal expression of support came from the United Kingdom. Robert Broadhurst, the singer's beloved "Tarah," bemoaned the fact that he and Roland had been out of contact for such a long time, but he wanted to assure his friend that he and many others of African ancestry throughout greater London were in total solidarity with him and his family.[29] Following Broadhurst's communication came a more formal letter of support signed by many important continental Africans and those of that ancestry, similar to the one the tenor had been given twenty-two years earlier. This letter, however, was far from congratulatory. It had as its basis an indictment against the United States and its regressive social policies regarding its African American citizenry:

> 5 September, 1942
> Mr. Roland Hayes
> 58 Allerton Street
> Brookline, Boston,
> Mass., U.S.A.
> Dear Mr. Hayes:
>
> We the undersigned, British Colonials of African descent in London, have heard with profound indignation of the cowardly assault made upon you and your family in Rome, Georgia. Permit us to avail ourselves of this opportunity to express to you and Mrs. Hayes our heartfelt sympathy.
> At a time like this when our two nations are supposed to be fighting to uphold democratic institutions and the Rights of Man, the disgraceful behavior of public officials in Rome and the cynical attitude of Governor Talmadge can only serve to undermine the faith of coloured peoples everywhere in the cause of the United Nations.[30]

As was the case with the October 1920 document, the most prestigious scholars, physicians, lawyers, diplomats, students, and businesspersons of African ancestry in London at the time signed it.

Among the signatories was the eminent Pan-Africanist George Padmore, who was to distinguish himself just three years later in 1945 at the Manchester Conference in London, where he, along with other attendees such as Kwame Nkrumah, Jomo Kenyatta, and W. E. B. Du Bois, would outline a strategy for decolonizing the African continent. Born Malcolm Ivan Meredith Nurse, Padmore was educated in the United States at Howard University and at Fisk. As a Fisk alum, he had seen Roland in concert in the 1920s while he studied medicine at the university. Robert Broadhurst signed the document as the Liberian minister – that is, as the representative of that West African republic.

Noël Sullivan, like so many others, also expressed his sympathies, dismay, and undying affection for his friend and his family. Sullivan was also discouraged, because he had believed that one of the positive things coming out of the Pearl Harbor invasion and World War II in general (which, of course, was raging as he wrote his letter) would be greater racial solidarity in the country against a collective enemy. Sullivan also extended another invitation for the singer to perform at the Carmel Arts Festival once again, as soon as his schedule would permit.

Roland's response to Sullivan revealed more in writing than he had apparently revealed to anyone else about the racial assault in Rome.

> I cannot help my adversaries by hurt nor hate, hence the only way to remind them of their brutality is to be kind to them. Dear Noël, I have been through many a scourge in my life, but never has my fortitude been put to such a test before as during that experience in Rome. As those brutal men, bent on cruelty, beat and battered me in the face and over the head, I could not but think of our Lord's experience on Calvary. Yes, Noël, it happened to me, but I have not been hurt – neither of body of heart nor spirit. Also, I am not afraid even, to still live amongst them. Repentance has already taken some of them by the heart and somehow I know that my remaining here at my post has meant a great deal to the rest of my Negro fellows who were bound to receive a harder treatment had I run away.[31]

Roland concluded his letter by mentioning his upcoming engagement at Carmel the following year and by saying he looked forward to seeing his friend.

Case number WB:SPM:JBT 144-19-8 was the official Justice Department's designation of the Roland Hayes incident in Rome, Georgia. Roland met with its officials, including Attorney General Francis Biddle and his assistant AG, Wendell Burge, on September 21, 1942, with Walter White and Thurgood Marshall of the NAACP also present. An official FBI report had been generated before the meeting, and White had communicated with Roland confidentially after reading it. Mocking portions of the report, his letter to the tenor said: "You certainly must have changed a lot since I last saw you to be the shouting, abusive, belligerent, and kicking individual which some of the white people there told the

FBI you are! And, from their accounts, the white people in Rome are the most polite, friendly, and just people who ever lived!"[32] After the meeting, White and Biddle dispatched Burge to Atlanta to meet with the FBI bureau chief and the U.S. attorney, a Mr. Sutherland (who was born near Rome). They then met with several people in Rome. Shamed by the negative national and international attention given to their city as a result of the Hayes episode, they were anxious not to have the ordeal taint their city any more than it already had. According to Walter White's November 9, 1942, letter to Roland, Chief Harris would fire the policeman who first struck Roland. After local action was taken against that officer, federal charges would then be made against him. Roland was free to return to Angelmo Farm, and if he encountered any negative situation, he was to contact Barry Wright in Rome to report it.

There turned out to be some collateral damage locally, which may or may not have been directly associated with the Hayes incident: Governor Eugene Talmadge lost his gubernatorial reelection bid to Ellis Arnall in 1942. He ran for the seat again in 1946 and won but died before taking office. But the primary contribution of the 1942 Rome affair was to famously, if only briefly, put a global spotlight on racism in Roland's home state and the region.

Some months after Roland experienced the most humiliating and overtly racial incident of his life, his friend Langston Hughes published an essay titled "My America."[33] In it, Hughes, with "clear and unprejudiced eyes," set out to assess social conditions in the 1940s United States, as it was defending democracy in Europe and in other parts of the world. In this somewhat toned-down reality check on the record of the country, Langston Hughes pointed out that while foreigners of European extraction could come to this country and become naturalized citizens, be guaranteed the right to travel throughout the land as they desired, buy food anywhere they chose, stay in a hotel anywhere where they were inclined to rest their head, buy tickets to concerts of their liking, attend theater productions anywhere in the land as they so fancied, travel on any railroad, and vote in Texas and Mississippi as it was their constitutional right to do so, *he,* as a native-born citizen of African ancestry, could not. Hughes then focused on the celebrated singer's Rome incident specifically:

America is a land where the best of all democracies has been achieved for some people – but in Georgia, Roland Hayes, the world-famous singer, is beaten for being Colored and nobody is jailed – nor can Mr. Hayes vote in the State where he was born. Yet America is a country where Roland Hayes *can* come from a log cabin to wealth and fame – in spite of the segment that still wishes to maltreat him physically and spiritually, famous though he is.[34]

TWELVE

"I Can Tell the World!"

1942–1950

AS DIFFICULT AS IT MIGHT BE TO IMAGINE, THERE WAS A
beneficial aspect of Roland's brutal assault by the Rome, Georgia, police:
the incident rapidly put Roland Hayes back in the limelight, and he knew
better than most how to use such attention to his advantage. Before the
media outlets, the tenor presented himself in the way an African American man of a certain age and stature was supposed to – that is, he was
dignified yet humble. Although he had been physically abused, he held
the moral high ground by forgiving his attackers for their misguided
ways (at least publicly). Above all, he appeared protective of his wife and
their young daughter, which presented him as a responsible family man.
Given the recent waning of his musical activities and his somewhat lag-
ging career, Roland could not have designed or imagined a better public
relations campaign.

Almost as if to do penance for its past criticism of the tenor, the
Baltimore-based *Afro-American* kept the assault in front of its readers,
just as it had the Lyric Theater incident in the city sixteen years earlier.
Several dedicated stories highlighted and addressed the inhumanity of
the assault, and the paper sent a special correspondent to Angelmo Farm
that summer to do an extensive story, with pictures, of Roland, Alzada,
and their child.

The publicity Roland received after his Georgia attack was a nearly
perfect lead-up to the release of his autobiography, *Angel Mo' and Her
Son, Roland Hayes,* as told to Dr. MacKinley Helm. Initially released
as a serial by the Boston-based literary magazine the *Atlantic Monthly,
Angel Mo'* appeared as a book by Little, Brown and Company in late 1942.

MacKinley Helm was an accomplished Brookline-based writer but, at the time, was not especially well known. Helm had written other books, but *Angel Mo'* seems to have been the only book that he wrote in this genre. Roland had always intended that his story be told. In the 1920s, the singer had asked the NAACP secretary, Walter White, to be his official biographer, but White had demurred. Roland later told his former Boston managers, William Brennan and George Judd, that he wanted the likes of Emil Ludwig to pen his story. Then Roland implied in one of his bids to attract financial backers for his autobiographical music drama that he had found an unnamed "Viennese playwright" to work with him on the biographical part of the drama. In the end, it would be Dr. Helm who would introduce the "official" Roland Hayes story to the world. *Angel Mo'* only hinted at the very savvy and shrewd business-man that Roland was, a man who, with the equivalent of a high school diploma, could negotiate very complex contracts and was on top of every aspect of his career.

It is unclear when Roland and his biographer were introduced to each other, but they must have worked on the book when Roland was in New England during the off-season, because there are no communi-cations to suggest that Helm traveled to Georgia.[1] To facilitate a fuller picture of his story, Roland had preserved thousands of pages of docu-ments (including the original contract, correspondence, and receipts pertaining to Fannie's ten acres in Georgia), personal and professional correspondence, photographs, scores, and other ephemeral material per-taining to his life and his work. Hayes and Helm signed a contract on June 2, 1942, with Little, Brown and Company to publish the work. The manuscript was likely in a later stage of development at the time of the June signing.

Angel Mo' presented many of the basic facts of Hayes's life, all in-tended to show him in a favorable light. Although he identified his broth-ers and his only sister, Mattie, there are no substantive details about them (for example, when and where they were born, their death dates, or any other information), which made it impossible for Helm to paint a full picture of their lives. There was also the complex issue of "Baby" Jesse Hayes. Roland left the issue of his youngest brother open for the reader's speculation. For example, in the book, he gives the impression that after the death of Fannie in September 1923, her final communication left her ten-acre farm in Georgia to Roland, Robert Brante, and Jesse.[2] By then, of course, Jesse Hayes had already tragically and mysteriously died. As Fannie had gone to New Jersey to bury her youngest son months earlier, she would not have referenced him in her final letter to Roland.[3] It is unlikely that this would have been an oversight on Helm's part; rather, Hayes may have tried to conceal the details of Jesse's demise.

As Roland recounted his rise to prominence, he acknowledged Fannie's influence on his success but made only slight reference to others who had helped along the way. Barely recognized in this account is the impact of W. Arthur Calhoun on his musical career. Duse Mohammed Ali appears as an associate and landlord during his early days in London, but nothing is said about his Pan-African or black nationalist leanings (not to mention Ali's association with Marcus Garvey). Despite their close friendship over the years, Robert Broadhurst was completely left out of *Angel Mo'*, as was Roland's dear friend Daisy Tapley. Hayes included Prince Tovalou, but it was mainly to substantiate his own claim to royal African ancestry based on his great-grandfather Abá 'Ougi.

Yet another personality dramatically played down in *Angel Mo'* is Joseph Salmon, introduced only as "M. Salmon."[4] While Roland gave some indication of the role that Salmon played in making him "Le Rage de Paris" in the early 1920s, he made no mention whatsoever of his wife, Maddie, who was equally influential in making bookings for him and advancing his career. Of course, based on Maddie's past support of Countess Bertha and Salmon's 1937 reprimand of Roland for not calling on him while in Paris, it is not surprising that Roland did not mention Maddie.

Roland was obviously guarded about certain autobiographical information – most notably concerning his relationship with Bertha – but even so, Roland dropped several hints in his book that point to their association. He mentioned a "Princesse de Colloredo-Mansfeld" among his early Parisian patrons in the 1920s,[5] but no such individual by that name could be located among the Parisian elite of that period. Of course, when he finally referenced his relationship with the countess, he described it as a strictly platonic one, with her acting as an inspirational muse.[6] There was no hint of intimacy nor the presence of the daughter they had parented together. This leaves open some questions: If Alzada had read the book, would not her curiosity have been raised about this unnamed lady? Or did she just accept that there were certain parts of her husband's life that she would not know about and realized it was better not to ask? Based on the communications from her to Roland, it seems that the latter was the position that she adopted.

Roland's portrayal in *Angel Mo'* of his relationship with Alzada is yet another area of interest. It leads the reader to conclude that they met as first cousins in Chattanooga when they were children in the early part of the 1900s and that they were somehow destined to be together as husband and wife. There is no mention of Alzada's sister Alma or any other serious romantic interest in his life prior to Alzada, save his girlfriend from Fisk who married within her station.

With regard to the limitations of *Angel Mo'*, Roland himself wrote to his dear friend Noël Sullivan after its release, telling him that Helm and the publishers had left out significant sections of the book. Among those exclusions were tributes to Sullivan, George Washington Carver, and Mary McLeod Bethune.[7] Roland noted that he was "chagrined" at this omission and implied that the aftermath of the Rome assault had prevented him from paying more attention to the book as it was in production.[8]

Despite the many omissions later research would reveal, Roland gave considerable information about his life, his philosophies, and the historical context in which he performed and operated. It is still an important contribution from the artist.

The reception of *Angel Mo'* by the public was strong, and the work received near universal acclaim for Roland. Some bought the book thinking that it would help compensate for the assault on him and his family in Rome, Georgia, earlier that year. Many African American and mainstream news outlets praised the work and encouraged their readers to purchase the book. They did.

Roland did his part too. He sent autographed copies to his many personal friends as well as to his strategic allies, including "Sister Mary" McLeod Bethune, George Washington Carver, President Franklin Roosevelt, and First Lady Eleanor Roosevelt. Roland also sent signed copies of *Angel Mo'* to personal friends like Walter White;[9] the Astors

in England; Henry Ford; Pearl S. Buck; Sterling Brown; Walter Damrosch; many governors, including those of Massachusetts, West Virginia,
Michigan, and Tennessee (but specifically not to the governor of Georgia); the Department of Justice officials who had been his advocates in
the Rome case; and many others in England, like Robert Broadhurst and
Louis Untermeyer.

The comments about the book were uniformly complimentary.
Some compared it favorably to Booker T. Washington's classic *Up from
Slavery,* and it was seen as a natural sequence to that celebrated autobiography.[10] Roland's friend and mentor George Washington Carver
praised the book but said that his health was so tentative that he could
sit inside and read it only in stages. He died within two months of his
letter to Hayes.[11]

The publicity from the Rome incident and the release of *Angel Mo'*
also boosted Roland's performance schedule. In January 1943, he was
on the West Coast for several engagements, including those in Carmel,
California, where he was with Noël Sullivan. He eventually arrived back
on the East Coast, where he was featured at a tribute to "Sister Mary,"
hosted by First Lady Eleanor Roosevelt at the Golden Gate Auditorium
in New York City. It was probably at this occasion when the First Lady
proposed that Roland go overseas to entertain the African American
troops in Europe later that year.

With his prominence freshly restored, Hayes sought to improve his
professional and financial situation. He switched from the Ray Halmans
Concert Management Agency in New York to the Boston-based Demeter Zachareff Agency, and to cut expenses, he offered to turn over the
management of Angelmo Farm to the Department of Agriculture for
the duration of the war. Rebuffed by the government, he began making
arrangements in 1943 with the agency of A. R. McDaniel of Calhoun,
Georgia, to sell half the acres. He required it to be a cash negotiation,
and McDaniel would have to absorb any advertising costs.[12]

In the midst of war raging in Europe, Roland returned to sing in the
United Kingdom twenty-three years after he first landed there in 1920. If
the singer's first trip was made in relative obscurity, the one that he made

in September 1943 was arranged and executed in near total secrecy. Mary McLeod Bethune, Walter White, and especially Eleanor Roosevelt, who had originally proposed Roland's trip to England to sing for the African American troops stationed there, used their influence to make the trip possible.

That fall, Roland was slated to perform with a chorus of African American soldiers in the greater London area. Not even his new manager, Demeter Zachareff, knew his whereabouts until after he had departed for England. Roland also informed his brother, Robert Brante, by letter on September 10 that he had already left for London by way of a U.S. Army military flight. In the event that anything "happened" to him, as he wrote his brother, he should contact his lawyer John P. Carr in Boston. Alzada had the keys to his strongbox.[13] He wrote a similar letter to Noël Sullivan on the same date informing him of his upcoming London appearances at the end of the month.[14]

Roland's arrival and military briefing in London took place over several days. He underwent a battery of medical tests after landing, which included tests and vaccinations for smallpox, typhoid, tetanus, typhus, and yellow fever. He also had to be declared free of any communicable diseases.[15] Once his tests were completed, word was released through the British press that he was in the country to hold several performances at the Royal Albert Hall at the end of the month.

The concert would be a grand affair for the war-torn British public as well as a publicity blitz for the U.S. Army. Londoners would be treated to a choral performance of African American soldiers, two hundred voices strong, accompanied by the London Symphony Orchestra. As the featured soloist, Roland was the icing on the cake. The performance was advertised as "The United States Army (the European Theatre of Operations) in collaboration with the *Daily Express* presents a U.S. Army Negro Chorus of 200 Voice with Roland Hayes and the London Symphony Orchestra conducted by Technical Sergeant Hugo Weisgall."[16] Although many of the choral participants were already seasoned musicians with extensive training and sight-reading abilities, many were not. PFC Kenneth Cantril, of Springfield, Missouri, who had a solo in one of the works to be presented, had already sung with the St. Louis Municipal Opera Association, for example, and continued his vocal studies in Britain when time allowed.

The director, Hugo Weisgall, was born in 1912 in Moravia (then a part of the Austro-Hungarian Empire), came to the United States as a child, and was raised in Baltimore. The talented musician was trained there at the Peabody Conservatory. He joined the military after Pearl Harbor and eventually became an aide-de-camp to General George Patton. He was serving in Europe when he was tapped to conduct Roland and the London Symphony Orchestra. This was the only time Roland sang under Weisgall's baton; Weisgall eventually became well known as an opera composer and conductor. He also was a professor of music at Juilliard, where he heard a young Shirley Verrett when she was a student there in the late 1950s. Weisgall subsequently invited her to star in his 1964 opera, *Athaliah,* based on the wicked biblical queen, which debuted in concert form in New York and was later staged at the New York City Opera.

Roland arrived more than two weeks before the concert because of the intense rehearsal schedule. Philadelphia native Corporal Marc Blitzstein had prepared the chorus prior to Roland's arrival and praised the enthusiasm of his soldier-musicians.[17] To preserve energy during the harsh war years, Roland, the London Symphony, and the chorus rehearsed in a cold Royal Albert Hall, requiring Roland to wear a coat throughout the rehearsals.

On the night of the performance, the chorus of African American soldiers walked onto the brightly lit stage with military precision, wearing sparkling uniforms and spit-polished shoes. The program began with Blitzstein's composition *Freedom Morning.* Appropriate for the occasion, the chorus then performed "Over My Head I See Trouble in the Air."

And then from a darkened stage, Roland confidently walked into a spotlight, decked out in a crisp U.S. Army uniform, to the cheers of a British public that had not seen him in their country in more than six years. Among the enthusiastic audience was his dear friend Robert Broadhurst, who openly wept with pride at the grand reception his countrymen were giving his dear "Cunjah."[18] Roland proudly saluted the audience, turned to salute the conductor and the soldiers, and then began. The tenor sang two well-known arrangements, "Go Down Moses" and "By and By," with the chorus.

After the intermission, the tenor continued with the encouraging and tuneful aria from Bach's Cantata 160, "I Know That My Redeemer Lives," well known to many Britons. This was followed by the recitative and aria "Though Sinful, I Surrender All" and "Now, O Lord, I Am Prepared" from the same work.[19] Hayes then performed the little-known "O Peace, Thou Fairest Child of Heaven" from Thomas Arne's obscure masque *Alfred*.[20] With the two-hundred-voice chorus, Roland then offered several spirituals, including "I Can Tell the World about This" and "Steal Away," and the night concluded with "Joshua Fit de Battle of Jericho." When the entire ensemble performed the obligatory United States national anthem, "The Star-Spangled Banner," the British audience stood respectfully. But the assemblage cheered when "God Save the King" ended the night's performance.

The concertgoers were spellbound, even under the threat of an air raid, and Roland too noted the "Power" of the performance when he later recorded his reflections of this joint accomplishment. He described the chorus, orchestra, and other soloists as "inspired" and believed that he had been spiritually transcended and "overpowered" by the entire experience.[21]

The night was hailed by London's *Daily Express* as an unqualified success. The reviewer said that "Colored American music did more . . . than a hundred pep talks" ever could, not to mention the role that it would play to advance "inter-racial understanding."[22] Present at the concert were many prestigious guests, including Lord and Lady Mountbatten; U.S. commanding general Jacob Devers; the U.S. ambassador to the Court of St. James, John S. Winant; and many others from the diplomatic corps, including representatives from the Soviet Union, Australia, Brazil, New Zealand, France, and India, among others.[23] The entire performance was repeated the following night and a few days later for members of the Allied Forces.[24]

Commentary on the entire undertaking was riddled with stereotypical remarks in print about African Americans' natural aptitude for music and other unintentionally insulting and unenlightened comments, such as "Negroes" were "Natural Actors" and did not "sing with [their] voice alone . . . all [their] emotions go into [the] song."[25] But the positive response to the concert resonated on both sides of the Atlantic, and there was talk of a short promotional film depicting the "magnificent presentation" of Roland Hayes and the African American chorus being made and distributed in the United States and the United Kingdom.[26]

The following week, Roland gave a sold-out solo recital at London's National Gallery with the eminent Dame Myra Hess at the keyboard, which was reviewed as "marvelous" by the British press. Hess's wartime concerts had also dramatically increased her standing throughout the United Kingdom. The Hayes/Hess duo also gave several private recitals, including one for the tenor's old friends Lord and Lady Astor in Plymouth.

Roland's singing engagement with the African American soldiers was not his only contact with the British-based American men of his race serving in the military. After arriving and completing the mandatory medical clearances, he had met the U.S. ambassador and was asked if he would participate in a field investigation with the goal of preventing any further racial outbreaks among the American enlisted ranks. As a special attaché for the U.S. military, he would investigate the complaints of racial discrimination registered by several African American soldiers stationed throughout the United Kingdom. Roland's own high-profile Rome, Georgia, assault was well known and was, to be sure, a factor in his invitation by U.S. military officials to England.

At the heart of the African American soldiers' complaint was their resentment of the treatment they received from white superior officers and countrymen, whom they derisively called "Paddies."[27] Roland spent more than ten days traveling throughout the country and meeting African American soldiers, including stops in "Salzburg" (code for an undisclosed military base in the United Kingdom),[28] Bristol, Severnake, Plymouth, and, of course, the greater London area. The soldiers' comments were generic but all-too-familiar to the tenor. While they found their contact with the British citizenry to be receptive of their presence in the country, if not friendly, the white American soldiers were quick to discourage any contact and used all available means to prevent it. If it meant humiliating the black soldiers by spreading false and demeaning racial stereotypes (for example, that black men had tails like monkeys, had an instinct for violence, and were natural sexual predators, especially where white women were concerned), they did it. On other occasions, according to the complaints, the military police were used against them inappropriately. Also, officers were encouraged to restrict African

Americans' liberties on trumped-up charges or vague suspicions at the urging of white enlisted men.

Roland's official report to Ambassador Winant and the military personnel cited a personal anecdote related to his travels to Lord and Lady Astor's residence with an African American officer, Colonel Thrasher.[29] When they had arrived at the Astors' home in Plymouth, they encountered two low-ranking white American soldiers who neglected to salute the superior officer until they were prompted, although they should have done so immediately upon realizing that they were in the presence of a superior.[30]

True to his past practice of not really challenging Jim Crow segregation, Roland did not advocate for outright desegregation in the military ranks (which did not take place until the Truman administration) but simply argued that those rules that were in place should be enforced. In practical terms, the singer opined that since the soldiers knew there was segregation within the military, they should not resist it.[31] However, he urged in his report that the military structure needed to be consistent with its existing regulations and not allow blatant instances of racial animus to go unchallenged. Further, he suggested that the military place "handpicked" sensitivity officers, to whom the African American soldiers could go if they felt they had been overtly aggrieved, on base. It would be the role of these "trusted" officers to enforce military regulations when cases of abuse could be demonstrated. This "equal treatment" among the ranks, Roland argued, would go a long way toward softening the racial tensions that he had observed throughout his investigation.[32]

As an added suggestion, Roland proposed that the two-hundred-voice African American chorus that he had recently performed with be kept in place by the military and allowed to perform throughout the United Kingdom. This, he felt, would be a gesture of goodwill and would demonstrate to the British population and to white American soldiers alike the accomplishments of the spit-polished black soldiers. It probably never entered Roland's mind that this particular suggestion – that blacks be allowed to entertain whites, as they had done throughout the history of the United States – was, in many ways, at the core of the African American soldiers' complaints. Most white Americans saw their black countrymen as "natural" performers and entertainers, and these were seen as acceptable roles for them. The black soldiers, on the other hand, wanted respect as fighting men. To what extent Roland's suggestions, however watered down they may have seemed (especially by today's standards), were acted on is not known.

Apparently unbeknownst to the U.S. military based in Britain or to the American embassy personnel, after his return to the United States Roland took a semi-anonymous letter written to him and forwarded it directly to First Lady Eleanor Roosevelt at the White House. In his preface to the letter, Roland wrote her about his recent trip to Great Britain. He reported on the success of his concerts and supported his assertion with thank-you letters that he had received from the U.S. ambassador and the military officers and the glowing reviews of his engagements. He then reported on his "invited" assignment to the First Lady and saw it as his "patriotic duty" to bring the situation of the African American soldiers to the attention of the president and to her.[33]

The letter from the anonymous African American corporal reiterated the complaints of the black soldiers who felt fundamentally disrespected by their white countrymen. They also believed the military structure facilitated the white enlisted men's oppression of them. In extreme instances, the anonymous corporal complained, white American soldiers attempted to keep them out of the "pubs" and resorted to violence when they attempted to enter. He said there were instances when it was necessary for black soldiers to "cut" some of the white soldiers to prevent them from carrying out violence against them.[34] The corporal's letter to Roland was nearly a desperate plea for his intervention, even though he knew the tenor was not a military man. But the corporal felt that the voice of the singer – a prominent African American figure who had recently suffered the humiliation of racial animus that they routinely experienced – would resonate louder than theirs. Surely, he would be able to identify with their plight and could get to higher levels of the government than could any of them. In forwarding the letter, the tenor had not only identified with his brethren but had acted.

The First Lady responded in a letter dated November 23 in which she expressed her concerns about racial discrimination among the military ranks and said that she would report this directly to the president, General George Marshall (U.S. military chief of staff), and "Mr. McCloy." She also agreed with Roland that it was the white people who needed to be educated but acknowledged the difficulty of that challenge.[35] A month after receiving the response from Mrs. Roosevelt, Roland wrote his friend Noël Sullivan in California reporting that he had kept his "pledge to our men in Arms to report their situation to men in the high places of our Nation."[36] This was Roland at his most racially conscious and patriotic height.

There were, of course, many instances of outstanding bravery and valor demonstrated by African American soldiers throughout World War II in the European and Pacific theaters. Roland's appeals to Mrs. Roosevelt for reform and recognition went largely unheeded. No African Americans soldiers were recommended for the singularly important Medal of Honor. The top-down, unwritten directive was that no African Americans would receive the recognition, although several white commanders had recommended individual black soldiers for the honor. There had been close to sixty African American Medal of Honor recipients in the country's previous wars. This glaring injustice was not corrected until the Clinton administration in the early 1990s. First Lieutenant Vernon Baker, who passed away in 2010, was the only living recipient at the 1997 ceremony.[37]

Roland's delay in England caused him to miss several scheduled engagements back home. His October 20 concert at Baltimore's Sharp Street Memorial Church had to be postponed "due to the fact that air transportation from overseas could not be arranged in time."[38] The *Afro-American* urged Baltimoreans to attend Hayes's rescheduled engagement to show support for his performances in the United Kingdom, and the October 27, 1943, recital drew more than two thousand concertgoers. Hayes was uniformly praised in the media (especially in the black press) for his heroic contribution to the war effort by singing with the African American soldiers in England.

Roland's concert schedule continued to blossom in 1944 in the capable hands of his new manager, Demeter Zachareff. However, apart from friendly places like Fisk University and Morehouse College and Baltimore (which did not consider itself as part of the "South"), he avoided engagements in the southern United States.[39] In yet another instance of appeasement for the Rome, Georgia, incident, he was asked to promote a film being produced by the March of Time, *Tolerance – An American Problem*, which dealt specifically with racial and religious intolerance.

Roland scored another major success at his October Carnegie Hall recital. The reviewer, Olin Downes, identified the vocal limitations of the fifty-seven-year-old singer, but as most reviewers did, he was quick to acknowledge the tenor's artistic skill in handling the repertoire and the languages.[40]

By May 1945, the war in Europe was won. Roland had received a bump in his performing schedule but was still averaging between five hundred dollars and seven hundred dollars per engagement, and most of these recitals were in smaller towns and venues. He spent a two-week residency at Black Mountain College in North Carolina, which had a more progressive policy in terms of admitting black and white students and supported a more forward-looking approach to education. Roland was also awarded yet another honorary doctorate, this one from Morehouse College in Atlanta.

After the liberation of Europe, Roland managed to reestablish contact with several of his friends in France. Among them was Lilly Goldschmidt, who was another one of his early supporters from the 1920s. She reported to the tenor that his estranged friend and most important Parisian advocate, celebrated cellist Joseph Salmon, had died a few years earlier in 1943 in Toulouse. His wife, Maddie, and their daughter, Jacqueline, were still in that city. Roland never reconciled with Joseph Salmon before his death and seems to have had no use for Maddie thereafter.[41]

The early part of 1946 found the Hayes family mostly at their Brookline home. In the spring of the year, he performed at Carnegie Hall. Nearing his fifty-ninth birthday, a *New York Times* reviewer noted accurately that although he was past his vocal prime, his artistry was still at its zenith. Roland spent most of the summer on the West Coast. After fulfilling two California engagements in Oakland (in June) and at Carmel (July), he spent time at Noël Sullivan's Holly Hills residence, where, away from his family, he worked on his next major publication, a dedicated book of spirituals, which was also published by Little, Brown and Company.

Roland completed the sale of Angelmo Farm in Georgia in 1947 (minus some land for Robert Brante and Fannie's original ten acres) and then bought a smaller farm in West Newberry, Massachusetts. The

former Merrill Farm on Crane Neck Hill was given the nearly comic
sounding, if not minstrelized, name "Rolalza" Farm, which was, of
course, a combination of his and Alzada's names. The intended purpose
of "Rolalza" was for general farming and raising livestock, but Roland
also meant for a vocal studio and community playhouse to be established
there.[42]

In early June the tenor turned sixty years old but showed no sign
of giving up his career. Engagements included singing at the inauguration of Charles S. Johnson, the recently installed first African American
president of his alma mater, Fisk University.

Fall 1947 marked a milestone in the tenor's career: it had been thirty
years since he had taken the audacious action of renting Boston's Symphony Hall for a solo recital. Roland highlighted the occasion with another recital and set out to identify several of the attendees who had
taken a chance on the young and unknown singer three decades earlier.
Roland received letters from several of these loyal patrons who had since
been his steadfast supporters. Also marking the thirtieth anniversary
milestone, the Boston-based *Christian Science Monitor* did a feature story
on the tenor.[43] After summarizing his early experience in Georgia and
Tennessee (including the obligatory information about his onetime enslaved mother) and his subsequent arrival in Boston, Roland addressed
himself to issues of racial equality and parity. His statement to the *Christian Science Monitor*'s Laura Haddock seemed to summarize his long-
held views on this delicate and controversial issue:

> I feel 95 percent of the Negro-white problem is the responsibility of the Negro. It
> is not enough for the Negro to say, "I have certain gifts. Why am I not permitted
> to contribute and develop them to the full?" He must prove he has these gifts
> and that they are worthy of taking their place alongside the good and great
> contributors of all races. . . . I could have fought prejudice in words and actions
> all my way, but how far would it have gotten me? I had to prove myself and my art
> as being worthy of what I sought.
>
> Now I have the satisfaction of seeing that it has paved the way for others – four
> or five of my race who are fine artists.[44]

It was such statements – that African Americans needed to prove themselves "worthy" of white people's respect – that caused Roland to drift
again and again into troubled waters with many in the African American
civil rights community at the time. At times when he had had the op-

portunity to stand up to Jim Crow in a forceful way, he had not done so, despite the level of protection his popularity would have given him. The idea of taking the blame from where it belonged and placing it with African Americans seemed backward to many civil rights activists. Others likened him to being the supreme "Uncle Tom," dressed in his obligatory servant's tuxedo.

Roland's regressive position on such matters (even by 1940s standards) caused his legacy to suffer among African Americans, especially when compared to the reputations of Paul Robeson and Marian Anderson. Anderson and Robeson were at least *perceived* as having taken stands on important racial issues (whether rightly or wrongly). Although Hayes's career and reputation was as big as Anderson's, if not bigger, and certainly bigger than Robeson's, he has yet to achieve certain standard recognitions, like having a Black Heritage stamp issued in his name. Many lesser-known African Americans have already been awarded such recognition, but as of this writing, Hayes has not.

The November 16 Sunday evening concert marking the tenor's thirtieth anniversary was well attended, as were most of his hometown appearances. The occasion was marked by the presence of Massachusetts's lieutenant governor, Arthur W. Coolidge, who happened to have been present at Roland's November 15, 1917, concert thirty years earlier. Coolidge offered brief remarks before the concert's intermission.[45]

Just after Christmas 1947, Roland and Reginald Boardman returned to the recording studio in Boston, using the Telavix Corporation facilities in the city. They recorded several works, including "Scandalize My Name," "Plenty Good Room," and "Were You There?" The recording session extended into January, but it is not clear if Boardman played for him at the January session.[46] These recordings were intended to be released on the newly created Angel Mo' label but were issued some time later.

Roland's February 1948 letter to Robert Broadhurst, his beloved "Tarah," was somewhat bittersweet. Over their twenty-eight-year friendship, Broadhurst had watched his friend develop from an obscure and hungry singer to an internationally acclaimed artist and symbol for the African diaspora. He also had seen his friend's star diminish with the onset of the depression in the 1930s but nonetheless had presented him to the likes of the exiled emperor Haile Selassie in England in 1937. Ultimately, in 1943, he had wept when Roland strode on the Royal Albert Hall stage in military uniform with two hundred African American soldiers and stirred the mostly white audience of war-weary Britons to hold firm against Hitler and the Nazi war machine in Germany. Broadhurst had written Roland after that 1943 appearance and recalled an incident from their earlier years in the United Kingdom. A white American who had insulted Roland years before had remorsefully offered him an apology for the offense. Roland's simple reply, according to Broadhurst's letter, was that he was above such small-minded insults.

Yet Roland's February 23 letter to his friend in London asked for his assistance in helping to get some furniture to him that a mutual friend of theirs had willed the tenor after his death. It was also a letter of soul-bearing. Roland informed Broadhurst that he had sold Angelmo Farm for a smaller piece of land in the Northeast, closer to his Brookline home. This particular piece of news must have represented something of a defeat for Broadhurst vis-à-vis his lofty ideals for his friend. Robert Broadhurst had once envisioned Roland taking "their" African homeland by storm and the singer becoming the ultimate symbol of African achievements worldwide. Later, as the architect of Angelmo Farm, Broadhurst had foreseen this experiment as the preeminent artists' colony that would carve a new path for the African race and would serve as a model for educating colonized Africans throughout the continent.

As he was already ill in February 1948 when Roland wrote him, Broadhurst was unable to assist the tenor with his request to get his furniture sent to the United States. With both of his dreams involving Roland left unfulfilled, the proud and fierce Pan-African idealist Robert "Tarah" Broadhurst died a few months later. Fate and circumstances had denied him both the hopes he had for the tenor. Nor had Roland made it to the African continent (although Broadhurst had attempted to get him there many times), and by the time of his February 1948 letter, the sixty-one-year-old singer had sold Angelmo Farm for the inglorious and far less ambitious "Rolalza" Farm in Massachusetts.

Emmie Tillett (formerly Bass) had begun working as a secretary at the British-based Ibbs and Tillett Agency, and after the death of Robert

Leigh Ibbs, she had married John Tillett. She became the major force within the agency and wanted to explore the possibility of bringing Roland back to England for a two-month tour the following spring. Roland was agreeable to her suggestion but told her it would not be practical for less than fifteen thousand dollars. He told her he would not be available before April 1949 and could stay until June. Emmie Tillett also informed Roland of her husband's tentative health after his recent return from the United States. John Tillett subsequently died in late 1948, leaving his wife in control of the influential booking agency. His death was the most probable reason for Emmie and Roland to postpone negotiations for the tenor's return to the UK.

In October 1948, Roland's second major publication, *My Songs: Aframerican Religious Folk Songs Arranged and Interpreted,* was released by Little, Brown and Company, the company that had first published *Angel Mo'* six years earlier. He dedicated the work to Alzada and Africa as well as to his "friend, fellow artist, and great patron of music, Noël Sullivan, on whose 'Hollow Hills Farm,' Carmel, California, this book was prepared."[47] The work was very different from *Angel Mo'* and in certain ways was a truer reflection of Roland's philosophy and his sense of race consciousness.

For example, he used the term "Aframerican" in the foreword of *My Songs* because he saw the term "Negro" as a "misnomer" and believed that "Aframerican" better reflected those Africans transplanted to the United States.[48] At face value, this was a remarkable gesture for the late 1940s, when most black Americans were still inclined to run away from their African ancestry because of the many negative stereotypes they had been fed about it through their American experience. Roland had not even intimated such language in *Angel Mo'.*

Roland gave considerable background on several songs that he had learned in his childhood or that were associated with some other part of his life. He compared a number of the thirty songs in the edition to their original African sources and offered an opinion on how they were transformed into songs by their "Aframerican" counterparts. It would have been difficult to conclude that Roland had not been to the continent and done extensive ethnomusicological fieldwork in the preparation of this volume. When he referred to well-known names like James Weldon Johnson and others of African ancestry, he took care to refer to them as "Aframericans." This was truly a revolutionary work.

My Songs is full of Roland's personal journeys (whether it was his American concert tours or his engagements throughout Europe, the Soviet Union, or South America), his Christian conviction, and their place in a wider multicultural human experience. In telling the story of "You're Tired, Chile" (alternately known as "Sit Down"), for example, he likened it to the story of his beloved mother, Fannie.[49]

The reviews of *My Songs* were not of the same scale of those of *Angel Mo'* but were mostly positive. Carl Van Vechten (as did all other reviewers) quickly took note of the tenor's use of the term "Aframerican" folk song as opposed to "Negro" spiritual.[50] All believed that Roland's thirty songs and piano arrangements were simple and accessible for most singers and that his commentary was an outstanding part of the volume. The *Boston Herald* reviewer was the most complimentary when he called it a notable contribution to the literature of the Aframerican spiritual.[51]

Unfortunately, the *My Songs* volume did not sell well. After a single edition, it was withdrawn. The work may have been a little forward-looking at the time, and there was the question of whether African Americans (at the time still using the acceptable terms "Negro" or "Colored") were ready to embrace the term "Aframerican" to describe themselves or their experience.

Roland would receive yet more recognition in the spring of 1949. The French government awarded him the Palmes Officier d'Academie for his service to French music. He was given the award by the French consulate in Boston.[52]

Apart from a March Jordan Hall engagement in Boston, Roland's spring schedule was relatively light. In May, however, Roland was approached by the playwright Maxwell Anderson and eventually by the composer Kurt Weil and stage director/producer Rouben Mamoulian about a musical stage work. Anderson visited Roland to talk about an upcoming project that he and Weil would be refining over the next several months, a musical adaptation of Alan Paton's *Cry, the Beloved Country,* set in pre-apartheid South Africa. By the time Anderson had visited Roland in Brookline, the script was ready, and a copy was left with the tenor. He was being considered for the role of the longsuffering rural minister Stephen Kumalo, the protagonist of the novel.

Roland read the Paton novel as well as the script. He wrote someone (possibly his lawyer Roland E. Shaine, although it is not clear if the letter was actually sent) expressing the profound impact that the book had on him, but he did not see the nobility of Stephen Kumalo manifested in the Weil/Anderson script that he saw emerge from the Paton novel. He recognized that the character Kumalo needed to be humble, but his feeling was that the play had made him appear too submissive. In the end Roland expressed his disappointment in what Weil, Anderson, and Mamoulian had conceived.[53]

The Kurt Weil/Maxwell Anderson musical adaptation, which was to be called *Lost in the Stars,* was scheduled to premiere on Broadway in October 1949, and despite Roland's dissatisfaction with the script, he went to New York in mid-May to formally audition for the role. Anderson had invited him to bring his accompanist, Reginald Boardman, because they wanted Roland to sing as well as read lines. Completely prepared for his audition, Roland had memorized his scenes and sang for the composer, playwright, and producer. *Lost in the Stars* did open on Broadway in October to acclaim, but not with Roland playing Stephen Kumalo.[54] The role would be assigned to the dashing and vibrant baritone Todd Duncan, who some years before had premiered the role of Porgy in the Gershwin opera *Porgy and Bess* in 1936.

One month after Roland auditioned for Anderson and Weil in New York, he wrote Noël Sullivan to describe the entire episode to him. In his letter, Roland told Sullivan that initially the composer, playwright, and stage director were pleased, if not enthusiastic, about his audition. However, two weeks after they were supposed to contact him, he had heard nothing. Roland ultimately chalked it up to "Hollywood tactics – hot to the burning point one day, and icy cold the next."[55]

The year 1949 was significant for yet another reason, although it is unclear if and when Roland became aware of the events halfway around the world. By late 1948, his daughter Maya was a beautiful twenty-two-year-old woman. Although she was well educated through her private tutors and governesses, she had not been away from the small town of St. Lary for any greater exposure, apart from the occasional trip to Paris.

The countess had opened up her home to refugee Jews and Roma during World War II and to others in need before and after the world conflict.[56] Such was the case with a teenaged Russian refugee, Yuri Bogdanoff, who had come to the chateau in need. He had been in service to a Russian general, Murayev, who had to escape from the Soviet Union and took the boy with him to Spain.[57]

Young Yuri eventually had to flee Spain and crossed the Pyrenees Mountains into France and landed in the small village of St. Lary. He was taken in by Bertha when she realized that he had no other place to go.[58] Although he was two years younger than Maya, the two shared a passion for horses and spent endless hours riding together. By Maya's twenty-third birthday in February, Bertha noticed that her daughter's midsection was getting larger and larger and knew right away who was responsible for her "weight increase." She immediately located Yuri and gave him an old-fashioned *Ohrfeige* (a good hard slap across both cheeks).[59] In this case, the slap was to inform the stunned young man that he was now engaged to be wed. The pregnant Maya and Yuri were subsequently married.

On August 29, 1949, Maya gave birth to beautiful twin boys, Igor and Grichka – Roland Hayes's very first grandchildren. Exactly when Roland became aware of his new status cannot be determined, as he had kept most of his life with his older daughter and her mother secret. But he knew of his grandsons. They were barely out of their toddler phase when the twin boys met their distinguished grandfather for the first and only time.

Bertha, however, had very distinct plans for Maya and Yuri's baby boys. They quickly became the apple of their grandmother's eye, and she assumed a major role in raising them. Although Maya may have objected on occasion to her mother overruling her parental decisions, Yuri acquiesced to the will of his mother-in-law, who assumed the dominant role in his sons' lives. Bertha came to see the arrival of her twin grandsons as the realization of her unfulfilled ambition initially envisioned for Maya, had she been a boy. It seemed that Bertha's dream of a new order years before had simply been delayed a generation.

As the 1950s were ushered in, Hayes encountered yet again Alan Paton's *Cry, the Beloved Country*. The Kurt Weil/Maxwell Anderson musical adaptation of the novel, *Lost in the Stars,* had opened as scheduled on October 30, 1949, and ran until the following July, but, according to Roland, the South African author of the novel was dissatisfied with the results. Roland wrote Noël Sullivan in February 1950 that Paton was so "mortified" with the Weil/Anderson musical adaptation of his work that he wanted a more "faithful" version of the novel done on film.[60] Paton enlisted the services of the Hungarian-American film director Zoltan Kurda to oversee the filming of the work on location in South Africa. According to what Roland wrote Sullivan, the eminent director was "after" him to play the role of Stephen Kumalo in the film version, which Paton would produce. He was scheduled to meet the director in New York in early March. He told his friend that he had been given the script of the movie, and if he "decided" to do the film, he would be shooting on location in South Africa the following May and June.

The very language that Roland used in his letter to Sullivan (that the highly regarded Kurda was "after" him; if he "decided to do the film" he would be in South Africa) made quite plain, once again, that he was exaggerating his importance in this entire scenario. There are no known communications between Roland and the Hungarian-born Kurda to suggest that the director was "after" him or even considering him for the role and no letters or telegrams from the South African novelist.[61] In the final analysis, the part of Stephen Kumalo was played in the 1951 film version of *Cry, the Beloved Country* by the veteran African American actor Canada Lee, and his costar was a young Sidney Poitier.

Not all of the news was disappointing for Roland at the end of the 1940s into the 1950s. In 1948, he was awarded an honorary doctorate from Boston University and crystallized a relationship with Edwin Booth of the university's theology department. Booth interviewed Roland in a series of radio programs, and the tenor used the opportunity to promote his *My Songs* volume and to speak about his life and philosophies in general. In April 1950, Boston University announced through a press release that Roland would join the voice faculty of the College of Music. According to the arrangement, Roland would teach four months of the year (January and February and July and August, which were traditionally his non-touring periods). He would accept only advanced students whom he would be coaching primarily (although not exclusively) in German lieder.[62]

In addition to paying Roland a salary for his services, the institution would establish a scholarship in his name and take over the management of his career, including the handling of his bookings, his recording ventures, and other aspects of his professional life. The appointment was made by the outgoing president of the university, Daniel Marsh, and the dean of the College of Music, Warren Freeman. There was even a suggestion that one of the buildings on the campus would be named after him. After receiving yet another honorary doctorate (the latest from Howard University in Washington, D.C.) Roland must have looked at the arrival of this new decade with some justifiable optimism.

THIRTEEN

Struggles in Remaining Relevant

1950–1959

BY THE EARLY 1950S, ROLAND WAS IN HIS MID-SIXTIES AND WAS seen by many as an elder statesman of the concert stage. As such, he advised, coached, corresponded with, taught, and generally showed interest in the next generation of African American concert singers. Among those with whom he had contact (including giving lessons) included Rawn Spearman, Seth McCoy, Elmer Dickey, Ellabelle Davis, McHenry Boatwright, Georgia Laster, and John Patton Jr. Other well-known names with whom he dealt in the early 1950s were William Warfield and Leontyne Price.

In June 1951, his daughter Afrika (as she had then begun spelling her name) graduated from Brookline High School and had been admitted to Keuka College in upstate New York. She stayed at the small college for two years before transferring to Westminster Choir College in New Jersey, where she pursued undergraduate and graduate degrees in music education.

In September 1951, after being out of touch with each other for many years, Roland and Roger Quilter reestablished communication and their long-held friendship. The septuagenarian composer reminded the tenor of when he and Lawrence Brown had first come to England more than thirty years earlier and of the pleasant times they had enjoyed. Quilter reminded Roland of the occasion when Roland had sung "He Never Said a Mumberlin' Word" at the home of composer Norman O'Neill with such feeling that the audience members had moved away to the corners of the room so as not to show their emotions in response to his touching performance. It was on that occasion that the tenor had first met Joseph

Salmon.[1] Quilter told Roland that his health had been tentative but he was feeling better. He wanted Roland to write soon because he was ready to begin working on his memoirs and was keen to use their early meeting as one of several vignettes in his proposed book. In Roland's response to the composer, he recalled the events that had taken place and added a few memories of his own.

The veteran singer also informed Quilter of his teaching arrangement with Boston University, which included scouting performance opportunities in Europe for his advanced students. Hayes believed that this part of his job could theoretically bring him back to London. Still inclined to exaggerate about his performing schedule and his general importance, however, Roland informed Quilter that he had between fifty and sixty concerts scheduled throughout the United States and Canada during the 1951–52 season, when the actual number was closer to ten. Roland also said that he had not seen his former accompanist Lawrence Brown since 1943, when he was last in London. Finally, Roland reported on Alzada and Afrika. His daughter, he said, at five foot eight inches tall, was looking down on both of her parents.[2]

In the end, however, there would be no Roger Quilter memoir, because after the death of his nephew in World War II, the composer drifted in and out of mental stability (part of which was brought on by his struggle with his homosexual identity). He was able to write Roland in his more lucid moments, but his mental incoherence continued. There is no evidence that Roland had even the slightest awareness of his friend's difficulties. The tenor had, of course, always known the composer to be a physically fragile and emotionally sensitive man, but on September 21, 1953, yet another of Roland's friends from his early days in England passed away.[3]

Boston University's arrangement had been set up for a fruitful association with the tenor. The incoming president of the university, Dr. Harold C. Case, had authorized the establishment of the Roland Hayes Fund the previous June to develop Roland's projects related to his teaching, recordings, and concert work. Roland had also secured private funding from his Canadian friends Doug and Dorothy Henderson, as well as from the Rockefeller family in New York.[4]

The earliest sign that a breach had occurred in Hayes's relationship with the university came in a letter that Roland sent Dr. Case in late December 1951 complaining about the poor promotion and subsequent postponement of his November 18 Symphony Hall recital. In it, he said that his reputation had suffered and that there were financial damages to himself and to his manager, Demeter Zachareff. Furthermore, he wanted to know how the president would address this fiasco.[5] Case's January 8 response (apparently lost) evoked a more spirited response from Roland informing the president that he had agreed to the arrangement with Boston University under the conditions that the institution take over the handling of his concert work, which had been done "poorly." He further said that there were financial implications. He reminded Case, once again, that he, Roland, had secured five thousand dollars for the institution from the Hendersons in order to develop his recording projects. To complicate matters, Roland sought the assistance of his lawyer Roland E. Shaine, who began drafting the letters that Roland sent to the university.[6] There were several letters from Shaine to Hayes concerning the Boston University situation from December 1951 through March 1952. Dorothy Henderson also wrote President Case complaining about the treatment of Hayes. She was sent back her five thousand dollar contribution minus costs, which had already been expended for a recording project.

It boiled down to the tenor wanting additional compensation above his five thousand dollar salary to cover his losses for the Symphony Hall concert promotion, which ended up being postponed. (There is no record of this concert being rescheduled.) Roland's formal relationship with Boston University ceased at the end of his contract on June 30, 1952. He wrote Noël Sullivan in March of that year to tell him that his association with BU had been one of the "GREATEST deceptions of my life."[7]

In early 1952, Roland was contacted by Arthur E. Knight, a young record collector and recordist. He and his partner, Dominic Rocha, had heard the tenor in concert in Rhode Island and had become dedicated admirers. Knight, in fact, became part of the tenor's effort to preserve his recorded legacy from the mid-1950s forward.

It was apparent to Roland by then (as he was approaching seventy years old) that he had made a tactical career error by not recording more while he was in his vocal prime. Roland no doubt had realized the potential of records in his early career but had turned away from the medium, ostensibly because it did not represent his voice to its full capacity. Certainly he understood how Paul Robeson had used the medium and appeared to have leveraged that into movie roles. Marian Anderson had also made effective use of recording. By the early 1950s, she and Robeson had surpassed Roland with regard to their celebrity and followings.

Roland asked Arthur Knight if "he knew anything about phonograph recordings." Although Knight seems to have been more interested in collecting Roland's vintage recordings from London for discography purposes, he was being asked to consider another role in the tenor's life. Roland explained in one of his letters to Knight that years earlier, the Columbia label had refused to have him as a regular artist because of the objections of white tenors on the label. This implied, of course, that the white tenors were afraid of the competition that Roland would have presented. However, there is evidence to suggest that the record label was motivated more by its profit margin and, when requested, had supplied the tenor with everything he needed to know in order for him to record under one of the label's personal recording arrangements. Knight responded that he and Rocha had no recording experience but could refer him to Stephen Fassett, who wound up playing a role in the tenor's final recordings.[8]

Roland's claim to Knight about his Columbia experience appears to be another one of his exaggerations in an effort to remain relevant. But Roland and Knight ultimately developed a friendship as Knight came to truly admire the tenor's legacy. In 1954 he produced an article on Roland that included the most comprehensive discography of the tenor to date.[9]

Roland's spring 1953 schedule included two Jordan Hall appearances in Boston, and he went as far south as Atlanta, where he performed at Spellman College. He also performed at Keuka College in New York, where Afrika was as a student at the time. Roland was not above reaching out for performance opportunities when he saw possibilities. Just prior to his January inauguration, president-elect Dwight Eisenhower received a patriotic letter from Roland, who reminded the former general that he had performed for him some years ago and was ready to step forward to serve the country once again.[10]

Spring 1953 also brought Roland more management drama. Claiming Zachareff owed him eighty-eight dollars, Roland left his manager and sought other representation. He reached out to the Frieda Rothe Agency, but Rothe declined the opportunity to represent him full-time, believing he was too far past his prime to be a viable client. She recommended Caesar Searchinger, director of the Frieberg Agency in New York, but Rothe also cautioned Searchinger about Roland's precipitous break from Zachareff.[11] Her plan was to limit her part to advancing his publicity aims, but she seems to have had a transitory role with Roland between managements. With his Boston-based lawyer, Roland Shaine, in the background, the tenor entered a management agreement with Caesar Searchinger that initially lasted about two years. Immediately after engaging Roland as a client, Searchinger was in the delicate position of having to negotiate certain concert plans that Demeter Zachareff had arranged or was in the process of working on when Roland left his management. As many of the Zachareff dates were based on a prospective client list that Roland had developed and supplied, the tenor believed that *he* was as much responsible as Zachareff for whatever came out of any such scenario.[12] And then there was the matter of arranging Roland's proposed European tour the following spring, which was already in negotiation while Roland was still with Zachareff.

Roland's biggest engagement during the fall 1953 season was his Carnegie Hall appearance on November 29. For this recital he sent complimentary tickets to his benefactor John D. Rockefeller Jr., among other strategic associates. Like clockwork, Noël Sullivan sent his congratulatory telegram to his friend on the day before the recital.[13]

Roland also heard from another longtime friend prior to his Carnegie Hall recital: his former accompanist Charles J. Harris, who had known him from their student days in Boston in the early 1910s. Harris had retired from South Carolina State College in Orangeburg, where he had brought Roland to perform several times. He had since moved to Durham, North Carolina, where he was teaching private piano lessons.[14] When Roland responded to him a few weeks later, he informed Harris about the success of his Carnegie recital and proposed that they see each other when he was next in the Boston area. Charles Harris and Roland remained in contact with each other for the next twenty-three years.[15]

By January 1954, although Caesar Searchinger was handling Roland's recital affairs, the tenor was, as always, involved with all matters concerning his career. He sought the advice of Nora Douglas Holt, the singer, composer, and founding member of the National Association of Negro Musicians. She had been Roland's longtime supporter and believed that many within the African American religious community did not know he was still actively performing. He sought her assistance in locating the appropriate medium for distributing information about him and his management to this particular community. Holt proposed that he develop a postcard-sized circular with information about his availability and contact details and send them to leading African American Greek letter organizations, churches, civic organizations, and historically black colleges and universities.[16] As she was soon embarking on a cruise, she offered to take the circulars with her and distribute them strategically at various ports of call in the Mediterranean and North Africa. She also graciously offered to fund the cost of the postcard promotion.

Always mindful of cultivating high-profile contacts for performance opportunities, Roland also wrote the celebrated Spanish Catalan cellist Pablo Casals. He broke the ice by reminding Casals that he had loaned him his accompanist twenty-nine years earlier, in 1925, for his tour of Spain. He informed the renowned cellist that he would be performing in Europe soon and gave him the venues and approximate dates of his engagements. Of course, he included his management's contacts in the various countries where he would be concertizing, in the event that Casals might be available to attend a performance. Roland also wrote that he would like to attend Casals's upcoming music festival to be staged in Prades (in southwestern France near the Pyrenees) that coming June, but what he was really after (though he did not explicitly say so) was an invitation from Casals to perform at the festival.[17]

As Roland had been announcing to friends and colleagues since the previous fall, a European tour was scheduled for May and June 1954. He would perform in Copenhagen, The Hague, Amsterdam, London (two dates), Berlin, Frankfurt, Wiesbaden, Stuttgart, Munich, and Salzburg. He also had an engagement in Paris in June. The tour was sponsored, in part, by the U.S. Department of State (and the USO) and was in response to the patriotic letter the tenor had written to President Eisenhower volunteering his services the year before. Roland contacted his "Old World" team, which included Emmie Tillett in the United Kingdom, Leo Riemens in Holland, and Charles Kiesgen in France to handle his engagements in their respective countries. Initially, another British manager, Van Slyck, was to handle Hayes's engagements in London, but when Tillett voiced her dismay at this arrangement, Hayes returned to her. Van Slyck, however, did get a percentage of Hayes's Wigmore Hall engagement.

Kiesgen informed Roland that he could book him in the more intimate theater of the Champs-Élysées and that the concert would be under the auspices of the Lowenguth Chamber Society. Several of his engagements, including those in Wiesbaden, Stuttgart, and other locations, were for him to perform for the U.S. military and other government personnel, as specified in his agreement with the State Department.[18]

Roland and Reginald Boardman departed by air for the Continent as scheduled at the end of April. Roland remarked in a letter to Noël Sullivan from Copenhagen that an entire generation of Europeans had grown up without having seen him perform live.[19]

On June 20, 1954, Roland again wrote Sullivan, from Poitiers, France, updating him on the progress of his European tour and his schedule.[20] He said that because his June 12 concert at the small Theatre des Champs-Élysées had not been well advertised, there was a small audience. But "*what* an audience!" he proclaimed in his letter. He said the concertgoers truly appreciated his art and were so enthusiastic that at the end of the concert, the director of the series, Alfred Lowenguth, himself came out on the stage and announced to the audience his reengagement for the following May.[21]

Roland failed to mention in his letter to Sullivan that among the "enthusiastic" audience members was a sixty-four-year-old Bertha, the Countess Colloredo-Mansfeld, his twenty-eight-year-old married daughter, Maya Kolowrat Bogdanoff, and her twin sons, Igor and Grichka, who were quickly approaching their fifth birthday.

The boys had sat in the audience, quietly mesmerized by the white-haired, "mythological" black figure singing on the stage. His countenance, although much darker, was very similar to theirs. Bertha, their grandmother, had also appeared spellbound as he sang. During the concert, the twins recalled seeing her shed a tear, as if she had been taken back to an earlier period in her life – to a place she had not been in years. "Issten," the twins' nickname for their grandmother, had done everything in her power to reinforce the Roland Hayes mystique and described their grandfather as a "prince of art."[22] She had told them of his storybook life and how he had traveled throughout Europe on a private train with other great musicians. She said he had sung for royalty and other dignitaries throughout the Continent. He had dined with the elite in the great courts of Europe. Igor and Grichka were raised to respect this "statue" of a man.[23]

At the end of the concert, the family had all gone backstage. A few well-wishers had arrived before them, seeking autographs. Bertha and Maya went in to see Roland first and left the twins just outside of his dressing room door with instructions not to misbehave. They stood very quietly, holding hands in their smart matching navy-blue velvet suits with white lace-trimmed collars. The most memorable aspect of the evening for Grichka, as he recalled years later, was the discomfort of the new pair of tight-fitting black patent leather shoes, which had not been fully broken in.

Inside the dressing room, a very different scene began to play itself out. Even before Roland embraced his daughter, tears began flowing from her eyes, and seeing her tears, he began to shed them as well. Their embrace was warm, emotional, and profound. Maya fought hard not to cry, but seeing his tears let her know it was all right to let go. So she stood and wept with her father.[24]

It was the reunion she had played out so many times in her mind. It was the dream to which she had retreated in her most desperate moments as a child and young adult during the war when she had believed that her father would somehow come and take her away from the misery of being and feeling different in southern France. Maya had not seen him since he had last been in Paris in 1937, when she was eleven, but that memory was crystal clear.

Standing at a respectable distance so as not to intrude on this long-awaited reunion was the tenor's former love interest and the twins' grandmother – Bertha. The now fully white-haired singer, whose dark skin was a little more wrinkled but every bit as smooth as she had recalled in her mind, then took a step back from his daughter to formally acknowledge her mother. He stood almost at attention as if he would salute. Graciously, however, he gently bowed and took her right hand and kissed it, which was the formal custom of the day.[25]

Once again, Roland Hayes was in the presence of the woman who thirty years earlier had been his "revealer of wonders," his muse, and the person most responsible for his artistic manhood. He had just kissed the hand of the one who had once inspired him to "read Goethe, Schiller, and Bismarck" in preparation for singing Schubert, Schumann, Beethoven, Brahms, and Hugo Wolf.[26] This was also the woman who had first made him a father and now a grandfather of the two boys standing nervously outside of his dressing room. If there were any bad feelings that may have existed between them, they evaporated, at least for those few moments.

Roland took a moment to dry his eyes and make himself presentable. When Maya opened the dressing room door, the tenor greeted his grandsons. He was momentarily given to break down in tears again, but instead he reached down and kissed and embraced the pair. He then stood back up and applauded them, telling them what beautiful boys they were. The four-year-old Igor and Grichka both proudly smiled. Standing as a dutiful mother hen, Maya admired this tender scene. Tears, once again, began flowing from her eyes. Even though she had pent-up resentment for all the years he had not been in her life, for the moment Roland's very grandfatherly reception of her twin sons seemed to make up for it.

The June 12 meeting at the Theatre des Champs-Élysées was some years in the making. As early as 1952, Maya had told her boys that they would all be going to America to live with her father – their grandfather. They would take a long trip on a boat and settle there for some time. The little boys were thrilled at the prospect of traveling such a long distance. As their Russian grandfather (Yuri's father) was totally absent from their lives, they at least had their mythological maternal grandfather, whose image was fiercely protected by their grandmother. Yet they also saw the pain that Maya felt because of his absence. Although she had something of a relationship with her father throughout the years, it was mostly through coded letters and the occasional gift.

When the boys finally met their grandfather, the pain of the tight shoes suddenly vanished, replaced by excitement. All little Grichka could manage to get out at the time was "Félicitations sur votre concert" (Congratulations on your concert). They avoided calling him *grand-père*, thinking that it was not entirely appropriate. They simply referred to him as "Monsieur." It was respectful but, given his relationship to them, somewhat formal. Grichka asked their celebrated grandfather if he would sing something *just* for them. The tenor complied with a brief vocal scale, at which they smiled and applauded warmly. After some discussions and somewhat superficial chatter, Bertha, Maya, and the twins left with the plan to spend the following day with Roland at his hotel. The group stayed at the Paris apartment of the boys' godmother and Maya's dear childhood friend, Monique David, who had also attended the concert at the Theatre des Champs-Élysées.

Dressed a little less formally, the twins, Maya, and Bertha went to the Hotel Continental on June 13, where they had an elaborate lunch served in Roland's room. For Bertha, it was strangely reminiscent of the days when she and Roland had dined alone, fearful of being seen together in public. After they ate lunch, Roland asked his grandsons if they wanted ice cream, to which the boys enthusiastically responded, "Oui, Monsieur."

While Maya and her father sat on his bed talking, Bertha sat in a chair to the side, attempting to give the father and daughter some physical space in order to catch up on their many years apart. Roland remarked on his daughter's flawless English, which she spoke without a hint of an accent. This was clearly the influence of Bertha, who had insisted that their daughter know the language of her father, as well as several other languages.[27]

As the afternoon passed, Maya asked her father (most probably at the urging of Bertha) if he would assist her financially with the twins, his grandsons. It was a time of financial stress for Bertha, who was supporting her daughter, her son-in-law, and their children on a stipend. Although it was a generous amount, it had been intended for one person. To his daughter's request, Roland offered his standard diplomatic yet noncommittal response, "I'll think about it." Maya had had no experience with her father to realize that such a response typically meant "no," but he was too polite to say that outright. As the years passed, however, there was no financial assistance for this daughter, which surely contributed to the pain (if not bitterness) that Maya felt about not having her father in her life in a meaningful way.

The reality, however, was that Roland was not in a position to financially assist his daughter. The very tour that he was currently on throughout Europe at the time had, by and large, been heavily subsidized by the U.S. Department of State. As such, he was required to sing for U.S. soldiers in Germany and other parts of Europe as a part of his agreement with the agency. Maya knew none of that, and Roland did not volunteer any information that might make him appear less important and affluent. Perhaps if he had told her the reality of his financial circumstances, she might have at least understood. But, either because of pride or because he did not want to appear less prestigious, Roland, in the end, said nothing.

The twin's all-too-brief meeting with their celebrated "Monsieur" ended quickly, but the memory of the encounter has lasted for more than five decades. It was the only time that the boys met their celebrated grandfather. It was also the final time that Maya saw her father. And, perhaps most important, it was the last time that Bertha saw the man for whom she had sacrificed her reputation, position, and family.

Roland had raised the possibility of coming back to Paris the following year and that his "American" family (Alzada and Afrika) would meet his "French" family.[28] In the end, however, there would be no American and French family meeting. It would be the tenor's last time to the French capital and to the country. Maya, Bertha, and Igor and Grichka would be left only with memories.

The very personal June meeting at the Hotel Continental aside, Roland had health issues that needed attention while he was in Europe. He was hospitalized for more than ten days at the U.S. Air Force base in Wiesbaden with a case of pneumonia but continued his tour after he recovered.[29] Roland had discussions with Emmie Tillett, Charles Kiesgen, and a Mrs. Beeks in Holland about returning to Europe the following year, but negotiations broke down and the trip did not materialize.

After returning to the United States, Roland had one last fling with the idea of Hollywood producers representing his life on the big screen. He had been approached by screenwriters Helen Yates and Louis Stanton about putting his story on film. After having been through such a scenario before, Roland contacted New York lawyer Edward Rumley[30] to find out about the legitimacy of their claim. Rumley wrote Roland several letters in August advising him not to move forward with any arrangement with the two, believing them to be bogus.[31] Rumley even proposed that the pair could be involved in some kind of McCarthy-styled leftist attempt to damage his name and could do so without his realizing what had taken place. The attorney volunteered his services to help find funding for a motion picture, but nothing came of any such effort.

Most of Roland's schedule kept him in the New England area in the fall of 1954. The Vanguard label issued two of his recordings. The first was a Christmas album on which he performed holiday songs from various countries around the world; the other contained the songs that appeared in his 1948 volume, *My Songs*.

Roland also sent a surprise package to Robert Brante in Georgia for his family. His brother acknowledged the gifts that Roland had sent him, his wife, and their seven children in late October.[32] As always, he signed his letters to Roland "Devotedly."

Robert Brante *was* devoted to his renowned younger brother. He had been Roland's right-hand man in the Angelmo Farm experience, and when it failed, Robert Brante remained in the area with his family to manage the land given to him by Roland as well as the ten acres that their mother, Fannie, had left both of them. Having lost the use of the left side of his body after a stroke, Robert Brante was not slowed in his ability to do manual work and play the keyboard. According to his sons, he played better with one hand than many could play with two. Devout and God-fearing, as he had been raised by Fannie, Robert Brante did not allow card playing in the house. There was also no pitching pennies and definitely no playing or listening to blues or jazz.[33]

He proudly drove his family around in his 1937 Chevrolet and occasionally traveled north to Chattanooga. Even without a fully functioning left arm, Robert Brante could keep up with any other man when it came to farming, and he taught his sons to respect the dignity of farmwork. As a fulltime resident of Gordon County, Georgia, Robert Brante had better knowledge of southern protocol than his "northern" brother. Had that ugly situation in Rome, Georgia, in July 1942 occurred to Robert Brante, he would have been obliged to handle it differently than his more celebrated brother had.

As an otherwise healthy and hearty man, he was out chopping firewood in the afternoon of December 23 but stopped to go back inside to rest because he was not feeling well. His wife, Margaret, wanted him to go see a doctor, but he insisted that he would feel better after resting on the sofa. In practically no time, it seemed, Robert Brante suffered a massive cardiac episode and died soon after. Several of his children were standing nearby as he passed away in the late afternoon. His oldest son, Robert, who worked eight miles away, was sent for, only to be greeted with the sad news when he arrived. Dr. Lane, the area physician, came sometime after 6:00 PM to pronounce him dead.[34]

This news hit Roland like a thunderbolt. No illness had preceded Robert Brante's sudden death. Roland left immediately for Curryville to assist his late brother's family, who would have a sad Christmas that year. On his train trip south to Chattanooga, where he was met by Robert Brante's oldest son, he had time to reflect on what had occurred. At sixty-seven years old, he was now the sole surviving child of William and Fannie Hayes. Funeral arrangements were carried out in Rome, Georgia. Roland had left Boston on such short notice that he had to inform several of his friends of the trip south to bury his "last and most favorite brother" after arriving in Curryville.[35]

Roland did not stay in Curryville as long as he would have liked because he was required to travel to New York to attend Marian Anderson's historic Metropolitan Opera debut in Verdi's *Un ballo in maschera* on January 7, 1955. The reviews of her performance were kind, pointing out the historical significance of Anderson being the first African American to sing a solo role at the country's premiere opera house, but many acknowledged that vocally she was well past her prime. Roland apparently did not offer a public opinion on her performance, but he had been a longtime supporter of and mentor to Anderson. He also wrote to Francis Robinson of the Met to secure tickets for the debut of Robert McFerrin, the second African American singer to appear in a solo role at the opera house. Unlike Anderson, however, McFerrin was in his prime when he assumed the role of Amonasro in Verdi's *Aida* toward the end of January. Robinson, or "Mr. Metropolitan" as he was commonly known, called on Roland for the next several years, and the two became quite friendly.

When Roland had said "I'll think about it" in response to his daughter Maya's request for financial assistance the year before, he had left her with the impression that he might eventually provide such. By early 1955, it was increasingly unlikely that he could. Roland had once again switched personal managers. The latest (and his final) representative was William Lane of Leominster, Massachusetts. Lane had demonstrated his concern about Roland and his career, so in a rare moment of total vulnerability, Roland revealed to Lane the severity of his financial situation.[36] The letter laid out his monthly expenses, including Afrika's college expenses; he was barely meeting his needs. The reality of the situation made it clear that Roland was *obliged* to keep singing, although his voice, at sixty-seven years old, had shown clear signs of strain.

In his effort to remain relevant, the tenor called on old acquaintances, hoping to generate performance opportunities. Before going to Europe in 1954, Roland had contacted cellist Pablo Casals, indirectly informing him of his availability to perform in a renowned summer festival. After there was no response, Roland made a more direct request to the organizers for an appearance at the 1955 Prades festival: "If you should have an interest for a concert by me with you this next June I would be glad to know as soon as possible so that it may be the first of my appearances in Europe during the festival period."[37] Some weeks later, Casals wrote Roland back, graciously declining his offer to perform. He informed him that the brochures were already printed and the plans were already in place but remembered with pleasure the tenor's performances in Barcelona some thirty years earlier.[38]

Approaching the age of sixty-eight, Roland continued to reach out to other associates. The year 1955 also marked the occasion of Maestro Pierre Monteux's eightieth birthday. Roland saw it as an opportunity to step back into the limelight, as the celebrated maestro had been involved in his history-making debut with the Boston Symphony Orchestra thirty-two years earlier.

Following a BSO press conference in which the issue of Maestro Monteux's birthday came up, Roland wrote a letter to a BSO board member proposing that he sing at the concert honoring the maestro. He had been asked to provide a "birthday greeting," but the tenor wanted to appear on the symphony stage, singing on the program. When there was no response from the board member to his suggestion, Roland took matters a step further.

In March 1955, Maestro Monteux was conducting Gounod's *Faust* at the Metropolitan Opera House. Roland contacted his friend at the company, Francis Robinson, and asked him to deliver a personal letter to the maestro from him.[39] In the message to the elderly conductor, Roland wrote a flowery note praising Monteux for his courage in giving him such an opportunity in 1923 and proposed that he perform at the upcoming BSO Pension Fund concert the following month. Furthermore, he would even do so "free of charge!"[40] A few days later, Maestro Monteux wrote Roland an equally gracious response telling him that the program had already been set and that it would be broadcast (a medium that he knew Roland disliked), so he would have to decline his offer.[41]

In yet another "outreach" effort, Roland wrote to his contacts at the State Department in Washington, who proposed a sponsored trip to Pakistan. Roland received a letter from the U.S. Embassy in Karachi but did not make the trip after all. His health and age were factors that needed to be considered. Because he had been hospitalized while in Europe the previous year, there were valid concerns about his ability to endure such an undertaking. In late June, however, Roland did a recital in Bermuda. He returned in early July, where he spent the remainder of the summer preparing for his 1955–56 concert season.

Roland's first concert of the 1955–56 season was at the First Unitarian Church in Baltimore. The October 25, 1955, issue of the *Afro Magazine* (a weekly magazine version of the Baltimore-based *Afro-American* newspaper) printed a story on Roland commemorating the "thirtieth" anniversary of the tenor's Jim Crow incident in the city. (The Lyric Theater incident had actually occurred in January 1926, so it had not been quite thirty years.) The story also commented that Roland had not returned to the city for another recital until 1933.[42]

Roland's schedule was relatively light throughout the spring of 1956. As in past years, he seldom performed outside of the New England area (with the exception of a recital in upstate New York). The engagements were mostly invitations from churches. But as always, Roland was the consummate professional, even when there was poor attendance.

Roland had been out of touch with Noël Sullivan for over a year when he received a June birthday greeting from him and news of his collaboration with the San Francisco–based impresario Dr. W. Hazaiah Williams. Roland wrote him on August 29, 1956, to thank him for the birthday wishes, beginning with the usual apology for not having written sooner and updating his friend of nearly thirty-five years on Afrika's budding interest in choral conducting.

The most distressing part of Roland's letter to Sullivan dealt with his visit to France two years earlier, in 1954, when he had attempted to reclaim his stored possessions from the Thomas Cook warehouse in Paris. All his things had been sold at auction for nonpayment. Roland maintained that he had not received any notes for unpaid charges during the war and apparently had made no inquiries about his stored materials. Among the things that he lost were six trunks of music and most of his European correspondence. Also lost were the teaching notes that his former Fisk professor, Jennie Robinson, had willed him. He said that he was still recovering from the shock of the loss.[43] He had briefly considered taking legal action against Thomas Cook but was advised against it. He also informed Sullivan that he had sold the farm in West Newberry, Massachusetts, a few years before. He closed his letter with the usual warm greetings reserved for Sullivan:

> With devoted, affectionate, greetings to you. I do not know who is with you now of my acquaintance, but whoever is there or whoever you see that I know, please tender my kind thoughts. Alzada joins in all I have said with respect to love and devotion.
>
> As ever,
> Roland[44]

As Roland sent this letter via airmail, Sullivan would have received it in a matter of days and would have had the opportunity to reflect, once again, on the sincerity and deep commitment of the tenor's friendship. Barely two weeks after his letter to Sullivan was sent, Roland received the following telegram dated September 16, 1956:

> God called Noel Sullivan to himself at 7:30 PM after a coronary occlusion.
>
> Brenda Doyle Ferrari (his niece)[45]

Roland immediately sent back a telegram extending his heartfelt condolences to the entire family and offering whatever assistance he could.[46] The death of Noël Sullivan was almost as painful to Roland as the loss of his brother Robert Brante nearly two years earlier. He had revealed things to Sullivan that he had not shared with anyone else, and Sullivan had also been with him from his early days in Europe through thick and thin. Sullivan had, in many ways, reinforced Roland's belief in the "other race." Although he and Roland were keenly aware of their racial differences, at a certain level they had transcended those barriers and respected each other as men and as friends.

Roland did not travel to his friend's funeral but certainly grieved this death. He wrote Langston Hughes (who had also benefited from Sullivan's largesse) a very pained letter about the passing of their mutual friend, but Hughes was already aware of it.[47] One month after Sullivan's death, Roland was informed that his late friend had left him a one thousand dollar "bouquet" of love in his will.

Among others whom Sullivan had similarly recognized in his will was the German opera singer Frieda Hempel, whose talent he had admired nearly as much as Roland's. Born in 1885, Hempel had actually died a year before Sullivan in 1955, but he had apparently not updated his will to reflect the change. Others so recognized were Lotte Lehmann, Povla Frijsh, and Elena Gerhardt.[48]

After having lost so many who had been close relatives and friends over the years, Roland contacted Dr. Karlis Osis of the Parapsychology Laboratory at Duke University in North Carolina. The spring 1957 communications between the two indicated that Osis had conducted some sort of séance with Roland at which his mother, Fannie, appeared.[49] How long the relationship continued is unclear, but Alzada must have been aware of the otherworldly contact, because Dr. Osis sent her greetings as well.[50]

That spring, Roland had fewer than five paid public engagements. As such, he wrote the attorneys of Noël Sullivan to politely inquire about the status of the one thousand dollar Sullivan bequest. He immediately received a note back from the law firm that his legacy would be received within one week.[51] Although the fall 1957 portion of Roland's schedule was slim, William Lane managed to set up several engagements for

Roland in the spring of 1958, including dates in Ohio, Illinois, Georgia, Tennessee, and of course Massachusetts.

As Roland turned seventy-one years old in June of 1958, his daughter Afrika completed her master's degree in music from Westminster Choir College. He contacted several colleagues and associates at various historically black colleges and universities to see about their assistance in securing her a teaching position. She was eventually offered a job at Virginia State College (now Virginia State University) outside of Petersburg and taught there a short time before moving to another teaching job in North Carolina.

By the end of the 1950s, Roland was still fostering the budding singing careers of several African American students, including the California-based tenor John Patton and contralto Louise Burge from Tennessee. Several came to sing for him in Brookline. A student recommended to him by Laura Wheatley, his dear friend from Baltimore, was a young baritone named Daniel Comegys.[52] After studying with Roland in Brookline, Comegys eventually traveled to France to study with Nadia Boulanger, who kept Roland informed of his progress. While pursuing a music career, Comegys always found time to check back in with his elderly teacher and did so for the next seventeen years.

FOURTEEN

"I Wanna Go Home"

1960–1977

BY THE EARLY 1960S ROLAND'S DAY AS A CELEBRATED performer and artist had unquestionably passed, yet he was determined to remain in the public eye. His skill as a teacher and as an adviser to a younger generation of singers, however, continued as it had the previous decade, and he was regularly consulted for career advice. Those skills were more in demand than his appearances on the concert stage. Often it was no more than a formal (or informal) audition, a letter of recommendation, or basic career moves that were sought. The septuagenarian singer heard from the likes of the up-and-coming lyric tenor Seth Mc-Coy and Odetta Felious. Better known to the world simply as "Odetta," she had nursed operatic ambitions when she auditioned for Roland. His letter to her was quite encouraging and complimentary.

As a teacher, he wanted his students to have a clear understanding of the texts they were singing, not just of the translations beneath the original language and the notes but an independent translation. He then wanted his students to read about the lives of each composer whose works they essayed – obviously a practice that developed out of his work with the countess.[1] Before students could perform a specific song or aria for him, they had to persuade the seasoned veteran that they had command of the translation of the work as well as some knowledge of the life of the composer who created it and of the context in which the work was created. In conversation with students, the master teacher especially wanted to know what personal experiences his young singers were bringing to the performance.

He also instructed on program building and how to come up with the right balance in constructing vocal concerts (that is, the different periods, languages, and styles represented). He exposed his students to the vocal literature from the Renaissance, baroque, pre-classical, classical, romantic, post-romantic, and twentieth-century periods.[2] Roland's paramount vocal approach focused on blending the pitch, vowel, and resonance, which he referred to as the "Father, Son, and Holy Ghost" of singing. He often coached his African American students (like Baltimorean Daniel Comegys, to whom he referred as "Comegazes") in the correct interpretation of African American spirituals, including several of his arrangements and those of his former accompanists Percival Parham, William Lawrence, and Lawrence Brown.[3]

Roland instructed by example. He told his students they were primarily vessels through which musical expressions flowed. He often conveyed his instructions in spiritual, if not religious, terms. Musical interpreters, according to him, opened themselves up to the spirit (which had been given from a divine source) and in turn communicated the message of the music to their audience.[4]

The majority of his students were European Americans. With his African American students, however, he emphasized that they be proud of the achievements of the race, because there was so much that "we" had won despite great odds.

Even in his seventies, Roland remained well read on many subjects. He read biographical essays of great composers and kept track of current events, especially those on the African continent, where dramatic changes were taking place. He remained a lifelong admirer of Emperor Haile Selassie and often spoke of him as the ideal African leader right up until the time of the deposed Ethiopian monarch's death in the mid-1970s. Roland followed with great interest the independence movements in Africa from the late 1950s into the 1960s. Although he repeatedly received invitations to visit countries like the newly independent Ghana, Ivory Coast, and Nigeria, he never set foot on the African continent.

Through his contact with Francis Robinson at the Metropolitan Opera, Roland was invited to judge the National Council Regional Auditions for the company's opera association. He was recognized by the organization's New England chapter by being made the lead judge. Although he was, by far, the best-known name among the judges, Roland had not once sung in an opera throughout his distinguished career. In 1925, a Berlin impresario, Dr. Peter Sirota, had made his bid through the Ibbs and Tillett Agency for Hayes to sing the title role in Verdi's *Otello*, offering the tenor an additional fifty engagements.[5] Apart from the fact that Roland had no immediate plans to appear in an opera, Otello, even at his vocal height, would have been an unsuitable role for him because it traditionally required a much larger voice, given the orchestral demands. It was only because Roland had the right skin color to portray Verdi's adaptation of Shakespeare's tragic Moorish general that Sirota had made such a proposal. Sirota's offer would not have been taken seriously anyway, because he was offering only two hundred dollars for a performance, too low for Roland to consider as he neared the height of his celebrity.

In any case, Robinson had maintained that if times had been different (that is, if the opera world had been integrated), his friend could have had a magnificent career on the opera stage.[6] Robinson suggested specifically that Roland could have mastered the role of Des Grieux in Massenet's *Manon*. The tenor aria "En fermant les yeux" (Closing my eyes), had been a signature piece in Roland's early career. Little did Robinson know that Hayes had purposely avoided the opera stage.

Not willing to give up on his career, Roland continued to solicit singing engagements. His long-held philosophy was that spreading his message by word of mouth was his most effective tool in generating interest in and selling tickets to concerts.[7] When rumors began to surface of his retirement, he quickly denounced them as "lies" (although he was nearing his seventy-fifth birthday). In October 1960, he sang at Boston's Jordan Hall, although instead of clarifying that he had engaged the hall through personal funds or those of his benefactors, he put out the statement that he had "been engaged" by the venue. His tried and tested technique of telling prospective concert bookers that they needed to decide quickly on his services as his calendar was filling up no longer yielded the results that it once had.

In 1961, however, Roland had a moderately extensive tour sponsored by the Association of American Colleges that took him south to Virginia, Tennessee, and Texas; to the lower and upper Midwest, including Ohio,

Iowa, Nebraska, and Minnesota; and finally out west to California. It was his first time to the far western state since receiving the news of Noël Sullivan's death in 1956. Roland had made the acquaintance of the celebrated photographer Ansel Adams (who had also photographed him) and had sent him tickets to his recital in California, but Adams was unable to see the tenor during his trip there. The audiences to whom Roland sang on this tour were relatively small but always very appreciative. For him, it was a matter of being before the public and continuing to spread his musical message.

If 1961 was moderately successful, 1962 brought Roland attention he had not received for some time. The year marked his seventy-fifth birthday, and in March, the 75th Hayes Birthday Committee was formed. A grand tribute and concert at Carnegie Hall on the tenor's birth date, June 3, was planned. Although the great cellist Pablo Casals had turned down Roland's request to perform at the Prades Music Festival some years earlier, he accepted the honorary role of co-chair of the Hayes birthday committee. He shared this responsibility with Dr. Warner Lawson of Howard University, who did the bulk of the work. Other distinguished names on the committee were Ralph J. Bunche of the United Nations, Roy Wilkins of the NAACP, Langston Hughes, singer Carol Brice, and president of Fisk University Dr. Stephen J. Wright, among others.[8]

In addition to making arrangements for the Carnegie Hall event in June, various committee members contacted old acquaintances of Roland's, including several of those who had been members of the Fisk Jubilee Singers with him in the 1910s. Among them, Charles W. Kelley wrote the elderly tenor a very gracious note with his apologies for not being able to attend the birthday concert in New York.

The Sunday afternoon concert marking Roland's seventy-fifth birthday was a grand affair. The major sponsor of the event was the American Missionary Association, which had supported Roland early in his career and for which the elderly tenor had given benefit recitals over the years. In fact, his June 3 concert also functioned as a fund-raiser on behalf of several historically black colleges and universities, including Dillard University, Huston-Tillotson College (now University), Le Moyne College, Talladega College, and Tougaloo College (and several of those institutions' chief executive officers were also members of the birthday committee). Roland was awarded the AMA's first prestigious Amistad Award on the occasion.[9]

Roland received congratulatory notes from far and wide. Metropolitan Opera soprano Leontyne Price sent a special greeting, and although she had to rush off for a recording date in Italy, she invited the tenor to see her at the Met later that year when she starred in Verdi's *Ernani*.[10] Although Pablo Casals had agreed to lend his name to the birthday event, he was unable to attend the Carnegie Hall recital but offered his heartfelt congratulations to the singer. As always, Roland was gracious and receptive. Telegrams were received from the likes of former First Lady Eleanor Roosevelt and Helen Henschel (the daughter of the late Sir George, one of Roland's teachers from his early days in England). There was also a letter from a Will Anthony Madden, who did attend the New York concert. He reminded the tenor that he had presented him in concert in the city forty-five years earlier. In his letter to the elderly singer, Madden said that he had attended a Carnegie Hall program in October 1912 when Roland appeared at the hall singing in Mendelssohn's *Elijah* with Minnie Brown, Daisy Tapley, and Harry Burleigh.[11] Madden recalled that former president Theodore Roosevelt was also in attendance at the performance.

Of course, Roland Hayes performed at the birthday celebration. The mini-recital included Beethoven's impassioned lied "Trocknet nicht, trocknet nicht" (Dry not, dry not [tears of eternal love]). At seventy-five, the tenor was still able to deliver a solid performance of the song because the range was not especially demanding, and he could create a stunning effect in the climatic final four measures of the work, "Tränen unglücklicher Liebe" (Tears of unhappy love). His emphasis on the final "Liebe" could still send chills through his listeners. Something of his incomparable artistry was still intact. He also did several spirituals, including "I Can Tell the World!," "Ezekiel Saw de Wheel," and his arrangement of "Swing Low, Sweet Chariot."

The recital was a resounding success: it drew a respectable audience, raised money for a worthy cause, and restored Roland to a spotlight that he was born to be in. It would be the largest audience for which Roland would perform for the remainder of his career.[12]

Roland's spring 1963 performing schedule took him to the West Coast again for recitals in California (including San Francisco and Sacramento); Richmond, Indiana; and Baltimore (a concert at Morgan State College, now University). As he had before, the tenor exaggerated in a letter to the sculptor Richmond Barthé, saying that it was a coast-to-coast tour.[13]

The real news in the Hayes family that year came from thirty-year-old Afrika. She had left her teaching position at Virginia State College and taken up one at North Carolina Central College (now University), where she taught voice, drama, and theater. While there, she met a very handsome and slightly younger student, Joseph Lambe, who was an especially gifted actor. The department staged a production of Sophocles's *Antigone* in which he was cast as Creon opposite Afrika in the title role.

A relationship between the two eventually developed. Afrika eventually followed Joseph Lambe, who left North Carolina for New York, where he pursued acting and a modeling career. They were secretly married in 1963 and began pursuing professional careers in the city.[14] Roland had an occasion to be in Brooklyn for a concert, and Afrika arranged to be in attendance. After her father's performance, Afrika introduced a very nervous Joseph Lambe to her father as her new husband.[15] Roland's reaction was surprisingly mild. In the past, the protective father had wanted to know the specifics of his daughter's suitors, including who their "people" were.

Although Afrika had musical ambitions, hers were very different from those of her father, and he often expressed his disapproval of certain choices she made along such lines.[16] When she had intended to appear in a locally staged musical (as opposed to a more serious genre), he was critical and found such decisions to be "beneath" her, professionally.

In April 1963, Roland received news of the death of MacKinley Helm of a cardiac episode in Santa Barbara, California. In addition to *Angel Mo' and Her Son, Roland Hayes,* Helm had written several other biographies as well as a few travel-related books. As Roland had given up on realizing his story on the big screen, he turned his attention to having his once-celebrated biographical narrative *Angel Mo'* reissued. It took some years after Helm's death for Roland to finally receive exclusive rights to the work from the biographer's widow, but eventually an agreement between the parties was reached. The New York–based publisher, Greenwood Press, reissued a limited run of *Angel Mo'* in 1969, but Roland had hoped for a more established publishing house like Little, Brown to take up the project.[17]

Roland stayed close to home in early 1964 to look after Alzada, who suffered from diabetes, among other ailments. A New York concert was given in his honor, but he appeared to have no recital dates early in the year. Roland rekindled his relationship with Demeter Zachareff in 1964, however. "Zee" was instrumental in arranging for the tenor to sing a concert at Goucher College in Towson, Maryland (outside Baltimore), where he would also have a three-week residency. His stay there began and ended with a public concert. In between, he coached several singers in arias and other repertory.

During Roland's three-week stay at Goucher, the celebrated maestro Pierre Monteux, who had retired to Hancock, Maine, and had established a conducting institute there, died on July 1, 1964. When a memorial service was held later in the year, a seventy-seven-year-old Roland sang at it and eulogized the conductor in the most flattering terms, praising Monteux as someone who was far ahead of his time.

Afrika's husband, Joseph Lambe, had long held the view that his wife had a significant vocal talent and urged her to develop it and put it on display before the public. At some point, the idea of a father and daughter joint recital came up between Roland and Afrika as a way of exposing Afrika's vocal ability. The two negotiated the repertory for the recital over the next several months in preparation for their joint concert at Jordan Hall in Boston. The April 4, 1965, afternoon concert was moderately attended, but it was recorded. Roland's voice showed signs of strain, especially in the louder passages and upper register. However, the reviewers were more critical of Afrika's singing than his. One reviewer praised Roland's singing and artistry but found Afrika's voice "rough."[18] The duo wanted to repeat the concert in New York, but they were not successful in securing a venue. They subsequently performed together again in Boston and in October 1966 gave another recital at Berry College in Mount Berry, Georgia.

It became increasingly challenging for Afrika to travel, because at thirty-two, she had become a new mother. Her daughter, Zaida Christine Lambe, was born on February 24, 1966, and Roland was, once again, a grandfather. He and Afrika gave another joint recital at Jordan

Hall in November under the auspices of the Longy Music School in Cambridge.[19]

Roland was fighting the flu close to the performance date, and there were questions about whether that concert would take place.[20] After the recital, he was hospitalized for another bout with pneumonia and remained there for over a month.[21] His general health became increasingly precarious. By the mid-1960s, Roland required thick trifocal glasses (which he always took off before performing), and his memory had noticeably deteriorated. He informed Afrika that because of his failing memory, he had to hear the accompaniments many times in order to make his entrances correctly.[22]

Roland sometimes offered Afrika advice about her solo performances, such as one in Baltimore in late 1966. He commented on her beautiful singing but advised that what "you ABSOLUTELY MUST DO is to keep sending the vowels in every word to the front of your mouth and not so backwards."[23]

Roland's health remained tentative in the spring of 1967, and he occasionally required assistance when moving around. As he neared his eightieth birthday, a Friends of Roland Hayes Committee formed to celebrate the occasion. The committee was co-chaired by Louis Speyer, recently retired oboist of the Boston Symphony, and A. Fred.[24] Among the honorary sponsors were Senator Edward Brooke (Massachusetts's first African American senator), Senator Edward M. Kennedy, and Erich Leinsdorf, music director of the BSO).[25] Roland's friend of fifty-six years, Charles Harris from Durham, North Carolina, contacted the tenor to tell him that he would do his best to be at the eightieth birthday event.[26]

In June 1967, the town of Brookline and the Friends of Roland Hayes Committee honored their distinguished citizen of the artistic stage. Fred Prager emceed the afternoon event. The first person to speak was a seventy-year-old Marian Anderson.[27] Senator Brooke spoke, and there was a surprise visit from the Massachusetts governor, John A. Volpe. He hailed the singer an "ambassador of music and song and a symbol of determination."[28] The governor presented Roland with a Paul Revere bowl and a proclamation marking the occasion.

The tenor's eightieth birthday was officially declared "Roland Hayes Day" in Boston. Hayes sang a brief concert at the Isabella Stewart Gardner Museum. As always, he was gracious to his guests and wrote a grateful note to the co-chairs of the event. Proudly sitting next to her husband of thirty-five years was Alzada, who was referenced by several of the guest speakers. A very pregnant Afrika, with her toddler, Zaida, also in attendance, sang on the occasion honoring her beloved father. Two months later, Afrika gave birth to another daughter, Erika.

In Cambridge on November 8, 1967, Roland gave another concert at Radcliffe College and asked that certain people like Fred Prager, Afrika and her husband, and his manager, William Lane, be given complimentary tickets. The following month, however, he sent Lane a letter, dated December 11, 1967, terminating their contract. In part the letter said:

> I am writing you regarding the arrangement set forth in my letter to you, January 3, 1956.
>
> As you know, termination by written notice is available to either of us. I feel that the time has come, for reasons which I know are well understood by you, for me to give you notice of termination which I now ask you to consider as hereby given you. . . .
>
> As you have the opportunity, I will be glad to hear from you.
>
> Cordially,
> Roland Hayes[29]

What is not entirely possible to discern from this notice is whether it was a "friendly" termination based on Roland's obvious advanced age, failing memory, and generally weakened capacity or a break due to some perceived disagreement with Lane. The former would appear to be the case because of the relatively "soft" tone of the letter, but given Roland's track record with managers and personal representatives, the latter cannot be entirely ruled out. In 1969, Lane signed a waiver discharging his former client from any indebtedness.[30]

In 1968, Roland was recognized for his career achievements with several honorary degrees. On April 25 he received his third honorary degree from Fisk University; on June 2, one day before his eighty-first birthday, he received an honorary doctor of oratory sciences degree from Curry College in Milton, Massachusetts; two days after that he was back in Tennessee, where he received an honorary doctorate from the University of Chattanooga (now University of Tennessee at Chattanooga) on June 5; and the following day, he received an honorary doctorate from the University of Vermont. He wrote a friend about the receipt of all the recognitions, saying, "It has been a spring of awards for me. BUT, I am still Roland Hayes living at 58 Allerton Street, Brookline, Mass, and am happy that this is so."[31]

Still not willing to give up spreading his musical message on the stage, Roland journeyed south in March 1969 to give recitals at Berry College in Georgia and in Austin, Texas, which he described to his student Daniel Comegys as enthusiastically received by the audience.[32] In 1970, Roland received a six thousand dollar gift from Mrs. Magaretta "Happy" Rockefeller to pay off the mortgage of his Brookline home. In his letter to the attorney handling the transaction on behalf of Mrs. Rockefeller, the tenor bemoaned the fact that his November 1970 concert dates in Boston and Washington, D.C., had been canceled out of economic necessity.[33]

Roland was able to manage only a few more engagements over the next few years. One took place at Glencairn Museum in Bryn Athyn, Pennsylvania, on April 30, 1972. As always, Reginald Boardman was at the piano. The program was not vocally demanding, and Roland performed Purcell, Handel, Monteverdi, Schubert, and Quilter, which he had sung on hundreds of occasions. He also included four Aframerican religious folk songs, "Didn't My Lord Deliver Daniel?," "O Rise, Shine for the Light Is a-Comin'," "I'll Make Me a Man," "You Mus' Come In by an' Thro' de Lamb." His vocal production was marginal, but the reception from his audience was very respectful.

The following year, Roland sang once again, this time at the Longy School of Music in Cambridge. The 1973 fund-raising engagement was the tenor's last public performance and was memorable, but not for its artistic merit. With Boardman at the keyboard, Roland delivered a program similar to one he had given the year before at Glencairn in Pennsylvania, adding several selections from his *Life of Christ* song cycle to the end of the program. He made it through the Monteverdi, the Purcell, the lieder, and the French songs with no difficulty, but when he came to his signature song from the *Life of Christ* cycle, "Lit'l Boy," he ran into trouble. When Roland reached the final verse, beginning "The last time the little boy was seen, he was . . . ," suddenly there was silence. He had forgotten the rest of the verse and could not remember his spot in the music to restart. He stood on the stage very composed but was clearly confused. After a few seconds, the singer turned slightly to the right toward Boardman for prompting. His accompanist whispered the words, "The last time the little boy was seen, he was standing on Mount Olivet green," but Roland could not hear Boardman's prompting. Alzada and Afrika and her two daughters were in the audience. Looking at her husband standing silent on the stage, Alzada began to shake like a leaf. Afrika decided to take matters into her hands. She stood and rhythmically spoke out the words, "The last time the little boy was seen, he was standing on Mount Olivet green . . ." Roland quickly recovered his spot in the music. He smiled, looked at Boardman with a confident nod, began the last verse, and completed the song.

After assisting her father from the audience, Afrika sat down, and then *she* became nervous. She believed that her actions had been disrespectful and remembered the incident as one of the worst moments of her life.[34] All of a sudden, Roland's forty-year-old daughter felt the crashing reality of just how frail and human her father really was. After the concert was over, the family drove home in total silence. Even though Afrika's daughters were only seven and six, they knew something was grave about this ride to 58 Allerton Street.[35] Once they arrived, Afrika told her somewhat despondent father, "Daddy, you have to stop, now!" Alzada then joined in, "Buddie, you have given to people all these years, now it time for you to live a little." Roland was eighty-six years old.

Roland had been invited to give several master classes on the West Coast in 1974 under the sponsorship of Dr. W. Hazaiah Williams. The California engagement came with a fee of two thousand dollars, which he had not been offered for an engagement since the late 1920s. Roland, however, was in no condition to accept. After his very public memory loss on the stage, as well as his general health decline, the idea of him traveling to the West Coast was impossible.

The impact of Roland's 1973 Longy concert seemed to have accelerated his mental decline, because he simply had nothing to do. There was nothing to occupy his mind. Although a diagnosis of Alzheimer's disease was not formally made at the time, he began displaying the classic symptoms. He occasionally went into his wife's bedroom in the middle of the night and asked her, "Where is Mother?" (that is, Fannie). Every morning, he took daily walks around the neighborhood. He began to lose his way and would have to be guided home by the Brookline police or some kindly neighbor.[36] He was, at least, well known to all of them.

Alzada, in the meantime, was also having health issues. She required cataract surgery on both eyes, and because of Roland's decline, he was unable to assist her. While Alzada recuperated at a private rehabilitation facility, Afrika and her daughters looked after the elderly man. The three eventually moved into Roland and Alzada's Allerton Street home because Afrika and Joseph Lambe had amicably separated and eventually divorced. Afrika and her daughters managed to keep Roland's deteriorating mind somewhat engaged by playing board games with him that required him to use his cognitive abilities.

Afrika's divorce from Joseph Lambe had not been contentious in the least. In fact, she recalled it as the friendliest divorce that one could ever imagine. He remained on the best of terms with his mother- and father-in-law, whom he affectionately called "Mom" and "Dad." Sometime in 1974, Joseph Lambe became ill and was eventually diagnosed with Hodgkin's disease. Since he was from Durham, North Carolina, he decided to return there for treatment at Duke University Hospital, but his condition was apparently too advanced for effective treatment.[37]

A few months before his death in the spring of 1975, he contacted Afrika and told her he wanted to come to Brookline to see his daughters and Roland and Alzada. Once he arrived in Brookline, Lambe's worsening condition required him to take frequent naps, which he did while he stayed at his former in-laws' Allerton Street home. Roland came downstairs at one point and saw Lambe napping on the sofa and did not recognize him. He went to Alzada and said, "Mahmmy, there is a man sleeping on the couch."

She calmly said, "That's all right. That's Afrika's husband, Joe."

He seemed to have understood her and smiled approvingly and walked away. Ten minutes later, Roland came back to his wife and said, "Mahmmy, there is a man sleeping on the couch." Shortly thereafter, Joseph Lambe returned to Durham and died on March 25, 1975.[38]

In the meantime, Roland's health situation continued to decline. By the fall of the following year, he had become more unstable and eventually had to be hospitalized for pneumonia. Afrika went to see him, only to be told that he had been a difficult patient. While his daughter was with him, he removed the intravenous tubes to his arm. A young nurse came in and lightheartedly said, "Roland, you need to stop pulling those . . ."

"Excuse me," Afrika interrupted, "this man is old enough to be your father. Please call him *Mr. Hayes.*"

The nurse quietly bandaged his hands in gauze to prevent him from pulling out the tubes again. After recovering from his most serious illness, Roland was transferred to a nursing home for convalescence. As in his hospital stay, Roland was not a cooperative resident at the nursing facility and had to be physically restrained in a wheelchair.

By the time Thanksgiving arrived, Alzada, Afrika, and the girls had not seen Roland for some time and decided to spend the holiday with him at the nursing home. They were all shocked to see the normally immaculately groomed Roland sitting restrained in a chair, unshaven, with unkempt hair and wearing a dirty robe. His granddaughter Zaida did not recognize him at all.[39] He had also been heavily sedated.

The shock of seeing her father like that was too much for Afrika, who quickly walked back out of his room. When she composed herself, she reentered and feigned a cheery greeting, "Hi, Daddy." His response was a high-pitched incoherent squeal with a forced attempt at smiling. Unable to contain her emotions, Afrika again left her daughters and her mother in the room with the unrecognizable and demoralized Roland.[40] His distressed eyes followed her out of the room, but he could not verbalize more than that unrecognizable vocalization. Alzada, however, remained. She and her granddaughters had Thanksgiving dinner with her husband of forty-four years. She quietly and dutifully fed the drooling man his meal and kept him company. This was the worst condition in which she had ever seen him in all the years they had been together.

A few weeks later, Alzada and Afrika discussed the possibility of going to the nursing facility to spend Christmas with Roland, but Alzada ruled out the visit. She concluded that it would be better to remember him as he had been and not as that shadow of a man she had spent Thanksgiving with. They both instinctively knew the end was near.

A few days after Christmas, Alzada received a call that her husband had been taken to Massachusetts General Hospital because of some respiratory complication. Shortly after midnight in the newly arrived 1977, a physician from Massachusetts General called. Roland Wiltsie Hayes, the great-grandson of the African Abá 'Ougi; the last surviving child of William and Fannie Hayes; the brother of William Jr., Mattie, Nathaniel "Tench," John, Robert Brante, and Jesse, died alone at the age of eighty-nine years old. His widow was told that he had died of a pneumonia-related illness. The official cause of death, however, was upper gastrointestinal bleeding.[41]

Late in the morning of New Year's Day, Alzada and Afrika went to the hospital morgue to identify Roland's body. Afrika glanced at her father's still form and very quickly left. Alzada stayed behind and spoke to her lifeless husband's remains. She had known that his end was near, but the reality of his death was no less painful.

News accounts appeared in the *Boston Globe* and the *Boston Herald* before being picked up by other national papers. The *New York Times'* January 2, 1977, story about Roland's death quoted the Associated Press's January 1 announcement that the "acclaimed concert tenor died yesterday."[42] This left the erroneous impression that he had passed away on December 31, 1976, as opposed to January 1, 1977. For some years, the error was left uncorrected. Some biographical sources indicate a 1976 death date and others 1977.

Condolences were sent to Alzada from far and wide. Among the mourning notices she received were those from the Fisk Jubilee Singers and the distinguished historian and Fisk alum Dr. John Hope Franklin.[43]

Alzada and Afrika planned a relatively simple funeral. The service was held on January 4 at Ebenezer Baptist Church near Roxbury, as his mother's had been fifty-three years earlier. His older brother John had also been "sent home" from the church. The service was led by Dr. Rafe M. Taylor. Roland's former student Clay Douglas sang at the funeral with the deceased tenor's trusted accompanist of thirty-five years, Reginald Boardman, at the keyboard. Douglas performed the very songs that had been sung at the funerals of Roland's father and mother, "Roun' about de Mountain," and "Sit Down." Some in attendance recalled the racially mixed service as being dignified and very uplifting – almost like a concert.

Dutifully in attendance was Roland's friend Charles J. Harris, whom he had met in the same city more than sixty-five years earlier. Nearing ninety-two years of age, Roland's oldest living colleague had flown to Boston from Durham, North Carolina, to attend his departed friend's service. Harris took a flower from Roland's casket after the funeral and held on to it for the remaining eleven years of his life.[44]

Roland Hayes's earthly remains were committed at Mount Hope Cemetery in Roslindale, Massachusetts. Not far away were those of his beloved mother, Fannie, and his brother John. He wanted to be placed in eternal repose near them. Fannie's marker summarized the Hayes family legacy:

HERE LIES THE BODY OF
FANNIE HAYES
BORN IN GEORGIA A SLAVE, ABOUT
THE YEAR 1842 AND DIED IN BOSTON
SEPTEMBER 26, 1923
HER SPIRIT
A PERMANENTLY SACRED AND
HELPFUL INFLUENCE REMAINS ALERT
AND BLOOMING IN OUR HUMAN GARDEN
WIFE OF
WILLIAM HAYES (DEC.)
MOTHER OF
WILLIAM JR. (DEC.)
MATTIE (DEC.)
NATHANIEL (DEC.)
JOHN (DECEASED AND LYING HERE)
ROLAND
ROBERT
JESSE (DEC.)

With Roland's transition in January 1977, Fannie had all of her children with her – in the afterlife.

A poem Charles Harris had written on the occasion of Roland's eightieth birthday seemed to apply to his passing:

Sing on and on till the last –
May a golden chariot await you at life's end.
May the sublimest steeds waft you from one eternity
To another with ceaseless opportunities to sing on through infinite time.[45]

Epilogue

THE HAYES LEGACY

THE ROLAND HAYES STORY HAS CONTINUED LONG AFTER HIS death and burial. While Alzada, Afrika, Zaida, and Erika mourned the loss of their beloved husband, father, and grandfather in Boston, others did the same across the Atlantic. Within a day of Roland's death, Bertha read about his passing in a Parisian paper. Roland's oldest grandsons, Igor and Grichka (who were twenty-seven at the time of their grandfather's death), confirmed that he had communicated with their grandmother and their mother throughout the 1950s, but the communications seemed to have stopped at the end of the 1960s.[1]

Once Bertha absorbed the news of Roland's death, she wrote a condolence letter to Afrika expressing her sorrow at her father's demise. She informed her that his other daughter, Maya, and his European grandchildren shared in her grief. Bertha also asked Afrika if she could return the letters that she had sent Roland over the years, as they were very personal to her. After some time, she received a "very nice handwritten" letter from Afrika acknowledging the condolence letter.[2] To Bertha's surprise, Afrika did not know of her, Maya, or Maya's children, and she was completely unaware of any letters written to her recently deceased father. While initially embittered by this spectacular lack of disclosure to his "American" family by Roland, Bertha concluded in the end that her relationship with him was still the best thing she had ever done in her life. Specifically, she said, "To me, it has meant so much, so tremendously much. The sin with which I approached it [that is, the relationship with Hayes] must be forgiven [that is, on earth]. Also, in heaven it must be forgiven."[3]

In light of their veiled father/daughter relationship, Maya seemed to have had mixed feelings about her father's death. To her, he once appeared to be her one lingering hope for a different life, but by the time of his death, all of those hopes were lost. Maya learned the news of Roland's passing after her mother did. It was especially painful for her to read in the news accounts that he was survived by an "only" daughter and two granddaughters. Apart from the twins, whom he had met as boys in 1954, Roland had not met any of her subsequent children: Laurette, Geraldine, Véronique, and François. The late Roland Hayes had in fact been survived by *two* daughters and eight grandchildren and a number of great-grandchildren that is at one dozen and counting.

To describe Maya's life in southern France as sad would be a dramatic understatement. She had endured a complicated relationship with her mother, her relationship with her husband had been rocky, and of course there were the many unresolved issues with her father.[4] By all accounts, she was a devoted mother to all of her children, but Bertha's strong personality seems to have overwhelmingly influenced her daughter's life. Maya worked for a time as a secretary, but in spite of her command of five languages, she was never afforded the opportunity to advance her considerable potential.

Maya's oldest sons, Igor and Grichka, witnessed the pain she experienced because of her absent father. Her inability to resolve those feelings led to her complex and difficult relationship with her mother. Bertha was fond of saying that her daughter had received all her father's negative characteristics but none of his positive ones.[5] The combination of Maya's fantasy/fascination with American Indians and the increasingly evident rejection by her father led to Maya's lack of interest in her African American heritage over the years.[6] Bertha never fully understood her antipathy toward this important part of her ancestry. Determined to honor that heritage, Bertha took over the raising of her daughter's twins sons, which understandably caused strain in her and Maya's relationship.[7]

As an adult man, Igor Bogdanoff was generous when he described the mother/daughter relationship as conflicted.[8] Dreaming of blending the black and white races, Bertha, who had already given birth to four sons, had expected another boy when she became pregnant with Roland's child. Maya's birth was a disappointment, as Bertha knew firsthand the limitations her society placed on girls – especially on one who was biracial. When Maya's twin sons were born in August 1949, Bertha's vision was revived. Maya *had* become the instrument to realize the "cause" she had intended to bring about with Roland. The two beautiful baby boys – *not* her daughter – would fulfill the mission that she had foreseen years before.

"Issten" lavished affection and attention on these "special" boys who she believed were destined for greatness. Among the things to which she exposed them were flying lessons, which the twins put to good use. She was determined to see that they had these lessons even when there was little food on the table. Unlike her daughter, who seemed to have all but rejected her African American heritage, Bertha was determined that her grandsons would embrace theirs. Once when Sammy Davis Jr. was performing in Paris, she exhausted all means to track him down in the city to arrange for Igor and Grichka to meet the celebrated musician.[9] Even though she could not always afford what she lavished on the twins, she would "fund-raise" as necessary. At one point, the teenaged Igor and Grichka reproached their grandmother for having had the affair with Roland, which accounted for their being perceived as different. They also accused their absent grandfather of not being a good father to their mother, who had obviously suffered from this missing part of her life. Bertha softened these negative feelings by reminding them that if it were not for her relationship with Roland, they would not have come into the world. She then showed them the letters that Roland had written to her and Maya and reminded them of how happy and impressed they had been when, not yet five years old, in Paris in 1954, they met their celebrated grandfather.

When Igor and Grichka were in their early teens, Bertha's nephew Ernest Kolowrat visited them in St. Lary for the first time.[10] As a little boy, he had previously met his eccentric aunt when she briefly visited his father – her younger brother Heinrich – before the outbreak of World War II at their family palace in Prague. Following the Communist takeover in Czechoslovakia in 1948, the family immigrated to the United States and settled in Massachusetts. As soon as the young Kolowrat had a job and the wherewithal – having completed his studies on a scholarship at Yale and served as an officer in the U.S. Navy – he returned on a vacation trip to Europe to reestablish relations with various relatives he left behind, including his aunt Bertha. He continued his European visits over the next twenty years, during which he established a close relationship with the entire contingent at St. Lary. "You are one of the rare people to whom I feel I can talk to, without being misunderstood or considered a poor old fool," Bertha wrote him in May 1967. "Something must be done to exploit my experiences. I feel that, before I die, I must leave something to the world – all that I lived and suffered and saw and 'digested' has a certain human interest . . . and then I see myself as a universally respected and recognized person, free of all material anguish, and the perpetual phantom of our ruin no more hovering over us." By then Kolowrat, intending to write a book, had equipped himself with a recorder for his visits, and his aunt had no hesitation in sharing with him details of what she sarcastically called "that so terrible thing I did."[11]

She also urged him to visit Roland at his Massachusetts home at 58 Allerton Street to get his side of the story. "I bought nearly all the furniture in that house," she said. "We bought beautiful Spanish furniture, because at that time, he was easily doing ten thousand dollars[12] an evening. I arranged to have it all shipped to Boston."[13] Noting that it would be just a short ride for her nephew from his own Massachusetts home, she advised him to take a chance and not call in advance. Roland was terribly afraid of his wife, she explained, and most likely would not consent to receive him. Alzada was the ultimate gatekeeper where her husband and his affairs were concerned. Although Hayes seems to have communicated his fear of Alzada to the countess, he kept Alzada in the dark about his and Bertha's relationship. Bertha had once dismissively referred to Alzada as Roland's "glorified housekeeper."[14]

One late afternoon on a wintry day in 1969, Kolowrat knocked on the door of Roland's Brookline residence. After a few moments a slight figure appeared in the dim twilight and from behind a screen door asked, "Are you the gentleman from the [*Boston*] *Globe* I talked to on the phone?"

Kolowrat quickly introduced himself as the nephew of the Countess Colloredo-Mansfeld, adding, "I hope I am not intruding."

Roland's first reaction was to invite his unexpected guest to come in. But as he began to open the screen door, he checked himself as if having a second thought. "Oh, we're having some guests just now," the octogenarian Roland explained, partly closing the screen door in front of him.

"I'm sorry, I didn't mean to interrupt," Kolowrat again apologized. "I'll be on my way. I only stopped by to say hello."

"No, no, no, no," Roland rejoined. His basic suspicion seemed to yield to inherent courtesy. He stepped outside to join Kolowrat in the cold on the porch, closing the screen door carefully after him.

After a few moments of uneasy silence, Kolowrat volunteered that he would again be visiting his aunt the next summer. "How is she, how is your aunt?" Roland asked with a touch of affected joviality. But before Kolowrat could respond, Roland launched into an impersonal monologue about the beauty of the countryside where Bertha had her chateau, "especially in the spring when everything is in bloom. . . . Say, did you ever visit the cathedral in Auch? It's magnificent, magnificent. The choir seat is one of the finest in the world. It is magnificent work." Without even a slight pause, Roland diverged into inquiring about the health of Kolowrat's father, whom he had not even met.

Kolowrat realized he might as well have been the reporter from the *Boston Globe* rather than a conduit to Roland's family in France. As Kolowrat wrote shortly after the visit, "Though eminently polite and solicitous, Roland Hayes deliberately wanted to remain impersonal."[15] For Kolowrat, however, merely being in the presence of Roland Hayes, whom he had heard so much about from his aunt, was more than making the visit worthwhile. In his starched white collar and elegant charcoal gray suit, he looked exactly the way he ought to have looked. Whether it was the sound of his voice, the shade of his skin, or those fragile hands his aunt had revered, everything was precisely the way it ought to have been. His individual features formed an indivisible whole, a total impression of the public image that was Roland Hayes. This was undoubtedly the man who once enthralled audiences all over the world.

Roland's monologue was interrupted by a throaty, grumpy voice from beyond the screen door, deep within the house. "Roland? What is it, Roland? What are you doing?"

"I'm coming, Mahmmy," he called back, "I'm coming."

Kolowrat reacted by again taking his leave, and this time Roland did not try to stop him.

"It was a pleasure meeting you," he said with genuine warmth. "You're a mighty fine-looking young man."

Without thinking it through, Kolowrat sought to repay the compliment.

"You have some mighty fine-looking grandchildren," he volunteered.

Roland stiffened. "Grandchildren!?"

"Why, your daughter's children in France."

As Kolowrat subsequently noted, "In an instant that perfectly composed image shattered into a grotesquely human face. His eyes darted back and forth from [me] to the inside of the door, and his nostrils began to pulsate . . . his lips were tightly compressed, but even so, trembled visibly." Kolowrat recalled, "I could feel the nervous power within him thrust in my direction, as if intent on assault." Was this the image of the other Roland that Kolowrat's aunt came to know during his emotional tirades against her? Or was his rarely displayed but legendary temper about to be unleashed?

Kolowrat was distressed. How could he have been so tactless? he thought to himself. He feared his thoughtless blunder could even trigger a heart attack in this frail octogenarian. "I'm sorry, I'm terribly sorry," Kolowrat half-stammered.

Roland struggled to retain his composure. He hesitated and then retreated behind the screen door, holding it slightly ajar.

From within the house came another call in that matriarchal voice. "I'm coming Mahmmy, I'm coming," Roland again responded but made no move to withdraw. Hoping to retrieve the situation, Kolowrat pulled out from his coat pocket the latest photo he had taken of Maya and the twins and held it in the small opening in the screen door. For a split second Roland glanced at it, then turned away as if it brought back a painful memory. With an abrupt, almost violent move he closed shut the screen door.

Realizing he had only compounded his original faux pas, Kolowrat again apologized. "Maybe I should have never come," he said, "but my aunt wants me to write about this . . . this whole affair. I don't have to tell you, she often sees things entirely her way. I thought maybe . . . well, maybe if I had your version, I could write a more meaningful account."

For a long moment of uneasy silence the two faced each other through the screen door. "I have no version," Roland finally said quietly. His voice now was calm and composed. He seemed to be again his public, dignified self. Focusing his eyes directly on his visitor, he nodded as if in acknowledgment and said, "It's all water under the bridge." He paused, then repeated, "It's all water under the bridge." He nodded again as if to reinforce his statement, then excused himself and disappeared within the house.

Back in France, twin brothers Igor and Grichka began their undergraduate studies in applied mathematics at the Institute of Political Science and at the École Pratique des Hautes Études in Paris, with their grandmother not far away. She was so determined to ensure that their obvious academic talent was given every opportunity to flower that she moved in with them in a small Parisian apartment. In the 1970s, as their American grandfather neared the end of his life, they were hitting their stride with a series of well-received science fiction books, including *Clefs pour la science-fiction* (The Key of Science Fiction) and, more recently, *Avant le big bang* (Before the Big Bang) and *Au commencement du temps* (At the Beginning of Time), as well as with a half-dozen other books, among them several best-sellers. The pair also hosted several popular television shows, including *Temps X, Rayon X,* and *A deux pas du future* (Two steps from the future). The twins have been national celebrities in France for the past quarter-century.[16]

Their fame, however, has not come without controversy. Grichka received his doctorate in applied mathematics in 1999, and Igor received his in theoretical physics in 2002. The brothers' story became better known to the world when a 2002 article about them and their cosmic theories appeared in the *New York Times*. The "Bogdanoff affair," as it became known in the world of scholarly physics, attracted prominent advocates from around the globe who supported the twin brothers' scientific claims as well as detractors who saw their claims as false positing.

After embracing their American heritage, the twins readily acknowledged Roland Hayes as their African American grandfather. As a result of their celebrity, American members of the Hayes family came to discover their European relatives' story, well after their famous grandfather's death.

The twins' road did have other challenges. On January 28, 1982, Igor and Grichka's very influential grandmother, Countess Bertha Katharina Nadine Kolowrat Colloredo-Mansfeld, died in Auch, not far from the southern province where they had grown up, exactly five years after Roland. Her funeral, in the wintry month of February in St. Lary, was a solemn occasion. One of her sons from her marriage to Hieronymus, Fritzi, was the family member from that aristocratic clan who attended the funeral. Josef (the *Fürst* – a title that distinguished him as the oldest son and de facto head of the family) did not come to his mother's funeral because he was scheduled for elective shoulder surgery.[17] Not hesitating to voice his feelings, Fritzi made clear that his mother had followed her own rules and in the process had caused his father, his brothers, and other Kolowrat and Colloredo-Mansfeld family members untold suffering. "Look at the disaster that she is leaving here," Fritzi observed to his American cousin Ernest Kolowrat, who had come for the funeral. Fritzi glanced at Maya and her children, saying, "More victims of my mother's crackpot schemes to save the world."[18]

Fritzi addressed his half-sister, Maya, in the formal *vous* form, probably reflecting the reality that he did not know this sister well at all. Although he may not have specifically intended to do so, Fritzi depressed, if not humiliated, his already devastated half-sister, whose bowed gray head was covered with a black shawl, even more. The real shocker was the announcement that his mother's monthly stipend of two thousand Swiss francs would be reduced to five hundred francs a month.[19] Maya, her husband, and their minor children all knew immediately that this meant even greater economic hardship than they had endured – including the pending foreclosure on Issten's St. Lary chateau.[20]

As the countess's small coffin arrived at the chateau to begin the procession to the church, her prized grandsons, Igor and Grichka, arrived dramatically piloting a helicopter. Their grandmother, no doubt, would have approved of their loud and flamboyant arrival. Just in time, they joined the funeral cortege and entered the small church where their beloved Issten was praised as *une grande dame* by the elderly priest who celebrated her requiem mass. Her heroics during World War II, when she had hidden refugee Jews from the Nazis, were praised, but there was no mention of the circumstances surrounding her fall from grace, which had been responsible for bringing her to the small village of St. Lary. To the throngs of villagers who had assembled to mourn her passing, she was reverently known as *la comtesse*. At the time of her death, she had been a resident of the area for the better part of sixty years.[21]

Later, in tribute, Igor and Grichka acknowledged their late grandmother's influence. According to them, she foresaw what they would become. They attributed their success to her because throughout their lives she had reinforced the idea that they were destined to make a significant contribution to humanity. They also came to embrace the reality that without Roland Hayes – and his greatness and his gene pool – they would not have achieved such success.[22]

The year 1982, however, was a tragic one for the twins and their siblings for yet another reason. Not four months after the death of their grandmother, their mother, Maya – Maria Dolores Franzyska Kolowrat-Krakowsky Bogdanoff, the first-born daughter of Roland Hayes, passed away of bone cancer on May 12 at the age of fifty-six. Fortunately, she did not have to endure the pain that her half-brother Fritzi had heaped on her the day of their mother's funeral for very long.

While the relationship between Roland and Maya had been complex, the relationship between Maya and her mother, Bertha, had at times been dramatic and rested somewhere between love and hate. She once confided to her American cousin that she was aware that she had been a disappointment to her mother. Maya also said that her greatest moments of joy had been the minutes following the birth of each of her children. Those moments, she calculated, had amounted to about two hours in total, or about twenty minutes for each child she had given birth to in her fifty-six years.[23]

Her oldest sons were not entirely surprised by her death, especially after Issten had died. According to them, the mother and daughter were alternately greatest enemies and best friends. They could not live without each other. As the dying Maya herself put it in a letter to her cousin from her hospital bed, "When Mamma was alive, I felt I was a planet trapped in a strange orbit I didn't like. Now [after her death], I feel as if the sun has gone out."[24] Of all the players in the "Roland and the countess" drama, Maya, without question, had suffered the most.

And so, within a span of five years, Roland, the countess, and the product of their "scandalous" union, Maya, were all gone.

Roland's death had an unexpected liberating impact on Afrika's musical development. Afrika characterized her father's well-intended vocal advice to her as somewhat stinging: "'Oh, this was very good dear, but . . .' I couldn't stand the 'buts,'" she said.[25] Her concert career continued after her father's death, but her true desire lay in teaching. Afrika Hayes Lambe had a long and productive career in the Boston Public School system and retired as a successful and highly regarded educator. She sang in the chorus of the Boston Opera directed by Sarah Caldwell, among other musical activities.[26] At eighty-one years old, she continues to play keyboard for dance classes in the Newton, Massachusetts, area.

As the only surviving daughter of Roland Hayes, Afrika Hayes Lambe has been the principal advocate in keeping the Hayes legacy alive. In 1982, she was present when the Roland W. Hayes Concert Hall was dedicated at the University of Tennessee at Chattanooga campus (where her father had been given an honorary doctorate in 1968, when the institution was still known as the University of Chattanooga). She was also on hand for other posthumous recognitions. She proudly accepted the honor, for example, when the Georgia Music Hall of Fame inducted her father into that organization in 1991.

Prior to that there were other efforts to keep the Hayes story relevant for a younger generation. The Boston-based Friends of Roland Hayes Committee commissioned Professor Robert Hayden to produce a biography of the singer to coincide with the centennial of his birth in 1987. The result of that undertaking was *Singing for All People,* published by Corey and Lucas Publications in 1989. The intended target audience for that work was high school students. Hayden subsequently began work on what would have been the first comprehensive scholarly biography of the legendary singer but was compelled to abandon the project for other professional opportunities.[27]

In 1990, the University of Wisconsin at Madison produced a public broadcast documentary titled *The Musical Legacy of Roland Hayes* with the highly regarded actor Avery Brooks narrating the televised program. It included appearances by the tenor's daughter, Afrika; the late bass-baritone William Warfield; Reginald Boardman, Roland's longtime accompanist;[28] and tenor George Shirley.[29] The genesis and creative spirit behind the program, however, was tenor Paul Spencer Adkins, who was also featured performing some of Hayes's repertoire in the documentary. Adkins had been exposed to the name Roland Hayes in 1977 (the year of Roland's death). While he was an artist-in-residence at the Madison campus in the late 1980s, he came up with the idea of producing the documentary. The arrival of the Hayes PBS documentary revived interest in the late singer's career and musical legacy, generating momentum for a formal recognition of Hayes's career. The Roland Hayes Museum was established in Calhoun, Georgia, and he was posthumously elected to the Georgia Music Hall of Fame, among other recognitions throughout the country.

In 1996, the Boston Symphony Orchestra commissioned the work *Lilacs,* scored for voice and orchestra, to celebrate the life and achievements of Roland Hayes. The work was conducted by then BSO music director Seiji Ozawa. George Walker, the composer of *Lilacs,* received the 1996 Pulitzer Prize for Music for his composition. Walker further honored Hayes by using a musical quote from "Lit'l Boy" in the composition.[30]

Afrika's daughters, Zaida and Erika, have also contributed in their respective ways to sustaining the Hayes legacy. After years of overseeing the annual Roland Hayes Memorial Concert in Boston, Afrika turned over the responsibility to Zaida, who has semiprofessional musical ambitions. She sings gospel, spirituals, and other popular music with several Boston-area choral ensembles, realizing that her grandfather would not have approved of some of her musical choices.[31] But as her mother's daughter, Zaida has struck out in her own direction. In fact, she has decided to follow her mother as a professional educator and specialize in early childhood education.[32]

Afrika's younger daughter, Erika, has had more direct involvement with the arts. As a professional dancer, she had a career with several companies, including the Dance Theater of Harlem (where she was mentored by the company's premiere dancer, Virginia Johnson) and the Miami Ballet in Florida. She ended her formal dance career with an eleven-year stint with the Boston Ballet, the company with which she started as a child. Erika quite early identified with some of the discriminatory practices that her grandfather experienced when as a ten-year-old dancer she was denied the role of Clara in the company's annual production of

Tchaikovsky's ballet *The Nutcracker*. When her mother questioned the management about the casting decision, she was offered the explanation that it was a "period piece" (that is, it would have been out of place for an African American child to play the role of a late nineteenth-century German girl).[33]

Afrika suffered another hurt eleven years after losing her father when, on February 8, 1988, her mother, Helen Alzada Mann Hayes, died in Brookline, Massachusetts, of bronchopneumonia. Like Roland, she had also suffered from Alzheimer's disease in her final years. As she had for her father, Afrika held a simple funeral at Ebenezer Baptist Church for her mother, the same church community that had sent off her grandmother and her uncle years earlier. In the obituary, Afrika described her mother's "quiet strength" and the support that she had provided for her husband, the celebrated tenor Roland Hayes, to whom she was married for forty-five years. On a snowy February 12, Alzada was reunited with her beloved Roland at Mt. Hope Cemetery. To be sure, Alzada was a quiet woman publicly, but the inside consensus was that she had clear control over the Hayes household before and after her husband's death.

After her mother's passing, Afrika made plans to sell the Allerton Street homestead, but not before reaching an arrangement with the E. Azalia Hackley Collection of the Detroit Public Library (DPL) to house Roland's vast collection of papers, scores, correspondence, and other ephemeral materials. Some years before he had died, the tenor had left certain materials to the Hackley Collection in memory of the Detroit-based singer Azalia Hackley. Although a few researchers were allowed to review the materials over the years (after receiving written permission from Afrika), the collection was not fully processed until 2007, and the current authors were the first to gain access to the more than 75,000 documents that are housed in the DPL.

Dr. Maurice Wheeler, then curator at the DPL, met Afrika at a National Association of Negro Musicians around 1987, and after several exchanges, the terms under which the collection could be used were spelled out in an agreement. It is only to be opened to "serious researchers." Wheeler recalled receiving a request from a woman who wanted to write a play based on the relationship between Roland and the countess. Fearing that this might be an embarrassment to the Hayes family at the time, he denied the request for access to the collection and later conferred with Afrika. She concurred with Wheeler's decision.[34]

Because it houses the largest collection of Roland Hayes materials anywhere, the DPL has been in the vanguard of promoting Hayes's legacy for the last two decades. In the 1990s it established the Roland Hayes Trail Blazers Awards to honor African American artists whose careers mirror the high artistic goals set by Roland Hayes.[35] In 2000, the DPL and the Ford Foundation jointly commissioned the Grammy-nominated composer Patrice Rushen to create a work honoring Hayes. In February 2014 the DPL and the E. Azalia Hackley Collection premiered Rushen's "The Legacy of Roland Hayes," featuring the renowned tenor George Shirley as the soloist.[36]

In the legendary singer's home state, the Roland Hayes Committee, which was responsible for his induction into Georgia's Music Hall of Fame, evolved into the Roland Hayes Guild. The guild established a museum in his honor in Calhoun, Georgia, in what was once known as Curryville. In 1995, the guild also oversaw the erection of a historical marker placed in Roland's honor in Calhoun under the auspices of the Georgia Department of Natural Resources. In 2000, the Roland Hayes Museum opened in the Harris Arts Center in Calhoun. Concerts continue to be held annually in his honor. Similar dedicatory concerts are held throughout the country, especially in the Boston area, where schools and other collections were established in tribute to the late tenor's musical genius.

The Calhoun-based Roland Hayes Guild has, for the last several years, been the driving force behind the movement to have the U.S. postmaster general issue a Roland Hayes commemorative stamp in the U.S. postal service's Black Heritage Series. Stamps have been produced to commemorate many lesser known names, but to date there has been no Roland Hayes stamp. Those for whom he paved the way, including Paul Robeson and Marian Anderson, have already been so honored. The application is still pending.

Roland Hayes's most important direct musical legacy has begun but is still developing. On the stage of Paris's Opera Bastille, in December 2008, a handsome, blond-haired, blue-eyed fourteen-year-old, Wenceslaus, made his debut as one of the *drei knaben* (three spirits) in Mozart's *Magic Flute*. His strong soprano voice was vibrant and clear, and his musicality is instantly recognizable, even for someone his age. The boy's ambition is to be an opera singer, and he has already built up an impressive repertory. Among his favorite songs are John Dowland's "Come Again" and Roland Hayes's arrangement of "Lit'l Boy."

Wenceslaus Bogdanoff, Igor's youngest son, is perfectly aware of his great-grandfather's extraordinary musical career and confidently proclaimed at the age of eight, "I will sing like my great-grandfather."[37] To that end, he has embraced Roland's legacy with pride. By the age of ten, he had already traveled around the world, and like his forebear, he has a flair for the recording studio. How far he progresses will most likely be decided by his determination to succeed. The talent is obviously there. If Roland had had the opportunity to hear his young progeny, he would have approved of the boy's career ambitions. Wenceslaus, who now sings bass, is a student at the New England Conservatory in Boston. He will no doubt sing on the stage of Jordan Hall during his tenure as a student. He will do so knowing that this is a venue that his great-grandfather had once dominated.

Acknowledgments

THIS HAS CLEARLY BEEN THE MOST AMBITIOUS WORK OF MY career, thus far, and the results would not have been possible without the alliance that Robert Sims and I formed for the purpose of telling this important story. Sims and I came to this work from different backgrounds and viewed this historical figure through different prisms. Yet he and I are obliged to acknowledge those people and institutions that have played a role in reviving the name and legacy of Roland Hayes.

At the top of this long list is Afrika Hayes Lambe, who has waited a long time (and endured more than one effort) to see her father's story finally told. In addition to offering us early access to the Roland Hayes Collection at the Detroit Public Library, she also gave us access to additional materials in her basement, which enhanced an already rich story and career. Lambe's daughters, Zaida Lambe and Erika Lambe Holland, were also helpful in sharing their reflections on their celebrated grandfather.

While Robert and I were in Georgia, we met other Hayes family members: Roland Robert Jr., William, and Toussaint Hayes, all nephews of the tenor. Roland Robert took us to the site where Angelmo Farm had once been in Gordon County, as well as to Mount Zion Baptist Church, which was pivotal to the life and development of young Roland Hayes. We are also grateful to Edward and Alice Mann Simpkins, who were able to supplement historical information about the Mann family and its importance to this story.

Nearly as important as the input of the Hayes family members was our relationship with Ernest Kolowrat. His involvement and contribution to this work cannot be understated. There is little question that without his generous and eager assistance, this would have been a very different work. Thank you, Ernest.

As the Roland Hayes story unfolded with many twists and turns, it was necessary for Robert and me to travel either individually or jointly to the United Kingdom and France and throughout the United States. In France, the contribution to this story of the celebrated twin grandsons of Hayes, Drs. Igor and Grichka Bogdanoff, has been of critical importance. Not only did they share their recollection of meeting the celebrated tenor when they were children, but they represent the European legacy of Roland Hayes. They also encouraged others to share their memories of the complex circumstances surrounding their late mother, Maya, and grandmother Bertha, the Countess Colloredo-Mansfeld. Their godmother, Monique Symphorien David, and Igor's son Wenceslaus and his daughters Sascha and Anna were also helpful during our stay in France. Luc Charliot and Philomena Scotch Coste were also of invaluable assistance while we researched and interviewed those in the greater Paris area. In the United Kingdom, the scholarship of Jeffrey Green and Valerie Langfield clearly informed this work. Aside from consulting with me on a regular basis, Jeff also secured rights for me to access several UK libraries and was of immense assistance when it came to researching Afro-Britons in the early twentieth century.

In the United States, several institutions assisted us in collecting, corroborating, and retrieving information. Our respective universities, Virginia Commonwealth University and Northern Illinois University, deserve profound acknowledgment and thanks. At VCU, several of my colleagues played significant roles, including Patricia Cummins, Kathryn Murphy-Judy, Paul Dvorak, Noel Boaz, Amy Rector Verrelli, Edward Abse, Christopher Stevenson, Matthew Pawlowicz, and John Ulmschneider, the university librarian who assisted me with housing the large amounts of materials necessary for this work. I am also grateful to the VCU College of Humanities and Sciences for providing me with early support to complete this book. Several on the VCU library staff, including John Glover and Alex Lorch, also provided necessary assistance. From the School of World Studies, James Greg Hellman helped scan the pictures for inclusion in this volume. My former dean, Bob

Holsworth, funded my research trip to France, and the former provost, Stephen Gottfredson, also provided immeasurable encouragement.

At Northern Illinois University, we gratefully acknowledge Dean Rich Holly of the College of Visual and Performing Arts and Paul Bauer, director of the School of Music. We also thank James Tucker, formerly of the NIU Opera Program, who directed the PBS documentary *The Musical Legacy of Roland Hayes,* which was so crucial to this process, and Diane Ragains, who substituted for Robert on numerous occasions while he traveled on Hayes-related business.

Apart from our personal institutions, there were many others who contributed to the successful completion of this book. We are pleased to thank David Kessler of the Bancroft Collection at the University of California at Berkeley; James Lay of the Gordon County Historical Society; Georgette Frazier of the Roland Hayes Commemorative Stamp Committee; Ricardo Morris, formerly of the Roland Hayes Museum; and Crystal DePerro of the Harris Arts Center in Calhoun, Georgia. My friend of many years Jessie Carney Smith, head librarian at Hayes Fisk University, had an obvious interest in this project and provided me with a sounding board and materials for inclusion. Vanessa R. Smith of the Fisk Special Collection and Deborah A. Wright of the Avery Research Center for African American Culture and Life at the College of Charleston made their unique contributions. Sharon L. Jarvis of the New York Public Library's Schomburg Center for Research in Black Culture was a very helpful resource person and pointed us to other collections that were beneficial. I am also grateful to Ja-Zette Washburn, archivist for the *Afro-American* in Baltimore, and Barbara Bauer and Jan Warzyn of Four Seasons Arts. Robert is grateful to Sam Edwards and Lyvonne Chrisman of the Friends of Negro Spirituals.

Several editorial hands came to our aid. Jay Whaley, my longtime Richmond editor; Carole Hall; Bob Daniels; Thomas J. Brown; and James Moffitt all lent their expertise throughout various stages of writing. Late in the process, we had the good fortune to meet Jane Kupersmith, formerly of Indiana University Press. Jane was assigned to "shave down" a manuscript well in excess of the contracted word count. What I feared would be a contentious relationship turned out to be a very fruitful one. I look forward to continuing our work together. We are also grateful to copy editor Julie Bush, who carefully combed through every line of this manuscript.

I am always proud to say that I had several students (present and former) who contributed to my scholarship, and this project has been no exception. Katherine Blanche-Shallit has now contributed to six of my major publications. Because of her facility with French, she translated an all-important letter from the E. Azalia Hackley Collection of the Detroit Public Library that confirmed what other sources had maintained about Roland Hayes's life and career in Europe. I also had assistance from Christopher Yeamans, Kelsey O'Neill, Jara Connell, and Alexander Burkard. Robert had the assistance of several of his students, including Alex Buda and Taylor Thompson.

We salute the staff of the Detroit Public Library, which was so cooperative with us at the start of the research for this book. Because I made more than ten trips between Richmond and Detroit to work there, I was on a first-name basis with many staff members, specifically Anne Savides and Romie Minor, assistant manager of the Special Collections Department and former director of the E. Azalia Hackley Collection, who deserves special mention as he fostered Robert and me through the early stages of this process. Our many conversations and work with Romie resulted in a very meaningful collaboration. Thank you, Romie. We hope you are pleased with the results.

I could always count on my colleague and friend Tim Brooks when it came to Roland Hayes recordings and related matters. He also made available several vintage Hayes recordings. We also are grateful to Steve Robinson, general manager of WFMT (Chicago), who provided us with several hours of digitally transferred personal recordings of Roland Hayes from the 1960s. This allowed us to hear the tenor's philosophies and opinions spoken in his own voice. The Wisconsin Public Television Service (PBS) provided us with a copy of the Hayes documentary, which informed this work tremendously.

There were others who added insight in one way or another that had the effect of enhancing this story. We are grateful to Daniel Comegys (a former student of Roland Hayes), Simon Estes, George Shirley, Willis Patterson, Brenda Jeffers, Alice Mahoney, Patricia A. Murray, and Diane

Ota. Paul Spencer Adkins, the star and producer of the PBS documentary *The Musical Legacy of Roland Hayes*, wasn't aware of this project until the wrap-up stages but was phenomenally supportive, as was Maurice Wheeler, who was responsible for securing the Hayes Collection for the DPL.

There are several important people who did not survive to see this work in print, and yet their presence is felt throughout these pages. Among them are the legendary soprano Shirley Verrett, jazz musician Joe Evans, and the equally legendary Odetta (who auditioned for Roland Hayes in Boston in the 1950s). Others whose souls have departed are Edna Williams, Nicole Fournier, and the great singers Ben Matthews and William Warfield. My dear friend Patricia Turner departed in March 2005, two years before this work was formally underway. She had given me an original copy of the Hayes biography *Angel Mo' and Her Son, Roland Hayes*, which I treasured throughout this process. I have often wondered while writing this book if she, in her quiet wisdom, planted the seed from which this work grew.

Of course we are grateful to our agent, Claudia Menza of the Menza/Barron Agency, for her skillful negotiations and belief in this project. And not to be forgotten are the many dedicated professionals at Indiana University Press who also believed in this work, including acquisitions editor Raina Polivka, her assistant Jenna Lynn Whittaker, and production coordinator Dan Pyle. We are enormously grateful to Nancy Lightfoot of IUP who kept us on task with regard to meeting our schedules. Julie Bush, Jamison Cockerham, and Tony Brewer also helped make this a stress-free process.

There is an area that we have identified as "general support" that may appear a little vague, but without it, this work might not have the breadth and depth that it has achieved. For that support we are pleased to thank Richard LeSueur, Ken Flaherty, Morris Henderson, Sonja Baker, Karen Savage, Olivia Mosely, Harriet Mack Golding, Louise W. Greene, James Harkless, Christopher Commins, Charles Hackett Jr., David and Rahab Kimani, Collen Callahan, Pangeline Edwards, Gerald Waldman, Marian Dora Howe-Taylor, Ruth and Theodore Howe, Louis Mabre-Cargill, Bernth Lindfors, Barbara Newell, Marva Jones Williams, Shirley Hamilton-Nehring, Charles Parker, Byron Sean, Deeann Mathews, David Edelfelt, Susheel Bibbs, Dorothy Canady, William Reitwiesner, and Marie Turner-Wright.

Many family and close friends have, in their own way, walked this path alongside Robert and me. It has been a multi-year journey, but we have arrived nonetheless. Robert's parents, Bennierene Sims Castile and William C. Sims Sr., have been more than loyal endorsers. Other supporters include William Sims Jr., Paul Garrison, Arthur White, Everton Swearing, Risa Hernandez, Paul Hamilton, Alicia Wilson, Jacqueline Hairston, Lena McLin, Cynthia Clarey, Alison Buchanan, Ysaye Barnwell, and David Farrar.

I am equally grateful to my family and friends who have been steadfast throughout this process and my chief advocates throughout my career. I am grateful to my brother Lowry M. Brooks Sr., who has demonstrated the power of faith; my sister and brother-in-law Joyce and Thomas Brown (Joyce actually played a small role in the Hayes story that she was not aware of); my sisters Bernetia Brooks and Cheryle Brooks Johnson; and my son, Arthur. My sister and brother-in-law Eileen and John Brown from Farmington Hills, Michigan, were also early supporters of this project when I traveled between Richmond and Detroit. My Zimbabwean sister Brenda Kahari has once again pitched in to keep things in perspective, and I am ever grateful to Denise Bethel of Sotheby's, who keeps me on the straight and narrow where photographs are concerned. We have clearly benefited from her expertise in this book. Again, we thank all of you.

Christopher Brooks

Roland Hayes

An die ferner Geliebte
Bußlied
Ich liebe dich
Mailied
Mit einem gemalten Band
Neue Liebe
Sehnsucht
Trocknet nicht, trocknet nicht
Wonne der Wehmut

BEMBERG, HERMAN
A toi
Mainacht

BERLIOZ, HECTOR
Absence
L'île inconnue
Le repos de la sainte famille – *L'Enfance du Christ*
Le spectre de la rose
Sur les lagunes
Villanelle

BERNARD, A.
By an' By

BOARDMAN, REGINALD
The Great Wonder
Lay Dis' Body Down
Michieu Banjo
The Music Had to Be
Pourtant tu t'en iras
The Stars Looked Down
There's a Little Wheel
To an Autumn Wind
To a Sparrow

BOATNER, EDWARD
I Done Done What You Told Me to Do
Mount Zion
Oh, What a Beautiful City
Wade in de Water

BONONCINI, GIOVANNI BATTISTA
Bella vittoria
Cara si, tu mi consumi
Lungi da te ben mio
Per la gloria

BROGI
Visione Veneziana

BRAHMS, JOHANNES
Am Sonntag Morgen
An die Nachtigal
Auf dem Kirchofe
Bei dir sind meine Gedanken
Botschaft
Dein blaues Auge
Es träumte mir
Der Gang zum Liebschen
Heimkehr
In Waldeseinsamkeit
Die Kränze
Lerehengesang
Die Mainacht
Mondenschein
Nachtigal
Nicht mehr zu dir zu gehen
O, komme, holde sommer Nacht
O wüßt Ich doch den Weg zurück
Ruhe, Süssliebchen
Sonntag
Wiegenlied

BRÉBEUF, JEAN DE
'Twas in the Moon of Wintertime

BROWN, LAWRENCE W.
African Maid
Bye and Bye
Every Time I Feel de Spirit
Joshua Fit de Battle of Jericho
Longing
Nobody Knows
No More
Song of the Sea
Steal Away

BURLEIGH, HARRY THACKER

Ahmed's Song of Farewell – *Saracen Songs*
Benediction of Peace
By an' By
By the Pool
Come with Me
Deep River
Don't You Weep When I'm Gone
Go Down in de Lonesome Valley
Go Down Moses
The Hour Glass
Is There Anybody Here Like Weepin'
  Mary?
I Stood on de Ribber ob Jerdon
Memory
My Lord What a Mornin'
Oh! Didn't It Rain
Oh! My Love
O Rock Me, Julie
Peter Go Ring-a Dem Bells
Scandalize My Name
Swing Low, Sweet Chariot
Three Shadows
Were I a Star
When I'm Gone
You May Bury Me in de East
The Young Warrior

CACCINI, FRANCESCA

Per la più vaga

CACCINI, GIULIO

Amarilli
Tu ch' hai le penne, amore

CADMAN, CHARLES

Call Me No More
Moonlight Song

CALDARA, ANTONIO

Alma del core
Come raggio di sol
Selve amiche
Vaghe Luci

CAMPBELL-TIPTON

Le cri des eaux

CAREY

Saw You the Nymph

GASPARINI, F.

Caro laccio

CAVENDISH

Finetta, Fair and Feat

CESTI, ANTONIO

Adori si sempre
S'io non vedo Alidoro

CHANLER, THEODORE

Eight Epitaphs

CHAPIN, LOUIS

Injunction

CHERUBINI, LUIGI

Ahi! Che forse

COLERIDGE-TAYLOR, SAMUEL

African Dances No. 2 and No. 4
The Evening Star
The Lee Shore
Life and Death
Hiawatha's Wedding Feast
Song of Proserpine
Thou Art Risen

COOK, WILL MARION

Down Lovers' Lane
Morning

COWELL, HENRY

The Donkey
The Fairy Fountain
The Little Black Boy

DANYEL, JOHN

Eyes, Look No More

DAWSON, WILLIAM
My Lord, What a Morning

DEBUSSY, CLAUDE
Beau soir
Les cloches
Colloque sentimental
En sourdine
Fantoches
Le faune
Mandoline
La mer est plus belle
L'ombre des arbres
Recitative and Air of Azael – *L'enfant prodigue*
Recueillement
Romance

DELMORE, HARRY A.
Afterward
Goin' to Ride Up in de Chariot

DENSMORE, JOHN H.
Kiss Me Goodnight

DOLMETSCH
Have You Seen a Whyte Lily Grow

DONIZETTI, GAETANO
Una furtiva lagrima – *L'elisir d'amore*

DOUGHERTY, CELIUS
A Minor Bird

DOWLAND, JOHN
Come Again, Sweet Love
Flow Not So Fast, Ye Fountains
Time Stands Still

DUNI, EGIDIO
Ariette – *De la fée urgele*

DUPARC, HENRI
Extase
L'invitation au voyage
Phidyle

DURANTE, FRANCESCO
Danza, danza

DVOŘÁK, ANTONÍN
Biblical Song No. 7
Biblical Song No. 10
By the Waters of Babylon

FAIRCHILD
The Red Cockatoo

FAURÉ, GABRIEL
Après un rêve
Claire de Lune
En prière
J'ai presque peur – *La Bonne Chanson*
Prison
Le secret
Sylvie

FOSTER, FAY
The Little Ghosts
Winter

FOURDRAIN, FÉLIX
Chanson Norvégienne
Chevauchée Cosaque

FRANCK, CÉSAR
Nocturne
La procession
Sie nur still

FRANZ, ROBERT
Für Musik

FROMM
The Shepherd of Palestine

GABRIELI, GIOVANNI
Vuoi tu, ch'io speri amore?

GABRIELLI, DOMENICO
Bellezza Tirana – *Clearco in Negroponte*

GALUPPI, BALDASSARE

Eviva Rosa bella – *La calamità de' cuori*

GASPARINI, FRANCESCO

Caro laccio, dolce nodo

GLENN, KATHERINE

Twilight

GLIERE, REINHOLD

O, That Thou Couldst Know

GLUCK, CHRISTOPH WILIBALD

Ah, quel tourment – *Armide*

GRETCHANINOFF, ALEXANDER

Missa oecumenica

The Wounded Birch

GRIEG, EDVARD

A Dream

GRIFFES, CHARLES T.

By a Lonely Forest Pathway

Come Love, across the Sunlit Land

The Dreamy Lake

A Feast of Lanterns

In a Myrtle Shade

The Lament of Ian the Proud

Phantoms

Rose of the Night

So-Fei Gathering Flowers

Symphony in Yellow

GUEDRON, PIERRE

Cette Anne si belle

HALL, FREDERICK

Day Is Done!

Git Up Chillon, Go 'Roun' de Wall

How Long fo' de Sun Go Down?

Lord, How Come Me Here?

Po' Me!

HANDEL, GEORGE FRIDERIC

Ah, spietato! – *Armidgi*

Alma mia – *Floridante*

La bella pastorella

Cara selve – *Atalanta*

Dolcimente in tuon leggiadro – *Alexander's Feast*

The Elves' Dance – *The Triumph of Time and Truth*

Figlia mia, non pianger no – *Tamerlano*

From Celestial Seats – *Hercules*

Grüne Matten, kühle Haine

Invocation to Happiness

Messiah

Oft on a Plat of Rising Ground – *Il Peneseroso*

Pack, Clouds, Away!

Pastorello d'un povero armento – *Rodelinda*

Rend'il sereno al ciglio – *Sosarme*

Selve amiche

Sweet and Graceful the Sounds of Music – *Alexander's Feast*

Total Eclipse – *Samson*

Voglio dire al mio tesoro – *Partenope*

Waft her Angels to the Skies – *Jephté*

Where'er You Walk – *Semele*

Would You Gain the Tender Creature – *Acis and Galatea*

HARRIS, ROY

Fog

HABLER, HANS LEO

Walvogelein's Bitte (Nurnberg)

HAYDN, JOSEPH

Gegenliebe

Heller Blick

She Never Told Her Love

The Spirit's Song

Stets barg die Liebe Sie

HAYES, ROLAND

The Angels Are Waiting at the Door
As One People
By an' By
Camp Meeting
Certainly Lord
Chilly Water
Come Along and Let's Go to Heaven
Come Out of the Wilderness
Dat's All I Want
Dat Same Train
Death Now Has Come to the Homeland
The Deceivers
Deep River
Der's a Little Wheel a-Turnin' in My Heart
Didn't My Lord Deliver Daniel?
Did You Hear When Jesus Rose?
Dip Your Finger in the Water
Don't Grow Weary Traveler
Don't Mind What Satan Say
Dry Bones
Eagle's Wings
Early in the Morning
Eve, Where Is Adam?
Ezekiel Saw de Wheel
Four an' Twenty Elders
Gi' Me a Little Time to Pray
Gi' Me Yo' Han'
Give-a-way Jordan
The Glory Manger
God Is God
Goodbye
Good News
Go Tell It on the Mountain
Great Camp Meetin'
Heaven
He Never Said a Mumberlin' Word
He Raised Po' Lazarus from the Dead
    Here'm I How Is It wid Me?
I Believe I Will Go Back Home (The
    Prodigal Son)
I Can Tell the World!
I Can't Stay Away
I Done, Done
If You Want to Go to Heaven

I Got a Well Made Up Mind
I Just Can't Keep from Cryin' Sometimes
I Know the Other World's Not Like This
I'll Make Me a Man
I'm Goin' Build
I'm So Glad
I'm Troubled
In a Dat Mornin'
I Stan' and' Fol' My Arms an' I Cry
It's Me, Standing in the Need of Prayer
I've Got a Home in That Rock
I've Got a Robe
I Wanna Go Home
I Want Two Wings
Joseph Begged His Body
Judgement Will Find You So
Keep-a Yo' Lamps Trimmed an' Burnin'
Keep Me from Sinkin' Down
Lay Dis Body Down
Le' Me Shine
Let My People Go
Lit'l Boy
Lit'l David
Lit'l Girl, Lit'l Girl! Yes, Mam
Live a-Humble
Lord, How Come Me Here?
Lord, I Wish I Had-a Come
My God Is So High
My Lord What a Mornin'
My Time Is Come (The Last Supper)
Nobody Knows Who I Am
No More, No More
O Hallelu
Oh Gi' Me Yo' Han'
Oh My Lit'l Soul's Goin' to Shine
O Mary Don't You Weep
On Our Knees
O Rise, Shine for the Light Is a-Comin'
Over My Head, I See Trouble in the Air
Plenty Good Room
Po' Lazarus at the Rich Man's Table
Poor Sinner's Found a-Home
Po' Pilgrim
Prepare Me One Body
Quiet Hallelujah to the Lord

Reform
Ride On!
Rise Mourner
Rock-a My Soul
Roll, Jordan Roll
Roun' about de Mountain
Same Train
The Shepherds and the Angel
Sister Mary Had-a but One Chile
Sit Down (You're Tired, Chile)
Six Songs
So Glad
Somebody's Knockin' at Your Door
Sometime I Feel Like a Motherless Child
Steal Away
Sweet Water from the Fountain
Swing Low, Sweet Chariot
They Led My Lord Away
To My Jesus' Campground
Too Late
Train Done Gone
Waiting for the Lord's Command
Wait 'til I Get On My Robe
Watch Yo' Close Friends
Way Up in Heaven
Were You There? (Crucifixion)
What a Beautiful City
What Man That Jesus Was
When the Stars Began to Fall
Where You Been a-Hidin' Sinner?
Who Betrayed My Lord?
Who Is Dat a-Writin'
Who Is Dat-a Yonder?
A Witness
You Better Mind
You Hear de Lambs a-Cryin'?
You Mus' Be Pure and Holy
You Mus' Come In by an' Thro' de Lamb
Zion Weep-a-low

HEILMAN

In-a Dat Day
New Born Again

HENSCHEL, SIR GEORGE

The Angels Dear
A Melody from Purest Sphere
Morning Hymn
My Weary Heart Can Find No Rest
She Comes Not
Siehst du das Meer?

HOLST, GUSTAV

The Heart Worships

HOLT, NORA DOUGLAS

Florida Night Song
My Love Is Like a Cry
Who Knows

HOPEKIRK, HELEN

Over All the Hilltops Is Peace
Thought Takes Off
To People Who Have Gardens

HOWARD

Love in Thy Youth

HÜE, GEORGES

J'ai pleure en rêve

JACOBSON, MYRON

Reverie

JAMBOR, AGI

He Who Knows

JAMES, WILLIS L.

He's Got de Whole Worl' in His Han'
Pity a Po' Boy

JENSEN

Murmuring Zephyrs

JOHNSON, HALL

Hold On
Jesus, Lay Yo' Head in de Winder
Way Up in Heav'n

JOHNSON, J. ROSAMOND
Lil' Gal
The Little Pickaninny's Gone to Sleep
Nobody Knows de Trouble I See
Since You Went Away

KLEMM, GUSTAV
I Feel Like My Time Ain't Long
It's Me, O Lord

KOECHLIN, CHARLES
Le thé

KREIN, ALEXANDER
Grief and Sorrow Is Your Lot, O Israel

KRIEGER, ADAM
Der Augen Schein

LAWRENCE, WILLIAM
Let Us Break Bread Together

LEONCAVALLO, RUGGERO
Vesti la giubba – *I Pagliacci*

LISZT, FRANZ
Du bist wie eine Blume

LOEWE, CARL
Der heilige Franziscus

LOTTI, ANTONIO
Pur dicesti,

LOUD, JOHN A.
If You Knew
In Maytime

LULLY, JEAN-BAPTISTE
Charmants ruisseaux
Fermez vous pour jamais, mes yeux
Soyez fidéle

MACHAUT, GUILLAUME DE
Douce dame jolie

MASSENET, JULES
En fermant les yeux . . . – *Manon*
Ah! Fuyez douce image – *Manon*
Que l'heure est donc brève

MATSUYAMA, YOSHINORI
Japanese Love Song
Sakura

MAUDE, CAROLINE
Clothes of Heaven
Magdalen

MAZZOCCHI, DOMENICO
Piu non sai

MEDTNER, NIKOLAI
Serenade

MÉHUL, ÉTIENNE
Champs paternels – *Joseph*

MENDELSSOHN, FELIX
Elijah
The May-bell and the Flowers

MILHAUD, DARIUS
Chant d'amour

MONTEVERDI, CLAUDIO
Con che soavità (Canzone)
Maledetto sia l'aspetto – *Scherzi musicali*
Vi ricorda – *Orfeo*

MORHARDT, J. E., JR.
Requiem

MOZART, WOLFGANG AMADEUS
An Chloë
Dies Bildnis – *Die Zauberflöte*
Gesellenreise
Or che il dover
Per pietà, non ricercate
Quando miro
Ridente la calma
Si mostra la sorte

Tali e contanti sono
Un'aura amorosa – *Così fan tutte*
Unglückliche Liebe
Warnung
Wie unglücklich bin ich nicht

MUSSORGSKI, MODEST
The Night
Phantasie
Song of Solomon

NICKERSON, CAMILLE
Micheu Banjo

NILES, JOHN JACOB
I Wonder as I Wander

PAOLO, DON
Fra duri scoglio

PARADISI, PIETRO DOMENICO
Arietta

PARHAM, RICHARD PERCIVAL
The Creation
Done Made My Vow to the Lord
God's Trombones
Goin' Home to Live with God
I'll Make Me a Man
I've Known Rivers
Life for Me Ain't Been No Crystal Stair
Mother to Son
Not Those Who Soar
O Le' Me Shine
Roun' 'bout de Mountain (And She'll Rise
   in His Arms)
Swing Low, Sweet Chariot
We Will All Sing Together
You Better Min'

PEARCE, COOPER W.
Alone I Live and Sigh for One

PETRIDIS, PETRO (ARRANGER)
O If Only I Were a Sunbeam (an ancient
   Greek melody)

POLLONI
Domani

PONCHIELLI, AMILCARE
Cielo e mar – *La Gioconda*

PORPORA, NICOLO
So ben, che la speranza

POULENC, FRANCIS
Air vif

PUCCINI, GIACOMO
Che gelida manina – *La bohème*
Ch'ella mi creda libero e lontano – *La
   fanciulla del West*

PURCELL, HENRY
I Attempt from Love's Sickness to Fly
If Music Be the Food of Love
Let Each Gallant Heart
O Solitude
Sylvia, Now Your Scorn Give Over
Urge Me No More
When I Am Laid in Earth – *Dido and
   Aeneas*

QUILTER, ROGER
Blow, Blow, Thou Winter Wind
Brown Is My Love
Cherry Valley
Dream Valley
Drink to Me Only with Thine Eyes
Fair House of Joy – *Shakespeare Songs*
Go Lovely Rose
It Was a Lover and His Lass
I Will Go with My Father a-Ploughing
I Wish and I Wish
Love's Philosophy
Love Will Find Out the Way
The Night Piece
O Mistress Mine – *Shakespeare Songs*
Over the Mountains
Take, O Take Those Lips Away

RACHMANINOFF, SERGEI

Again Alone
As All Things Fade
In the Silence of Night
Songs of Georgia

RAMEAU, JEAN-PHILIPPE

Ariette – *Dardamus*
Waken, O Shepherds

RAVEL, MAURICE

La flûte enchantée – *Schéhérazade*
Tout gai!

REIMANN, HEINRICH

The Lanthorn
Leih' mir deine lantern
Tanzlied

RHODES, WILLIAM

The Garret
Little Brown Baby
When Malindy Sings

RING, MONTAGUE

Noontide Song

ROBINSON, AVERY

Didn't It Rain
Hail the Crown
Shadow
Water Boy

ROGERS, ALEX

Why Adam Sinned

RUBENSTEIN, ANTON

Es blinkt der Thau

RUMMEL, WALTER MORSE

Ecstasy

SAINT-SAËNS, CAMILLE

Danse macabre
Turnoiement – *Mélodies persanes*

SANTOLIQUIDO, FRANCESCO

Erinni
Persian Poem by Omar Khayyam
Persian Poem No. II
Persian Poem No. III by Abu-Said

SCARLATTI, ALESSANDRO

All'acquisto di gloria
Chi vuole innamorarsi
Dimmi qual prova – *Da bel volto d'Irene*
Già il sole dal Gange
Ingrato quanto sei
Scorgo il fiume
Sento nel Core
Su venite e consiglio

SCHOENBERG, ARNOLD

Erhebung

SCHUBERT, FRANZ

Abschied
Am Meer
An die Leier
Auf dem Wasser zu singen
Das sie hier gewesen
Du bist die Ruh
Eifersucht und Stolz
Erstarrung
Erster Verlust
Fischerweise
Die Forelle
Freude der Kinderjahre
Ganymed
Die Gebüsche
Gefrorne Tränen
Gute Nacht
Hoffnung
Ihr Bild
Der Jüngling an der Quelle
Die Krähe
Lebensmut
Der Leiermann
Die Liebe hat gelogen
Lied eines Schiffers an die Dioskuren
Der Musensohn

Nacht und Träume
Die Nebensonnen
Der Neugierige
O wie schön ist deine Welt
Die Post
Rastlose Liebe
Der Schmetterling
Schwanengesang
Das Sehnen
Sehnsucht
Seligkeit
Die Stadt
Die Taubenpost
Ungeduld
Der Vollmond Strahlt – *Rosamunde*
Vor meiner Wiege
Das Wandern
Wandrers Nachtlied
Die Wetterfahne
Wohin

SCHUMANN, ROBERT

Alte Laute
Aufträge
Aus den östlichen Rosen
Dichterliebe
Geisternähe
Ich hab' im Traum geweinet
Lied eines Schmiedes
Mein schöner Stern
Mondnacht
Der Nußbaum
Weh, wie zornig ist das Mädchen

SECCHI, ANTONIO

Lungi dal caro bene

SELMORE-STORER

Goin' to Ride Up in the Chariot

SHARP, CECIL

The False Night on the Road
The Lark in the Morn

SIBELIUS, JEAN

The Silent City
Swift the Springtime Passes

SLONIMSKY, NICOLAS

Autumn
La fuite de la lune – *Impressions*
My Little Pool
Silhouettes – *Impressions*

SPALDING, FLORENCE A.

Liebestraum

STEWART, HERBERT E.

Are You Ready

STILL, WILLIAM GRANT

Lis'en to de Lambs

STOREY-SMITH, WARREN

A Caravan from China Comes
Doors Where My Heart Used to Be

STRADELLA, ALESSANDRO

Ragion sempre addita

SWANSON, HOWARD

The Valley

TAILLEFERRE, GERMAINE

On a dit mal de mon ami

TANEYEV, ALEXANDER

The Fountains

TAPPERT, W.

Ich spring' in diesem Ringe

**TCHAIKOVSKY, PYOTR ILYICH
DON JUAN'S SERENADE WHY?**

Wohin, Wohin? – *Eugene Onegin*
Yearning, I Wait Alone

TELEMANN, GEORG PHILIPP

Die rechte Stimmung

THOMPSON, JACK

An Emblem

TIERSOT, JULIEN

L'amour de moi

Tambourin

TOMASI, HENRI

Rengaine

TORELLI, GIUSEPPE

Tu lo sai

TRUNK, RICHARD

An die Liebe

Der Feind

Ships That Pass in the Night

Tanzlied

VAUGHAN WILLIAMS, RALPH

The Roadside Fire

VERDI, GIUSEPPE

Celeste Aida – *Aida*

Solenne in quest'ora – *La forza del destino*

VILLA-LOBOS, HEITOR

Xango (a Brazilian African chant)

VON FULDA, ADAM

Apollo aller Kunst

VON LIEDERBUCH, WOLFLEIN

Mein Frewd möcht sich wol meren

Wach auf, mein Hort

WAGNER, RICHARD

Walther's Prize Song – *Die Meistersinger*
  von Nürnberg

Winterstürme – *Die Walküre*

WALTON, WILLIAM

King Herod and the Cock

WECKERLIN, JEAN-BAPTISTE

Dieu des enfers

WHELPLEY, BENJAMIN

I Know a Hill

WHITE, CLARENCE C.

Bear de Burden

WIDOR, CHARLES-MARIE

Mon bras pressait

WOLF, HUGO

Auf ein altes Bild

Auch kleine Dinge

Beherzigung

Benedeit die sel'ge Mutter

Daβ doch gemalt all' deine Reize wären

The Harper Songs

Lebe wohl

Der Musikant

Nun wandre, Maria

Der Tambour

Über Nacht

Verborgenheit

Wenn du zu den Blumen gehst

Zur Ruh

WORK, JOHN WESLEY, II

Go Tell It on the Mountain

My Soul Is a Witness for My Lord

ANONYMOUS

D'où viens-tu, bergère?

Die Heilige Joseph Siete

The Lamentation (East African songs)

The Little Chicken

O Elijah, Prophet Great

Sleep My Little One

Notes

INTRODUCTION

1. See the documentary *Songs of Triumph, Songs of Joy.*

2. We gratefully acknowledge the many conversations with Avery Brooks, which helped to tease out the subtleties of these conclusions.

PROLOGUE

1. Helm, *Angel Mo' and Her Son, Roland Hayes,* 3 (hereafter *AM*). Roland Hayes Parkway, Route 156, now marks the location of Curryville.

2. Ibid., 3.

3. Ibid., 34–38.

4. Ibid.

5. Ibid.

6. This genre of musical communication came to be known as "alert" songs.

7. Peter Weaver's mother was not named in the *AM* account but apparently was owned by the Mann family. It is mentioned that Charles Weaver/Abá 'Ougi raised his newborn son to the heavens and bemoaned the fact that, while he was born a free man, his son was born enslaved. *AM,* 42.

8. Ibid.

9. This information is based on 1880 U.S. census records. The information on Fannie Hayes's grave marker indicates that she was born "about" 1842.

10. *AM,* 45.

11. Ibid., 42.

1. A NEW JERUSALEM (1887–1911)

1. Helm, *Angel Mo' and her Son, Roland Hayes,* 13–16 (hereafter *AM*).

2. Ibid.

3. Ibid.

4. Ibid.

5. Ibid.

6. Ibid.

7. Ibid., 22.

8. The 1900 census records suggest a more complex picture of the family at best and provide grossly inaccurate information at the least, with inaccuracies related to Fannie, William, Jesse, and possibly Roland's reported ages.

9. In a series of radio interviews that Roland gave to promote his book of arranged spirituals, *My Songs, Aframerican Religious Folk,* in the late 1940s, he went into greater detail about the impact that his father had on his musical development than he had in *AM* earlier in the decade..

10. Hayes Papers of the Hayes Collection, Detroit Public Library (hereafter DPL). See letter dated September 13, 1949. This is an excerpt from the late

1940s interviews that Roland Hayes did with Edwin Booth of Harvard's School of Theology.

11. Roland Robert Hayes, personal communication, July 2007. See also this story mentioned in the prologue.

12. *AM*, 51–52.

13. Ibid., 27.

14. Ibid., 56.

15. Mullett, "World-Famous Singer."

16. Mabel Ansley Murphy, "He Stood before the King" (no further information available).

17. *Christian Science Monitor*, June 6, 1962.

18. *AM*, 57; also see Warren Marr II, "Roland Hayes," *Black Perspective in Music*, 2, no. 2 (Autumn 1974): 186–90.

19. *AM*, 31.

20. Ibid., 60.

21. The Fort Wood area of Chattanooga dated from the Civil War era as a Confederate stronghold. In the 1880s, the area began to be developed by investors and eventually became one of the more prestigious suburbs of Chattanooga. There was a small African American section of Fort Wood where those who worked in service-related areas for nearby white families lived.

22. *AM*, 66–91.

23. Ibid.

24. Ibid.

25. Ibid.

26. Ibid., 68.

27. Mullett, "World-Famous Singer," 27.

28. *AM*, 69.

29. Ibid. Hayes interview (interviewer unknown), New York City, June 1962, Hayes private papers, courtesy of Afrika Hayes Lambe.

30. *AM*, 71.

31. Ibid.

32. Hayes Papers, DPL. See letter dated September 13, 1949.

33. *AM*, 72.

34. Ibid.

35. In *AM*, Hayes said that he had taken a job at another iron foundry, Casey-Hedges. In other accounts, he suggests it was the Price-Evans Foundry.

36. Ibid.

37. Murphy, "He Stood before the King."

38. *AM*, 76.

39. Mullett, "World-Famous Singer," 27.

40. Ibid.

41. Murphy, "He Stood before the King"; Hayes interview (interviewer unknown), May 1962 (?), Hayes private papers, courtesy of Afrika Hayes Lambe.

42. Qtd. in Mullett, "World-Famous Singer," 27.

43. *AM*, 78.

44. Murphy, "He Stood before the King."

45. Ibid.

46. Mullett, "World-Famous Singer," 27.

47. Ibid. Calhoun recalled the year being 1904 in a 1937 letter to Hayes. In Mary B. Mullett's 1925 *American Magazine* article, Hayes recalled the year as 1904. More than sixty years later, in a 1968 letter to William Stone's grandson, Robert H. Solem, Hayes said the year was 1905.

48. Ibid. However, in issue 55 of *Guideposts* (1947) magazine, Hayes said it was Calhoun who first played the recordings for him. Given the cost of the machine, the Stone scenario is likely more accurate.

49. Enrico Caruso recorded the aria from *I Pagliacci* on three occasions: in 1902 (Italy), 1904, and 1907. Since the 1904 version was recorded in the United States (with orchestra), there is a possibility that Hayes heard that performance at the Stones'.

50. Hayes later sought to purchase that monumental gramophone and, after

having been in touch with Stone's sister, Ethel Carter, after Stone's death, it was given to him. Hayes Papers, DPL. See undated 1962 letter from Ethel Carter.

51. Ibid. See letter dated October 12, 1937. Calhoun eventually relocated to New York, where he was the principal organist and choirmaster for the Williams Institutional CME Church and taught private lessons in voice, piano, organ, and music theory. On his stationery he advertised himself as "Roland Hayes First Music Teacher."

52. Hayes Papers, DPL.

53. Hawkins, *Nashville Metro.*

54. Mullett, "World-Famous Singer," 110.

55. Hayes Papers, DPL. See material dated January 1937.

56. The AMA's forerunner was involved in the *Amistad Africans v. US Government,* which was resolved in 1841 when the Supreme Court ruled in favor of the continental Africans. The organization was also instrumental in the founding of such higher learning institutions as Atlanta University and Howard University.

57. *AM,* 83.

58. Downes, "Roland Hayes, Colored Singer." Based on the context, Stubbs must have had enough musical ability to accompany Hayes's audition selections for Jennie Robinson. In the account offered by Mabel Ansley Murphy in "He Stood before the King," Robinson's reaction to Hayes's performance was different than reported. According to Murphy, Miss Robinson had "a lump in her throat, her eyes bright with unshed tears." Also, in that account, Hayes sang the spiritual "Steal Away."

59. Mullett, "World-Famous Singer," 110.

60. *AM,* 85.

61. Mullett, "World-Famous Singer," 110.

62. Ibid.

63. Hayes indicated in *AM* that he worked for the Childresses for two years, but in the above referenced article, Hayes indicated that he was with them for a year.

64. Seroff, "Singing of the Old Tunes." Also see the *Fisk University News,* vol. 10, no. 4, December 1919.

65. *Fisk University News,* vol. 10, no. 4, December 1919.

66. Seroff, "Singing of the Old Tunes," 15.

67. Work was well known for his compositions and arrangements.

68. Seroff, "Singing of the Old Tunes," 33.

69. Mullett, "World-Famous Singer," 110.

70. *AM,* 86.

71. Ibid., 87.

72. Hayes private papers, courtesy of Afrika Hayes Lambe.

73. *AM,* 91.

74. Hayes private papers, courtesy of Afrika Hayes Lambe.

75. Seroff, "Singing of the Old Tunes," 33.

76. See the documentary *Songs of Triumph, Songs of Joy.*

77. *AM,* 86–89. Hayes indicated on p. 89 that the celebrated chorus had no formal association with the music department at the time.

78. Such a communication came from Charles W. Kelley, who went with the Jubilee group when they traveled to Boston in 1911. Hayes Papers, DPL.

79. *Nashville Globe,* April 23, 1909.

80. Seroff, "Singing of the Old Tunes," 37–39.

81. Mullett, "World-Famous Singer," 110.

82. *AM,* 89.

83. Ibid.

84. Mullett, "World-Famous Singer," 110.

85. *AM,* 89.

86. Mullett, "World-Famous Singer," 110.

87. *AM,* 90.

88. Ibid., 162.

89. Lulu Vere Childers was a Kentucky-born African American musician who had also studied voice and keyboard at Oberlin Conservatory of Music. Although she had a career as a singer (contralto), her greatest claim to fame was her establishment of the Howard University music department, which she led between 1909 and 1942. It was probably through her connections that Hayes went to Louisville and maintained contact with her for a portion of his early career.

90. After his international reputation was well established, Childers embarked on a plan for the tenor to tour with Howard University's chorus performing Samuel Coleridge-Taylor's choral masterpiece *Hiawatha,* but he was unable to meet the commitment because of a scheduling conflict. He did, however, agree to give a benefit recital for the institution.

91. The Pendennis Club is still an active organization after 127 years. A strict dress code is still enforced (i.e., no jeans, short pants, or shirts without collars).

92. Mullett, "World-Famous Singer," 112.

93. Ibid.

94. Hayes Papers, DPL. See letter dated March 18, 1911.

95. According to Hayes, Jennie Robinson stayed away from the May 1911 commencement exercise when he also sang (*AM,* 92). Also see Seroff, "Singing of the Old Tunes." Seroff makes a point that Hayes was a scapegoat in the ideological standoff between Jennie Robinson and John W. Work II. In 1925, fifteen years after

the event, Hayes simply said he was summoned to the department, informed of his dismissal, and told he was not the type of student that the department wanted. He related this version without mentioning any names. It was only in his later telling of the story that he indicated that it was his teacher Jennie Robinson who had informed him of his dismissal and did so in very unsympathetic tones. In 1925, Hayes was perhaps attempting to spare the memory of his recently deceased former teacher in initially recounting his earth-shattering moment. In his later account, he named Robinson as the person who delivered the devastating body blow.

96. *AM,* 90–91.

2. ROLAND'S WORLD IN BOSTON (1911–1920)

1. *The New York Times,* January 22, 1911.

2. In Helm's *Angel Mo' and Her Son, Roland Hayes* (hereafter *AM*), Hayes said that he had met Henry Putnam in Louisville (97), but in his 1925 account (in Mullett, "World-Famous Singer") he said that the message was handed to him by a manager from the Pendennis Club.

3. *AM,* 97–99.

4. Ibid.

5. Ibid.

6. Roland also sang for Arthur Foote, who assisted him with interpretation of certain songs, and Benjamin Whelpley. Theodore Parker listened to Hayes and offered no comment whatsoever. *AM,* 97–98.

7. Ibid.

8. Ibid., 100.

9. Ibid.

10. Charles Harris offers an account of his interactions with Hayes during the early Boston days in *Reminiscences of My Days with Roland Hayes.* This self-published work provides more information

and detail, in many ways, than Hayes's own about this period in Boston. Harris's written communications with Hayes began in the early 1950s and substantiate much of what he said in his 1944 account. It was also Harris's account that provided information on the deaths of people like Jennie Robinson, John W. Work, Arthur Hubbard, and Henry Putnam, among others, all of whom were dead by 1944. Harris, *Reminiscences*, 6.

11. Harris mistakenly refers to the opera as *The Bohemian Girl* composed by Balfe when the actual aria that Hayes sang was from *Martha* by von Flotow.

12. Harris, *Reminiscences*, 4.

13. *AM*, 101.

14. Ibid.

15. Mullett, "World-Famous Singer," 112.

16. Francesco Lamperti had been a celebrated teacher throughout much of the nineteenth century. He produced a highly successful singing book, *A Treatise on the Art of Singing* (revised and translated by J. C. Griffith [New York: Schirmer, 1980]), which was critical of teachers who allowed their students to perform before being thoroughly trained in the art of bel canto, or beautiful singing, which focused on the beauty and smoothness of the vocal line. He had taught a number of celebrated singers, including Arthur Hubbard, using those techniques. Lamperti's approach to the male voice was that there was a chest voice (used for speaking) and a mixed voice (typically used for singing in the upper part of one's register). This was Hubbard's approach to teaching Hayes.

17. Olin Downes, "Roland Hayes, Colored Singer, First of Race to Sing in Symphony," *Boston Sunday Post*, September 23, 1923, A4. This account said that it was Henry Putnam who paid for Hayes's lessons with Hubbard, but this is the only account that made such a claim.

18. *AM*, 100.

19. Hayes letter, 1965, from private papers courtesy of Afrika Hayes Lambe.

20. Work apparently believed in Hayes's singing talent enough to invite him to participate in the recording project, even though he had not returned to Nashville with the other Fisk singers at the end of the missionary conference. Among the works that were included in the recording were Work's choral arrangements of spirituals including "Swing Low, Sweet Chariot," and other standards like "Roll, Jordan Roll," "My Soul Is a Witness for My Lord," and "All Over This World."

21. This information is courtesy of Tim Brooks of Greenwich, Conn.

22. Seroff, in "Singing of the Old Tunes," maintains that in this recording, Hayes is featured in the selection "Shout All Over God's Heaven/Little David"; we do not agree that it is Hayes but someone else, possibly John W. Work II.

23. *AM*, 104.

24. Ibid.

25. This recital has been reported elsewhere as a solo recital of Hayes's, but it was, in fact, a joint effort.

26. Harris, *Reminiscences*, 10. White and Richardson were also Boston-based musicians. Like Hayes, they also advertised in the *Crisis* magazine, which was the media vehicle of the NAACP.

27. Ibid.

28. Hayes suggested that they met in 1914, but personal correspondence makes clear that they knew each other at least two years before then.

29. Among others singers who routinely performed Burleigh's art songs were Marian Anderson, Irish tenor John McCormack, Paul Robeson, and the Polish opera singer Marcella Sembrich.

30. Burleigh might have been instrumental in forming the quartet because in 1912, his name recognition was stronger than the other singers', with the possible exception of Tapley. Hayes Papers of the Hayes Collection, Detroit Public Library (hereafter DPL). See letter dated June 10, 1962. Will Anthony Madden's 1962 letter written to Roland on the occasion of his seventy-fifth birthday recalled hearing the quartet in performance at Carnegie Hall in the fall of 1912.

31. Brooks, *Lost Sounds.* The recording, with Carroll Clark, of the hymn "I Surrender All" made by Columbia Records is the only extant recording of Tapley. She performed in England and was hosted by the preeminent composer Samuel Coleridge-Taylor, who proclaimed her one of the most talented musicians he had ever met. *Indianapolis Recorder,* October 19, 1912.

32. Samuel Coleridge-Taylor had a significant following among African Americans by the turn of the last century and had died in September 1912. He made at least three trips to the United States, where he was hailed as the "African Mahler."

33. Simpson, *Hard Trials,* 57. This 1913 meeting was perhaps the earliest contact between Hayes and Du Bois.

34. F. Taylor, "Black Musicians in 'The Philadelphia Tribune,'" 138.

35. Hayes Papers, DPL. See letter dated December 28, 1914.

36. Ibid. See letter dated August 10, 1913.

37. Harris, *Reminiscences,* 13–22. Harris gave considerable detail to some of his and Hayes's exploits over the course of this tour. For example, they ran into a former girlfriend of Hayes's from Fisk, met Harris's family in Augusta, and made a stop in Chattanooga to meet Hayes's first teacher, Arthur Calhoun.

38. The *Afro-American Ledger* was the forerunner of Baltimore's *Afro-American,* which is still an active newspaper. It is one of the sources that documented Roland Hayes's presence in various locations around the country during the 1910s, paying special attention to his activities in the Baltimore area.

39. *Afro-American Ledger,* May 16, 1914.

40. *AM,* 106–108.

41. Narins, *African American Almanac,* 17–18.

42. *AM,* 108.

43. Harris, *Reminiscences,* 22.

44. Ibid.

45. Nettles, *African American Concert Singers,* 170.

46. *Afro-American Ledger,* December 5, 1914, quoting from the *Boston Herald.*

47. Ibid.

48. Ibid.

49. Brooks, *Lost Sounds,* 440.

50. Southern, *Music of Black Americans,* 259.

51. *Fitchburg (Mass.) Daily Sentinel,* February 9, 1915.

52. Hayes Papers, DPL. See program dated April 15, 1915.

53. *AM,* 110.

54. Other than that he attended Fisk and was on the faculty of Howard University, no other information was supplied on this musician.

55. See the Roland Hayes scrapbook in the Roland Hayes Collection at the Boston Public Library (hereafter BPL).

56. Hayes Papers, DPL. See multiple performance requests 1916–17.

57. We would like to thank Bob Daniels for supplying us with the location of this institution.

58. Perhaps his programming of this work was to appeal to provincial taste.

Such songs do not appear on any of his programs at Jordan Hall or any similar A-level venues.

59. Hayes private papers, courtesy of Afrika Hayes Lambe.

60. Ibid. At the time of this program, Alice Dunbar had married and divorced her second husband, physician Henry Callis. The month after the concert (April 1916), she married her third husband, Robert Nelson.

61. In "Singing of the Old Tunes," Seroff maintains that the correct date of this performance should be 1915, if this was a performance conducted by John Work. We, however, have relied on Hayes's recollection of the date.

62. *AM,* 110.

63. Ibid., 108.

64. Brooks, *Lost Sounds,* 204.

65. See photo collection in Hayes Papers, DPL. Also see Seroff.

66. Hayes Papers, DPL. See 1916 letter from A. Hubbard, undated.

67. *Afro-American Ledger,* November 8, 1914.

68. Keiler, *Marian Anderson,* 36.

69. Hayes scrapbook, Roland Hayes Collection, BPL.

70. *AM,* 111.

71. Brooks, *Lost Sounds,* 465.

72. There is no information as to who sang the soprano part in this Boston *Elijah* performance.

73. Brooks, *Lost Sounds,* 440.

74. *AM,* 112.

75. Ibid.

76. Mullett, "World-Famous Singer," 112.

77. Simpson, *Hard Trials,* 88.

78. *AM,* 113.

79. According to Tim Brooks (personal written communication, 2008), Hayes did a test recording for the Victor label just after his recital on November 19, 1917, but

he was unsure if the recording was made in New York or Boston. Hayes made a Victor trial recording of "A Fragrant Flower," identified as a composition of Hayes, which could have been purchased for $.25.

80. *Afro-American* (Baltimore), December 1, 1917. A communication leading up to the Baltimore engagement came from an African American local arts enthusiast, Laura Wheatley, who became a promoter and Hayes supporter in the Baltimore area. In her letter to him dated September 25, 1917, she asked him to do his upcoming engagement at Bethel AME Church for $100 because that would be all the pastor could afford. She guaranteed that he could have a two-hundred-voice chorus to back him up and that the event would be well worth it. Hayes Papers, DPL.

81. "Graphophone" was the forerunner of the more commonly used "gramophone."

82. Brooks, *Lost Sounds,* 441. The absence of a date and language like "Replying to your inquiry of recent date" suggests that Hayes was sent a form letter; it does not have his name on it. Letter in the Hayes Papers, DPL. In a personal written communication, Tim Brooks suggested a date of November 19, 1917, as the date of Hayes's first recording venture but questioned the exact date because those records are not available.

83. Brooks, *Lost Sounds,* 443.

84. Ibid.

85. Ibid.

86. Hayes Papers, DPL. See Roland W. Hayes stationery, 1917–19.

87. Ibid. See multiple performance requests, 1916–17.

88. Burleigh was represented by G. Ricordi Publishers.

89. Ibid. This also suggests that Hayes was working with a secretary who was

assisting him in some capacity with such correspondence.

90. *AM,* 114–15.

91. Hayes papers, DPL. See letter dated March 28, 1918. Also see *AM,* 118.

92. Hayes reported that with the exception of seeing her relatives in Chattanooga and her son Robert Brante on the West Coast, Fannie did not enjoy the tour. There was an occasion in which she left the boardinghouse where they were staying in order to purchase a train ticket to Los Angeles, perhaps to stay with Robert. *AM,* 116–17.

93. Hayes papers, DPL. See performance request letters 1918–19.

94. Brooks, *Lost Sounds,* 443. There was certainly some significance in Hayes's recording.

95. Hayes private papers, courtesy of Afrika Hayes Lambe.

96. Dr. Wormley was also one of Hayes's more successful national distributors who bought and sold Hayes's recordings.

97. Brooks, *Lost Sounds,* 445. Also see Knight, "Roland Hayes," for additional information about the Hayes discography.

98. Advertisement, *Crisis,* May 1918, 42.

99. Hayes papers, DPL. It is likely that George Broome also received inquiries on Hayes's behalf, but those documents are not available.

100. Ibid.

101. Ibid.

102. As Lawrence Brown also appeared to have been on this trip, he may well have accompanied Hayes on the non-Burleigh works, similar to the arrangement that he and Burleigh had for his 1917 Symphony Hall concert in Boston.

103. Hayes papers, DPL. See program dated February 20, 1919.

104. *AM,* 125.

105. Ibid.

106. At this point, Hayes's version of his story gets somewhat confused, if not totally distorted. Roland maintained that he, Fannie, and Lawrence Brown were forced to remain on the West Coast throughout the balance of the year because of the 1919 "unholy year of race riots" in Chicago and several major southern cities with large African American populations. This could not have been accurate. In early May – specifically, the evening of May 9, 1919 – history placed Roland Hayes in Boston at the very venue in which he was first introduced to the city, Mechanics Hall.

107. Badger, *Life in Ragtime,* 218; also see Brooks, *Lost Sounds,* 288.

108. The account in *Angel Mo'* is most certainly inaccurate by more than a year. On pages 125–26, Hayes suggests that he was around when his brother John died in Boston, but private communications between him and Fannie Hayes indicate that he was already in England at the time.

109. *Evening Gazette* (Xenia, Ohio), October 24, 1919, 9. This is the same "Billy" King who was one of Marian Anderson's primary accompanists. This is also further evidence that Hayes did not remain on the West Coast through the end of 1919, as he maintained.

110. *Fisk University News,* vol. 10, no. 4, December 1919.

111. Ibid.

112. Ibid.

113. Hayes subsequently took the notes to his home in France, where they were lost in storage. Hayes's 1956 letter to his friend Noël Sullivan confirmed that the Robinson notes were among those that were lost in France. Sullivan Papers.

114. Hayes Papers, DPL. See program dated December 10, 1919.

115. Harris, *Reminiscences,* 27.

116. Hayes Papers, DPL. See program dated December 18, 1919.

117. Harris, *Reminiscences*, 27.

118. In *AM*, 128, Hayes suggested that it was Duse Mohammed Ali who facilitated the introduction to the agents Ibbs and Tillett. This could not have been true because he had been communicating with Ibbs and Tillett prior to arriving in London. He did not meet Ali until he arrived in that city.

119. Hayes Papers, DPL. See letter dated January 20, 1920.

120. Ibid. See letter dated March 1920.

121. *AM*, 126.

122. See Hayes's passport photo on *Ancestry.com*. The actual 1920 passport is in the Hayes private papers, courtesy of Afrika Hayes Lambe. His interest in Belgium stemmed from his desire to visit the Belgian Congo, which he considered a necessary stop.

123. Hayes Papers, DPL. See personal notes from Hayes to prospective patrons, spring 1920.

124. Hayes private papers, courtesy of Afrika Hayes Lambe.

3. ROLAND RULES BRITANNIA (1920–1921)

1. Maxtone-Graham, *Only Way to Cross*, 15–21.

2. Schomburg, "Negro Digs Up His Past," 237.

3. Afrika Hayes Lambe, personal communication, March 2007.

4. Helm, *Angel Mo' and Her Son, Roland Hayes*, 172 (hereafter *AM*).

5. Locke, *New Negro*.

6. Hayes private papers, courtesy of Afrika Hayes Lambe.

7. *AM*, 128.

8. Ibid.

9. Green, "Roland Hayes in London," 29.

10. *AM*, 128.

11. In 1912, Duse Mohammed Ali had Marcus Garvey working for him at the London-based paper. It is generally accepted that Garvey's Pan-Africanist views were fostered by his association with Ali.

12. Vincent, *Black Power*, 39.

13. Duffield, "Duse Mohammed Ali." Also see Green, "Roland Hayes in London."

14. Green, "Roland Hayes in London," 37.

15. *Times* (London), February 27, 1919, 7.

16. Hayes Papers of the Hayes Collection, Detroit Public Library (hereafter DPL). See letter dated May 12, 1920.

17. Once again, we thank Jeffrey Green for supplying this invaluable information.

18. Alan Rich, "A Bouncy Seventy-five: Roland Hayes, Despite His Age, Gives Concerts, Teaches and Reminisces," *New York Times*, June 3, 1962. The actual review that Hayes references in this interview has not emerged.

19. Hayes Papers, DPL. See letter dated June 23, 1920.

20. Lloyd, *Sir Dan Godfrey*. See also Thomas Lewis Johnson's entry on Godfrey in the *Oxford Dictionary of National Biography* and the website jeffreygreen. co.uk, p. 28. With thanks to Jeffrey Green for supplying this information.

21. Hayes Papers, DPL. See letter dated June 29, 1920.

22. Ibid. See letter dated August 2, 1920.

23. Foreman, *Music in England*, 111–13.

24. Hayes Papers, DPL. See letter dated July 12, 1920. This communication establishes that the singer was not in the country at the time of his older brother's death, as maintained in *AM*.

25. Ibid. See letter dated July 26, 1920.

26. Ibid. See letter dated August 5, 1920.

27. Ibid. See letter dated July 8, 1920.

28. Ibid. See letter dated October 10, 1920.

29. Ibid. See document dated October 28, 1920.

30. Pound, *Selected Letters of Ezra Pound,* 204.

31. Langfield, *Roger Quilter;* personal written communication from Professor Valerie Langfield, December 5, 2009. See also Dan O'Hara's review of Langfield's book in *The Gay and Lesbian Humanist* (Winter 2003–04).

32. Hayes Papers, DPL. See letter dated February 2, 1921.

33. *Musical Times,* March 1, 1921.

34. *West Africa* qtd. in Green, "Roland Hayes in London," 31–32.

35. Ibid.

36. *AM,* 132.

37. Olin Downes, "Roland Hayes, Colored Singer, First of Race to Sing in Symphony," *Boston Sunday Post,* September 23, 1923.

38. *AM,* 134–35.

39. *Times* (London), April 21, 1921. Also see the *Daily Telegraph* (London), April 23, 1921.

40. *Daily Telegraph* (London), April 23, 1921.

41. Hayes recorded the interview in June 1962 (interviewer unknown) a day after his seventy-fifth birthday concert at Carnegie Hall in New York. Hayes private papers, courtesy of Afrika Hayes Lambe.

42. *Times* (London), April 22, 1921.

43. *Daily Telegraph* (London), April 23, 1921.

44. *AM,* 136.

45. Ibid., 137; see also Green, "Roland Hayes in London," 29–41.

46. Qtd. in Green, "Roland Hayes in London," 35.

47. *AM,* 139.

48. Hayes Papers, DPL. See letter dated May 13, 1921.

49. Green, "John Alcindor."

50. Lewis, *W. E. B. Du Bois,* 580.

51. Hayes Papers, DPL. See program dated October 8, 1921.

52. Ibid. See letter dated June 17, 1921.

53. Adejumobi, "Pan African Congress."

54. Contee, "'Status' of the Pan-African Association of 1921."

55. C. Brooks, "Duro Ladipo and the Moremi Legend."

56. Hayes Papers, DPL. See letter dated July 8, 1921.

57. Ibid.

58. Duberman, *Paul Robeson,* 49.

59. Langfield, *Roger Quilter.* In a personal communication from Valerie Langfield, December 2009, she made an even stronger claim of a likely relationship between the composer and Brown.

60. Boyle and Bunie, *Paul Robeson,* 139.

61. Hayes Papers, DPL. See program dated October 8, 1921.

62. In a 1934 *Boston Transcript* interview, Hayes said he began working with Sir George in January 1922, but there is correspondence between them dating from November 1921. The vocal coach assists with language and interpretation. The voice teacher may also do this but focuses on vocal production, sound, and technique.

63. *Boston Transcript,* September 25, 1934.

64. Qtd. in Green, "Roland Hayes in London," 38.

65. Qtd. in ibid., 39.

66. Hayes Papers, DPL. See letter dated March 21, 1922.

4. "LE RAGE DE PARIS" (1921–1922)

1. Hayes Papers of the Hayes Collection, Detroit Public Library (hereafter DPL). See letter dated May 5, 1921.

2. Ibid. If Hayes met d'Indy, there is no record of it. In any case, he made no mention of it and was apparently not drawn to his vocal compositions.

3. Ibid. See letter dated May 28, 1921.

4. Ibid.

5. Helm, *Angel Mo' and Her Son, Roland Hayes*, 149 (hereafter *AM*). Hayes's account of the Mont Thabor Hotel incident is inconsistent with his personal communications, which state that he and Brown were so outraged by their treatment at the hotel that they immediately returned to England, vowing never to return to Paris. Several letters addressed to Hayes at the Mont Thabor Hotel were still being sent there, however, as late as June 22, 1921, indicating that they remained in Paris for at least three weeks. Hayes Papers, DPL.

6. Hayes Papers, DPL. See letter dated June 8, 1921.

7. Ibid. See letter dated June 21, 1921.

8. Hayes mentions Tovalou (referred to in their personal communications as "Tova") only once in *AM*, but their letters suggest that a far more complex relationship between the two existed.

9. *AM*, 35.

10. Hayes Papers, DPL. See letter dated August 21, 1921.

11. *AM*, 150.

12. Ibid.

13. Hayes Papers, DPL. See letter dated January 15, 1922.

14. Ibid. See letter dated January 25, 1922.

15. Hayes private papers, courtesy of Afrika Hayes Lambe.

16. Hayes Papers, DPL. See letter dated March 29, 1922.

17. Ibid.

18. Ibid.

19. Ibid. See letter dated March 23, 1922.

20. Ibid.

21. Ibid. See letter dated June 22, 1922.

22. *AM*, 151.

23. Ibid., 153.

24. Ibid.

25. Hayes Papers, DPL. See letter dated June 2, 1922.

26. Sullivan Papers. See letter dated January 4, 1932, among many others that document their close relationship.

27. Hayes Papers, DPL. See letter dated July 6, 1922.

28. Wagstaff, "André Messager." Messager had studied with Gabriel Fauré and Camille Saint-Saens.

29. *AM*, 154. The issue of Roland Hayes in opera is somewhat of a conundrum. During and after his vocal heyday, Hayes would have been a significant draw for several African American opera companies operating in the country. The opportunity was present and available had he wanted to pursue such an ambition. It will be clear in later chapters that he wanted his personal story to be musically dramatized (as in an opera) and would have taken part in such a production.

30. Ibid., 153–54.

31. Ibid.

32. Hayes private papers, courtesy of Afrika Hayes Lambe.

33. Hale's use of the phrase "bad disorder" was a reference to syphilis. This was the euphemistic way of referring to the sexually transmitted disease during this period. Hale's implication that Hayes could be seduced by some wealthy Parisian reflected the prevailing feeling at the time that most African American men desired a white woman.

34. Hayes Papers, DPL. See letter dated March 31, 1922.

35. Monteux, *It's All in the Music*, 115–16. Pierre Monteux gives a slightly different account; however, the personal communications found among Hayes's

private papers and those in the DPL substantiate the version here, as does a contract between Hayes and Brennan for a major concert that Roland sang in January 1923.

36. Lawrence Brown Papers. See letter dated September 19, 1922.

37. Ibid.

38. Hayes Papers, DPL. See letter dated November 7, 1922.

39. Duberman, *Paul Robeson,* 78–79.

40. Ibid.

41. Ibid.

42. Hayes Papers, DPL. See letter dated November 4, 1922.

43. Hayes private papers, courtesy of Afrika Hayes Lambe.

44. *AM,* 156.

5. "YOU'RE TIRED, CHILE" (1923)

1. Helm's *Angel Mo' and Her Son, Roland Hayes,* 157 (hereafter *AM*), suggests that the tenor returned to the United States in response to a letter he had received from Fannie. However, the communications indicate that Hayes also had to be back in the country to meet various performing engagements in January 1923.

2. Hayes private papers, courtesy of Afrika Hayes Lambe. Although we have edited Fannie Hayes's letters to her sons and others, the substance and quality of her thoughts have been retained.

3. Ibid.

4. Hayes Papers of the Hayes Collection, Detroit Public Library (hereafter DPL). See program dated January 7, 1923.

5. Ibid.

6. Lawrence Brown Papers.

7. Hayes Papers, DPL. See program dated January 7, 1923.

8. Hayes private papers, courtesy of Afrika Hayes Lambe.

9. Ibid.

10. Lawrence Brown Papers.

11. *AM,* 161–62.

12. Ibid.

13. Hayes Papers, DPL. See letter dated November 25, 1921.

14. Hayes private papers, courtesy of Afrika Hayes Lambe.

15. Hayes Papers, DPL. See letter dated February 15, 1923.

16. In *AM,* Hayes does not mention the fact that Jesse died, much less the circumstances surrounding his death.

17. Although unlikely, there is the possibility that Fannie did not immediately inform Hayes of Jesse's death. He would have learned of it at some point, but just when he learned is an open question. He would have obviously known of his brother's death by the time he arrived back in the United States in the fall of 1923. Why Hayes left the readers of *AM* (published in 1942) with the impression that Jesse was alive when Fannie Hayes died is unknown.

18. Hayes Papers, DPL. See program dated February 10, 1923.

19. This information is courtesy of Tim Brooks of Greenwich, Conn.

20. When compared, "Sit Down" as recorded by Hayes in 1923 was different from the spiritual "You're Tired, Chile" recorded by the tenor in 1941. Both versions are in minor tonalities, but the earlier version is slow and sustained as compared to the later version, which is upbeat with a far more elaborate keyboard accompaniment.

21. This is the story behind the version that Hayes recorded in 1941. The text differs significantly from the version he recorded in 1923. In both versions, however, there are the repeated references to "Sit down and rest a little while." Hayes, *My Songs,* 57.

22. Hayes Papers, DPL. See letter dated April 16, 1923.

23. Ibid. Hayes's letter dated April 19, 1923, in response to Fannie is available in the Hayes Papers, DPL, but Fannie's letter to him is apparently lost.

24. See reviews in *Wiener Allgemeine Zeignung*, April 26, 1923, and *Wiener Morgen Zeitung*, April 27, 1923, respectively.

25. Hayes private papers, courtesy of Afrika Hayes Lambe.

26. *AM*, 171.

27. Hayes Papers, DPL. See letter dated June 14, 1923.

28. Hayes private papers, courtesy of Afrika Hayes Lambe. In the letter dated August 28, 1923, and others, Fannie Hayes may have been referring to Felton Hayes, her only grandchild, as one of her sons. Or this could also fuel the speculation that she had not informed Roland of his younger brother Jesse's death.

29. Ibid. Roland Hayes surely had in mind his recent experience with Lawrence Brown when he instructed William Brennan on how to deal with William Lawrence on the question of fees. No doubt it was Roland who lined up Percival Parham, Arthur Calhoun, and probably one or two other accompanists as alternates if things had not worked out with William Lawrence.

30. Ibid.

31. *AM*, 172.

32. Fannie's letter to which Roland Hayes responded is apparently lost.

33. *AM*, 176. This is yet another instance of Roland's recollection not being accurate, because he said in *AM* that Fannie wanted to leave the farm in Georgia to "Jesse, Brantie, and me" (176). Not only had Fannie not said this in the letter, but he and she were well aware that Jesse Hayes was already dead by September 1923.

34. *Boston Sunday Post*, September 23, 1923.

35. *AM*, 172–73.

36. Ibid.

37. Ibid.

38. Ibid.

39. Hayes Papers, DPL. See telegram dated September 26, 1923.

40. *AM*, 174.

41. Lawrence Brown Papers.

42. Hayes, *My Songs*, 57. The text of the later version of the work shows a marked difference between the two versions. This version presents an upbeat, fast tempo compared to the early version.

YOU'RE TIRED, CHILE (SIT DOWN)

Oh sit down sister, I know you're tired. I know
you're tired, sit down.
'Cause you come a long way; sit down chile!
Sit down an' res' a lit'l while. (repeat)

Oh you come a long way, an' you had hard
trials.
I know you're tired, sit down chile,
Sit down an' res' a lit'l while.

Oh, you come a long way, an' the road was dark.
I know you're tired, sit down chile,
Sit down an' res' a lit'l while.

Tell me what you're waitin' for. I'm waitin' for
my mother.
'Cause I want to tell her howdy, sit down chile.
Sit down an' res' a lit'l while.
Tell me what you're waitin' for. I'm waitin' for
my neighbor.
'Cause I want to tell him howdy, sit down chile.
Sit down an' res' a lit'l while.

Oh, you come a long way, you had a big load.
I know you're tired. Sit down (repeat)

Oh sit down sister, I know you're tired. I know
you're tired, sit down.
'Cause you come a long way; sit down chile! Sit
down an' res' a lit'l while.
Oh you come a long way, an' you had hard
trials.

I know you're tired, chile,
(spoken) Sit down an' res' a lit'l while.

6. THE HAYES CONQUEST
(1923–1924)

1. Helm, *Angel Mo' and Her Son, Roland Hayes*, 197 (hereafter *AM*). Also see Kolowrat, *Confessions*, 151–52.

2. Evans and Cornwall, *Czechoslovakia*.

3. Ibid.

4. Kolowrat, *Confessions*, 151–52.

5. Ibid.

6. *AM*, 198.

7. Ibid., 177–79. The account offered in Kolowrat, *Confessions*, 153, indicated that it was Hayes who made the announcement in limited German. *Time* magazine (October 8, 1923) reported on the incident and said that it was Hayes's accompanist who made the announcement.

8. Ibid., 177–79.

9. Kolowrat, *Confessions*, 153.

10. Ibid.

11. Ibid.

12. *AM*, 179.

13. The incident was summed up in the November 5, 1923, issue of *Time* magazine under the heading "Czechoslovakia – 'Anti-Foreign.'" *Time* gave a brief summary of the incident without any of the nationalist implications and without mentioning the participation of Prague's mayor or the fact that Hayes had left the stage and then returned.

14. Kolowrat, *Confessions*, 153–54.

15. Ibid.

16. Count Leopold and Nadine von Huppman-Valbella were married in St. Patrick's Cathedral in New York on March 18, 1884, in a very fashionable wedding (*New York Times*, March 19, 1884). I am grateful to Ernest Kolowrat for providing me with the history of the Kolowrat and Colloredo-Mansfeld families. I also

want to acknowledge his assistance in graciously offering a copy of his book, *Confessions of a Hapless Hedonist*. In addition, he generously shared information about his hours of interviews with his aunt Bertha, made in the early 1960s through the late 1970s.

17. Ernest Kolowrat, personal communication, January 21, 2009.

18. Hayes Papers of the Hayes Collection, Detroit Public Library (hereafter DPL). See program dated November 15, 1923. Hayes indicated that the date was November 15. The forty-third season program supports the Friday, November 16, afternoon concert and the Saturday, November 17, 8:15 PM concert in Symphony Hall. In his biography of the conductor, *Pierre Monteux, Maître*, p. 71, John Canarina indicates the debut took place on November 16, 1923. As indicated, the same performance was on November 15, 16, and 17, which accounts for the discrepancy in dates from various sources.

19. Hayes private papers, courtesy of Afrika Hayes Lambe. Hayes recovered Fannie's letters written to her friends in order to keep them for posterity.

20. Ibid.

21. The reference to the "baby" is most likely Jesse, the youngest Hayes son, who was commonly known as "Baby" Jesse by his siblings (although he would have been in his twenties at the time of the will).

22. Hayes private papers, courtesy of Afrika Hayes Lambe.

23. This hair came into our possession as a part of the material that was given over to us by Afrika Hayes Lambe. It was among the many private papers found in the basement of her home in Newton, Mass.

24. The actual letters from this early period were left to rot in the countess's chalet in southern France. Ernest Kolowrat had

them in his possession at one point, but he returned them to his aunt at her request.

25. Hayes Papers, DPL. See program dated November 15, 1923.

26. *AM*, 185.

27. Hayes private papers, courtesy of Afrika Hayes Lambe.

28. H. I. Parker, *Boston Transcript*, November 1923.

29. *AM*, 185.

30. Janken, *White*, 101.

31. Ibid.

32. Heywood Broun's *New York World* review is quoted in Lankard, "Roland Hayes." Also see *AM*, 188.

33. Hayes private papers, courtesy of Afrika Hayes Lambe.

34. *Chattanooga Times*, December 12, 1923.

35. Hayes Papers, DPL. See program dated February 5, 1924.

36. Ibid.

37. Janken, *White*, 101–105.

38. Ibid.

39. Hayes Papers, DPL. See letter dated February 19, 1924.

40. *West Africa Magazine*, February 23, 1924.

41. Hayes Papers, DPL. See letter dated March 1, 1924.

42. Ibid. See letter dated March 20, 1924.

43. Ibid. See letter dated March 25, 1924.

44. Ibid. See letter dated April 10, 1924.

45. Kolowrat, personal communication, January 21, 2009.

46. The countess's nephew Ernest Kolowrat saw the letters and characterized them as increasingly passionate.

47. *AM*, 197–99.

48. Kolowrat, *Confessions*, 144.

49. Ibid., 151.

50. Ibid.

51. Ernest Kolowrat interviewed his aunt in Paris in 1978 (hereafter Kolowrat/Colloredo-Mansfeld interview).

52. Kolowrat, personal communication, January 21, 2009.

53. Ibid.

54. Kolowrat/Colloredo-Mansfeld interview.

55. Ibid.

56. Ibid.

57. Ibid.

58. Ibid.

59. Ibid.

60. Ibid.

61. We are grateful to Ernest Kolowrat for making a copy of this letter from Hayes to the countess available for use in this work.

62. *AM*, 199.

63. Hayes Papers, DPL. T. C. White's letter indicates that he was a "Charge d'Affaires ad interim," but it does not specify of what. The letterhead indicates the concert director, Leopold Adler, but right of that is handwritten "Legation of the United States of America, Prague, April 2, 1924." Perhaps a copy of the letter was also sent to that foreign mission.

64. Ibid.

65. Ibid.

66. Hass, "German Science." The German opposition to having continental Africans as a policing force also found support among southern white Americans, including President Woodrow Wilson. There has also been the suggestion by some scholars who believe that the imposition of the continental Africans was, in part, a retaliation for the atrocities that the Germans had carried out against the Herero, an ethnic group nearly wiped out in southern Africa (modern day Botswana) twenty years earlier.

67. Ibid., 333.

68. Hitler, *Mein Kampf*. Also see Scheck, *Hitler's African Victims*.

69. Roland Hayes, "God Sings Thru Me," *Guideposts* 55 (1947). In *AM*, 210, Hayes said that this performance took place in the early fall of 1924, but that is not possible. He had returned to the United States by mid-August of that year, and there is no evidence to support that he returned to Berlin, did this concert, and returned to the United States to begin his next American tour by early October. The fact that the Berlin incident was reported in the September 15, 1924, issue of *Time* magazine perhaps added to the confusion. In describing the incident, it said, "Some weeks ago, Roland Hayes, Negro tenor, gave a concert . . ." It perhaps should have said "Some *months* ago." In any event, several who have written about this well-known episode in Hayes's career (see Keiler's *Marian Anderson,* among other accounts) mistakenly followed the information presented in *AM*. A postcard from Hayes to Charles Harris is dated May 10, 1924. The European dating system (which Hayes was apparently observing) has the date "10/5/24." This could have been misunderstood by an American observer as "October 5, 1924."

70. *AM,* 211.

71. Hayes, "God Sings Thru Me."

72. Ibid.

73. *AM,* 212.

74. Translations by David Evans Thomas, 1998.

75. *AM,* 212.

76. Ibid.

77. *Berliner Montag Post,* May 12, 1924.

78. "Beaten in Georgia, Says Roland Hayes," *New York Times,* July 17, 1942. The Nationalsozialistische Deutsche Arbeiterpartei was founded in Germany on January 5, 1919.

79. Hayes private papers, courtesy of Afrika Hayes Lambe.

80. "Negroes Present Medal to Singer – Award Made in Absentia as Roland Hayes Sings Before King George," *Philadelphia Public Ledger,* July 2, 1924.

81. Arsenault, *Sound of Freedom,* 37. Also see Janken, *White,* 89–103.

82. *AM,* 197–98.

83. Ibid.

7. ROLAND AND THE COUNTESS (1924–1926)

1. The countess also suggested the practice of doubling the *m* for words like *madre* to refer to the Virgin Mary.

2. Helm, *Angel Mo' and Her Son, Roland Hayes,* 198 (hereafter *AM*).

3. Ernest Kolowrat, taped interview with Bertha Colloredo-Mansfeld, Paris, 1978 (hereafter Kolowrat/Colloredo-Mansfeld interview).

4. Kolowrat, personal communication, January 21, 2009. Also, Igor Bogdanoff, written communication, April 8, 2008.

5. According to a communication from Igor Bogdanoff, the recombination was to be a melting of the old aristocracy and a new black lineage. See also Kolowrat/ Colloredo-Mansfeld interview.

6. Kolowrat, *Confessions,* 155.

7. Ibid.

8. Hayes Papers of the Hayes Collection, Detroit Public Library (hereafter DPL). See letter dated May 9, 1924.

9. Ibid. Letter September 23, 1924.

10. Martin, *Race First,* 115. The name of the organization was in response, in part, to Tovalou's personal experience in Paris. The year before, the prince had been assaulted in a Parisian nightclub by several Americans. The prince sued the club, and courts ruled in his favor. Citing the propensity toward racial violence by American tourists, the French government

banned overtly racist films such as *The Birth of a Nation* from being shown in French theaters. Also see Stovall, *Paris Noir,* 73.

11. W. E. B. Du Bois Papers, MS 312.

12. There is evidence to suggest that Hayes and Garvey might have interacted, but the singer would have also kept that relationship, had it existed, somewhat concealed for the reasons that he and Prince Tovalou seem to have parted company. According to Robert Hill in *The Marcus Garvey and the Universal Negro Improvement Association Papers, Volume X,* Tovalou fell out of grace with the UNIA for a time. He returned to France and in 1932 married the African American singer Roberta Dodd Crawford in Paris. Prince Tovalou died in 1938. Some sources indicate that Roberta Dodd Crawford studied with and was mentored by Hayes, but her name did not appear in the records of the Detroit Public Library during the examinations by the authors. She had a somewhat limited career in Europe and eventually returned to Texas, where she was born, and died there in 1954.

13. Hayes Papers, DPL. See letter dated August 11, 1924.

14. Hayes private papers, courtesy of Afrika Hayes Lambe.

15. Hayes Papers, DPL. See letter dated November 18, 1924.

16. Ibid. See letter dated November 25, 1924.

17. Ibid.

18. Ibid

19. Ibid.

20. Ibid. See letter dated December 4, 1924.

21. Ibid. See letter dated September 10, 1924.

22. Ibid. See letter dated December 26, 1924.

23. "Roland Hayes' Third Recital," *Musical America,* January 20, 1925.

24. Ibid.

25. Hayes Papers, DPL. See letter dated January 30, 1925.

26. Brooks, *Lost Sounds,* 257.

27. Hayes Papers, DPL. See letter dated January 8, 1925.

28. Ibid.

29. *San Francisco Call,* February 27, 1925.

30. Ibid. On the subject of opera, Hayes heard continually from European impresarios jostling to get him as a client.

31. Hayes private papers, courtesy of Afrika Hayes Lambe.

32. Hayes Papers, DPL. See letter dated April 24, 1925.

33. *AM,* 216–23.

34. Ibid.

35. Ibid.

36. Kolowrat/Colloredo-Mansfeld interview.

37. Ibid.

38. *AM,* 198.

39. Kolowrat/Colloredo-Mansfeld interview.

40. Kolowrat, *Confessions,* 151. The countess recalled when interviewed about this, "An affair would have been easier to hide," but Bertha saw herself as "a one-man woman and could not be with one man for breakfast and another for tea."

41. Ibid.

42. Kolowrat/Colloredo Mansfeld interview.

43. *AM,* 213–14. Roland said that Leo Rosenek was his accompanist, but all other information suggests that it was Eduardo Gendron on this tour in Germany. According to a handwritten contract dated July 16, 1925, in Vienna, Austria, Roland engaged Rosenek to accompany the balance of his European concerts.

44. Ibid.

45. Ibid.

46. Ibid.

47. Ibid.

48. Ibid., 233.

49. Hayes private papers, courtesy of Afrika Hayes Lambe. See document dated February 25, 1925. Also see *AM*, 234.

50. Hayes private papers, courtesy of Afrika Hayes Lambe.

51. Ibid. While he was in Evanston, Illinois, performing at Northwestern University, Hayes stayed with his former employer, Professor Warren G. Waterman. Roland met with Waterman this time as his own man and as an international celebrity. However, the "master/servant" dynamic was still evident. Waterman addressed his former butler as "Roland," and the tenor addressed his former employer as "Professor Waterman." It may, however, been have an issue of showing deference to Waterman because of the age difference.

52. *Pittsburgh Courier,* January 2, 1926.

53. *New York Evening Sun,* December 31, 1925.

54. Walton Crocker wrote a tribute to Hayes simply called "The Conquest of Hayes," which includes vignettes from his birth up to the height of his fame in the mid-1920s.

55. Hayes Papers, DPL. Hayes's schedule of performances indicates that he was in the Boston area at the time.

56. Kolowrat, personal communication, January 21, 2009. This was a direct quote from the taped interview that Kolowrat conducted with his aunt. Hayes had accused her at one point of having seen another man and questioned whether Maya was in fact his child.

57. Kolowrat, *Confessions,* 155–56.

58. Ibid.

59. Hayes private papers, courtesy of Afrika Hayes Lambe. The Swiss birth document is from vol. 1926, no. 323.

60. Ibid.

61. Ibid.

62. Hayes Papers, DPL. In an October 12, 1937, letter to Hayes from his former teacher Arthur Calhoun, the latter jokingly recalled Fannie Hayes's often-quoted relationship advice to her son.

63. Hayes private papers, courtesy of Afrika Hayes Lambe. The abbreviation "Gfin." stands for *Gräfin,* the German word for "countess."

64. Ibid.

65. Ibid.

66. *Afro-American* (Baltimore), January 8, 1927. In this panel, the countess's name is misspelled as "Helena Kollorydo, of a high born Austrian family, formerly of the Kaiser's court."

67. *AM*, 199.

68. Maya was never taken on any of these family outings but was left in the care of a governess in St. Lary. Ernest Kolowrat, personal communication, February 2011.

69. Kolowrat/Colloredo-Mansfeld interview.

70. Kolowrat, *Confessions,* 154.

71. Kolowrat/Colloredo-Mansfeld interview.

72. Ibid.

73. Ibid. William Lawrence was considered a very handsome man at the time. His looks aside, Hayes might have harbored some insecurity where his accompanist was concerned.

74. Ibid.

75. Kolowrat, *Confessions,* 154.

76. This opinion was expressed by Ernest Kolowrat about his aunt.

77. Ibid.

78. *AM*, 197.

8. THE CONQUEST
SLOWS (1926–1930)

1. *Time* magazine, December 7, 1925. The French expression from the late eighteenth century is applicable here. At

the time of the opulent court of Louis IX, the expression "Plus royaliste que le roi" (More royal than the king) was frequently heard. In the case of Roland Hayes, he was required to know the music of Western art music composers (whether he was singing German lieder, French *melodie*, or Italian songs) as well as, if not better than, his European and European American counterparts. He then had the additional requirement, which to some degree still exists among African American vocal concert artists, to know and interpret African American spirituals with equal facility.

2. Hayes Papers of the Hayes Collection, Detroit Public Library (hereafter DPL). See letter dated January 8, 1926.

3. *Washington Daily American,* January 6, 1926.

4. *Washington Tribune,* January 6, 1926.

5. Ibid.

6. Helm, *Angel Mo' and Her Son, Roland Hayes,* 201 (hereafter *AM*). Once again, the account in *AM* contrasts with other versions of these events. In Hayes's account, he arrived in Baltimore the day of the concert; however, in several other accounts (i.e., newspaper reports and other private correspondence), he arrived the day before and stayed in the Wheatley home. Also see the account reported in the *Afro-American* (Baltimore), January 9, 1926.

7. *Afro-American* (Baltimore), January 9, 1926.

8. Ibid.

9. The secretary on this trip was not Howard Jordan but someone named H. D. Mann. It may have been a relative from Chattanooga, Tennessee, temporarily performing this role.

10. *AM*, 201. See also the *Afro-American* (Baltimore), January 16, 1926. Other live accounts indicate that there was a disturbance inside the theater similar to that which Hayes had experienced at the 1924 Berlin recital.

11. *Afro-American* (Baltimore), January 9, 1926.

12. Ibid.

13. Ibid., January 16, 1926.

14. Ibid.

15. Ibid. Despite what Laura Wheatley wrote in her editorial, she and Hayes were fully aware of the Jim Crow situation that he was going to confront at the Lyric Theater and, for reasons that were not entirely clear, chose to go forward with the recital.

16. All of the comments are from ibid.

17. Hayes Papers, DPL. See letter dated February 2, 1926.

18. *New York Times,* February 8, 1926.

19. Hayes Papers, DPL. See letter April 20, 1926.

20. Ibid.

21. Ibid. See letter dated August 30, 1926.

22. Ibid. Hayes narrated his activities of the summer of 1926 to William Brennan in a lengthy letter at the end of the summer.

23. Ibid.

24. Ibid.

25. Ibid. See program dated September 5, 1924.

26. *AM*, 200.

27. Hayes Papers, DPL. See program dated October 13, 1926.

28. *AM*, 235.

29. Hayes private papers, courtesy of Afrika Hayes Lambe.

30. Ibid.

31. *Times* magazine, April 11, 1927, quoting from the *Pittsburgh Courier.*

32. Hayes Papers, DPL. See sketch and note by R. Broadhurst, March 11, 1930.

33. Ibid.

34. Barry's last name is unknown.

35. Ibid. See letter dated February 1, 1927.

36. Ibid.

37. Hayes private papers, courtesy of Afrika Hayes Lambe.

38. *Afro-American* (Baltimore), January 8, 1927.

39. Hayes private papers, courtesy of Afrika Hayes Lambe.

40. Hayes Papers, DPL. See letter dated March 7, 1927.

41. Ovington, *Portraits in Color,* 1927.

42. Ibid., 234. There are several inaccuracies in the chapter as well. For example, it states that "Hayes lost his mother in 1924," when Fannie Hayes in fact had died the year before.

43. Ibid., 240–41.

44. We are grateful to Tim Brooks for providing us with the information on the Hayes recordings.

45. *AM,* 236. Count Chigi Saracini was later associated with the founding of the Chigana Music Academy in Florence.

46. Ibid., 240; Hayes private papers, courtesy of Afrika Hayes Lambe.

47. Hayes private papers, courtesy of Afrika Hayes Lambe.

48. Hayes Papers, DPL. At one point, Arthur Calhoun was even prepared to play for his former student, if William Lawrence had not accepted the proposed terms. In a letter dated June 2, 1925, Brennan and Judd politely declined an offer from Calhoun to accompany Roland for the 1925–26 season.

49. Ibid. See letter dated October 18, 1926.

50. Ibid.

51. Ibid.

52. Hayes letters to Noël Sullivan, Sullivan Papers.

53. *AM,* 246–62. Hayes's account of his travels in the Soviet Union offered in *AM* is somewhat sanitized when compared to the typewritten version found in his papers in the Detroit Public Library.

54. Hayes Papers, DPL. See Hayes's typewritten day-to-day journal from January 28 to March 1, 1928.

55. Ibid.

56. Ibid.

57. Ibid.

58. Harindranath Chattopadhyay (also known as "Herin") was a celebrated Indian actor, poet, and politician. Various biographical accounts do not explain his presence in the Soviet Union in the late 1920s. *AM* indicates that he was a little more than a wanderer. But further inquiry confirms that Harindranath came from a prominent family of artists, revolutionaries, and social activists. His brother Virendranath Chattopadhyay aligned himself with the Germans during World War I with the goal of forcing the British out of India. In the early 1920s, Viren (or "Chatto," as he was commonly known) went to the Soviet Union and aligned himself with the Communist Party (which probably accounts for how his brother Herin was in the USSR in the late 1920s with Hayes). Viren's political activism eventually led to his execution by the Soviet state in 1937 by the Stalin government. Herin's sister Sarojini Naidu was also a celebrated poet and social activist, as was Herin's wife, Kamaladevi Chattopadhyay, who was also a women's rights activist and social reformer. She and Herin had a son but eventually divorced. In his later years, Herin would become known as an actor in plays and in movies. It was through Herin that Hayes received an invitation to perform in India from Mahatma Gandhi (*AM,* 249). Hayes was prepared to make the trip, but Gandhi was arrested and imprisoned, causing Hayes to scrap the trip. There is no indication that Herin and Hayes maintained contact with each other after the Soviet Union meeting. Harindranath later became known as a

politician and an actor. In 1973 he received
the Padma Bhushan award (India's
third highest civilian award given by the
president).

59. Hayes Papers, DPL. See Hayes's
typewritten day-to-day journal from
January 28 to March 1, 1928.

60. Ibid.

61. In his detailed account, Hayes said
that he and Herin often took long walks
when they reached a new town. This relationship is somewhat complex, because
Herin shared the same room and train
berth with Hayes. This was a remarkable
gesture on Hayes's part for someone whom
he had just met.

62. Sullivan Papers.

63. Ibid.

64. Ibid.

65. Howard Jordan letters to Noël
Sullivan, Sullivan Papers. Jordan was also
writing Sullivan, informing him of his
movement with Hayes as well as his personal feelings for Sullivan. It is unclear if
there was a relationship between the two,
but some of the letters are very intimate
and romantic in nature.

66. Hayes Papers, DPL. See Hayes's
typewritten day-to-day journal from
January 28 to March 1, 1928.

67. Ibid.

68. Ibid.

69. Ibid. Also see *AM*, 249.

70. Hayes private papers, courtesy of
Afrika Hayes Lambe.

71. Sullivan Papers. In a letter to Noël
Sullivan, Howard Jordan tells him of
Hayes's brief return to New York to deal
with the "hated issue." The specifics of this
are unknown. He did go to Boston while
he was there.

72. Hayes private papers, courtesy of
Afrika Hayes Lambe. Sir Ofori Atta was
the first continental African to be knight-
ed by King George V. The spring 1928

knighting also gave the African traditional
ruler the opportunity to broadcast from
London to the citizens of his country. It is
not known if Hayes sang for the African
ruler when they met in London.

73. Hayes Papers, DPL. See letter dated
April 11, 1928.

74. Ibid.

75. Ibid.

76. Ibid.

77. Ibid.

78. Ibid.

79. Ibid.

80. Ibid.

81. Roland Hayes Collection, Boston
Public Library.

82. *New York Times,* November 16, 1928.

83. Hayes Papers, DPL See letter dated
January 21, 1930.

84. Ibid. See letter dated January 26,
1929. Also see Hayes private papers, courtesy of Afrika Hayes Lambe.

85. Hayes Papers, DPL. See letter dated
January 21, 1930.

86. Sullivan Papers.

87. Ibid.

88. Hayes Papers, DPL. See letter dated
November 20, 1929.

89. Ibid. See letters dated November 26
and December 18, 1929.

90. Ibid. See letters dated October 4
and December 5, 1929.

91. Ibid. See letter dated November
1929.

92. Sullivan Papers. See telegram dated
January 21, 1930.

93. Hayes Papers, DPL. See proclamation dated February 18, 1930.

94. Ibid. See letter dated November
16, 1930. It is not clear whom Roland was
referring to here as "My dearest." It could
have been a letter to Bertha in Europe, but
it is more likely to have been Alzada Mann,
who had begun to emerge prominently in
the singer's life.

95. The second wife of Robert Brante Hayes was named Margaret, as was his first wife, whom he divorced.

96. Hayes Papers, DPL. See letter dated December 21, 1930.

9. "HARD TRIALS, GREAT TRIBULATIONS" (1930–1935)

1. Hayes Papers of the Hayes Collection, Detroit Public Library (hereafter DPL). See letter dated July 27, 1930.

2. Ibid. See letter dated March 2, 1931.

3. Ibid. See letter dated March 5, 1931.

4. Ibid.

5. *Washington Post*, April 27, 1930, A3. Also see *Washington Post*, January 18, 1931, and January 25, 1931, respectively.

6. Keiler, *Marian Anderson*, 186.

7. P. Hayes, "White Artists Only." Also see Arsenault, *Sound of Freedom*, 92.

8. P. Hayes, "White Artists Only."

9. Ibid.

10. "Negro Spirituals Win Hayes Praise," *Washington Post*, February 1, 1931, M12.

11. Ibid.

12. Arsenault, *Sound of Freedom*, 91.

13. See Keiler, *Marian Anderson*, 186–211, for a more detailed discussion of the events leading to the Marian Anderson incident.

14. Ernest Kolowrat, taped interview with Bertha Colloredo-Mansfeld, Paris, 1978 (hereafter Kolowrat/Colloredo-Mansfeld interview).

15. Ibid.

16. This is a summation based on Kolowrat's interview with his aunt in Paris in 1978. The actual letter was kept by Hayes, who presumably lost or destroyed it.

17. It is likely that the countess went to Maddie and Joseph Salmon for financial assistance to travel back to St. Lary.

18. Kolowrat/Colloredo-Mansfeld interview.

19. Ibid.

20. Hayes private papers, courtesy of Afrika Hayes Lambe. Among the private papers were official forms indicating that Hayes was prepared to adopt baby Maya within months of her birth.

21. Because the countess saw neither Hayes nor the "other" woman, there is a strong probability that no one other than Hayes was present at the time. Informing the servants to deliver such a message could have been nothing more than a ploy to deter Bertha from attempting to enter the residence.

22. Helm, *Angel Mo' and Her Son, Roland Hayes*, 270 (hereafter *AM*).

23. Ibid.

24. Fradella, *Jack Johnson*.

25. Hayes would have also faced disdain among African Americans at the time who would have viewed him as a traitor to the race by being famous and going outside the race to marry.

26. Hayes private papers, courtesy of Afrika Hayes Lambe.

27. Ibid. Among these papers was a large envelope that had once been sealed (which was opened prior to our receiving this material). On the front of the envelope was the handwriting of the elderly Roland Hayes, "This envelope is to be opened ONLY by my – wife Helen Alzada Hayes – Otherwise, it must be destroyed without being opened by anyone [signed] Roland W. Hayes." As this envelope had been opened (and it cannot be ascertained whether it was done before or after Hayes's death) by the time it reached us in the spring of 2008, the recipient, presumably Alzada Hayes, apparently chose not to destroy its contents. The documents inside establish the birth and attempted "adoption" of Hayes and Bertha's daughter,

Maya. They also record how their daughter had been ruled as the illegitimate daughter of the Countess Colloredo-Mansfeld (although she was married to the count when the child was born) by a tribunal in Switzerland. Also found in the envelope were several letters written by Bertha to Hayes and his representative attempting to conceal their relationship in the late 1920s, as it had begun to appear in news accounts in Europe and the United States.

28. Sullivan Papers. In his August 1, 1931, letter to Sullivan, Hayes did not indicate that it was the result of financial reasons that he gave up the house in Paris but said it was simply a matter of inconvenience for him to try and maintain it.

29. Hayes Papers, DPL. See letter dated June 1931.

30. Kolowrat/Colloredo-Mansfeld interview.

31. Hayes Papers, DPL. See B. Watson business card.

32. Ibid. See letter dated October 16, 1932.

33. *AM,* 271.

34. The deceased Daisy Tapley might have also been a factor in Roland's idea of being raised up by the "eternal woman." Although there is no evidence to suggest that their relationship was anything more than platonic (as Daisy was in a domestic relationship with Minnie Brown), there is no question that she was a powerful female influence in his life. Yet another woman who played a pivotal role in Hayes's life would have been Jennie Robinson, his voice teacher from Fisk University. Although their relationship had at one point been antagonistic, Hayes credited her with raising him up from near illiteracy to give him a sound musical foundation, and he identified that negative encounter as one of the major epiphanies

in his life on his road to becoming a great artist.

35. Hayes Papers, DPL. See letter dated December 24, 1931.

36. Ibid.

37. Ibid. This information is also available in Hayes private papers, courtesy of Afrika Hayes Lambe.

38. *Boston Chronicle,* March 19, 1932.

39. Hayes private papers, courtesy of Afrika Hayes Lambe.

40. There was little evidence of any Mann family opposition to the developing love relationship between the first cousins Roland and Alzada. As he was taking care of her at his Brookline home and she apparently was looking after his well-being, little was said. Even family members were not immediately aware of the romantic development. Robert Brante, among others, indicated as much. When writing her, Roland addressed the envelope "Helen Alzada Mann." As Alzada had excellent clerical skills, among others, she became his official secretary. In official correspondence, he referred to her as his secretary, "H. A. Mann."

41. Hayes Papers, DPL.

42. Ibid.

43. Ibid.

44. Ibid. Sullivan sent Hayes a birthday greeting at the beginning of June, marking the occasion of Roland's forty-fifth birthday.

45. Sullivan Papers.

46. Hayes Papers, DPL.

47. Ibid. It is not known what is meant by "broadcast greetings." Prior to this, Roland had adamantly opposed the idea of broadcasting over the radio. His feelings were that it was not true art and that the technology distorted the vocal production so much as to make it unrecognizable.

48. Within a few years, Ormandy became the associate conductor of the

Philadelphia Orchestra and eventually replaced Stokowski as principal conductor, a position he kept for the next forty-four years.

49. Hayes Papers, DPL. See program dated November 25, 1932.

50. Ibid. See letter dated September 18, 1932.

51. Sullivan Papers. See letter dated August 1, 1931.

52. Hayes Papers, DPL. See letter dated December 14, 1932.

53. Ibid. See letter dated February 3, 1933.

54. Ibid.

55. Ibid. See letter dated February 4, 1933.

56. Emil Ludwig was a renowned German writer and biographer. He had also interviewed Joseph Stalin and Benito Mussolini in 1931 with the intent of developing their stories. It is unknown if he and Hayes actually met.

57. Hayes Papers, DPL. See letter dated February 4, 1933.

58. Ibid. See letter dated March 29, 1933, to cousin Cora, who was attempting to bring Hayes to Chattanooga for a concert.

59. Ibid. See letter dated April 24, 1933.

60. Ibid. See letter dated April 26, 1933.

61. Sullivan Papers. See letter dated March 16, 1933.

62. Hayes Papers, DPL. See letter dated March 27, 1933.

63. Ibid. See letter dated May 1, 1933.

64. Ibid.

65. Ibid. See letter dated May 6, 1933.

66. Ibid. See letter dated June 27, 1933. RKO had an interest in inserting parts of Hayes's story in the plot that the studio was developing about a story on Stephen Foster. Hayes declined such an idea, as he felt it would weaken the autobiographical account that he wanted to tell.

67. Ibid.

68. Ibid. See program dated August 3, 1933.

69. Ibid. See letter dated August 5, 1933.

70. Ibid. See letter dated August 8, 1933.

71. Ibid. See letter dated September 11, 1933.

72. This is the *official* birth date of Africa, but based on a letter dated November 2, 1932, there is a question about the baby's true birth date. Alzada had concluded that letter with "All our love . . . Africa and Mother," which meant that she was probably pregnant with Africa (Roland's second daughter) when she and Roland had married in February 1932. It would also explain all the secrecy surrounding their marriage. The child's middle name, "Fanzada" was a combination of "Fannie" and "Alzada."

73. Hayes Papers, DPL. See letters dated December 18, 1933.

74. Ibid.

75. Hayes private papers, courtesy of Afrika Hayes Lambe. The journal or newspaper in which this review appeared is not named.

76. Ibid.

77. *Boston Chronicle,* January 20, 1934.

78. Ibid.

79. Ibid.

80. *Pittsburgh Courier,* January 20, 1934.

81. Hayes Papers, DPL. See letter dated March 19, 1934.

82. Ibid. See letter dated March 20, 1934.

83. "Roland Hayes May Not Sing on Radio, for He Scorns Offering Art Cheaply," *New York Amsterdam News,* February 22, 1933.

84. Hayes Papers, DPL. See letter dated May 15, 1934.

85. Ibid. See letter dated April 28, 1934.

86. Ibid. See letter dated August 8, 1934.

87. Ibid.

88. Ibid. See letter dated October 30, 1934.

89. Ibid. See letter dated November 3, 1934.

90. Ibid. See letters dated November 6 and 15, 1934.

91. Ibid. See letter dated November 21, 1934.

92. Ibid.

93. This would include George Judd, Aaron Richmond, and Frank Andrews. It is not known when or how Ruth Cowan left Hayes's management "team."

94. Erlmann, *African Stars,* 112–55.

95. Hayes Papers, DPL. See letter dated January 16, 1935. Note there is an error in the date of the letter, which was corrected by the Hackley Collection personnel who processed the collection.

96. Ibid.

97. Ibid. See letter dated February 21, 1935.

98. Hayes private papers, courtesy of Afrika Hayes Lambe.

99. Hayes Papers, DPL. See letter dated April 12, 1935.

100. Ibid. See letter dated May 14, 1935.

101. Ibid. See several letters to this effect between July and November 1935.

10. RETURN TO EUROPE (1936–1942)

1. Hayes Papers of the Hayes Collection, Detroit Public Library (hereafter DPL). See letter dated May 30, 1935.

2. Ibid. See letter dated January 20, 1936.

3. Ibid. See letter dated January 19, 1936.

4. Ibid. See letter dated February 12, 1936.

5. *Washington Tribune,* February 4, 1936.

6. *Afro-American* (Baltimore), September 5, 1936.

7. Hayes Papers, DPL. See letter dated April 14, 1936.

8. Hayes had actually traveled to Canada in 1934. Given the quick and free access that Americans had to Canada at the time, many almost considered the country a part of the United States.

9. [Delaware?] *Journal and Guide,* March 21, 1936.

10. Hayes Papers, DPL. See letter dated November 12, 1936.

11. Ibid.

12. Ibid. See letter dated January [day not specified], 1937.

13. Ibid. See letter dated January 5, 1937. Also see Hayes's February 18, 1937, letter to Noël Sullivan in Sullivan Papers.

14. Hayes Papers, DPL. See letter dated January 5, 1937. Hayes's later estimates were considerably longer.

15. Ibid. See letter dated January 15, 1937.

16. Ibid. Presumably this was from the correspondence from the late 1930s.

17. Ibid.

18. Ibid.; Hayes private papers, courtesy of Afrika Hayes Lambe.

19. Hayes Papers, DPL. See letter dated January 11, 1937.

20. Ibid. See letter dated March 5, 1937.

21. Hayes private papers, courtesy of Afrika Hayes Lambe. Letter dated April 4, 1937.

22. Personal communication, April 2007.

23. Hayes Papers, DPL. See letter dated May 16, 1937. Roland was a secret supporter of the Abyssinia Affair boycott. Additional material located in Hayes private papers, courtesy of Afrika Hayes Lambe.

24. Hayes Papers, DPL. See letter from Kahn to Hayes, October 1937.

25. Hayes private papers, courtesy of Afrika Hayes Lambe.

26. Hayes Papers, DPL. See letter dated May 24, 1937. We are grateful to Katherine Blanche for identifying this letter as she was translating the French correspondence found in the collection.

27. Ibid. See several letters between Pieta and Soviet government concert officials between late April and early June 1937.

28. *New York Times,* October 10, 1937. The reviewer was somewhat understated in his evaluation of Hayes's performance and noted at the start of the review that, "since this recital was a benefit, detailed criticism would be out of place."

29. Hayes Papers, DPL. See letter dated October 12, 1937.

30. Ibid.

31. Ibid. See letter dated November 12, 1937.

32. Ibid. See letter dated November 23 and December [exact day unknown], 1937.

33. Management with Copley did not last very long because of his sudden death.

34. Hayes Papers, DPL. See letter dated January 28, 1938.

35. Ibid. See letter dated February 23, 1938.

36. Ibid.

37. Ibid. See letter dated March 8, 1938.

38. Ibid.

39. Ibid. See letter dated March 12, 1938.

40. Helm, *Angel Mo' and Her Son, Roland Hayes,* 286.

41. Ibid.

42. Hayes Papers, DPL. See the letter from Parham [without a specific date], 1938.

43. *New York Times,* September 21, 1938.

44. Personal communication, April 2007.

45. Sullivan Papers. See letter dated October 4, 1938.

46. Hayes Papers, DPL. See the letter from Monteux dated December 12, 1938.

47. Ibid. See letter dated March 17, 1939.

48. Ibid. See letter dated August 25, 1939.

49. This information was provided courtesy of Tim Brooks.

50. Among the other things that he recorded were "Maledetto sia l'aspetto" from *Scherzi musicali* (1632) by Monteverdi; "Eviva Rosa Bella" from *La Calamità de' cuori* by Galuppi; "Lungi da te ben mio" by Giovanni Battista Bononcini; "L'amour de moi," a French chanson of the thirteenth century; "Le rêve" ("En fermant les yeux") from *Manon* by Massenet; "It Was a Lover and His Lass" from *As You Like It* by Shakespeare/Roger Quilter; "Bist du bei mir" by J. S. Bach; and "Crucifixion" and "He Never Said a Mumberlin' Word," unaccompanied African American spirituals.

51. Ibid. See letter dated February 29, 1940.

52. Hayes Papers, DPL. See letter dated April 9, 1940. The letter was actually dictated to Bethune's assistant and signed "per Fannie B."

53. Hayes Papers, DPL. See the Stokowski letter dated December 8, 1939, and the Walter White letter dated December 18, 1939. Maestro Stokowski was a maverick in this area. Years later, he lived up to his promise to Walter White to use more African American artists when he gave an opportunity to a young singer, Shirley Carter (who became internationally renowned as "Shirley Verrett"), in 1960 when he appeared with the Philadelphia Orchestra after a nineteen-year absence. After signing her to sing with him and the Houston Symphony Orchestra (which he directed at the time), he had to rescind the offer because the orchestra board did not want to hire an African American singer. Carter's appearance with Stokowski in Philadelphia turned out to be a far more

prestigious engagement and was a major boost to her career.

54. Sullivan Papers. See letter dated May 3, 1940.

55. This information is courtesy of Tim Brooks.

56. Hayes private papers, courtesy of Afrika Hayes Lambe.

57. Hayes Papers, DPL.

58. Hayes private papers, courtesy of Afrika Hayes Lambe. See Maya's letter to Hayes dated January 1942.

59. Ibid.

60. Ibid.

61. Ibid. Although Maya's recollection was off by one year, she was referencing his 1937 concert at the Salle Gaveau.

62. Ibid.

63. Ibid. Bertha's letter to Hayes was dated December 25, 1941, and continued into January 1942. According to the note written by the countess, a photo was included in the envelope, but it was not present when we were given access to this material.

64. Ibid.

65. Ibid.

66. Ibid.

11. ROME, GEORGIA (1942)

1. *Time*, July 27, 1942.

2. Afrika Hayes Lambe, personal communication, April 2007.

3. Ibid. Lambe recalls the clerk specifically saying, "Niggers aren't allowed to sit under the fan."

4. *Time*, July 27, 1942.

5. Hayes Papers of the Hayes Collection, Detroit Public Library (hereafter DPL). See Alzada's official statement dated August 4, 1942.

6. Lambe, personal communication, April 2007.

7. Hayes Papers, DPL. See Alzada's official statement dated August 4, 1942.

8. Ibid. It was the practice in the American South to call African American women by their first name, regardless of their age or status, instead of by such titles as "Mrs." or "Miss."

9. *New York Times*, July 17, 1942.

10. Ibid.

11. Ibid.

12. Hayes Papers, DPL. See letter dated July 17, 1942.

13. Ibid. See telegram dated July 18, 1942.

14. Hayes private papers, courtesy of Afrika Hayes Lambe.

15. Hayes Papers, DPL. See letter dated July 28, 1942.

16. *Time*, July 27, 1942. This article recounted the fundamental highlights of the story but prefaced it with information about two previous racial incidents prior to the Hayes assault.

17. Hayes Papers, DPL. See letter dated July 25, 1942.

18. If Roland received negative mail, which certainly was a strong possibility, he seems to have discarded such communications.

19. It was the *Time* magazine story that reported that the governor's office said that Chief Harris should handle the case himself and the *New York Times* story that indicated the opposite.

20. Hayes Papers, DPL. See letter dated August 4, 1942.

21. *Time*, July 27, 1942.

22. Hayes Papers, DPL. See Walter White letter dated August 21, 1942.

23. There are several communications relating to this case to be found among the Hayes Papers at the Detroit Public Library in the folder "Rome, Georgia." Also, there are more sensitive documents relating to the Rome incident among the private Hayes papers made available to us by Afrika Hayes Lambe.

24. This issue became popularly known as the "Cocking Affair." The accrediting Southern Association of Colleges and Schools responded to Talmadge's interference by removing the Georgia state system's accreditation. This was one of the issues that led to Talmadge's 1942 defeat in his reelection bid. The "Cocking Affair" was subject of a 2007 opera by Michael Braz, *A Scholar under Siege.* Walter Cocking was eventually reinstated as the law school dean.

25. Although this statement was not in the Hayes official document, Afrika clearly remembers hearing it said.

26. Afrika Hayes Lambe recalled sitting on a bench outside of the cell where her parents were (personal communication, April 21, 2007). Hayes's written statement suggested that she was left alone in an outer lobby.

27. Hayes Papers, DPL. See letter dated August 4, 1942.

28. Ibid. See letter dated August 28, 1942.

29. Ibid. See letter dated August 26, 1942.

30. Ibid. See letter dated September 5, 1942.

31. Sullivan Papers. See letter dated September 6, 1942.

32. Hayes private papers, courtesy of Afrika Hayes Lambe. See letter dated September 17, 1942.

33. L. Hughes, "My America."

34. Ibid.

12. "I CAN TELL THE WORLD!" (1942–1950)

1. There are no communications between the singer and Helm that demonstrate the relationship prior to the late 1930s in the Hayes Papers of the Hayes Collection in the Detroit Public Library (hereafter DPL) or among the private papers of Afrika Hayes Lambe.

2. Helm, *Angel Mo' and Her Son, Roland Hayes,* 176 (hereafter *AM*).

3. Ibid. Although it is a letter referenced in this section (see p. 176), the context does not even hint at Jesse's demise, which Hayes could have kept from Helm.

4. Ibid., 149–51.

5. Ibid.

6. Ibid., 197–99.

7. Sullivan Papers. See letter dated October 21, 1942.

8. Ibid.

9. In Hayes's personal letter to Walter White, he proposed that he turn Angelmo Farm over to the U.S. Department of Agriculture for the duration of the war. He further proposed that because of the animal husbandry techniques that had been experimented with on the land, among other groundbreaking activities, the government might be interested in developing it and seeing what the African American workers were capable of. He did stipulate that if the offer was accepted, the farm would come under the direct supervision of the federal government with no Georgian state or county government association or interference at all. Hayes Papers, DPL. See letter to Walter White dated October 29, 1942.

10. Ibid. See letter from *Atlantic Monthly Press* dated October 19, 1942.

11. Ibid. See letter from Carver dated November 20, 1942.

12. Hayes private papers, courtesy of Afrika Hayes Lambe. See letter dated May 17, 1943.

13. Hayes Papers, DPL. See letter to Robert Hayes letter dated September 10, 1943.

14. Sullivan Papers. See letter dated September 10, 1943.

15. Hayes Papers, DPL. See letter dated September 17, 1943.

16. Hayes private papers, courtesy of Afrika Hayes Lambe. See Royal Albert Hall playbill, dated September 28, 1943.

17. *Afro-American* (Baltimore), October 9, 1943.

18. Hayes private papers, courtesy of Afrika Hayes Lambe. See letter dated October [date unspecified], 1943.

19. Royal Albert Hall playbill, September 28, 1943.

20. Ibid.

21. Hayes Papers, DPL. See Hayes's "Power" reflection dated September 29, 1943, after the second London performance. In this personal reflection, Hayes commented that these gallant African American singing soldiers, if given the right equipment and motivation, would gladly defend the United States with total commitment.

22. *Daily Express,* September 30, 1943.

23. "Negroes Sing in London," *New York Times,* September 29, 1943.

24. "Coloured Soldiers Give a Concert at the Albert Hall," *Picture Post Magazine,* October 16, 1943, 18. A white soldier from Rome, Georgia, Hiram Swain, wrote Roland while he was in England and attempted to explain to the tenor that they had met once before on his farm when Swain had driven a bank cashier from Rome to Angelmo Farm some years earlier. Swain apologized for not being able to attend the singer's concert in London.

25. Ibid., 19.

26. *Afro-American* (Baltimore), November 27, 1943.

27. Traditionally, "Paddy" was a pejorative term for persons of Irish descent, but in this instance it was used to refer to all of the European American troops. The African American soldiers were called by the derogatory term "Spook."

28. G. Smith, *When Jim Crow Met John Bull.* Others who were called on in a similar capacity were General Benjamin O. Davis Sr., Lena Horne, and the boxer Joe Louis. We are grateful to Jeff Green for the information.

29. Despite efforts, we could find no other information about the U.S. officer.

30. Hayes Papers, DPL. See letter to Ambassador Winant dated November 10, 1943.

31. This was yet another manifestation of Hayes's racial accommodationist views, which were similar to those advanced by Booker T. Washington from the 1910s.

32. Hayes Papers, DPL. See letter to Ambassador Winant dated November 10, 1943.

33. Ibid. See letter to Eleanor Roosevelt dated November 8, 1943.

34. Ibid.

35. Ibid. See letter from Eleanor Roosevelt dated November 23, 1943.

36. Sullivan Papers. See letter dated December 18, 1943. In this letter to Sullivan, Hayes also described the destruction of various parts of London and other parts of the country by the German bombing campaign.

37. Brooks et al., "Military," 1469.

38. *Afro-American* (Baltimore), October 16, 1943.

39. Hayes Papers, DPL.

40. Olin Downes, "Recital by Hayes Delights the Audience," *New York Times,* October 16, 1944.

41. It is not likely that Hayes reached out to Madeleine, the wife of Joseph Salmon, after hearing of his death. We are of the opinion that he regretted not mending fences with his early French benefactor.

42. Hayes private papers, courtesy of Afrika Hayes Lambe.

43. Roland Hayes as told to Laura Haddock, "'My Song Is Nothing!' Roland Hayes Calls His Voice the Tool of a More Important Mission – Racial Harmony," *Christian Science Monitor,* November 22, 1947, 6.

44. Ibid. This opinion also smacks of the elitist view that he expressed about other African American singers, particularly Paul Robeson and Julius Bledsoe. He acknowledged their "natural talent" but did not consider them to be in his category because they had not refined their talent as he had (i.e., by learning the languages and about the lives of the composers and such). He believed Marian Anderson had done this.

45. "Roland Hayes Observes an Anniversary," *Christian Science Monitor,* November 17, 1947.

46. This information is courtesy of Tim Brooks.

47. Hayes, *My Songs.*

48. Ibid., foreword. In other settings, we have maintained that it was Roland who coined the term "Aframerican," but subsequent inquiries make clear that the term was used as early as the late nineteenth century, if sparingly.

49. Ibid., 57.

50. Van Vechten, "Soul of a People Lifted in Song."

51. Rudolph Elie, "American Spirituals Given New Settings by Roland Hayes" (review), *Boston Herald,* November 21, 1948. Also see "Point, Counterpoint" (review), *Book Review,* December 19, 1948.

52. "France Honors New Englanders," *Boston Herald,* May 21, 1949.

53. Hayes Papers, DPL. This communication is undated, but it was apparently sent to someone, as it was with the other correspondence regarding the Kurt Weil/ Maxwell Anderson work.

54. The role of Stephen Kumalo was portrayed by a younger and more dashing, physically imposing baritone, Todd Duncan. Apparently, Weil and Anderson had envisioned Paul Robeson for the role, but when he was unavailable they briefly considered Hayes, although the singing part had been written for a voice lower than his. Todd Duncan was no newcomer to Broadway at the time. He had premiered the role of Porgy in the Gershwin opera *Porgy and Bess,* which had also been produced by Rouben Mamoulian.

55. Sullivan Papers. See letter dated June 9, 1949.

56. Kolowrat, *Confessions,* 179.

57. Ibid.

58. Ibid., 180.

59. Ibid.

60. Sullivan Papers. See letter dated February 23, 1950.

61. This statement is based on an examination of the Hayes Papers in the Hackley Collection, DPL; the private papers of Hayes in the Boston Public Library's Hayes Collection; and the Hayes private papers courtesy of Afrika Hayes Lambe. If there was information to support Hayes's assertion of his being courted by Kurda, Alan Paton, or anyone else regarding the movie, it has been lost.

62. Boston University press bulletin no. 49–157, April 25, 1950, in Hayes private papers, courtesy of Afrika Hayes Lambe.

13. STRUGGLES IN REMAINING RELEVANT (1950–1959)

1. Hayes Papers of the Hayes Collection, Detroit Public Library (hereafter DPL). See Quilter letter dated September 7, 1951.

2. Ibid. See Hayes letter, undated, September 1951.

3. Langfield, *Roger Quilter, 1877–1953.*

4. Hayes private papers, courtesy of Afrika Hayes Lambe. See letter from Warren Freeman about the establishment of the Roland Hayes Fund dated June 12, 1951.

5. Ibid. See letter from Hayes Fund dated December 31, 1951.

6. Ibid. See letter from Hayes to Harold Case dated January 10, 1952.

7. Sullivan Papers. See letter dated March 25, 1952.

8. Hayes Papers, DPL. See Hayes letter to Arthur Knight, dated February 19, 1952, and Knight's February 25 response.

9. Knight, "Roland Hayes."

10. Hayes Papers, DPL. See Hayes letter to Dwight D. Eisenhower dated January 19, 1953.

11. Ibid. See letter from Frieda Rothe dated April 23, 1953.

12. Ibid. See letter from Caesar Searchinger dated October 5, 1953.

13. The Columbia Artist Agency, which had booked Carnegie Hall for Hayes for his November 29, 1953, recital, had to pursue him for several months before receiving the $418 that it cost to reserve the recital hall for Hayes.

14. Hayes Papers, DPL. See letter from Charles J. Harris dated November 24, 1953.

15. Ibid. See Hayes letter to Charles J. Harris dated December 19, 1953.

16. Ibid. See Hayes letter to Nora Douglas Holt dated February 23, 1954, and her response to him dated February 25, 1954.

17. Ibid. See Hayes letter to Pablo Casals dated March 3, 1954.

18. Hayes private papers, courtesy of Afrika Hayes Lambe.

19. Sullivan Papers. See letter dated May 5, 1954.

20. Ibid. See letter dated June 20, 1954.

21. Ibid. If this was yet another of Hayes's exaggerations, it is not clear. He rarely, if ever, wrote to anyone that he had delivered a poor performance and that the audience was anything other than truly appreciative.

22. This section is based on information we obtained from interviewing Drs. Igor and Grichka Bogdanoff in Paris, October 15, 2008 (hereafter Bogdanoff interview). See also Ernest Kolowrat, taped interview with Bertha Colloredo-Mansfeld, Paris, 1978 (hereafter Kolowrat/Colloredo-Mansfeld interview).

23. Kolowrat/Colloredo-Mansfeld interview.

24. Ibid.

25. Bogdanoff interview.

26. Helm, *Angel Mo' and Her Son, Roland Hayes,* 199.

27. Kolowrat/Colloredo-Mansfeld interview.

28. Ibid.

29. Material courtesy of Patricia A. Murray, the granddaughter of Charles Harris, August 2013.

30. Our assumption is that Edward Rumley was a lawyer. Efforts to discover more information about him and his background did not yield significant findings.

31. Hayes Papers, DPL. See Hayes letter from Edward Rumley to Hayes dated August 17, 1954.

32. Ibid. See Hayes letter to Robert Brante Hayes dated October 24, 1954.

33. This information was based on an interview with Roland Robert, William, and Toussaint Hayes, August 2007, in Calhoun, Georgia. We are grateful for this firsthand account of Robert Brante. In the conversation with the brothers, they referred to one another as "Brother Robert," "Brother William," and "Brother Toussaint" and to Robert Brante as "Father."

34. Ibid.

35. Hayes Papers, DPL. See Hayes letter to Doug and Dorothy Henderson dated January 3, 1955.

36. Ibid. See Hayes letter to William Lane dated February 9, 1955.

37. Ibid. See Hayes letter to Pablo Casals dated February 14, 1955.

38. Ibid. See Casals letter to Hayes dated March 2, 1955.

39. Ibid. See Hayes letter to Francis Robinson dated March 8, 1955.

40. Ibid. See Hayes letter to Pierre Monteux dated March 9, 1955.

41. Ibid. See Monteux letter to Hayes dated March 14, 1955.

42. "Roland Hayes," *Afro Magazine,* October 25, 1955, 6.

43. Sullivan Papers. See letter dated August 29, 1956.

44. Ibid.

45. Hayes Papers, DPL. See telegram to Hayes dated September 16, 1956.

46. Ibid. See handwritten note from Hayes to Sullivan family dated September 16, 1956.

47. Hayes private papers, courtesy of Afrika Hayes Lambe.

48. Hayes Papers, DPL. See letter from Ben Duniway, attorney to Hayes, dated October 16, 1956.

49. Ibid. See several letters between Hayes and Karlis Osis, February 1, 1957. Some of the letters in this exchange were undated. Just how Fannie appeared at the séance and what she communicated could not be discerned from the letters.

50. Dr. Osis produced several works on the subject of near-death and out-of-body experiences. See Osis, "Apparitions Old and New," 74–86. Also see Osis and Haraldsson, *At the Hour of Death.*

51. Hayes Papers, DPL. See letter from Hayes to Sullivan attorney dated May 13, 1957, and the response dated May 17, 1957.

52. As of this writing, Daniel Comegys is the only former student of Roland Hayes whom we were able to locate. Comegys provided us with the most comprehensive information about the tenor's late career, as well as about his teaching methods and singing philosophy.

14. "I WANNA GO HOME" (1960–1977)

1. Daniel Comegys, personal communication, November 7, 2007.

2. Ibid.

3. Although he claimed several arrangements as his, Hayes's piano playing skills were limited, and the more likely scenario is that the arrangements were co-ventures between him and Percival Parham or perhaps one of his other accompanists. The pianism in some of the arrangements was far too sophisticated for Hayes's keyboard abilities.

4. Daniel Comegys, personal communication.

5. Hayes Papers of the Hayes Collection, Detroit Public Library (hereafter DPL).

6. Hayes private papers, courtesy of Afrika Hayes Lambe.

7. Daniel Comegys, personal communication.

8. Hayes private papers, courtesy of Afrika Hayes Lambe.

9. Hayes Papers, DPL. See letter from Wesley Hotchkiss to Hayes dated June 5, 1962.

10. Hayes private papers, courtesy of Afrika Hayes Lambe. See Hayes letter to Leontyne Price dated November 11, 1962.

11. Hayes Papers, DPL. See letter from W. Madden dated June 10, 1962. After Tapley's death, it is not known what happened to Minnie Brown. Her singing career did not flourish, and she probably went into obscurity.

12. Ibid. Hayes spoke with an unnamed interviewer the day after his Carnegie Hall performance in New York. Although the date on the reel-to-reel tape indicated May 23, 1962, the conversation between Hayes and the interviewer made clear that it took place the day after his New York recital (which would have been June 4, 1962). The information on the tape also indicated that the interviewer was Alix Williamson, a well-known classical music publicist who had clients such as Frederica von Stade and Richard Tucker. However, Williamson was a woman, and the person on the tape interviewing Hayes was a man. Among those who came backstage to greet Hayes after the Sunday afternoon concert was a twenty-eight-year-old George Shirley, the up-and-coming tenor who had made a highly anticipated Metropolitan Opera House debut the year before. Throughout the 1960s and early 1970s, Shirley sang several leading roles with the company. He told Hayes on this occasion that his parents had taken him to see the older tenor in performance when he was a young boy in Detroit. Shirley interviewed Hayes in the mid-1970s at his Brookline home and told Hayes that his performance had inspired him to pursue a musical career. George Shirley, personal communication, November 2012.

13. Hayes Papers, DPL. See letter to Richmond Barthé dated March 18, 1963.

14. On several occasions they had to rely on Hayes for financial assistance. The couple also at times ran afoul of the guidelines that he had given them for the repayment of their debt.

15. Afrika Hayes Lambe, personal communication, April 2007. A formal wedding announcement issued from Roland and Alzada Hayes indicates Afrika and Joseph Lambe were married in Baltimore in January 1963. Hayes private papers, courtesy of Afrika Hayes Lambe.

16. Hayes Papers, DPL. See letter to Afrika dated March 18, 1963.

17. Ibid. See letter from Roland Shaine to Hayes dated May 5, 1971. Also see Jennifer Hildebrand, "Two Souls, Two Thoughts, Two Unreconciled Strivings: The Sound of Double Consciousness in Roland Hayes's Early Career," *Black Music Research Journal* 30, no. 2 (Fall 2010): 273–302.

18. Hayes Papers, DPL.

19. Hayes private papers, courtesy of Afrika Hayes Lambe. See letter to R. Walter dated September 30, 1966.

20. Clifford Barnes, "'Good Room' for a Father and a Daughter," *Christian Science Monitor*, November 8, 1966. This review was more charitable of Afrika's performance. It also commented on her singing to her eight-month-old daughter, who was in the audience. Also see Daniel Rosen, "Two Hayeses in Concert at Jordan Hall," *Boston Herald*, November 8, 1966. The reviewer once again was laudatory of Hayes while referring to Afrika's singing as "a shade on the coarse side." The *Boston Globe* reviewer, Michael Steinberg, November 8, 1966, also lavished praise on Hayes but said Afrika "had a voice of animal excitement.... [There] is some insecurity about high notes and Miss Hayes has a tendency to pull out all the stops too soon."

21. Hayes private papers, courtesy of Afrika Hayes Lambe. See letter to R. Bleecker dated January 7, 1967. The letter from Ruth Bleecker, who was a curator at the Boston Public Library, was seeking a donation of some of his memorabilia.

22. Hayes Papers, DPL. See letter to Afrika Lambe dated October 14, 1966.

23. Ibid.

24. Louis Speyer played in the Boston Symphony between 1919 and 1965. Just three years younger than Hayes, he had been a member of the symphony orchestra when Hayes made his historic debut in 1923 under the direction of Maestro Monteux. On the occasion on Hayes's eightieth birthday, Speyer commented that he had never been so moved by a performance as he had been by Hayes's interpretation of the Berlioz *L'Enfance du Christ*. Hayes private papers, courtesy of Afrika Hayes Lambe.

25. Hayes Papers, DPL. See Friends of Roland Hayes stationery and letter dated March 6, 1967.

26. Ibid. See letter from Charles Harris to Hayes dated April 4, 1967.

27. Although Anderson's "official" age was sixty-five, it became well known that she had taken five years off and was, in fact, ten years young than Hayes instead of the fifteen years that she held out to the world.

28. Hayes private papers, courtesy of Afrika Hayes Lambe.

29. Hayes Papers, DPL. See letter from Hayes to William Lane dated December 11, 1967. The agreement between Hayes and Lane was signed in January 1956, but Lane had begun working with Hayes the year before. Hayes had routinely "tested" out a manager before he signed an exclusive agreement.

30. Ibid. See letter waiver signed by W. Lane dated June 5, 1969. Apart from the 1969 release, there were no more communications from William Lane to Hayes.

31. Ibid. See letter from Hayes to Dr. Thompson dated July 8, 1968.

32. Daniel Comegys, personal communication. In the interview, Comegys said that Hayes told him, "My people don't ask for me anymore, but I still have a message to deliver."

33. Hayes Papers, DPL. See letter from Hayes to Dana S. Creal dated December 9, 1970.

34. Afrika Hayes Lambe, personal communication, March 2007.

35. Zaida Christine Lambe, personal communication, July 16, 2009.

36. Afrika Hayes Lambe, personal communication, March 2007

37. Ibid.

38. Zaida Christine Lambe, personal communication. Afrika Hayes Lambe described the funeral of Joseph Lambe in very real terms. She explained to her daughters that they needed to cry while they were in Brookline, but when they went to Durham to funeralize her late former husband, they must conduct themselves with dignity and restraint.

39. Ibid.

40. Afrika Hayes Lambe, personal communication.

41. Hayes private papers, courtesy of Afrika Hayes Lambe. This information was listed on the estate tax records.

42. Associated Press, January 1, 1977.

43. Hayes Papers, DPL. The are numerous letters, notes, and telegrams of condolences.

44. Charles J. Harris was two years older than Roland. Because of his incessant concern about his health (i.e., not eating white sugar and preferring raw vegetables over cooked ones, among other dietary practices), he lived to be 103 years old. He frequently offered Roland, among others, advice about his health and diet regimen, including personalities like Mahalia Jackson. Patricia A. Murray, personal communication, November 14, 2012.

45. Hayes private papers, courtesy of Afrika Hayes Lambe.

EPILOGUE

1. Igor and Grichka Bogdanoff, interview, Paris, October 15, 2008 (hereafter Bogdanoff interview).

2. Ernest Kolowrat, taped interview with Bertha Colloredo-Mansfeld, Paris, 1978 (hereafter Kolowrat/Colloredo-Mansfeld interview).

3. Ibid.

4. Contributing to the instability in Maya's marriage was the fact that she had strayed outside the relationship and had two children with another man before returning to the marriage.

5. Kolowrat, *Confessions*, 156.

6. Ibid., 182. See also Maya's letter to Hayes dated January 1942 in Hayes private papers, courtesy of Afrika Hayes Lambe. When we spoke with Igor Bogdanoff's daughters in Paris (Maya's granddaughters), they were more interested to know about the Native American part of their heritage vis-à-vis Hayes than the much stronger African American blood that they shared in common with him.

7. Kolowrat, *Confessions*, 182.

8. Igor Bogdanoff, personal communication, May 2008.

9. Kolowrat, *Confessions*, 182.

10. Ernest Kolowrat, personal communication, January 2009. Kolowrat's meeting with his aunt Bertha in many ways was pivotal to creating a multidimensional picture of the Roland Hayes story. The account of the meeting between Kolowrat and Hayes is based on a close adaptation of Kolowrat's written unpublished record he made shortly after the visit. We are grateful to Ernest Kolowrat for making this encounter available to us.

11. Kolowrat, *Confessions*, 151.

12. No doubt an exaggeration on the part of the countess.

13. Kolowrat/Colloredo-Mansfeld interview.

14. Kolowrat, personal communication, January 2009.

15. Kolowrat, written communication regarding his 1969 meeting with Hayes. It was perhaps after this encounter with Kolowrat that Hayes assembled all of the papers documenting his relationship with the countess and the birth of their child and the communications from her asking his lawyer to deny the existence of such a relationship. The envelope was sealed and was not to be read by anyone other than his wife, Alzada.

16. Kenneth Overbye, "Are They a) Geniuses or b) Jokers? French Physicists' Cosmic Theory Creates a Big Bang of Its Own," *New York Times*, November 9, 2002. Their fame, however, did not come without controversy. In the mid-1990s, both brothers began to pursue doctorates initially at the University of Bordeaux but moved to the University of Burgundy. On the social scene, Igor recently remarried a direct descendant of Louis XIV, Amélie de Bourbon-Parme; the wedding was held in her ancestors' castle, today a fabled national monument, Chateau Chambord. Like their grandmother, the twins have encountered financial difficulty in their efforts to sustain a storybook medieval chateau not far from the one Issten had lost, a luxurious townhouse in Paris, and a late-model jet helicopter of their own. Their father (Maya's husband), Yuri Bogdanoff, passed away in 2012.

17. Kolowrat, *Confessions*, 399–402.

18. Ibid., 401.

19. Ibid., 400.

20. Ibid., 400–401.

21. Ibid., 402.

22. Bogdanoff interview. This belief on the part of the twin brothers was their personally expressed view.

23. Kolowrat, *Confessions*, 179.

24. Ibid., 403.

25. "Interview Afrika Hayes: Growing Up with Roland Hayes," *Fidelio* 3, no. 2 (Summer 1994): 3.

26. Among the productions that Afrika Lambe sang in were Verdi's *Aida* and Bellini's *Norma,* both of which starred Shirley Verrett.

27. "Interview Afrika Hayes: Growing Up with Roland Hayes." Hayden's materials were donated to Afrika Hayes Lambe and eventually to the E. Azalia Hackley Collection in Detroit. This information was confirmed in a telephone conversation with Professor Hayden in May 2009.

28. Despite several efforts, we were unable to locate specific biographical information on Reginald Boardman. It is assumed that he is deceased as of this writing.

29. In addition to George Shirley and the late William Warfield, Paul Spencer Adkins interviewed the late Todd Duncan for the documentary. Because of Duncan's declining eyesight, however, he refused permission to have his interview aired. Marian Anderson was also scheduled to participate in the program but was ill and had to cancel her involvement. The executive producer was Deborah Mims. Paul Spencer Adkins, personal communication, September 3, 2012.

30. Geoff Gehman, "*Lilacs* Reveals a Composer's Life," *Morning Call,* February 21, 1999. Walker's mother, an ardent admirer of Hayes, encouraged the teenage Walker to hear the singer in concert in his native Washington, D.C.

31. Zaida Christine Lambe, personal communication, July 16, 2009.

32. Ibid.

33. Erika Lambe, personal communication, July 18, 2009.

34. Maurice Wheeler, personal communication, April 12, 2013.

35. We are aware of the award being given out only once so far, however.

36. Detroit Public Library, "Detroit Public Library's E. Azalia Hackley Collection Concert Features Patrice Rushen Musical Score," February 7, 2014, press release.

37. Bogdanoff interview.

Bibliography

MANUSCRIPT COLLECTIONS,
ARCHIVES, AND LIBRARIES

Bethune, Mary McLeod, Papers. 1922–1955. Bethune-Cookman College Collection. Bethune University, Daytona Beach, Fla.

Brown, Lawrence, Papers. Schomburg Collection. New York Public Library.

James Cabell Library. Virginia Commonwealth University. Richmond.

Du Bois, W. E. B., Papers. Special Collections and University Archives. University of Massachusetts Amherst Libraries.

Fisk University Special Collections. Nashville, Tenn.

Hayes, Roland, Collection. Boston Public Library.

Hayes, Roland, Papers. E. Azalia Hackley Collection of African Americans in the Performing Arts. Detroit Public Library.

Lawrence, William, Papers. College of Charleston, S.C.

Library of Virginia. Richmond.

Maryland Historical Society. Baltimore.

Moorland-Spingarn Research Center. Howard University, Washington, D.C.

NAACP Papers. Library of Congress, Washington, D.C.

Schomburg Center for Research in Black Culture. New York Public Library.

Sullivan, Noël, Papers. Bancroft Collection. Bancroft Library. University of California, Berkeley.

University of Wisconsin, Madison.

Virginia State University Library. Petersburg.

West Sussex County Library. United Kingdom.

INTERVIEWS CONDUCTED
BY AUTHORS

Paul Spencer Adkins
Grichka Bogdanoff
Igor Bogdanoff
Avery Brooks
Tim Brooks
Joyce Brooks Brown
Daniel Comegys
Philomena Scotch Coste
Monique Symphorien David
Mattiwilda Dobbs
Simon Estes
Joseph James Evans Jr. (deceased)
Nicole Fournier (deceased)
Jeffrey Green
James Harkless
Robert Hayden
Roland Robert Hayes Jr.
Toussaint Hayes
William Hayes
Erika Lambe Holland

Brenda Jeffers
Ernest Kolowrat
Afrika Hayes Lambe
Zaida Lambe
Valerie Langfield
Ben Matthews (deceased)
Patricia A. Murray
Odetta (deceased)
Willis Patterson
John Patton (deceased)
George Shirley
Alice Mann Simpkins
Edward Simpkins
Edgar A. Toppins (deceased)
Patricia Turner (deceased)
Marie Turner-Wright
Shirley Verrett (deceased)
William Warfield (deceased)
Maurice Wheeler
Edna Williams (deceased)
Barbara Wright-Pryor

PERIODICALS

African and Orient Review
Afro-American (Baltimore and Washington editions)
Afro-American Ledger (forerunner to *Afro-American*)
American Magazine
Amsterdam News
Atlanta Daily Word
Atlantic Monthly Press
Berliner Montag Post
Black Music Research Journal
Boston Chronicle
Boston Globe
Boston Herald
Boston Sunday Post
Boston Transcript
Chattanooga Times
Chicago Defender
Christian Science Monitor
The Crisis
Daily Express (London)
Daily Telegraph (London)

Daily Washington American
Evening Gazette (Xenia, Ohio)
Fidelio
Fisk University News
Fitchburg (Mass.) Daily Sentinel
Gay and Lesbian Humanist
Guideposts
Indianapolis Recorder
Issvestya (Soviet Union)
Journal and Guide (Delaware)
Musical America
Musical Times
Nashville Globe
New York Amsterdam News
New York Evening Sun
New York Times
New York World
Philadelphia Public Ledger
Philadelphia Record
Phylon
Picture Post Magazine (London)
Pittsburgh Courier
Pravda (Moscow)
San Francisco Call
Time
Times (London)
Virchirniaya (Moscow)
Washington Daily American
Washington Post
Washington Tribune
West Africa Magazine (London)
Wiener Allgemeine Zeignung (Berlin)
Wiener Morgen Zeitung (Berlin)

BOOKS AND ARTICLES

Abbott, Lynn. "'Play that Barber Shop Chord': A Case for the African-American Origin of Barbershop Harmony." *American Music* 10, no. 3 (1992): 289–325.
Adejumobi, Saheed A. "The Pan African Congress." In *Organizing Black America: An Encyclopedia of African American Associations,* edited by Nina Mjagkij. New York: Garland, 2001.

Agnew, Hugh Lecaine. *The Czechs and the Lands of the Bohemian Crown*. Stanford: Hoover Institution Press, 2004.

Anderson, William L., ed. *Cherokee Removal: Before and After*. Athens: University of Georgia Press, 1991.

Aptheker, Bettina. "Review of *Race Woman: The Lives of Shirley Graham Du Bois*, by Gerald Horne." *Women's Review of Books* 18, no. 7 (April 2001): 9–10.

Arsenault, Raymond. *The Sound of Freedom: Marian Anderson, the Lincoln Memorial, and the Concert That Awakened America*. New York: Bloomsbury Press, 2009.

Badger, R. Reid. "James Reese Europe and the Prehistory of Jazz." *American Music* 7, no. 1 (1989): 48–67.

———. *A Life in Ragtime*. New York: Oxford University Press, 1995.

Bardolph, Richard. "The Distinguished Negro in America, 1770–1936." *American Historical Review* 60, no. 3 (April 1955): 527–47.

———. "The Negro in *Who's Who in America*, 1936–1955." *Journal of Negro History* 42, no. 4 (October 1957): 261–82.

Barron, Mary Jo Sanna. "In Retrospect: Bessie Jones; Singing for the Ancestors." *Black Perspective in Music* 13, no. 1 (Spring 1985): 91–114.

Beilke, Jayne R. "The Changing Emphasis of the Rosenwald Fellowship Program, 1928–1948." *Journal of Negro Education* 66, no. 1 (Winter 1997): 3–15.

Belles, A. Gilbert. "The College Faculty, the Negro Scholar, and the Julius Rosenwald Fund." *Journal of Negro History* 54, no. 4 (October 1969): 383–92.

Benjamin, Ionie. *The Black Press in Britain*. London: Trentham Books, 1995.

Boas, Franz, and C. Kamba Simango. *Tales and Proverbs of the Vandau of Portuguese South Africa*. Columbus, Ohio: American Folk-Lore Society, 1922.

Boyle, Sheila Tully, and Andrew Bunie. *Paul Robeson: The Years of Promise and Achievement*. Amherst: University of Massachusetts Press, 2001.

Brignano, Russell C. "Autobiographical Books by Black Americans: A Bibliography of Works Written since the Civil War." *Negro American Literature Forum* 7, no. 4 (Winter 1973): 148–56.

Brooks, Christopher A., et al. "Military." In *African American Almanac*, 11th ed., edited by Christopher A. Brooks, 1469. Farmington Hills, Mich.: Cengage/Gale Publishers, 2011.

Brooks, Tim. *Lost Sounds: Blacks and the Birth of the Recording Industry, 1890–1919*. Chicago: University of Illinois Press, 2004.

———. "'Might Take One Disc of This Trash as a Novelty': Early Recordings by the Fisk Jubilee Singers and the Popularization of 'Negro Folk Music.'" *American Music* 18, no. 3 (2000): 278–316.

Brown, Sterling A. *A Son's Return: Selected Essays of Sterling A. Brown*. Boston: Northeastern University Press, 1996.

Buck, Christopher. *Alain Locke: Faith and Philosophy*. Los Angeles: Kalimat Press, 2005.

Burlin, Natalie Curtis. *Songs and Tales from the Dark Continent: Recorded from the Singing and Sayings of C. Kamba Simango, Ndau Tribe, Portuguese East Africa and Madikane Cele, Zulu Tribe, Natal, Zululand, South Africa*. New York: G. Schirmer, 1920.

Campbell, Clarice T. *Civil Rights Chronicle: Letters from the South*. Jackson: University Press of Mississippi, 1997.

Canarina, John. *Pierre Monteux, Maître*. Newark, N.J.: Amadeus Press, 2003.

Carby, Hazel V. *Race Men*. Cambridge, Mass.: Harvard University Press, 1998.

Carter, Marva Griffin. "Roland Hayes: Expressor of the Soul in Song (1887–1977)." *Black Perspective in Music* 5, no. 2 (Autumn 1977): 188–220.

Chafe, William H. "Presidential Address: 'The Gods Bring Threads to Webs Begun.'" *Journal of American History* 86, no. 4 (March 2000): 1531–51.

Cheatham, Wallace McClain, and Sylvia Lee. "Lady Sylvia Speaks." *Black Music Research Journal* 16, no. 1 (Spring 1996): 183–213.

Clayton, Buck, and Nancy Miller Elliott. *Buck Clayton's Jazz World.* New York: Oxford University Press, 1986.

Contee, Clarence G. "The 'Status' of the Pan-African Association of 1921: A Document." *African Historical Studies* 3, no. 2 (1970): 409–17.

Cook, Mercer. "The Negro Spiritual Goes to France." *Music Educators Journal* 40, no. 5 (April–May 1954): 42–44, 48.

Cooper, Michael. *Slave Spirituals and the Jubilee Singers.* New York: Houghton Mifflin, 2001.

Dalfiume, Richard M. "The 'Forgotten Years' of the Negro Revolution." *Journal of American History* 55, no. 1 (June 1968): 90–106.

de Lerma, Dominique-Rene, Doreene McKenzie, and Leroy Vlaun. "A Concordance of Scores and Recordings of Music by Black Composers." *Black Music Research Journal* 4 (1984): 60–140.

Deutsch, Monroe E. "Equality in Life as Well as in Death." *Journal of Negro Education* 23, no. 4 (Autumn 1954): 496–501.

Duberman, Martin Bauml. *Paul Robeson.* New York: Alfred A. Knopf, 1988.

Duffield, Ian. "Duse Mohammed Ali: Afro-Asian Solidarity and Pan-Africanism in Early Twentieth-Century London." In *Essays on the History of Blacks in Britain,* edited by I. Duffield and J. S. Gundara. Aldershot, U.K.: Avebury, 1992.

Dyer, Richard. "A Legacy Lost? Roland Hayes Recordings Should Be Preserved, but Nobody Seems to Be Interested." *Boston Sunday Globe,* July 1, 1969.

Embree, Edwin R. *American Negroes.* New York: John Day, 1942.

Erlmann, Veit. *African Stars: Studies in Black South African Performance.* Chicago: University of Chicago Press, 1991.

Evans, Robert, John Weston, and Mark Cornwall. *Czechoslovakia in a Nationalist and Fascist Europe: 1918–1948.* London: Oxford University Press, 2007.

Fabre, Genevieve, and Michel Feith, eds. *Temples for Tomorrow: Looking Back at the Harlem Renaissance.* Bloomington: University of Indiana Press, 2001.

Fabre, Michel. "Rene Maran, the New Negro and Negritude." *Phylon* 36, no. 3 (1975): 340–51.

Fields, Dorothy Jenkins. "Tracing Overtown's Vernacular Architecture." *Journal of Decorative and Propaganda Arts* 23 (1998): 323–33.

Fikes, Robert, Jr. "African Americans Who Teach German Language and Culture." *Journal of Blacks in Higher Education,* no. 30 (Winter 2000–2001): 108–13.

Foreman, Lewis. *Music in England 1885–1920.* London: Thames, 1994.

Forrest, Leon. "An Avalanche of Creation." *Callaloo* 13, no. 4 (Autumn 1990): 703–26.

Fradella, Salvatore James. *Jack Johnson.* Boston: Branden, 1990.

Frazier, E. Franklin. "Ethnic and Minority Groups in Wartime, with Special Reference to the Negro." *American Journal of Sociology* 48, no. 3 (November 1942): 369–77.

Gates, Skip G. "Of Negroes Old and New." *Transition,* no. 46 (1974): 44–50, 52–58.

Geary, Lynnette G. "Jules Bledsoe: The Original 'Ol' Man River.'" *Black Perspective in Music* 17, no. 1/2 (1989): 27–54.

Green, Jeffery P. *Black Edwardians: Blacks in Britain, 1901–1914.* London: Frank Cass Publishers, 1998.

———. "John Alcindor (1873–1924): A Migrant's Biography." *Immigrants and Minorities* 6, no. 2 (1987): 174–89.

———. "Requiem: 'Hiawatha' in the 1920s and 1930s." *Black Music Research Journal* 21, no. 2 (Autumn 2001): 283–88.

———. "Roland Hayes in London, 1921." *Black Music Research Journal* 10, no. 1 (Spring 1982): 29–42.

Handy, W. C., and Eileen Southern. "Letters from W. C. Handy to William Grant Still." *Black Perspective in Music* 8, no. 1 (Spring 1980): 65–119.

Harris, Charles. *Reminiscences of My Days with Roland Hayes.* Orangeburg, S.C.: self-published, 1944.

Harris, Leonard, ed. *The Philosophy of Alain Locke: Harlem Renaissance and Beyond.* Philadelphia: Temple University Press, 1989.

Hass, Francois. "German Science and Black Racism: Roots of the Nazi Holocaust." *Journal of the Federation of American Societies for Experimental Biology* 22 (2008): 332–37.

Hawkins, Bret W. *Nashville Metro: The Politics of City-County Consolidation.* Nashville: Vanderbilt University Press, 1966.

Hayes, Patrick. "White Artists Only." *Washingtonian,* April 1989, 95–103.

Hayes, Roland. *My Songs, Aframerican Religious Folk Songs Arranged and Interpreted.* Boston: Little, Brown, 1948.

Haynes, George E. "The Church and Negro Progress." *Annals of the American Academy of Political and Social Science* 140 (November 1928): 264–71.

Heaton, Margaret M. "Stereotypes and Real People." *English Journal* 35, no. 6 (June 1946): 327–32.

Helm, MacKinley. *Angel Mo' and Her Son, Roland Hayes.* Boston: Little, Brown, 1942.

Herskovits, Melville J. "Negro Art: African and American." *Social Forces* 5, no. 2 (December 1926): 291–98.

Hickerson, Joseph. "Alan Lomax's 'Southern Journey': A Review-Essay." *Ethnomusicology* 9, no. 3 (September 1965): 313–22.

Hill, Robert. *The Marcus Garvey and the Universal Negro Improvement Association Papers, Volume X.* Oakland: University of California Press, 2006

Hitler, Adolf. *Mein Kampf.* Translated by Ralph Manheim, with introduction by Abraham Foxman. Boston: Houghton Mifflin, 1943.

Holly, Ellistine Perkins. "Black Concert Music in Chicago, 1890 to the 1930s." *Black Music Research Journal* 10, no. 1 (Spring 1990): 141–49.

Holmes, D. O. W. "The Negro Chooses Democracy." *Journal of Negro Education* 23, no. 4 (October 1939): 496–501.

Hughes, C. Alvin. "We Demand Our Rights: The Southern Negro Youth Congress, 1937–1949." *Phylon* 48, no. 1 (1987): 38–50.

Hughes, Langston. *I Wonder as I Wander: An Autobiographical Journey.* New York: Rinehart, 1956.

———. "My America." *Journal of Educational Sociology* 16, no. 6 (February 1943): 334–36.

James, Willis Laurence. Review of *The Meaning of Negro Folk Music: Negro Slave Songs,* by Miles Mark Fisher. *Phylon* 15, no. 1 (1954): 100–102.

Janken, Kenneth Robert. *White: The Biography of Walter White, Mr. NAACP.*

Raleigh: University of North Carolina Press, 2003.

Johnson, Charles A. "Camp Meeting Hymnody." *American Quarterly* 4, no. 2 (1952): 110–26.

Johnson, Guy B. *Annals of the American Academy of Political and Social Science* 190 (March 1937): 245–46.

Johnson, James Weldon. *Along this Way: The Autobiography of James Weldon Johnson*. New York: Da Capo Press, 2000.

Jones, James Nathan, Franklin F. Johnson, and Robert B. Cochrane. "Alfred Jack Thomas: Performer, Composer, Educator." *Black Perspective in Music* 11, no. 1 (Spring 1983): 62–75.

Karger, Howard Jacob. "Phyllis Wheatley House: A History of the Minneapolis Black Settlement House, 1924 to 1940." *Phylon* 47, no. 1 (1986): 79–90.

Keiler, Allan. *Marian Anderson: A Singer's Journey*. New York: Simon and Schuster, 2000.

Kernfeld, Barry, and Howard Rye. "Comprehensive Discographies of Jazz, Blues, and Gospel." *Notes* 51, no. 2 (December 1994): 501–47.

Knight, Arthur E. "Roland Hayes." *Record Collector* 10, no. 2 (July 1955).

Kolowrat, Ernest. *Confessions of a Hapless Hedonist: An Inconvenient Discovery about the Meaning of Pleasure*. Bloomington, Ind.: Xlibris Publisher, 2001.

Langfield, Valerie. *Roger Quilter: His Life and Music*. Rochester, N.Y.: Boydell Press, 2002.

———. *Roger Quilter, 1877–1953: His Life, Times, and Music* Birmingham: University of Birmingham, 2004.

Lankard, Frank G. "Roland Hayes." In *Rising above Color,* edited by Philip Henry Lotz, 86–87. New York: Association Press, 1946.

Leininger-Miller, Theresa. *New Negro Artists in Paris: African American Painters and Sculptors in the City of Light, 1922–*

1934. New Brunswick, N.J.: Rutgers University Press, 2001.

Lewis, David Levering. *W. E. B. Du Bois: The Fight for Equality and the American Century, 1919–1963*. New York: Henry Holt, 2000; New York: Macmillan, 2001.

Lloyd, Stephen. *Sir Dan Godfrey, Champion of British Composers*. London: Thames Publishing, 1995.

Locke, Alain, ed., *The New Negro: An Interpretation*. 1925; New York: Atheneum, 1992.

Martin, Tony. *Race First: The Ideological and Organizational Struggles of Marcus Garvey and the United Negro Improvement Association*. Westport, Conn.: Greenwood Press, 1976.

Massaquoi, Hans J. *Destined to Witness: Growing Up Black in Nazi Germany*. New York: William Morrow, 1999.

Materer, Timothy, ed. *The Selected Letters of Ezra Pound to John Quinn, 1915–1924*. Durham: Duke University Press, 1991.

Maxtone-Graham, John. *The Only Way to Cross*. New York: Collier Books, 1972.

McGinty, Doris Evans, and Revella Hughes. "From the Classics to Broadway to Swing." *Black Perspective in Music* 16, no. 1 (Spring 1988): 81–104.

McGinty, Doris Evans, and Camille Nickerson. "Conversations with . . . Camille Nickerson: The Louisiana Lady." *Black Perspective in Music* 7, no. 1 (Spring 1979): 81–94.

McGuire, Phillip. "Black Music Critics and the Classic Blues Singers." *Black Perspective in Music* 14, no. 2 (Spring 1986): 103–25.

Meacham, William Shands. "The Newspaper and Race Relations." *Social Forces* 15, no. 2 (December 1936): 268–71.

Miller, Zell. *They Heard Georgia Singing*. Macon, Ga.: Mercer University Press, 1996.

Mohamed, Ali Duse. *In the Land of Pharaohs: A Short History of Egypt.* London: Stanley Paul, 1911.

Monteux, Doris G. *It's All in the Music.* New York: Farrar, Strauss, and Giroux, 1965.

Montgomery, Leroy J. *The Negro Problem: Its Significance, Strength and Solution.* New York: Island Press, 1950.

Moore, Gerald. *Am I Too Loud.* New York: Macmillan, 1962.

Moss, James Allen. "Negro Teachers in Predominantly White Colleges." *Journal of Negro Education* 27, no. 4 (Autumn 1958): 451–62.

Mullett, Mary B. "A World-Famous Singer Whose Parents Were Slaves." *American Magazine,* June 1925.

Myers, Kurtz. "Audio-Visual Matters." *Notes* 5, no. 2 (March 1948): 207–10.

Naddell, Martha Jane. *Enter the New Negroes: Images of Race in American Culture.* Cambridge, Mass.: Harvard University Press, 2004.

Narins, Brigham, ed. *The African American Almanac.* 10th edition. Detroit: Gale Group Publishers, 2007.

Nettles, Daryl Glen. *African American Concert Singers before 1950.* Jefferson, N.C.: McFarland, 2003.

Osis, K. "Apparitions Old and New." In *Case Studies in Parapsychology: Papers Presented in Honor of Dr. Louise E. Rhine,* edited by K. R. Rao, 74–86. Jefferson, N.C.: McFarland, 1986.

Osis, K., and E. Haraldsson. *At the Hour of Death.* Rev. ed. New York: Hastings House, 1986.

Ovington, Mary White. *Portraits in Color.* New York: Viking Press, 1927.

Rampersad, Arnold. *The Life of Langston Hughes: Volume 1: 1902–1941; I, Too, Sing America.* New York: Oxford University Press, 1986–88.

Ramsey, Guthrie P., Jr. "Cosmopolitan or Provincial? Ideology in Early Black Music Historiography, 1867–1940." *Black Music Research Journal* 16, no. 1 (Spring 1996): 11–42.

Robeson, Paul, Jr. *The Undiscovered Paul Robeson: An Artist's Journey, 1898–1939.* New York: John Wiley, 2001.

Robinson, D. S. "Report of the Annual Meeting of the Western Division of the American Philosophical Association." *Journal of Philosophy* 26, no. 10 (May 1929): 264–75.

Rudwick, Elliott M. "W. E. B. Du Bois in the Role of *Crisis* Editor." *Journal of Negro History* 43, no. 3 (July 1958): 214–40.

Rye, Howard, and Jeffrey Green. "Black Musical Internationalism in England in the 1920s." *Black Music Research Journal* 15, no. 1 (Spring 1995): 93–107.

Scheck, Raffael. *Hitler's African Victims: The German Army Massacres of Black French Soldiers in 1940.* London: Cambridge University Press, 2006.

Schomburg, Arthur A. "The Negro Digs Up His Past." In *The New Negro: An Interpretation,* edited by Alain Locke. 1925; New York: Atheneum, 1992.

Senghor, Léopold Sédar. "Standards Critiques De L'Art Africain." *African Arts* 1, no. 1 (1967): 6–9, 52.

Seroff, Doug. "Singing of the Old Tunes, in the Old Fashioned Way." Notes from *There Breathes a Hope: The Legacy of John Work II and His Fisk Jubilee Quartet, 1909–1916.* Archeophone 5020, 2010.

Shankman, Arnold. "Julian Harris and the Negro." *Phylon* 35, no. 4 (1974): 442–56.

Simpson, Anne Key. *Hard Trials: The Life and Music of Harry T. Burleigh.* Metuchen, N.J.: Scarecrow Press, 1990.

Sitkoff, Harvard. "Racial Militancy and Interracial Violence in the Second World War." *Journal of American History* 58, no. 3 (December 1971): 661–81.

Smith, Eunice Young. *A Trumpet Sounds: A Novel Based on the Life of Roland Hayes.* Westport, Conn.: Lawrence Hill, 1985.

Smith, Graham. *When Jim Crow Met John Bull: Black American Soldiers in World War II Britain.* London: Tauris, 1987.

Southern, Eileen. *The Music of Black Americans.* 3rd ed. New York: W. W. Norton, 1997.

Southern, Eileen, and William Clarence "Billy" Eckstine. "Conversations with . . . William Clarence 'Billy' Eckstine: 'Mr. B' of Ballad and Bop." *Black Perspective in Music* 7, no. 2 (Autumn 1979): 182–98.

Southern, Eileen, and Fela Sowande. "Conversation with Fela Sowande, High Priest of Music." *Black Perspective in Music* 4, no. 1 (Spring 1976): 90–104.

Spearman, Rawn Wardell. "The 'Joy' of Langston Hughes and Howard Swanson." *Black Perspective in Music* 9, no. 2 (Autumn 1981): 121–38.

Spencer, Jon Michael. "The Black Church and the Harlem Renaissance." *African American Review* 30, no. 3 (1996): 453–60.

Standing, T. G. "The Possibility of a Distinctive Culture Contribution from the American Negro." *Social Forces* 17, no. 1 (October 1938): 99–106.

Stewart, Gustavus Adolphus. "The New Negro Hokum." *Social Forces* 6, no. 3 (March 1928): 438–45.

Stovall, Tyler. *Paris Noir: African Americans in the City of Light.* New York: Mariner Books/ Houghton Mifflin, 1996.

Szucs, Loretto Dennis, and Sandra Hargreaves Luebking, eds. *The Source: A Guidebook of American Genealogy.* Salt Lake City: Ancestry Incorporated, 1997.

Taylor, Frederick Jerome. "Black Musicians in 'The Philadelphia Tribune,' 1912–20." *Black Perspective in Music* 18, no. 1/2 (1990): 127–40.

Taylor, Quintard. "Black Urban Development: Another View; Seattle's Central District, 1910–1940." *Pacific Historical Review* 58, no. 4 (November 1989): 429–48.

Tracy, Steven C. *Langston Hughes and the Blues.* Chicago: University of Illinois Press, 2001.

Van Vechten, Carl. "Soul of a People Lifted in Song" (review). *New York Herald Tribune Weekly Book Review,* November 21, 1948.

Verrett, Shirley, and Christopher Brooks. *I Never Walked Alone: The Autobiography of an American Singer.* Hoboken, N.J.: John Wiley, 2003.

Vincent, Theodore G. *Black Power and the Garvey Movement.* San Francisco: Ramparts Press, 1976.

Wagstaff, J. "André Messager." In *New Grove Dictionary of Opera,* edited by Sadie S. Macmillan. New York: Macmillan, 1997.

Walton, Lester A., L. H. White, A. W. K., and Lucien H. White. "Black-Music Concerts in Carnegie Hall, 1912–1915." *Black Perspective in Music* 6, no. 1 (Spring 1978): 71–88.

Washington, Ethel M. *Union County Black Americans.* Mount Pleasant, S.C.: Arcadia, 2004.

Watts, Marjorie S. "Intercultural English: An Experiment." *English Journal* 34, no. 2 (February 1945): 81–87.

Whalum, Wendell Phillips. "James Weldon Johnson's Theories and Performance Practices of Afro-American Folksong." *Phylon* 32, no. 4 (1971): 383–95.

White, Walter. "The Color Line in Europe." *Annals of the American Academy of Political and Social Science* 140 (November 1928): 331–36.

Woodgate, Leslie. "Roger Quilter, 1 November 1877–21 September 1953." *Musical Times* 94, no. 1329 (November,1953): 503–5.

DOCUMENTARIES

The Musical Legacy of Roland Hayes. Debra Mims, executive producer. Wisconsin Public Broadcasting, 1990.

Songs of Triumph, Songs of Joy: The Legacy of Roland Hayes. Produced by the Detroit Public Library, 2001.

UNPUBLISHED MANUSCRIPTS

Brooks, Christopher A. "Duro Ladipo and the Moremi Legend: The Sociohistorical Development of the Yoruba Music Drama and Its Political Ramifications." PhD diss., University of Texas at Austin, 1989.

Crocker, Walton L. "The Conquest of Roland Hayes." Boston, August 1927.

"Mann Clan Reunion." Unpublished Mann family history, 1994.

Sullivan, Noël. "Forty Years Remembered: A Letter in the Form of a Memoir to the Children of My Sister Gladys S. Doyle." 1954.

Index

CHRISTOPHER A. BROOKS is Professor of Anthropology at Virginia Commonwealth University and is a prolific author and biographer, producing the best-selling *I Never Walked Alone: The Autobiography of an American Singer* (with the late Shirley Verrett) and *Follow Your Heart: Moving with the Giants of Jazz, Swing, and Rhythm and Blues* (with the late Joe Evans). Brooks is also general editor of and a major contributor to the 1,600-page reference work *The African American Almanac* (11th ed.).

ROBERT SIMS is Professor of Voice at Northern Illinois University. He has received international acclaim for his interpretations of African American spirituals and has given numerous recitals throughout the United States, South America, Europe, Africa, and Asia. He was invited by Jessye Norman to participate in "Honor! A Celebration of the African American Cultural Legacy" at Carnegie Hall and has appeared as a soloist with the Mormon Tabernacle Choir. Sims is a contributor to *The African American Almanac* (11th ed.).